Genograms
Third Edition

Other Norton books by Monica McGoldrick

Living Beyond Loss: Death in the Family, 2nd Edition
(Edited with Froma Walsh)

Women in Families: A Framework for Family Therapy
(Edited with Carol Anderson and Froma Walsh)

You Can Go Home Again: Reconnecting with Your Family

A Norton Professional Book

Genograms
Assessment and Intervention
Third Edition

Monica McGoldrick

Randy Gerson

Sueli Petry

W. W. Norton & Company

New York • London

First edition published as GENOGRAMS IN FAMILY ASSESSMENT

For information about permission to reproduce selections from this book, write to
Permissions, W. W. Norton & Company, Inc., 500 Fifth Avenue, New York, NY 10110

Composition and book design by Paradigm Graphics
Manufacturing by Malloy Printing
Production Manger: Leeann Graham

Library of Congress Cataloging-in-Publication Data

McGoldrick, Monica.
Genograms : assessment and intervention / Monica McGoldrick, Randy Gerson, and Sueli
Petry. -- 3rd ed.
p. ; cm.
Includes bibliographical references and index.
ISBN 978-0-393-70509-6 (pbk.)
1. Genograms. I. Gerson, Randy. II. Petry, Sueli S. III. Title.
[DNLM: 1. Family Therapy--methods. 2. Family Relations. 3. Famous
Persons. 4. Pedigree. WM 430.5.F2 M4782g 2007]

RC488.5.M395 2007
616.89'156--dc22   2007001298

ISBN 13: 978-0-393-70509-6 (pbk.)

W. W. Norton & Company, Inc., 500 Fifth Avenue, New York, N.Y. 10110
www.wwnorton.com
W. W. Norton & Company Ltd., Castle House, 75/76 Wells St., London W1T 3QT
1 3 5 7 5 9 8 6 4 2 0

To our families, from whom we have received our strengths and to whom we leave the legacy of all our endeavors.

Contents

Expanded Contents

List of Illustrations

("C" refers to color insert)

Genogram Creation and Typologies

Acknowledgments

I AM EXTREMELY GRATEFUL TO W. W. NORTON for their support with this project throughout three editions and over more than twenty years. In particular, Deborah Malmud has been an enormous support and a great pleasure to work with. I am deeply grateful for her interest, creativity, and integrity in working with me over the years. Michael McGandy was an enormous help over the years, most of all in managing the complexities of this third edition, and I am very grateful for his help. Andrea Costella put enormous energy into the artwork and the book is a credit to her dedication. Casey Ruble was the most amazing copy editor I have ever known—checking the most complex information with a magnificent eye for detail and incongruities. I would also like to thank MonkeyGraphics (www.monkeygraphics.net), based in Hungary, for their superior work revising and upgrading the quality of the genograms throughout the book. The book is a credit to all their efforts.

I am grateful to many people for their help in the development of this project. I owe special thanks to Randy Gerson for the formative efforts he made to describe genogram patterns and to make them universally accessible through his creativity in computer applications. I thank my friend and colleague of many years, Michael Rohrbaugh, who challenged my assumptions and helped me clarify my thinking about genograms and their potential as a research and clinical tool.

My sisters, Morna and Neale, and my nephew, Guy Livingston, helped me develop the genograms in between their life adventures. My lifemates, Betty Carter, Froma Walsh, Carol Anderson, Nydia Garcia Preto, Paulette Moore Hines, Ken Hardy, Charlee Sutton, John Folwarski, Miguel Hernandez, Marlene Watson, Jayne Mahboubi, Eliana Gil, Nollaig Byrne, Imelda Colgan McCarthy, Vanessa Mahmoud,

Barbara Petkov, Vanessa Jackson, and Roxana Llerena Quinn have also been of immeasurable support to me in thinking about genograms and their implications for understanding families. My refound friend and soulmate, Fernando Colon, provided inspiration, help, and affirmation, particularly regarding the importance of nonbiological kin networks. I thank my friend Robert Jay Green for challenging my unquestioning belief in the relevance of genograms, helping me to clarify for myself the deepest meanings of family and of home. Mary Ann Ross has for many years generously offered her ideas, creativity, hard work, and good cheer in the research for this book. My colleagues Dee Watts Jones, Joanne Klages, Joan Marsh Schlesinger, Debra Chatman Finley, Eunjung Ryu, Robbin Loonan, Josianne Menos, Sybil Williams Gray, Robert Bonner, and many students have been an enormous support in every way for many years and have made all my efforts, including on this book, possible. I am very grateful for their support and critique. I also thank Irene Umbel, who keeps our office running smoothly, and Fran Snyder, my guardian angel at work, for freeing me by her efforts to do this work. I am ever grateful that she has come into my life. Roberto Zapata fell into my life at the exactly right moment and was a pleasure to work with and a joy to know for all his graphic skill, creativity, and diligence in creating genograms, and I thank him for his help in this endeavor. Gary Jaffe came on the scene just when we needed him and generously helped us to make the diagrams work. And Laura Benton fell into our laps at the end of our journey with a quiet creativity, intelligence, and diligence that was miraculous. She was an incredible help in bringing the manuscript to completion. We are so grateful for her help.

And most of all I am grateful to Sueli Petry for her dedication to genograms and specifically for the hard work that is finally bringing this third edition to fruition. She came first as a student with a strong interest in genograms and grew into a friend and colleague and a steadfast support in thinking through the issues of genograms.

Finally, my deepest thanks go to the closest members of my own genogram, Sophocles Orfanidis, my husband of 38 years, and John Daniel Orfanidis, my son, whose birth coincided with the first edition of this book and whose launching into adulthood coincides with this third edition. I look forward to how my own genogram will continue as the next generations expand our family. Of course there would have been no book without the underlying support of my parents and all my other family who have come before me—whether connected through biology, legal ties, or spiritual affinity—and who are a part of my genogram (see Figure 1.2). I stand on the shoulders of many supportive, creative, and generous kin, without whom I would not be writing this. With their support, I write for all those who will come after.

—Monica McGoldrick

WORKING WITH MONICA ON THIS BOOK has been an amazing journey. I am grateful for her belief in me. With her intellect, her stamina, and her serious work ethic, she challenged me to think ever more deeply about the families we treat and about how to track relationships, legacies, and the many family patterns that all come together to form current family stories. It has been an incredible experience for me to be a part of this process.

I first became interested in genograms and family patterns when I was in the first year of a master's graduate program in psychology and I saw Monica's videotape on the Legacy of Loss. I was moved by the family in that video and by Monica, who made their genogram come to life. That experience was so powerful that I knew I wanted to know more about family systems, and after completing my psychology program I went on to study family therapy. I sought out Monica and the Multicultural Family Institute, and we have been together for more than 7 years now. During the past 3 years we have worked very closely on this book to develop better genograms, consulting with colleagues, students, software developers, and family and friends. She is my mentor and my friend and I am ever grateful for her friendship, her energy, her joy of life, and her love and respect for the work.

I would also like to thank my parents. My mother, Catarina Separovich de Carvalho, changed her name to Catherine when she became an

American citizen. She always lived as an outsider, first as a child of immigrants from Yugoslavia in Brazil, then as an adult immigrant from Brazil in the United States. She and my father, Aristides Berilo deCarvalho, faced oppression daily, yet they transmitted the family patterns of hard work, love, and the belief that life is essentially good.

Finally, I am grateful for my husband and life companion, Karl Petry, who nurtured me with love and encouragement. Karl is a practical dreamer whose faith makes the improbable possible.

—Sueli Petry

Preface

THIS BOOK EVOLVED OUT OF A LONG INTEREST in the clinical, research, and instructional value of genograms. Over the past few decades use of the genogram as a practical tool for mapping family patterns has become increasingly widespread among healthcare professionals. A dream we had when we first thought of writing about genograms seems a real possibility in the near future: computer software that will create a database for studying genograms as well as for mapping them graphically. In the past three decades genograms have become widely used in geneology, medicine, psychology, social work, counseling, nursing, and the other healthcare and human service fields, and even in law and business. This third edition of *Genograms: Assessment and Intervention* reflects the growing and widespread use of genograms for clinical intervention, particularly the evolving use of family play genograms. The book attempts to better illustrate the diversity of family forms and patterns in our society and the many applications of genograms in clinical practice. The genogram is still a tool in progress. Based on feedback from readers and other developments in the field, we have expanded the book and slightly modified the symbols used since the second edition. We trust that the evolution of the genogram as a tool will continue as clinicians use genograms to track the complexity of family process.

Although a genogram can provide a fascinating view into the richness of a family's dynamics for those in the know, it may appear to be a complex arrangement of squares and circles on a page to those who don't know the players in the drama. Our solution to this dilemma has been to illustrate our points primarily with famous families, about whom we all have some knowledge, rather than with clinical cases. It should be noted, however, that we are family therapists, not historians, and thus the information we have gleaned about these families is limited. Most of the sources have been biographies, newspapers, and the Internet. Readers may have better information about some of the families than we were able to uncover from published sources. We apologize in advance for any inaccuracies in the material. Hopefully the descriptions sketched here will inspire readers to pursue further the fascinating stories of such families as the Eriksons, Fondas, Freuds, Kennedys, Robesons, Einsteins, and Roosevelts. Surprisingly, only limited family descriptions are available for many of history's most interesting personalities. We trust that future biographers will be more aware of family systems and use genograms to broaden their perspective on the individuals and families they describe.

Genograms
Third Edition

Genograms: Mapping Family Systems

T HE GENOGRAM HAS BEEN ESTABLISHED as a practical framework for understanding family patterns. The purpose of this book is to explicate the practical, theoretical, graphic, and clinical uses of the genogram and its potential for research. The standardized genogram format is becoming a common language for tracking family history and relationships (see the key printed on the inside front cover of this book). Despite the widespread use of genograms by family therapists, family physicians, and other healthcare providers, there was no generally agreed-upon format for genograms prior to the first edition of this book in 1985. Even among clinicians with similar theoretical orientations, there was only a loose consensus about what specific information to seek, how to record it, and what it all meant. The standardized genogram format used in this book was worked out in the early 1980s by a committee of leading proponents of genograms from family therapy and family medicine, including such key people as Murray Bowen, Jack Froom, and Jack Medalie. They became part of a committee organized by the North American Primary Care Research Group to define the most practical genogram symbols and agree on a standardized format. Since the format was originally published in 1985, there have been a number of modifications recommended by different groups around the world. We see the format included in this edition as a work in progress, as expanded use of genograms will undoubtedly extend the format further. For example, computers have led us to begin development of standard color coding for names, location, occupation, illnesses, and so on. The symbols will surely be further modified in the future just as they have been modified over the past four decades.

Genograms record information about family members and their relationships over at least three generations. They display family information graphically in a way that provides a quick gestalt of complex family patterns; as such they are a rich source of hypotheses about how clinical problems evolve in the context of the family over time.

In addition to presenting this standardized format, *Genograms: Assessment and Intervention* describes the interpretive principles upon which genograms are based, as well as possibilities for software, which can record genogram information and store it for retrieval for research purposes. In addition, the book outlines the application of genograms in many clinical areas. The genogram guidelines presented here have been developed over the past several decades in collaboration with many colleagues. These guidelines are still evolving, as our thinking about families in context progresses. This third edition defines even more of the symbols and conventions that make genograms the best shorthand language for summarizing family information and describing family patterns.

Genograms appeal to clinicians because they are tangible, graphic representations of complex family patterns. The need for such maps has reached such a point that the Salzburg Music Festival recently offered a kind of genogram to follow the family relationships of a Mozart opera (Oestreich, 2006). Had they known about genograms, of course, they could have done an even better graphic, such as the one we did for one of the most complicated opera plots ever, *Il Trovatore* (Figure 1.1)!

In this case, the Old Count Di Luna, thinking a gypsy had bewitched his younger son, had her burned at the stake. The gypsy made her daughter promise vengeance. The daughter, Azucena, meant to kill the Count's son but accidentally killed her own son and then raised the count's son as her own. The son grew up to become a troubadour and knight who fell in love with a young woman, Leonora, who was being pursued by his older brother, Count Di Luna the younger. In this genogram we have shown the son of the old Count Di Luna in all his incarnations (the apparently dead son of the count, adopted son of Azucena, and troubadour lover of Leonora). By the end of the opera, of course, all is revealed and the three personages are recognized as one.

Figure 1.1 Verdi's *Il Trovatore*

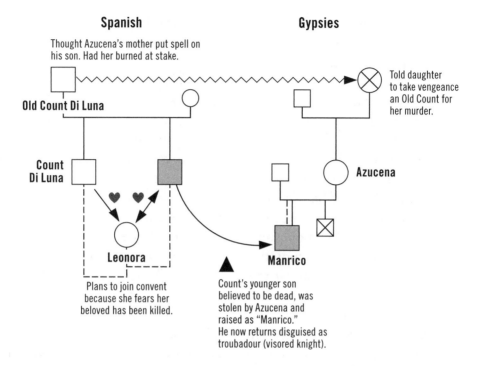

Genograms allow you to map the family structure clearly and to note and update the map of family patterns of relationships and functioning as they emerge. For a clinical record, the genogram provides an efficient summary, allowing a person unfamiliar with a case to grasp quickly a huge amount of information about a family and to scan for potential problems and resources. Whereas notes written in a chart or questionnaire may become lost in a record, genogram information is immediately recognizable and can be added to and corrected at each clinical visit as one learns more about a family. Genograms can be created for any moment in the family's history, showing the ages and relationships of that moment to better understand family patterns as they evolve through time. Soon software will allow clinicians to track the family's timeline or chronology—to follow the details of key developments in relationships, health, and so on over the entire life cycle of the family.

Genograms make it easier for us to keep in mind the complexity of a family's context, including family history, patterns, and events that may have ongoing significance for patient care. Just as our spoken language potentiates and organizes our thought processes, genograms help clinicians think systemically about how events and relationships in their clients' lives are related to patterns of health and illness.

Gathering genogram information should be an integral part of any comprehensive clinical assessment, if only to know who is in the family and what the facts of their current situation and history are. The genogram is primarily an interpretive tool that enables clinicians to generate tentative hypotheses for further evaluation in a family assessment. It cannot be used in a cookbook fashion to make clinical predictions. But it can sensitize clinicians to systemic issues, which are relevant to current dysfunction and to sources of resilience. Software will soon make it possible to study the genogram patterns of multiple families and to compare and contrast the profiles of all the cases in one's genogram database.

Thanks to the mind-boggling new field of genetic genealogy (Harmon, 2006), we all suddenly have access to our genetic histories in ways no one ever imagined possible, and we are just at the beginning of a whole new set of possibilities for learning about our family and cultural heritage—from our connection to Genghis Kahn or Marie Antoinette to the realities of our cultural and racial heritage, which may be deeply hidden by family lore. Being able to map out our family tree with the aid of computers is the only way we will be able to incorporate the complexities we are coming to know about our heritage, and this is absolutely the route for studying family patterns of relationship, functioning, and illness. Computers are the future of genograms!

Typically, the genogram is constructed from information gathered during the first meeting with a client/patient and revised as new information becomes available. The initial assessment forms the basis for treatment. It is important to emphasize, however, that clinicians typically do not compartmentalize assessment and treatment. Each interaction of the clinician with a family member informs the assessment and thus influences the next intervention.

Genograms help a clinician get to know a family. They thus become an important way of "joining" with families in therapy. By creating a systemic perspective that helps to track family issues through space and time, genograms enable an interviewer to reframe, detoxify, and normalize emotion-laden issues. Also, the genogram interview provides a ready vehicle for systemic questioning, which, in addition to providing information for the clinician, begins to orient clients to a systemic perspective. The genogram helps both the clinician and the family to see the "larger picture"—that is, to view problems in their current and historical context. Structural, relational, and functional information about a family can be viewed on a genogram both horizontally across the family context and vertically through the generations.

Scanning the breadth of the current family context allows the clinician to assess the connectedness of the immediate members of the family to one another, as well as to the broader system—the extended family, friends, community, society, and culture—and to evaluate the family's strengths and vulnerabilities in relation to the overall situation. Consequently, we include on the genogram the immediate and extended family members, as well as significant nonblood "kin" who have lived with or played a major role in the family's life. We also note relevant events (moves, life cycle changes) and problems (illness, dysfunction). Current behavior and problems of family members can be traced on the genogram from multiple perspectives. The index person (the "IP" or person with the problem or symptom) may be viewed in the context of various subsystems, such as siblings, triangles, and reciprocal relationships, or in relation to the broader community, social institutions (schools, courts, etc.), and sociocultural context. And soon, we will be able to explore an entire database of genograms for particular patterns: genetic patterns, illnesses, gender and sibling patterns of functioning, the likelihood of triangles in which one parent is close and the other is distant, loss or trauma in previous generations, correlations between various symptom constellations, and so forth.

By scanning the family system historically and assessing previous life cycle transitions, clinicians can place present issues in the context of the family's evolutionary patterns. The genogram usually includes at least three generations of family members, as well as nodal and critical events in the family's history, particularly in relation to the life cycle. When family members are questioned about the present situation with regard to the themes, myths, rules, and emotionally charged issues of previous generations, repetitive patterns often become clear. Genograms "let the calendar speak" by suggesting possible connections between family events over time. Patterns of previous illness and earlier shifts in family relationships brought about through loss and other critical life changes, which alter family structure and other patterns, can easily be noted on the genogram. Computerized genograms will enable us to explore specific family patterns and symptom constellations. All this provides a framework for hypothesizing about what may be currently influencing a crisis in a particular family. In conjunction with genograms, we usually include a family chronology, which depicts the family history in chronological order. A computerized program for gathering and mapping genogram information with a database will make it a lot easier for the clinician to track family history, because a chronology will be able to show events for any particular moment in the family's history.

Genogram applications range from simply depicting the basic demographic information about a family, which can be done in a 15-minute medical or nursing interview (Wright & Leahey, 1999), to multigenerational mapping of the family emotional system using a Bowen framework (see bibliographic section on Assessment, Genograms, and Systems Theory), to systemic hypothesizing for strategic interventions, to developing "projective" hypotheses about the workings of the unconscious from genogram interviews. Some have suggested modifications of the genogram format (see bibliography section on Genogram Variations and Sociograms), such as Friedman, Rohrbaugh, and Krakauer's (1988) "time-line" genogram, Watts Jones's (1998) genogram to depict the "functional" family, Friesen and Manitt's (1991) attachment diagrams, Burke and Faber's (1997) genogrid to depict the networks of lesbian families, or spiritual/religious genograms (see bibliography section on Spiritual Genograms). Some clinicians have stressed the usefulness of genograms for working with families at various life cycle stages (see Chapter 8 and bibliography on Family Life Cycle), for keeping track of complex relational configurations seen in remarried families (see bibliography on Divorce and Remarriage), for engaging and keeping track of complex, culturally diverse families (see Culture and Race section of bibliography), for exploring specific issues such as sexuality and the sexual history of the family with sexual genograms (Hof & Berman, 1986; McGoldrick, Loonan, & Wolsifer, 2006), and for making family interventions, as with family play genograms (see Chapter 10). Some have even used genograms as the basis for teaching illiterate adults to read, interviewing them about their genograms, transcribing their stories, and then teaching them to read their own narratives (Darkenwald & Silvestri, 1992). Others have used work and career genograms to facilitate career decisions (Gibson, 2005; Moon, Coleman, McCollum, Nelson, & Jensen-Scott, 1993) or to illustrate organizations such as a medical practice (McIlvain, Crabtree, Medder, Strange, & Miller, 1998). Some have creatively expanded the genogram concept with what they call a gendergram, which maps gender relationships over the life cycle (White & Tyson-Rawson, 1995).

The genogram has been used to elicit family narratives and expand cultural stories (Congress, 1994; Hardy & Laszloffy, 1995; McGill, 1992; Sherman, 1990; Thomas, 1998), to identify therapeutic strategies such as reframing and detoxifying family legacies (Gewirtzman, 1988), in solution-focused therapy (Zide & Gray, 2000), as validation for children growing up in child welfare and multiple homes and family constellations (Altshuler, 1999; McGoldrick & Colon, 2000; McMillen & Groze, 1994), to discover families' strengths and unique responses to problems (Kuehl, 1995), and to work with particular populations, such as children (Fink, Kramer, Weaver, & Anderson, 1993), the elderly, and couples in premarital counseling (Shellenberger, Watkins-Couch, & Drake, 1989). Many of these authors have called for more research using genograms. For example, Ingersoll-Dayton and Arndt (1990) have written persuasively about the research potential of genograms for gerontological social workers assessing and intervening with older adults or for professionals supporting caregivers of the elderly who are feeling burdened with their role. Makungu Akinyela uses genograms to teach an African-American Family course in the department of African-American Studies at Georgia State University in Atlanta. In this course students track their own family histories and place them in conversation with research literature on policy, history, migration, and cultural development of African-American families. In taking this approach, students are able to see the connection between scholarly research and their own families' lived experience.

In recent years much of the literature on genograms has focused on expanding their meaning to include the larger context, although the graphics of these expanded genograms have generally not been well developed. There has been much attention given to the "cultural genogram," referring to specific focus on the cultural aspects of a family's history, and to the religious or spiritual genogram, which focuses on a family's religious history and specific ways that religion and spirituality play out in family patterns. A whole book has been written on "community genograms," although the graphics do not resemble genograms and do not depict the three-generational family map as a basic context (Rigazio-DiGilio, Ivey, Kunkler-Peck, & Grady, 2005). Difficulty depicting expanded genograms flows from the problems in showing multiple dimensions on one genogram graphic, reflecting the age-old problem that diagram graphics always involve a tradeoff between the amount of information included and the clarity of the graphic. We will discuss some of these issues with the hope that in the future we will find creative ways to show and track expanded genogram information. We will try to at least stimulate discussion about how these issues can become visually depicted on genogram graphics. Of course, computer genograms attached to a database will have many more possibilities for depicting specific issues one or two at a time, or for making different graphics for different moments in family history.

It is worth noting that some family therapists (such as Haley, Minuchin, and White) have actually eschewed the use of genograms. Haley, for example, often said he did not believe in ghosts. However, although structural and strategic family therapists such as Minuchin, Watzlawick, Weakland, and Sluzki have not used genograms in their approaches, preferring to focus on the relationships in the immediate family, even they share a concern about hierarchical structures, particularly coalitions where generational boundaries are crossed. Michael White (2006) suggested that gathering genogram information is problematic because it "privileges" certain family of origin experiences over other relationships, which may disqualify or fail to honor these other people. On the other hand, he and the others in the narrative therapy movement have conveyed strong interest in the histories of members of society who have been marginalized. We believe that it is precisely this aspect—articulating historical patterns—that is one of the magical aspects of genograms. They can reveal aspects of the family that have been hidden from family members—secrets of their history. Such revelations help families understand their current dilemmas and provide future solutions. Indeed, one of the most exciting aspects of genograms is the way they lead families beyond the one-dimensional linear perspectives that have so often characterized psychological explanations. They actually teach people to think systemically, because, as soon as family members and clinicians notice one pattern, their vision is expanded by seeing other patterns as well. The very richness of the genogram graphic itself facilitates noticing more than one pattern at a time.

Family Medicine

It was family physicians who first developed the use of genograms to record and track family medical history efficiently and reliably (see bibliography section on Healthcare, Medicine, Nursing, Stress, and Illness; Campbell, McDaniel, Cole-Kelly, Hepworth & Lorenz, 2002; Jolly, Froom, & Rosen, 1980; Medalie, 1978; Mullins & Christie-Seely, 1984; Olsen, Dudley-Brown, & McMullen, 2004; Rakel, 1977; Rogers, Durkin, & Kelly, 1985; Rogers & Holloway, 1990; Sloan, Slatt, Curtis, & Ebell, 1998; Taylor, David, Johnson, Phillips, & Scherger, 1998; Tomson, 1985; Wimbush & Peters, 2000; Wright & Leahey, 1999, 2000; Zide & Gray, 2000). It was also family physicians who first proposed the standardization of genogram symbols (Jolly et al., 1980). Crouch (1986), one of the most influential family physicians in the promotion of genograms, was also one of the first in medicine to write about the value of working with one's own family for the sake of professional development, an approach that has been widely promoted by Bowen and his followers for many years (see bibliography on Coaching).

Within the field of medicine there has been much effort to incorporate genograms as a basic assessment tool. Scherger (2005) has written a call to arms about the current crisis in family medicine and the need to redesign the field to allow family physicians to offer truly family-oriented care, for which attention to genogram information could be a major part. He argues powerfully for using new information technologies to help track and deal with families in a contextual way as the only serious possibility for providing appropriate care to families in our society. First, however, we will have to develop the technology to address families systemically and train physicians to use it, if they are not to be overwhelmed by the morass of paperwork and insurance industry–driven services. In a classic article in the *Journal of the American Medical Association*, Rainsford and Schuman (1981) wrote about the importance of genograms and family chronologies especially for tracking complex, stress-ridden cases, which often require the most attention from the healthcare system. They offered an example of a multiproblem family, such as many that show up at every entry point of the healthcare system, in social service agencies, schools, and in the criminal justice system. It makes eminent sense to have clear and comprehensive ways of tracking the patterns of such families, as they can be a tremendous drain on any system. The authors showed the family members' stressful events and clinic visits over a 7-year period, illustrating the importance of the physician's having a longitudinal picture of all family members together in order to understand a single member's visit at a particular point in time. Genograms could allow clinics to track doctor visits in relation to other family stresses, not just for one patient, but for all other family members as well. With such mapping included in every assessment, it would be a great deal easier to see when extra resources are needed to prevent the ongoing ripples of serious dysfunction.

It is also important to show the context around the biological and legal family in order to understand a family in context. Figure 1.2 illustrates the informal kinship network of friends that has surrounded my own (MM) immediate family.

These are people, some long dead and some in my daily life, who live in my heart. They are people who could offer a loan, help out my husband

Figure 1.2 McGoldrick Family and Network

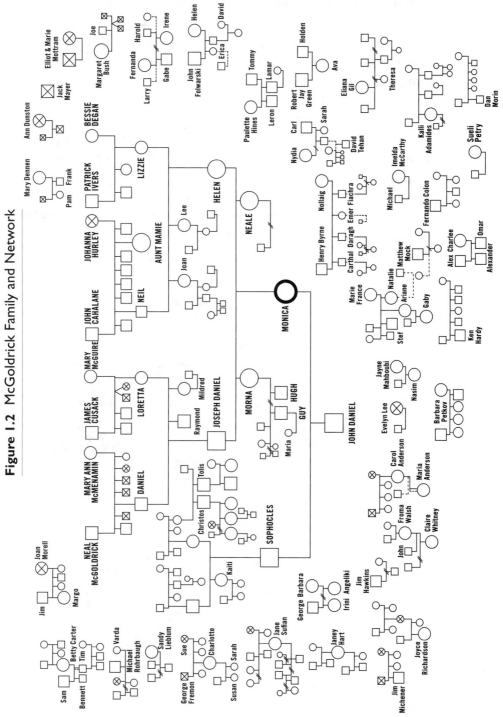

or son, or give me strength and courage if I were in a crisis. Genograms need to show not just the biological and legal members of a family, but also the network of friends and community essential for understanding the family. This includes current relationships as well as the relationships that came before and live in the person's heart, giving hope and inspiration in times of distress. It is this kinship network, not just the biological relatives and not just those who are alive now, that is relevant in developing an understanding of clients and their possible resources. Such genograms are an important part of illustrating in greater depth the context around the immediate family.

Figure 1.3 illustrates the fact that family genogram history always evolves in the context of larger societal structures—cultural, political, religious, spiritual, socioeconomic, gender, racial, and ethnic—which organize each member of a society into a particular social location.

Figure 1.3 The Genogram in Multiple Contexts

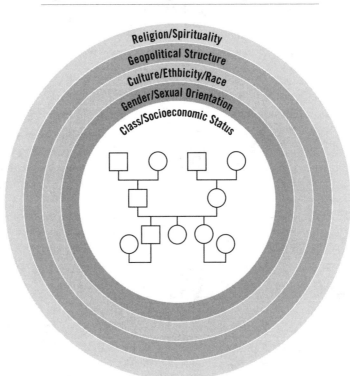

It is important always to think of the genogram in its broader context. At times we actually define the resources and institutions of the community to highlight families' access or lack of access to community resources (Figure 1.4). Many have been attempting to expand genograms to take these larger social structures into account in understanding genogram patterns. Some have tried to map the community or historical connections of national and cultural patterns, for example, using a genogram to illustrate the multigenerational, step-sibling and half-sibling relationships involved in the reunification of Germany, including "Uncle Sam" and "Mother Russia" to illustrate the multigenerational international connections that may impinge on the "sibling" relationships of East and West Germans today (Scharwiess, 1994). Rigazio-DiGilio and colleagues (2005) have suggested ways to depict the larger temporal and contextual community. These maps resemble ecomaps, illustrating around each person in a spherical grid various events and situations that have come to shape clients' experiences over time. Although they are not really genograms in that they are not family maps, they do attempt to depict aspects of the context within which people live. We look forward to the continued evolution of genograms to enable us to better illustrate the larger cultural levels along with the specific individual and kinship dimensions of family patterns.

Figure 1.4 Genogram Within Community Context

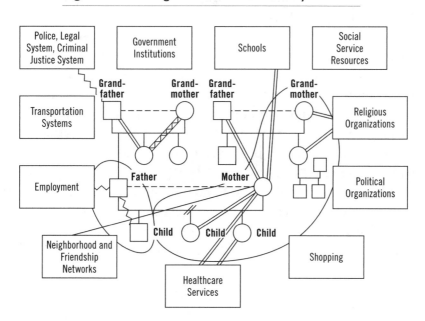

A Family Systems Perspective

A systemic perspective guides clinicians in using genograms for clinical assessment and intervention. This perspective views family members as inextricably intertwined in their lives and in death, and views all members of society as ultimately interconnected. Neither people, nor their problems, nor the solutions to their problems, exist in a vacuum. As Paolo Freire (1994, p. 31) has said, "No one goes anywhere alone, even those who arrive physically alone. . . . We carry with us the memory of many fabrics, a self soaked in our history and our culture."

All are inextricably interwoven into broader interactional systems, the most fundamental of which is the family. The family is the primary and, except in rare instances, most powerful system to which we humans ever belong. In this framework, "family" consists of the entire kinship network of at least three generations, both as it currently exists and as it has evolved through time (Carter & McGoldrick, 2005). Family is, by our definition, those who are tied together through their common biological, legal, cultural, and emotional history and by their implied future together. The physical, social, and emotional functioning of family members is profoundly interdependent, with changes in one part of the system reverberating in other parts. In addition, family interactions and relationships tend to be highly reciprocal, patterned, and repetitive. It is these patterns that allow us to make tentative predictions from the genogram.

A basic assumption here is that symptoms reflect a system's adaptation to its total context at a given moment in time. The adaptive efforts of members of the system reverberate throughout its many levels, from the biological to the intrapsychic to the interpersonal (i.e., immediate and extended family, community, culture, and beyond). Also, family behaviors, including problems and symptoms, derive further emotional and normative meaning in relation to both the sociocultural and historical context of the family. Thus, a systemic perspective involves assessing the problem on the basis of these multiple levels.

Families are organized within biological, legal, cultural, and emotional structures, as well as according to generation, age, gender, and other factors. Where you fit in the family structure, as well as in the larger context, can influence your functioning, relational patterns, and the type of family you form in the next generation. Gender and birth order are key factors shaping sibling relationships and characteristics. Given different family structural configurations mapped on the genogram, the clinician can hypothesize possible personality characteristics and relational compatibilities. Ethnicity (McGoldrick, Giordano, & Garcia-Preto, 2005), race, religion, migration, class, and other socioeconomic factors, as well as a family's life cycle stage (Carter & McGoldrick, 2005) and location in history (Elder, 1992), also influence a family's structural patterns. These factors all become part of the genogram map.

Families repeat themselves. What happens in one generation will often repeat itself in the next—that is, the same issues tend to be played out from generation to generation, though the actual behavior may take a variety of forms. Bowen termed this the "multigenerational transmission" of family patterns. The hypothesis is that relationship patterns in previous generations may provide implicit models for family functioning in the next generation. On the genogram, we explore patterns of functioning, relationship, and structure that continue or alternate from one generation to the next.

Clearly, a systems approach involves understanding both the current and historical context of the family. The "flow of anxiety" (Carter, 1978) in a family system occurs along both vertical and horizontal dimensions (Figure 1.5). For the individual, the vertical axis includes biological heritage and programmed behaviors such as temperament, as well as other aspects of genetic makeup. The horizontal axis relates to the individual's development over the lifespan influenced by whatever experiences may change this course—relationships, migration, health and illness, success, traumatic experiences, and so on.

At the family level, the vertical axis includes the family history and the patterns of relating and functioning that are transmitted down the generations, primarily through the mechanism of emotional triangling (Bowen, 1978). It includes all the family attitudes, taboos, expectations, labels, and loaded issues with which family members grow up. These aspects of our lives are the hand we are dealt. What we do with them is the question. The horizontal flow at a family level describes the family as it moves through time, coping with the changes and transitions of the family's life

Figure 1.5 Context for Assessing Problems

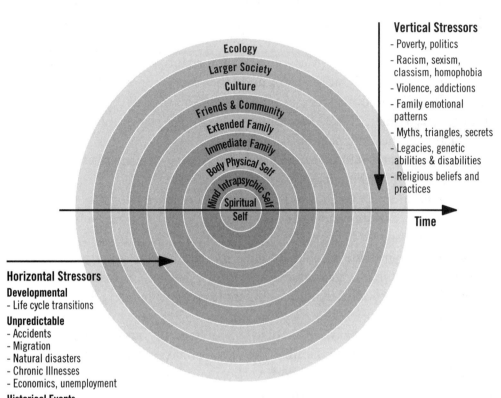

Vertical Stressors
- Poverty, politics
- Racism, sexism, classism, homophobia
- Violence, addictions
- Family emotional patterns
- Myths, triangles, secrets
- Legacies, genetic abilities & disabilities
- Religious beliefs and practices

Ecology
Larger Society
Culture
Friends & Community
Extended Family
Immediate Family
Body Physical Self
Mind Intrapsychic Self
Spiritual Self

Time

Horizontal Stressors
Developmental
- Life cycle transitions
Unpredictable
- Accidents
- Migration
- Natural disasters
- Chronic Illnesses
- Economics, unemployment
Historical Events
- Economic and political events

cycle. This horizontal flow includes both predictable developmental stresses and unpredictable events, "the slings and arrows of outrageous fortune," that may disrupt the life cycle process—untimely death, birth of a handicapped child, migration, chronic illness, job loss, and so on.

At a sociocultural level, the vertical axis includes cultural and societal history, stereotypes, patterns of power, social hierarchies, and beliefs, all of which have been passed down through the generations. A group's history, particularly a legacy of trauma, will have an impact on families and individuals as they go through life (e.g., the impact of the holocaust on the Jews and the Germans; the impact of slavery and colonization on African-Americans, Latinos, and those who benefitted from these exploitations;

the impact of homophobia on both homosexuals and heterosexuals; etc.). The horizontal axis relates to community connections, current events, and social policy as they affect the individual and the family at a given time. This axis depicts the consequences on people's present lives of a society's "inherited" (vertical) norms of racism, sexism, classism, homophobia, and ethnic and religious prejudices as they are manifested in social, political, and economic structures that limit the options of some and support the power of others (Carter & McGoldrick, 2005b). With enough stress on this horizontal axis, any family will experience dysfunction. Furthermore, stressors on the vertical axis may create additional problems, so that even a small horizontal stress can have serious repercussions on the system. For example, if a young Mexican mother has many unresolved issues with her mother or father (vertical anxiety), she may have a particularly difficult time dealing with the normal vicissitudes of parenthood combined with the racism she experiences in a U.S. community (horizontal anxiety). The genogram helps the clinician to trace the flow of anxiety down through the generations and across the current family context.

Coincidences of historical events or of concurrent events in different parts of a family are viewed not as random happenings but as occurrences that may be interconnected systemically, though the connections may be hidden from view (McGoldrick, 1995). In addition, key family relationship changes seem more likely to occur at some times than at others. They are especially likely at points of life cycle transition. Symptoms tend to cluster around such transitions, as when family members face the task of reorganizing their relations with one another in order to go on to the next phase (Carter & McGoldrick, 2005). The symptomatic family may become stuck in time, unable to resolve its impasse in order to reorganize and move on. The history and relationship patterns revealed in a genogram assessment provide important clues about the nature of this impasse—how a symptom may have arisen to preserve or to prevent some relationship pattern or to protect some legacy of previous generations.

There are many relationship patterns in families. Of particular interest are patterns of relational distance. People may be very close, very distant, or somewhere in between. At one extreme are family members who are distant, in conflict, or cut off from each other. At the other extreme are families who seem almost stuck together in "emotional fusion." Family members in fused or poorly differentiated relationships are vulnerable to dysfunction, which tends to occur when the level of stress or anxiety exceeds the system's capacity to deal with it. The more closed the boundaries of a system become, the more immune it is to input from the environment, and consequently, the more rigid family patterns become. In other words, family members in a closed, fused system tend to react automatically to one another, practically impervious to events outside the system that require adaptation to changing conditions. Fusion may involve either positive or negative relationships; in other words, family members may feel very good about each other or experience almost nothing but hostility and conflict. In either case, there is an overdependent bond that ties the family together. With genograms, clinicians can map family boundaries and indicate which family subsystems are fused and thus likely to be closed to new input about changing conditions.

As Bowen (1978) and many others have pointed out, two-person relationships tend to be unstable. Under stress, two people tend to draw in a third. They stabilize the system by forming a coalition of two in relation to the third. The basic unit of an emotional system thus tends to be the triangle. As we shall see, genograms can help the clinician identify key triangles in a family system, see how triangular patterns repeat from one generation to the next, and design strategies for changing them (Fogarty, 1975; Guerin, Fogarty, Fay, & Kautto, 1996).

The members of a family tend to fit together as a functional whole. That is, the behaviors of different family members tend to be complementary or reciprocal. This does not mean that family members have equal power to influence relationships, as is obvious from the power differentials between men and women, between parents and children, between the elderly and younger family members, and between family members who belong to different cultures, classes, or races (McGoldrick, 1998). What it does mean is that belonging to a system opens people to reciprocal influences and involves them in one another's behavior in inextricable ways. This leads us to expect a certain interdependent fit or balance in families, involving give and take, action and reaction. Thus, a lack (e.g., irresponsibility) in one part of the family may be complemented by a surplus (overresponsibility) in another part. The genogram helps clinicians pinpoint the contrasts and idiosyncrasies in families that indicate this type of complementarity or reciprocal balance.

A Caveat

Throughout this book, we make assertions about families based on their genograms. These observations are offered as tentative hypotheses, as is true for genogram interpretations in general. They are suggestions for further exploration. Predictions based on the genogram are not facts. The principles for interpreting genograms should be seen as a roadmap that, by highlighting certain characteristics of the terrain, guides us through the complex territory of family life.

Many of the genograms shown here include more information than our discussion can cover. We encourage readers to use these illustrative genograms as a departure point for further developing their own skills in using and interpreting genograms.

Genograms are obviously limited in how much information they can display, although computers will allow us to collect a lot more information on a genogram than we can display at any one time. Clinicians always gather more information on people's lives than can ever appear on any single genogram illustration. We will soon be able to choose what aspects of a genogram we want to display for a particular purpose, while having the capacity to maintain the whole history in a computer database.

2

Creating Genograms

GATHERING FAMILY INFORMATION AND CONSTRUCTING a genogram should always be part of a more general process of joining, assessing, and helping a family. Information is gathered and organized as family members tell their story. Although basic genogram information can be collected in a structured format as part of a medical record, the information should always be treated with respect and gathered for a purpose. Sharing a family's history is a sacred contract, not a matter of mere technical fact-gathering. The drawing, however, needs to conform to certain rules so that all clinicians have the same understanding of genogram language. This chapter explains the graphic dimensions of the genogram. Later chapters will explain the underlying patterns of this physical map as they pertain to specific family patterns, cultural patterns, and cultural issues, as well as the clinical and research implications of this map.

Genogram information can be obtained by interviewing one family member or several. Clearly, getting information from several family members increases reliability and provides the opportunity to compare perspectives and observe interactions directly. By interviewing several family members, we get multiple points of view, which together fill out the family's history—although, of course, we then have to deal with the added complexity of having multiple versions of family history.

Because family patterns can be transmitted from one generation to the next, the clinician should scan the genogram for patterns that have repeated over several generations. Such repetitive patterns occur in functioning, relationships, and family structure. Recognizing such patterns often helps families avoid repeating unfortunate patterns or transmitting them into the future. Tracking critical events and changes in family functioning allows us to make systemic connections between seeming coincidences (such as anniversary reactions), assess the impact of traumatic changes on family functioning, identify the family's resources and vulnerability to future stresses, and finally to put all of this into a larger social, economic, and political context. This tracking enables the clinician to promote resilience based on past sources of strength, helping family members modify past adaptive strategies that have become dysfunctional (Walsh, 2006).

Of course, seeing several family members is not always feasible, and often the genogram interview is used with just one person. The time required to complete a genogram assessment can vary greatly. Although the basic information can usually be collected in 15 minutes or less (Wright & Leahey, 1999), a comprehensive family assessment interview involving several family members may take an hour or two. It may at times even take much longer, as family members may not initially feel comfortable enough to reveal traumatic aspects of their history. Clinicians often prefer to spread the questioning out over time and develop the genogram as they progress in their work with families. What makes genograms such a rich tool is that information gets corrected and expanded as the clinician learns more about the family history. Thus, over time, the genogram itself becomes a more accurate and comprehensive map of the family's story.

Mapping the Family Structure

The backbone of a genogram is a graphic depiction of how different family members are biologically, legally, and emotionally related to one another from one generation to the next. This map is a construction of squares and circles representing people and lines delineating their relationships. In taking a genogram we usually go back to the grandparents of the index person (IP), including at least three generations on the genogram (or four or even five generations if the IP has children and grandchildren). The year that a genogram depicts is written in the upper left-hand corner. Usually the genogram depicts the current year, but a clinician might also use the genogram to freeze-frame a moment in the past, such as the time of symptom onset or critical change in a family. Depicting a genogram for a particular moment in the family history is extremely useful, as it gives a picture of family members' ages, who was living in the home at the time, and the state of relationships in that period. When we choose one date in a person's life, other information, like deaths, ages, and important events, is calculated in relation to that date. If the person is dead, the age at death is shown instead (Chapter 8 shows a number of Freud genograms for different dates in their life cycle, indicating the ages of family members at each point).

On the following pages we will build a sample genogram, using the typical format for genogram construction and expanding the genogram as the clinician learns more about family members. Refer to the key to symbols printed on the inside front cover of the book to decipher the genograms.

Each family member is represented by a box (male) or circle (female). For the index person or identified patient (IP) around whom the genogram is constructed, the lines are doubled. The figures representing family members are connected by lines that indicate their biological and legal relationships. Two people who are married are connected by lines that go down, across, and back up, with the husband on the left and the wife on the right. An "m" followed by a date indicates when the couple was married.

Figure 2.1 shows Jose Rodriguez and his parents. We can tell he is the IP by the double line around his symbol, which is square (showing he is male). His age (27) is shown inside his symbol, and his birthdate (1980) is written to the left, above his symbol. His symbol hangs down from a line that joins his parents. (Children of a couple are hung down from the couple line in order of their birth, left to right.) Once the basic family structure or skeleton of the genogram is drawn, we can start adding information about the family, particularly regarding demographics, functioning, relationships, and critical family events.

Figure 2.2 shows more information about Jose and his parents. It also includes his siblings, whose symbols are made smaller and higher than his own. Typically the IP is shown lower and a bit larger than his or her siblings, as you can see with Jose. Spouses of siblings are shown lower and smaller than the siblings themselves, so that the birth order remains clear, as will be seen in the next genogram. This allows you to clearly see the

Figure 2.1 Jose Rodriguez and Parents (2007)

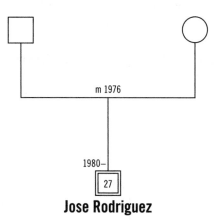

structure of the family, including birth order, gender, and distance in age between siblings, and to develop hypotheses related to it. Often we have no way of knowing for sure whether our hypotheses about a particular family are accurate, but hypothesizing about patterns on a genogram is a basic way to understand the family's history. We see that Jose is the 2nd of four siblings. (The small black circle on the far left indicates that Carmella had a miscarriage in 1978.) He has an older brother Peter, who has a high-school education and works in construction, and his younger twin siblings, David and Maria, are a law student and a nurse, respectively. Converging lines connect the twins to the parental line. If the twins are identical, a bar between their birth lines connects them to each other, as will be seen in the next genogram for Jose's nieces. Given the distance in age, we might assume that Jose and Peter, who is only a year older than he, would grow up as a pair and that perhaps the twins, being 4 years younger, would be another pair, though it could be that the three brothers would be a group and the sister the outsider. However, other factors may modify such alliance patterns; in this case, for instance, the two oldest brothers are different on major dimensions (sports and education).

We also see that Jose is a computer programmer with a BA, and that Jose's mother, Carmella, is 59 and works as an office manager whereas the father, Jorge, who is 58, is a cab driver. We may wonder what family dynamics led the younger siblings to receive more education and what impact educational and occupational differences may have on family relationships.

Figure 2.2 Rodriguez Nuclear Family (2007)

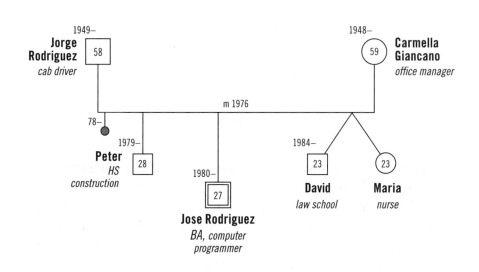

Figure 2.3 expands the genogram upwards to show the father's family of origin and downwards to show the next generation. For a person who is dead, an **X** is placed inside the symbol, as indicated for the paternal grandparents. Birth and death dates are separated by a dash above the symbol. The person's current age or age at death is usually indicated within the symbol, as we can see for the grandparents. In genograms that go back more than three generations, symbols for individuals in the distant past are not usually crossed out, as they are all presumably dead. Only untimely or traumatic deaths are usually indicated with an **X** on such genograms. Here, we see that the father, Jorge, is placed lower than his siblings to make clear his place in the sibling line. We learn also through this expansion that Jose is married to a Russian woman, Katya, and that they are expecting their first child (indicated by a triangle). We also see that his older brother,

Figure 2.3 Jose Rodriguez With Father's Family (2007)

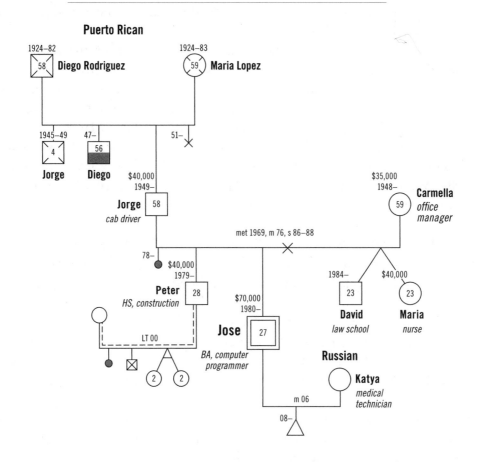

Peter, has 2-year-old identical twin daughters and that he and his partner, who have lived together since 2000, indicated by "LT 00," experienced both a miscarriage and then the stillbirth of a son prior to the twins' birth. Looking upwards we begin to learn about Jose's father. Jorge was the youngest child in his Puerto Rican family and was named for an oldest brother who died at age 4, the same year Jorge was born. Exploring family patterns of naming and birth order can reveal a great deal about relationships, as we will see. The second son, Diego, named for the grandfather, has an active alcohol problem, which is probably an ongoing stress on the whole family. We see also that the grandmother had an abortion of the final pregnancy in 1951 (indicated by an X). It seems she was so overwhelmed by the loss of her oldest son that she felt she could not bear to risk having another child whose loss would break her heart.

The genogram also includes the annual income of the immediate family members, indicating that Jose is currently by far the most financially successful. Making much more money than his older brother may create some distance between them. Finally, we learn that Jorge and Carmella met in 1969 and were separated from 1986 to 1988. Marriage, separation, divorce, and living together dates, along with dates when a couple met, are included above the couple line. Backslashes signify a disruption in the marriage—one slash for separation, two for divorce— and a slash in the other direction (creating an X) signifies reconciliation after a separation or divorce.

Figure 2.4 adds the mother's family of origin. We see that Carmella came from an Italian family that had a miscarriage and then twins who died at birth. Following these losses, they adopted a daughter (indicated by a dashed line next to the solid line), the same year the mother became pregnant and had Carmella. Another biological son was born when Carmella was 3, and in 1960 the couple took in a foster son (indicated by a dotted line). Shortly thereafter, Carmella's parents separated, when she was 12. The father had a live-in girlfriend from that time until his death in 1979.

The genogram also shows that Carmella's younger brother was gay and in a sexual relationship with an African-American man, and that Katya's parents were Russian Jewish immigrants.

Jose's presenting problem was free-floating anxiety to the point of almost incapacitating panic. His genogram may help us to develop some hypotheses about his anxiety. It is perhaps not surprising that he should become anxious shortly before the birth of his first child. From the genogram we can see that there was a loss of the first child for three generations: His father's oldest brother died at 4, and his mother's parents lost their first three children. His parents had a miscarriage before the birth of his older brother, and that brother experienced a miscarriage and a stillbirth before the birth of their twins. But there may be other factors operating as well. Jose's father, who was named for his dead brother, is now 58, the same age *his* father, Diego, was when he died. Coincidentally,

Figure 2.4 Jose Rodriguez With Mother's Family

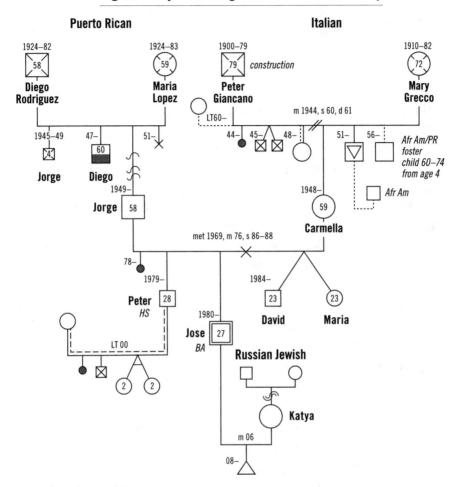

Jose's mother, Carmella, is 59, the same age as the paternal grandmother when she died. This could possibly create added anxiety for Jorge, who may be passing down the anxiety to his son, to whom he is very close.

Symbols Used to Denote Family Experiences and Relationships

Various symbols are used to show common family experiences and relationships. The Rodriguez family illustrates the use of many of these symbols (Color Figure 1). For example, you can see that Jose's father was an immigrant and had experience living in more than one culture. The single-wave line above his symbol reflects the 2 years he was in Vietnam in the military from 1967 to 1969. The double-wave line below this single wave indicates that after he returned from Vietnam, he immigrated to the mainland U.S. and has remained here ever since. The "SL" to the lower right of his symbol indicates that he is both a smoker and had difficulty with the English language as an immigrant. (His daughter-in-law, Katya, had the same difficulty.) The O beside the symbol of his older brother indicates that the brother is obese. We can also see that this brother is cut off from his father for many years, from 1966–1981, indicated by the line with a double slash between them. However, they repaired the cutoff (shown by the circle between the cutoff lines) the year before the father died.

This genogram also reveals a set of family relationships in which Jose may be pitted against his older brother, to whom the mother always felt very attached because he was born 3 months after her beloved father died. Carmella had a conflictual relationship with her older sister since childhood, just as her sons, Peter and Jose, do. Peter is athletic and good-looking, whereas Jose is short and uncoordinated, characteristics that we have also noted on the genogram. Other symbols reflect the nature of the relationships between other family members; refer to the key on the inside front cover to decipher them.

Mapping Couple Relationships with Multiple Partners

Couple relationships with multiple partners add a degree of complexity that is challenging to depict on a genogram. Figure 2.5, which diagrams the wives of King Henry VIII, shows one way of handling this.

The rule of thumb is that, when feasible, the different marriages follow in order from left to right if all members are deceased, but for current family members, the most recent partner would usually be shown closest to a spouse. In the case of Henry VIII, because all are deceased, the wives are shown in order from left to right: Catherine of Aragon, Ann Boleyn, Jane Seymour, Ann of Cleves, Katherine Howard, and finally Katherine Parr. The marriage and divorce dates should help to make the order clear. However, when each spouse has had multiple partners (and

Figure 2.5 Henry VIII and His Wives

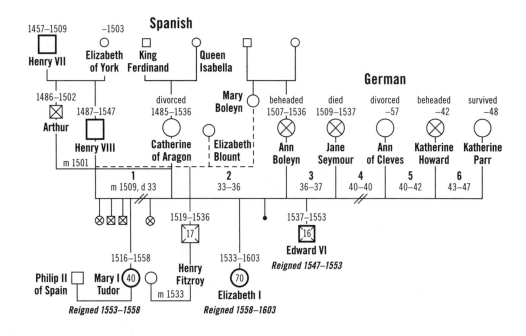

possibly children from previous marriages), mapping the complex web of relationships can be difficult indeed. In this case the genogram indicates two of Henry VIII's many affairs (shown by dotted lines): one with Elizabeth Blount, because it produced a son, and another with Mary Boleyn, because she was the sister of his second wife, Ann Boleyn. A further complication is that Henry's first wife, Catherine of Aragon, had previously been married to Henry's older brother, Arthur.

One solution to these types of problems is to place the relationship you are focusing on in the center and the partner's other spouses off to the side, as in Figure 2.6. Such situations can get very complicated when each spouse has had other spouses. If previous spouses have had other partners, it may be necessary to draw a second line, slightly above the first marriage line, to indicate these relationships, as is indicated for Roger Vadim and Tom Hayden.

Figure 2.6 Husband (Ted Turner), Wife (Jane Fonda), and Several Partners of Each

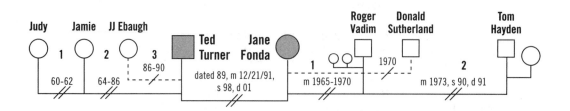

The next genogram, of Jane Fonda's father (Figure 2.7), is even more complicated. Each spouse had been married several times. Henry's first wife, Margaret Sullavan, had been married once before she married him, and she remarried afterwards. Fonda's second wife, Frances Seymour, had earlier been married to George Brokaw, who himself had previously been married to Clare Booth, who in turn later married Henry Luce. What cannot be seen on this genogram is that Henry Fonda and his wife Frances Seymour lived very near to his previous wife Margaret Sullavan and her next husband, Leland Hayward (who was Fonda's agent) when they were in California. The two families then moved next door to each other in Connecticut, so the marriage chronology does not tell the whole story.

Whenever possible it is preferable to show children from different marriages in their correct birth order (oldest on the left, youngest on the right). If there are many children in a family, an alternate method to show them is the one depicted in Figure 2.7. This method can be used to save space. The drawback of this method is that it becomes difficult to see the birth order. For example, Amy, perhaps Jane and Peter Fonda's half-sister, is shown to the left of Peter, even though she was many years younger than he. Jane and Peter's other half-sister, Pan, who was 5 years older than Jane and lived with them from age 5 until she went to college, is also not shown in birth order, as she was, in fact, the oldest of all. An alternative genogram showing all the Fonda siblings in birth order (Figure 2.8) could be relevant for understanding the siblings in relation to each other. Notice that in this case Brokaw's next wife, Clare Booth Luce, has been omitted to keep the graphic clear. With complex families, choices always have to be made between clarity and level of detail. Of course, with computers

Figure 2.7 Henry Fonda Marriages (1960)

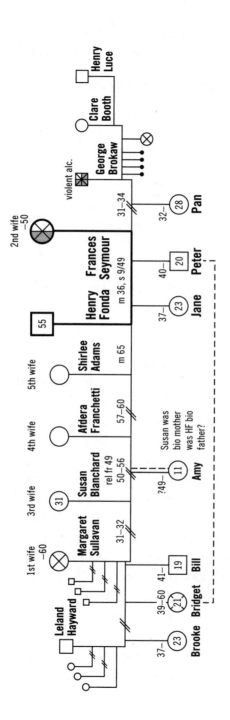

that can hold data on many relationships, choices can be made about whom to include on a particular genogram graphic.

Figure 2.8 Fonda Children in Birth Order (1956)

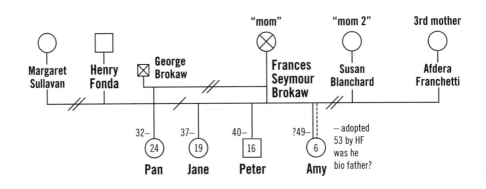

If a couple are involved in a love affair or living together but not legally married, their relationship is depicted with a line similar to that for married couples, except that the line is dotted rather than solid (as shown for Jane Fonda and Donald Sutherland in Figure 2.6). If they are in a committed relationship there can be a dotted and a solid line to show the permanency but that the relationship is not legal, as shown in Figure 2.9 for Jodie Foster's mother, Brandy, and her partner, Josephine. When spouses have had partners of both sexes, it may be necessary to draw the relationship lines at different levels to clarify who was connected with whom. When there have been a great many partners, it may also be necessary to be selective, showing only the most significant relationships.

Figure 2.9 shows the family of Jodie Foster. Her father, Lucius, fathered children by five partners: three wives and two other partners. (We have drawn lines down indicating the number and placement of children, but not their gender, as it was not our focus.) Recording the specific chronology of couple relationships can be significant in tracking family patterns, a process that will become much easier with computer software,

Figure 2.9 Jodie Foster

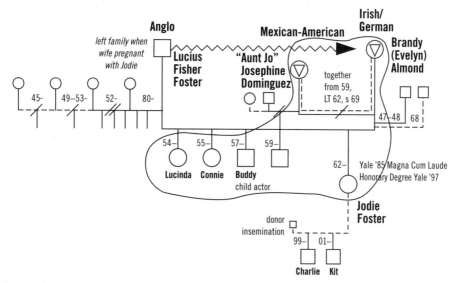

where the entire couple chronology could be charted but only certain information shown. Jodie, for example, was conceived and born 3 years after her parents separated—indeed, shortly before the divorce came through.

Jodie's mother was in a committed couple relationship with Jo Dominguez from 1959. The couple began living together in 1962 (LT 62). Jo's prominence in the family is indicated by depicting the couple line for Brandy and Jo just above that of the biological father. "Aunt Jo" became a haven of stability for the children, providing financial, physical, and emotional support to them for many years. Brandy and Jo separated in 1969. Jo's husband is shown smaller and higher, along with the woman he spent the rest of his life with. He never divorced Jo and was thus not free to marry again; his other relationship is indicated with a dotted line.

Single-parent adoption can be diagrammed as seen in Color Figure 2. This genogram shows the family of Mia Farrow, who had biological children (including twin sons, Matthew and Sasha, and a third son, Fletcher) and interracially adopted three children (Soon-Yi, Lark, and Daisy) with her second husband, Andre Previn. She adopted three more children during her relationship with Woody Allen (Moses, Dylan/Eliza/Malone, and Tam), the first two of whom he adopted as well, and they had a biological child together (Satchel, now called Seamus). Finally, she adopted four more children on her own: Thaddeus, Frankie-Minh, Isaiah, and Kaeli. If at all possible, the cultural background should be indicated, as it is an important part of anyone's history. Because this genogram is so complex, we have also offered color coding (blue for names, red for disabilities, green for location and cultural heritage, and other colors for other information.

When living situations are complicated, it is helpful to draw lines circling the different households. This is especially important in multinuclear families, where children spend time in various households, as in Figure 2.10 for Jackie Bouvier Kennedy and her sister Lee after their parents' separation when Jackie was 7. During the school year the sisters lived in New York City with their mother, maternal grandparents, and maternal great-grandmother. (The great-grandmother, however, was thought "uncouth" and kept upstairs most of the time. Furthermore, the grandparents, although never separated, did not speak to each other, despite the fact that they sat together at meals!) During the summers, Jackie and Lee spent time with their father's large extended family on Long Island, though their father appeared only occasionally.

When the "functional" family is different from the biological or legal family, as when children are raised by a grandparent or in an informal adoptive family, it is useful to create a separate genogram to show the functional structure (see Watts Jones, 1998). When children have lived as part of several families—biological, foster, and adoptive—separate genograms may help to depict the child's multiple families over time.

Color Figure 3 shows the changes in Louis Armstrong's family from the year he was born, 1901, through 1918. Louis Armstrong, perhaps the greatest jazz musician of all time, was an amazingly inventive, quick, and technically and creatively extraordinary musician who grew up in poverty and in shifting living situations from his early childhood in New Orleans. Luckily he found support for his phenomenal talents from a relatively early age and through his powerful intelligence was able to use his inventiveness to develop his talents. Soon after he was born he went to live with his father's mother, Josephine Armstrong, as his parents separated and his

Figure 2.10 Family of Jackie Bouvier Kennedy

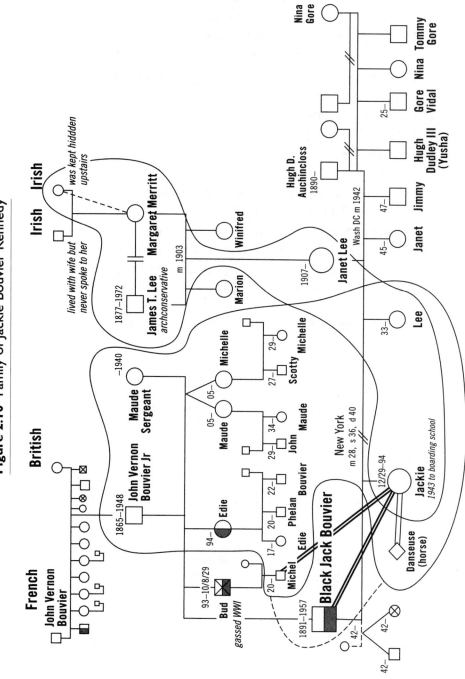

father went to live with another woman. The next year, however, his parents got back together, and in 1903, Louis's sister, Beatrice, was born. But Louis remained with his grandmother until 1905, when his parents separated, and he and his sister, who was called Mama Lucy, moved in with their mother. They lived with her and a number of boyfriends over the next several years. In 1912, when he was 11, Louis shot off a gun on a holiday, was arrested, and was sent to the New Orleans Home for Colored Waifs. He remained there for a couple of years until about 1914, when he went to live with his father and half siblings. But he soon returned to live with his mother, and he stayed with her until 1918, when, at the age of 17, he moved to Chicago to work with King Oliver's band.

Figure 2.11, which illustrates a lesbian couple with a child born to one of them, Sue, and adopted by the other, Ann, demonstrates how to diagram children conceived by donor insemination. The very small square indicated as the child's biological father is a sperm donor. The parents' previous relationships are also shown on the genogram. Sue had been

Figure 2.11 Donor Insemination and Lesbian Network

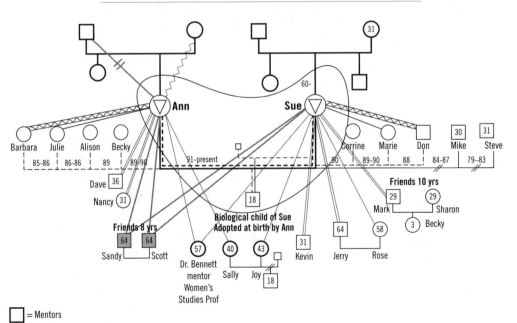

 = Mentors

= Couple Friends

married and divorced several times and Ann had had several live-in partners. Burke and Faber (1997) have suggested using a "genogrid," an adaptation of the genogram, to help to depict the liaisons, long-term bonds,
and social networks of lesbian couples. The genogrid distinguishes historical influences, primary emotional and social relationships, and intimate
relationships. This genogram reflects the relationships suggested by
Burke and Faber.

Missing Information

Information is always missing from genograms, but what information is
missing in itself may give clues to family secrets, cutoffs, and so on. When
only partial information can be unearthed, that is included. For instance,
in the Freud family, which we will discuss in Chapter 8, Sigmund's father
was married three times. We know that he had four children with his first
wife, two of whom died early, but nothing is known about them or his
second wife, Rebecca. One suspects something must have gone very
wrong for no one ever to mention the other children again or the wife,
especially because Sigmund's older half brothers, as well as the father,
would have known her.

Tracking Family Patterns on the Genogram

At times it is useful to create different genograms to show different kinds
of information, perhaps one for basic demographics, one for relationship
patterns, one for patterns of family creativity and dysfunction, one for the
family's community connections, and others to provide snapshots of key
points in the family's history, such as the point of symptom onset.

Demographic Information: Getting the "Facts"

In fleshing out the history of the immediate and extended families, our
initial concern is with getting the "facts" on each family member. These are
the vital statistics of the family, the type of objective data that can usually
be verified by public records. Demographic information includes ethnic

background, ages, dates of birth and death, whereabouts, income, occupation, and educational level. There is a specific place to put some of this information: Current age or age at death goes inside the person's symbol, the birth date goes above the person's symbol and to the left, the death date goes above the symbol to the right, and the person's current location and income go above the birth and death dates. Other demographic information goes near the person's symbol wherever there is room.

Color Figure 4 shows demographic information for the Fonda family. The following information would be relevant for each family member, though we do not have all such information for the Fonda family.

- dates of birth, marriage, separation, divorce, illness, and death (including cause)
- sibling position
- ethnic, class, and religious background
- any changes in class through education, income, or marriage
- current religious practices and changes in religion
- occupation and education
- current whereabouts
- state of current relationships (closeness, conflict, cutoff)

As the clinician collects more information about family events, certain gaps will appear in the history. The clinician can use the genogram to map the family's evolution through time and to broaden the historical perspective on the family. At times family members themselves become so interested in their story that they begin historical research to expand their perspective. Family members may learn more information by speaking to relatives, consulting family bibles, reading local or regional histories, or obtaining medical, genealogical, and other public records.

Patterns of Functioning

Information about functioning includes more or less objective data on the medical, emotional, and behavioral functioning of family members. Objective signs, such as absenteeism from work and drinking patterns, may be more useful indications of a person's functioning, although more commonly family members may start by indicating that the family member is "weird." Indicators of highly successful functioning should also be included. The information collected on each person is placed next to his or her symbol on the genogram. Using a software program with a database will allow the clinician to add details on the functioning of each individual in the family without crowding up the genogram, because they can be hidden or shown as the clinician chooses. The therapist might also indicate a global level of functioning on the genogram by each person's symbol and track changes in the functioning over time on a family chronology.

Addictions are shown by filling in the bottom half of the square or circle. Those in recovery from addiction have only the lower left half filled in. If they have attended therapy, Alcoholics Anonymous, or another recovery program, or if they have any strong institutional affiliation, such as with a church, fraternal organization, or other group, this can be indicated by a line out to a rectangle indicating the therapist or institutional connection.

Color Figure 5 shows information on the functioning of the Fonda family. On this genogram, rectangles linked to Ted Turner and Peter Fonda indicate their relationships with their therapists. The dates of treatment can also be shown. Suspected alcohol or drug abuse can be indicated by slanted lines on the bottom half of the symbol, as indicated for Peter Fonda. In Peter's case, he has acknowledged using drugs over many years, but sees himself as lucky that it never became an addiction (Fonda, 1998). Using genogram software, one could also track type of abuse (daily marijuana use, weekend binge drinking, etc.), in order to track the evolution of the substance abuse problem over time.

Serious mental or physical illness can be indicated by filling in the left half of the symbol. In general, the nature of the illness should also be indicated near the symbol. Genogram software will soon allow one to track illnesses, both physical and psychological, in considerable detail, and then choose to show particular illnesses for diagnostic purposes, or, on the other hand, to hide details in order to track other family patterns more easily. When a person has both an addiction and a mental illness, three-quarters of the symbol is filled in, as indicated for Jane and Peter's maternal grandfather, Eugene Ford Seymour. When he or she is mentally ill but in recovery from addiction, the left half is filled in and the lower right is empty with a horizontal line across the middle of the symbol.

The functioning of family members may repeat itself across several generations. In such cases, a particular style of functioning (whether adaptive or maladaptive) or of dealing with problems is passed down from one generation to the next. This transmission does not necessarily occur in linear fashion. An alcoholic father may have children who become teetotalers, and their children may again become drinkers.

Often the presenting problem of the family will have occurred in previous generations. Numerous symptomatic patterns, such as alcoholism, incest, physical symptoms, violence, and suicide, tend to be repeated in families from generation to generation. By noting the pattern repetition, the clinician may be helped to understand the family's present adaptation to the situation and to short circuit the process. For example, let's look again at Color Figure 5 for the Fonda family. Jane remembered that her mother had had plastic surgery to improve her figure and recognized that her mother undoubtedly had struggled with the same body image problems she struggled with herself (Fonda, 2006). Margaret Sullavan's daughter Bridget Hayward committed suicide less than a year after her mother had committed suicide herself. Given the evidence that one suicide seems to make suicide an option for others in the family, specific efforts at suicide prevention may well be indicated in such families.

The same can be said for preventive intervention in families with a history of such symptoms as sexual abuse and alcohol abuse. For example, Ted Turner (Color Figure 6) reached a crisis in 1991 at age 53, the same age at which his father had shot himself in the head with the gun with which he had taught Ted to shoot years before. Ted, like his father, had led a driven life of work and hard drinking. But Ted managed not to repeat his father's pattern. Instead, that age became for him a time of critical transformation of his life. It was the year he married Jane Fonda. Both of them gave up drinking, and Ted committed himself to expanding his life rather than letting his obsession with work drive him over the edge, as it had for his father.

Clinicians can track multigenerational patterns of resilience, strength, and success as well as failure (Walsh, 1995, 2006). All the families in this book should be assessed for their resilience as well as their problems.

Among the most amazing are the Hepburns (see Color Figure 17), who illustrate the repeated trauma of suicide and depression along with the resilience and power of strong women on their own; the Fonda/Turner families, which show an amazing ability to survive and transform themselves beyond the trauma of loss, suicide, silence, and mental illness, turning hardship into productivity and self-regeneration; the Bell family (see Figure 6.2), in which deafness is complemented by inventiveness and resourcefulness with sound; and Frida Kahlo (see Color Figure 9), who illustrates an amazing ability to transform cultural difference, disruption, loss, trauma, and physical disability into transcendent strength and creative energy. Another remarkably creative, resilient family is the Blackwell family (Figure 2.12), who show a dramatic pattern of strong and successful women. The parents were Dissenting Congregationalists who believed in equal education for women. This amazing family included the first woman physician and the first woman minister in the U.S., as well as numerous other successful woman physicians, ministers, artists, and suffragettes. Yet, as so often happens, patterns of success and failure coexist in the family. In each succeeding generation, along with all these outstandingly successful women, one daughter appears to have been an invalid. Of Samuel and Hannah's five daughters, Anna was a writer, Elizabeth the first woman physician in the U.S., Ellen, an accomplished artist, and Emily, another of the early women physicians. The second daughter, Marion, was always sickly. Their brother Samuel married Antoinette Brown, the first woman minister in the U.S., and together they also had five daughters: Edith and Ethyl became physicians, Florence became a successful minister, and Agnes became an artist. The third daughter, Grace, became an invalid. The three sons of Samuel and Hannah Blackwell who married were quite extraordinary in their own right, especially for marrying three remarkable women, Antoinette Brown, Lucy Stone (one of the most important early suffrage leaders), and Emma Lawrence (Lucy's cousin and another early suffrage leader). The next generation had 16 children altogether (not counting 3 infant deaths), 7 of them adopted, several by the unmarried daughters. The only adopted son, Paul, was given up because of family disapproval. In a family like this, one can't help but ask about the underlying gender constraints and empowerment mechanisms. It is interesting that none of the Blackwell daughters ever married.

Figure 2.12 Blackwell Family

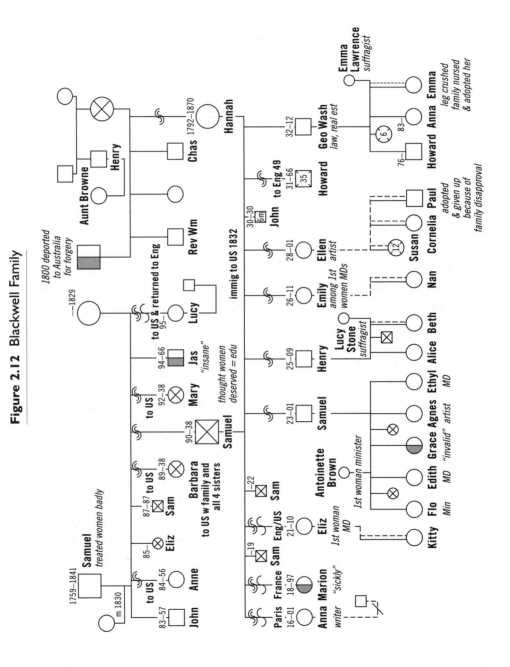

Only one sister, Anna, became engaged—to a "handsome, wealthy, educated, amiable and fascinating man"—and the family closed ranks against him, writing very strong letters to dissuade her from the marriage (Hays, 1967, pp. 52–53). When another sister, Marion, fell in love with a young man who was a friend of her brother's, Elizabeth wrote to discourage her, "The idea of your union seems to me now utterly impossible," offering herself as a substitute companion for her sister's romantic interest (Hays, 1967, p. 53).

Another common pattern of family functioning is success in one generation followed by remarkable failure in the next. This may be particularly true of the families of famous people, where children may rebel against pressure to live up to the reputations of their parents. The Adams family is a powerful example of that phenomenon, with all but one of the children of John Adams having serious problems (Figure 2.13). The same was true for the one successful son in that second generation, John Quincy Adams, whose first two sons had serious problems. Only in the fourth generation did the one successful son, Charles Francis Adams, manage to produce a group of children who were, except for one, relatively functional.

Many people may believe that they are almost fated by family circumstance for the path they take in life. For example, Martin Luther King (see Figure 5.6) said of himself: "Of course I was religious. I grew up in the church. My father is a preacher, my grandfather was a preacher, my great-grandfather was a preacher, my only brother is a preacher, my daddy's brother is a preacher. So I didn't have much choice" (Carson, 2001, p. 1).

Specific patterns of functioning may also be repeated across the generations. For example, a quick glance at the family of Carl Jung (Color Figure 7) shows again a preponderance of ministers: Jung's father, two paternal uncles, all six maternal uncles, the maternal grandfather, and three maternal granduncles. Next one sees that Jung was following in his forefather's footsteps in becoming a physician: Both his paternal grandfather, for whom he was named, and his paternal great-grandfather were physicians. Finally, Jung himself, who was from his youth attracted to alchemy and the supernatural, was again following a pattern of many other family members who believed in the supernatural, including his mother, maternal grandfather, and maternal cousin, Helena Preiswerk, who claimed to be a medium and whose séances Jung attended in his

Figure 2.13 Adams Family

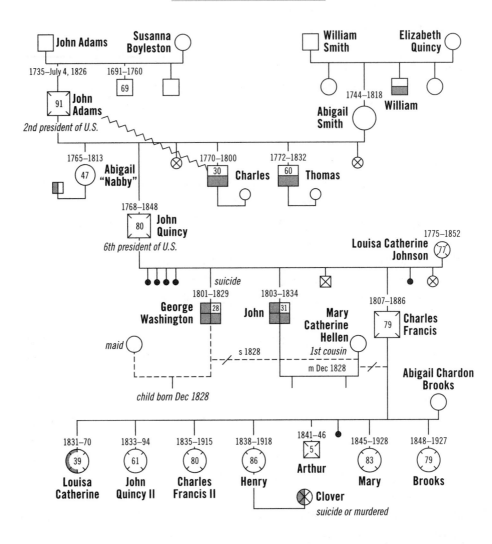

youth. It is not surprising then, that Jung became a physician with a profound interest in religion and in the supernatural. It fit with the predominant patterns in his family. One might be more surprised if he had ignored medicine, religion, and the supernatural in his own work. He also had fears of inheriting the mental illness of his mother and paternal great-grandmother, Sophie, and he did indeed suffer a breakdown in 1913.

Family Relationships and Roles

Delineating the relationships between family members is the most inferential aspect of genogram construction. Such characterizations are based on the reports of family members and direct observation. Different lines are used to symbolize various types of relationship between two family members. Although such commonly used relationship descriptors as "fused" or "conflictual" are difficult to define operationally and have different connotations for clinicians with various perspectives, these symbols are useful in clinical practice. Relationships in a family do, of course, change over time, so this aspect of genograms is one of the most subjective and most subject to change. Furthermore, one might argue that any conflictual relationship implies underlying connection, so that any highly conflictual relationship by definition reflects fusion as well as conflict. Cutoffs can also involve great conflict or silent distancing. Dominance or relationships in which one person focuses an enormous amount of energy on another can be illustrated by a heavy straight line with an arrow in the direction of the one who is focused upon. Other important relationships, such as hostile/dependent and ambivalent ones, are harder to depict on a genogram. Relationships involving physical abuse are depicted by a zigzag line ending in a solid arrow, indicating who was abused by whom. To indicate sexual abuse we use the same zigzag line and solid arrow, but with straight lines on the outside of the zigzag line to differentiate from physical abuse. Emotional abuse is shown by a zigzag line with the arrow not filled in.

Because relationship patterns can be quite complex, it is often useful to represent them on a separate genogram, which will be easier with genogram software. It will also be possible with the genogram software to indicate the timing of changes in relationship patterns, which may be very important in tracking family process. It is especially relevant to indicate the start and end dates on any cutoffs in the family, as cutoff is likely to ripple out into other patterns of illness or dysfunction.

Relationship Questions

There are many relationship questions you may want to ask to begin to get an understanding of the family, such as the following:

- Are there any family members who do not speak to each other or who have ever had a period of not speaking? Are there any who were/are in serious conflict?
- Are there any family members who are extremely close?
- Who helps out when help is needed?
- In whom do family members confide?
- All couples have some sort of marital difficulties. What sorts of problems and conflicts have you encountered? What about your parents' and siblings' marriages?
- How do you each get along with each child? Have any family members had particular problems dealing with their children?
- What are the power dynamics in family relationships? Are there certain family members who are intimidated by others? Are there certain family members who have more power to define what will happen in relationships? This refers not just to family members who have charisma or emotional power in the family, but also specifically to family members who have more power because of their status in the family and/or in society because of gender, race, skin color, socioeconomic status, age, and sexual orientation.

The clinician should get as many perspectives on family relationships as possible. For example, the husband may be asked, "How close do you think your mother and your older brother were?" The wife might then be asked for her impression of that relationship. The goal is to uncover differences, as well as agreements, about family relationships and to use the different perceptions of the family to enrich the genogram picture for both the clinician and the family.

From the relationships between family members, the clinician also begins to get a sense of the complementarity of roles in the family. Questions that elucidate the role structure include:

- Has any family member been focused on as the caretaker? The problematic one? The "sick" one? The "bad" one? The "mad" one? The "selfish" one? The strong one? The weak one? The dominant one? The submissive one? The successful one? The failure?

- Who is seen as warm? As cold? As caring? As distant?

Labels or nicknames used by family members are particularly instructive. Often, each family member has a family-wide label that describes and even circumscribes his or her position in the family—for example, the tyrant, the supermother, the star, the rebel, or the baby. Labels are good clues to the emotional patterns in the system.

Sometimes it is useful to ask how members of the present family would be characterized by other family members—"How do you think your older brother would describe your relationship with your wife?" or "How would your father have described you when you were 13, the age of your son now?" Again, gathering as many perspectives as possible enriches the family's view of itself and introduces channels for new information.

Relationship patterns of closeness, distance, conflict, and so on may also repeat themselves over the generations. Genograms often reveal complex relational patterns that would be missed if not mapped across a few generations. Recognizing such patterns can, it is hoped, help families avoid continuing the repetition in future generations. One example of such a repetition would be a family in which mother and son in each generation have a special alliance whereas father and son have a negative, conflictual relationship. Realizing the predictability of such patterns and the multigenerational programming involved, a son might choose consciously to change his relationship with his parents in order to change this pattern.

The family of the playwright Eugene O'Neill shows a multigenerational pattern of estrangement between father and children (Figure 2.14). Eugene's paternal grandfather deserted his family, returned to Ireland, and probably committed suicide. Both Eugene and his older brother Jamie felt estranged from their father, James, although they were both totally dependent on him emotionally and financially, and all of them blamed each other for the mother's drug addiction. In the next generation, Eugene, the playwright, refused to see or even mention the name of his daughter, Oona, after her marriage to Charlie Chaplin. He did the same with his son Shane after Shane's son died of neglect. O'Neill never even saw his oldest son, Eugene, Jr., until he was 12, and they were estranged at the time of Eugene Jr.'s suicide at age 40.

Figure 2.14 O'Neill Family Repetitive Patterns

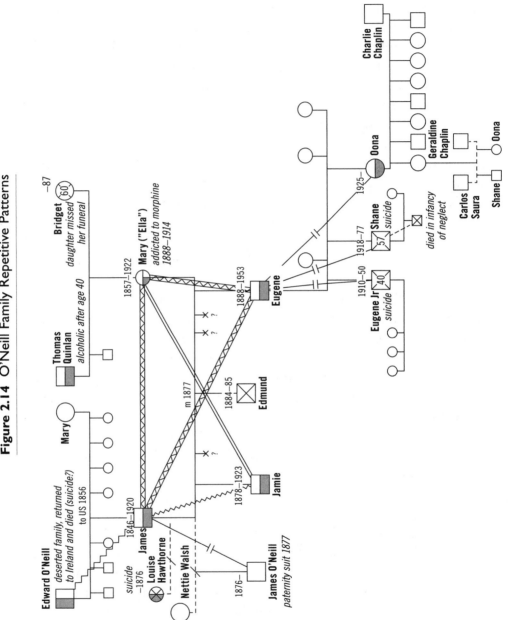

Adding Contextual Factors to Genograms

As the basic genogram is being drawn, it is important to make sure that the context of the family is indicated: their cultural, religious, socioeconomic, and community values and connections, including work and friend relationships. Although the complexity of these contextual factors is impossible to convey on a single graphic, some basic information about this context is essential and computers will soon make tracking these dimensions a bit easier by enabling us to record information and show it a little at a time. Meanwhile, we always indicate important friendships, work connections, religious affiliation, and cultural heritage, along with as much as possible about the other context of the family.

By asking in an open-ended way what other contextual forces may influence the person, it is possible to get a much broader range of responses, from "belief in social justice" to "shopping" or "music" to "social status." It is also important to ask whether any nonbiological or nonlegal members of the family belong on the genogram, as well as what other key influences should be included. We draw these factors as rectangles, as one does for institutional involvements such as AA, healthcare institutions, or religious communities. Lines can be drawn between family members and the influences that have been included. As can be seen for the Rodriguez family (Color Figure 8), such a contexual genogram can indicate both points of connection and points of tension for a family. In their case, hard work and holidays are strong points of similarity, whereas sports and education created tension between the two older brothers. Jose's wife's Judaism is a "hot" issue for his mother, which repeats a conflict she and her husband had between the Catholic church and Espiritismo.

Such connections can help families become aware of shared values and also point out connections that cause conflict, which may be important for clinical intervention. Contextual influences may include:

- *institutional affiliations*: religious, business, political, or community service institutions; fraternities; professional, military, self-help, athletic, choir, TV, Internet, and hobby groups
- *physical/psychological/spiritual activities*: working out, meditation, yoga

- *support systems* (those that support the family and those that are supported by the family): neighbors, housekeepers, accountants, lawyers, doctors/chiropractors or other caretakers, hairdressers, God, children, pets
- *business and governmental institutions*: legal system, political system, welfare system, social service, credit card companies, insurance companies
- *values or interests*: education, food, sports, music, art, outdoors, stock market

Cultural Genograms: Incorporating Ethnicity, Race, Religion, Spirituality, and Migration

Genograms should always depict information on clients' problems within a contextual framework that takes into account their cultural background (see bibliography on Cultural Genograms). Thus, all genograms should, in this sense, be cultural genograms. Clients in the U.S. are often disconnected from their cultural history; thus, genogram tracking that places them in class, gender, ethnic, racial, and religious context is part of helping them understand who they are, just as questioning around sibling patterns, untimely loss, and multigenerational triangles helps people see themselves in a family context.

Genograms help us contextualize our kinship network in terms of culture, class, race, gender, religion, family process, and migration history. When we ask people to identify themselves ethnically, we are asking them to highlight themes of cultural continuity and cultural identity to make them more apparent. The genogram is a practical, visual tool for assessment of family patterns and context as well as a therapeutic intervention in itself. Genograms allow clinicians to quickly conceptualize the individual's context within the growing diversity of family forms and patterns in our society. By its nature the process of doing a genogram involves the telling of stories and emphasizes respect for the client's perspective, while encouraging multiple views of different family members. By scanning the family system culturally and historically and assessing previous life cycle transitions, the clinician can place present issues in the context of the family's evolutionary patterns of geography, migration, and family process.

Color Figure 10 shows the cultural genogram of Frida Kahlo and Diego Rivera, who are typical of many people in the Americas in their complex mixture of cultural heritages. (See Color Figure 12 for a similar map of the cultural heritage of the British Royal family.) Kahlo appears to have had a very strong idea of the importance of this heritage, doing her own artistic version of a genogram, including family members who had died or been cut off, as can be seen in Color Figure 9. On her version you can see the cultural mix of her grandparents, as well as the son who died in infancy, and perhaps the half sisters who were extruded from the family and sent to a convent before the mother, Matilda, would agree to marry the father.

Spirituality, Religion, and Fraternal Organizations

Although religion and spiritual resources have, throughout world history, been a primary resource for families in responding to all distress, therapists have often tended to ignore this dimension in their clinical assessment. But religious practices and beliefs (and changes in those beliefs) are important markers of family process. We know that religious beliefs have a strong impact on clients' responses to illness and other stress, as well as on recovery from addiction. But spiritual beliefs also join and alienate family members. George Washington (see Figure 5.3), who kept all diaries and letters from the early age of 14 (amounting in the end to more than 20 volumes of papers), never once mentioned "Christ," though he was a nominal Christian. However, like most of the founding fathers, he was deeply invested in the fraternity of Freemasons, which was a major building block of the Revolution and of his views of government (Johnson, 2005, pp. 10–11). Such secret societies, with their religious, political, and social underpinnings, may have a strong influence on business, friendships, and family relationships. It is undoubtedly of some significance that in the 2004 presidential election, both candidates were members of another elite secret fraternity with religious undertones—the Skull and Bones society at Yale University, where members promise to keep their fraternal (and religiously connected) secrets until death. John Kerry was descended from one of the founders of the society; George Bush was one of at least twelve members of his immediate family who went to Yale, almost all of whom were also in Skull and Bones. This list included all four males of his father's generation, as well as the only daughter's husband, his paternal grandfather and great-great grandfather, and one of his two daughters. For several generations, close friends of the Bush family included members of Skull and Bones, many of whom were also connected in political, financial, war industry, and national intelligence (CIA) circles. As Color Figure 11 shows, membership in Skull and Bones had a profound influence on the family and provided a network of family relationships, such as a godfather for George W. H. and "uncles" for George W., as well as business and political relationships. It would be impossible to have a good clinical assessment of such a family system without understanding the power and privilege that comes with membership in such a secret society.

Undoubtedly such fraternal relationships, like less secret religious communities, have a profound if unseen influence on families. Thus, all fraternal organizations to which family members belong should be noted on a genogram. They are resources as well as influences on beliefs and behavior. Other religious issues to track on a genogram include conversions, disaffection or expulsion from a religious community, and family conflicts that center on religious differences. Bill Clinton, whose parents seem to have had little interest in religion, was first baptized at the age of 9 with one of his best friends and has had a very strong religious practice ever since. In his autobiography he discussed having been in the Masonic youth organization DeMolay, but he decided against becoming a Mason, "following the long line of distinguished Americans going back to George Washington and Benjamin Franklin . . . probably because in my twenties I was in an anti-joining phase. . . . Besides, I didn't need to be in a secret fraternity to have secrets. I had real secrets of my own, rooted in Daddy's alcoholism and abuse" (Clinton, 2005, p. 45). Both Clinton and Bush are born-again Christians, for different reasons and from different periods of their lives.

A strikingly different example of someone who felt very alienated and whose conversion probably had multiple meanings was Marilyn Monroe. She converted to Judaism when she married Arthur Miller, though neither he nor his family apparently cared about this issue, and she maintained her conversion until her death (Zimroth, 2002). In Monroe's case, in spite of her divorce from Miller, her conversion "took" and she maintained her Jewish identity until her death, perhaps because, as Zimroth (2002) suggested, it gave her a new sense of "outsider" identity and "historical destiny" through its connection to family and culture, as well as to guiding life principles. The particular function of a person's connection to a religious or spiritual community as well as the meaning of one's distancing from a community of origin, as we will see in Chapter 8 with Erik Erikson's disidentification with his partly Jewish roots, are always worth exploration.

Socioeconomic Status Genograms

It is important to include on any clinical genogram indicators of the education, occupation, and financial status of family members, because this information conveys a tremendous amount about the stresses and resources that play a role in any crisis. With a little graphic creativity, we can create genograms to illustrate the family's socioeconomic status and how it has evolved over time.

Figure 2.15 illustrates a family's changes in class over four generations. Although both sides of the family were generally upwardly mobile, it is interesting that in the second generation, the only children not to move up from working poor to working class were the youngest children of the two branches of the family that experienced the untimely death of a parent. In the next generation, all six children moved up to at least the

Figure 2.15 Socioeconomic Class Genogram

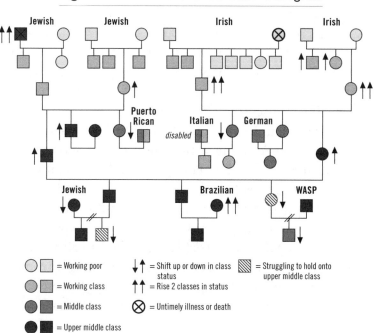

middle class, but the two daughters who married working class men had their middle class status threatened. Both women were teachers, and both of their husbands were blue collar workers. In the fourth generation, the children of two members of the third generation who had achieved upper middle class status had their status threatened: The son who married a working class woman was able to bring her up to his status, but the two daughters who married upper middle class men moved down in status as a result of divorce, and their children were not able to maintain their upper middle class status. This pattern repeated itself for the oldest daughter on the maternal side in the third generation; her children reverted to working class status after her Italian husband's early disability. Generally speaking, women move down in class in a divorce, whereas men do not. This family is no exception. Thus finances and untimely loss or separation can have long-range impact on family members. Such patterns are extremely important to show on genograms.

Religious/Spiritual Genograms

Religion, or at least religious practice, is more likely to change in each generation of a family, at least in the twentieth and twenty-first centuries in the U.S. Thus, religious genograms may be difficult to draw, because each family member may have a long spiritual trajectory throughout the life cycle. Furthermore, the point at which a conversion occurs may coincide with other life cycle events in ways that are important to assess. Hodge (2005a, 2005b) discussed a number of tools for spiritual assessment in clinical practice—from the spiritual lifemap (which tracks the spiritual life cycle of an individual along a timeline), to the spiritual genogram (which illustrates the patterns in a family across the generations), to spiritual ecomaps and ecograms (which depict clients' current and historical spiritual relationships)—to whatever degree is feasible on a single map.

The following questions gleaned from our own experience and the literature on spiritual genograms (see Religion/Spirituality section of the bibliography) may be helpful to clinicians in opening the questioning about spirituality and religion with a client. Mapping the responses graphically will take all the creativity a therapist or client can muster!

Spirituality Questions

- What meaning does religion or spirituality have for you in your everyday life? In your family's life? In times of danger or crisis?
- What religious or spiritual rituals or beliefs did you grow up with? Have you changed them? What or who influenced the development of your sense of spirituality?
- Are your religious/spiritual beliefs a source of connection or conflict between you and other family members?
- Who understands or shares your religious/spiritual framework?
- Do you participate regularly in religious services or other religious practices?
- What are your sources of hope?
- What are your beliefs about God?
- How do you deal with transgressions that violate your conscience? Forgiveness?
- Have you had premonitions concerning life events?
- What does your religion say about gender roles? Ethnicity? Sexual orientation? How have these beliefs affected you and your extended family?
- What role do music, prayer, meditation, reading, group participation, or good works have in your spiritual practice?
- Have any of your family members felt disillusioned about religion or had serious conflict with each other about religion?
- Have you or any of your family changed religion? If so, how did the family respond?
- Have you had spiritual experiences with friends or relatives who have died? Have you had encounters with spirits, ghosts, angels, or demons? Did you ever feel the intervention of a spirit on your behalf?

Community Genograms

The following are some questions to ask family members in order to gain understanding of their connectedness to their community.

Community Connection Questions

- What community institutions have members of your family belonged to?

- Where did they/do you go to socialize?
- What kinds of connections have you/they had with school? Work? Civic groups? Religious groups, fraternities or sororities?
- Were there ever groups you wanted to be part of but from which you were or felt excluded?
- Are there significant groups in which you and others in your family are not in the same position? Are there groups in which you and your family are not in the same position as most of your community, such as if you are a Democrat in a Republican family, the darkest skinned member of the family, the only family member who has gone to college, or the only Jewish family in a strongly Anglo community?

Because of the multiple dimensions of family members' relationships with their community, it is difficult to imagine a genogram that could visually depict these patterns clearly, but including community context in assessment and intervention with clients is extremely important (Rigazio-DiGilio et al., 2005). At best we can probably explore a few dimensions at a time. It is, nevertheless, worth trying to display graphically a family's connections, resources, and problems in a community context. This is important because, as Rigazio-DiGilio and her colleagues (2005) pointed out, without some mapping of the community context, it is hard to help clients to understand that this context influences their problems and is therefore an important resource in seeking solutions.

Although much has been said about expanding genograms to include issues from the larger social context (the sexual genogram, the cultural genogram, the religious or spiritual genogram, the community genogram, the ecomap, etc.), realistically, such mapping is extremely difficult to accomplish. This is because of the number of different people on even a simple genogram (at least 10) and the number of changing dimensions for each person over the course of a life, which may last 90 years! As noted earlier, any genogram always reflects a trade-off between clarity and complexity. Thus, mapping the sexual history of multiple family members on a genogram would very quickly become overwhelming, and there is probably no simple number of graphic descriptors that would make a clear graphic possible.

The same is true for culture; beyond a certain level of complexity, you cannot show even one cultural dimension—say, ethnicity—not to mention multiple dimensions such as class and religion on the genogram of families who have grown up in multiple countries, speak multiple languages, and have migrated into multiple cultural contexts. Even the ethnicity of an individual becomes prohibitively complex, not to mention that of the whole family. Tiger Woods, for example, is a quarter African-American, a quarter Chinese, a quarter Thai, an eighth Dutch, and an eighth American Indian. This would be very difficult to diagram. Now that he has married a Swedish woman, their children are an even more complex ethnic combination.

There quickly comes a point at which the complexity cannot be mapped in any graphic form. Thus, we must decide to highlight certain aspects of individual and family history while leaving others in the shadows in any particular graphic. The difficulty of drawing comprehensive graphics is not, however, a reason to ignore these important issues in genogram mapping.

Most of the writings about these contextual expansions of the genogram refer to a clinical process where the basic genogram map is used as the basis for the contextual inquiry about these various dimensions of life rather than as a graphic depiction. Computers will help us greatly with this, because they can capture many complexities of changes over time, which can then be shown for a moment or with a genogram of the family's educational history or cultural history, one or two dimensions at a time.

Issues Difficult to Capture on Genograms

Certain genogram patterns, although extremely important in the systems theory underlying genogram mapping, will remain very difficult to capture. These include:

- *Family members involved in family business.* It is extremely difficult to show the organizational relationships in relation to the family structural relationships of families where numerous family members serve on boards, as CEOs or managers, or as full- or part-time workers within a family business.

- *Family members' relationship to the healthcare system.* Mapping such relationships is difficult when different family members are involved at different moments in time with a variety of professionals and have differing relationships with these care providers.
- *Cultural genogram issues.* The variety of issues—such as reasons for migrating, holidays and special events, values about power, and myths and rules (as recommended by Congress, 1994)—makes drawing cultural genograms cumbersome.
- *Family secrets.* It could be easy to show who knows the secret and who does not, but usually when there is one secret, there are others, and showing how particular secrets are kept or shared through a family taxes any mapping process (although computers will be able to capture them and help us see how secrecy operates in families).
- *Particular family relationships.* The nuances of family relationships include complimentarity, unequal power, triangles, patterns of avoidance, intrusion, overfunctioning/underfunctioning, overresponsibility/underresponsibility, scapegoating, dependence/independence, and enmeshment/individualism/isolation.
- *Patterns of friendship.* Even patterns of friendship can quickly become difficult to manage on a genogram. It is easy enough to ask the members of a household to add their key friends, but once we ask about their parents' patterns of friendship it becomes more complex. What if the husband's mother always had a "best" friend but within a year or two had a dramatic cutoff that embroiled other friends and family? What if the parents have many "couple" friends but only a few with whom they have real intimacy? And what happens to this network if the couple gets divorced? The graphic will rapidly become very crowded and hard to follow!
- *Relationships with work colleagues.* The same problems emerge in mapping relationships with work colleagues. Over a whole lifetime these networks may tell a complex story, and if you add the stories of sibling and parents, the picture will quickly become very jammed. Yet these relationships may be key stressors or resources at critical moments in the family history.
- *Spiritual genograms.* A number of authors have written informative papers about working with couples and families around their spiri-

tual history (see the Religion/Spirituality section of the bibliography). Some have even drawn elaborate graphics of doves, bibles, and other religious symbols to illustrate religious visions, intensity of religious experience, and involvement in religious organizations. Practically speaking, however, even with a graphic artist and a very fancy computer to generate the graphic, the landscape of the genogram will quickly become overloaded in trying to track even one individual's spiritual history, never mind that of the whole family. Nevertheless, some notation on any genogram about key religious or spiritual affiliations, experiences and changes is essential, and such assessment of clients' spiritual and religious beliefs and history is necessary for effective clinical assessment. Furthermore, Hodge (2001) offered interesting genogram interview questions on whether clients have ever experienced angels, saints, demons, evil spirits, or the dead and, if so, what kinds of encounters they have had. Such experiences may be crucial to understanding a person's distress or sources of hope, and we need to accept the challenge to find ways to map these relationships on a genogram.

- *Community genograms.* Because connections to community groups, governmental structures, and so on are so complicated, they remain extremely difficult to map, though, as Rigazio-DiGilio and her colleagues (2005) pointed out, they are a very important aspect of genogram inquiry. If you do not take the larger context into account in assessment and in intervention, you marginalize it as a factor in human problems and thus mystify clients about the nature of much of their distress.

- *Tracking medical and psychological stressors.* This can also be very difficult to map concisely because of the potential complexity of each individual family member's medical or psychological history. Nevertheless, it is the most practically useful tool available for assessing patients in any healthcare setting. It is always necessary to know in outline the health history of all family members connected to the IP because of the resource role they will play in healthcare as well as the ripple effect of stress of an illness. Family members may be resources as caretakers; previous generations may provide role models for handling the stress of illness or may exaggerate a patient's fears of reliving previous negative illness scenarios.

- *Ecomaps.* In one of the classic attempts to contextualize genograms within an ecomap, Hartman (1995) offered 14 larger context institutions (such as social welfare, healthcare, extended family, and recreation) and five different types of connection lines (strong, tenuous, stressful, flow of energy toward family member, and flow of energy toward institution, organization, or group). Even with a small family, as mentioned earlier, the picture quickly becomes very crowded. Adding the institutions from the social context can become very challenging to depict graphically.

Despite the complexities that make it impossible to map all aspects of a family's context on a single graphic, we are at the start of a very exciting new era when, with the help of computers, we will soon be able to make amazing three-dimensional maps that will enable us to track complex patterns in ways we can barely imagine. We will be able to zoom in and track details in great depth on a particular dimension and then compare patterns of thousands of genograms at a time, just as we are now becoming able to study DNA patterns and compare people all around the planet. And we will be able to examine the impact of the broad social network of friends, family, and community over long periods of time. What is very exciting is that for the first time we will be able to examine complexities that go far beyond the individual's ability to hold onto the particulars of family patterns. That is, we'll be able to check out our hunches and intuitions about family patterns over a huge group of families and see whether our ideas are borne out, or find out about new links we have been missing in the relationships between human connections and health, resilience, and creativity.

3

The Genogram Interview

ENOGRAM INTERVIEWS MAY BE DONE in just a few minutes or over many hours, months, or years, depending on the purpose. This chapter offers a framework for thinking about the layers of information on a genogram in a comprehensive way. Readers will want to modify the collection of genogram information to suit the context in which they are working. Expanding Wright and Leahey's (1999, p. 261) recommendation, we believe that if all healthcare interviewers would embrace the simple postulate that "illness is a family affair," we could change the face of health- and mental health care. Indeed, the fragmentation of our society and the disconnection from our families and communities are responsible for many of the ills we witness. Thus, mapping our connections could be the first step toward healing.

We urge that genogram interviewing be incorporated into social service, education, and counseling services as well. Wright and Leahey (1999, p. 265) asserted that the basic genogram information can be gleaned in as little as 2 minutes! This information would include basic demographic information about age, occupation/school grade, ethnic and religious background, migration dates, current health status of family members who are in the household or closely connected to the IP, and key clinical connections and family resources.

This chapter provides a detailed framework for genogram questioning. This is not an outline for how to conduct an interview, which must depend on the purposes, circumstances, and the responses one gets as the interview proceeds. Rather, it provides a framework for thinking about the structure of the questions to consider. A further guide to genogram questions is provided at the end of each chapter in *You Can Go Home Again: Understanding Family Relationships* (McGoldrick, 1995), which provides a basic explanation of the theory of family systems and relationships that undergirds genogram interviewing.

The Family Information Net

The process of gathering family information can be thought of as casting an "information net" in larger and larger circles to capture relevant information about the family and its broader context. The net spreads out in a number of different directions:

- from the presenting problem to its larger context
- from the immediate household to the extended family and broader social systems
- from the present family situation to a chronology of historical family events
- from easy, nonthreatening queries to more difficult and possibly anxiety-provoking questions
- from obvious facts about functioning and relationships to judgments and hypotheses about family patterns

The Presenting Problem and the Immediate Household

In family medicine, genogram information beyond the most basic demographic data is often recorded as it emerges in office visits. In family therapy, individual family members usually come with specific problems, which are the clinician's starting point. At the outset, families are told that some basic information about them is needed to fully understand the problem. Such information usually grows naturally from exploring the presenting problem and its impact on the immediate household. In both a healthcare and a mental health setting it makes sense to start with the immediate family and the context in which the problem occurs:

- Who lives in the household?
- How is each person related?
- Where do other family members live?

The clinician asks the name, age, gender, and occupation of each person in the household in order to sketch the immediate family structure. Other relevant information is elicited through inquiring about the problem:

- Which family members know about the problem?
- How does each view it? And how has each responded?
- Has anyone else in the family ever had similar problems?
- What solutions were attempted by whom in those situations?
- When did the problem begin? Who noticed it first? Who is most concerned about it? Who is least concerned?
- Were family relationships different before the problem began? How have they changed? What other problems existed before this problem began? What other problems have developed since this problem began?
- Has the problem been changing? For better or for worse? In what ways?

This is also a good time to inquire about previous efforts to get help for the problem, including previous treatment, therapists, hospitalizations, and the current referring person.

The Current Situation

Next the clinician spreads the information net into the current family situation. This line of questioning usually follows naturally from questions about the problem and who is involved:

- What has been happening recently in your family?
- Have there been any recent changes in the family (e.g., people coming or leaving, illnesses, job problems)?

It is important to inquire about recent life cycle transitions as well as anticipated changes in the family situation (especially exits and entrances of family members—births, marriages, divorces, deaths, or the departure of family members).

The Wider Family Context

The clinician looks for an opportunity to explore the wider family context by asking about the extended family, social network, and cultural background of all the adults involved. The interviewer might move into this area by saying, "I would now like to ask you something about your background to help make sense of your current problem." The clinician then inquires about each side of the family separately, beginning, for example, with the mother's side:

- Let's begin with your mother's family. Your mother was which one of how many children?
- When and where was she born?
- Is she alive?
- If not, when did she die? What was the cause of her death?
- If she is alive, where is she now?
- What does she do?
- How far did she go in school?
- Is she retired? When did this happen?
- When and how did your mother meet your father? Did they marry, and, if so, when?
- Had she been married before? If so, when? Did they separate or divorce or did the spouse die? If so, when was that?
- Did she have children by any other relationship other than your father?
- What is she like?
- How is her health?
- How do you get along with her? How do others get along with her?

And so on. In like fashion, questions are asked about the father. Then the clinician might ask about each parent's family of origin. The goal is to get information about at least three or four generations, including grandparents, parents, aunts, uncles, siblings, spouses, and children of the IP.

Dealing With a Family's Resistance to Doing a Genogram

When family members react negatively to questions about the extended family or complain that such matters are irrelevant, it often makes sense to redirect the focus back to the immediate situation, until the connections between the present situation and other family relationships or experiences can be established. An example of how to deal with a family's resistance to revealing genogram information is illustrated on the videotape *The Legacy of Unresolved Loss* (available from www.Multicultural-Family.org). Gentle persistence over time will usually result in obtaining the information and demonstrating its relevance to the family.

Religious and Cultural History

It is essential to learn about the family's ethnic, socioeconomic, political, and religious background in order to place presenting problems and current relationships in context. When the questioning expands to the extended family, it is a good point to begin exploring issues of ethnicity. Exploring ethnicity and migration history helps establish the cultural context in which the family is operating and offers the therapist an opportunity to explore family attitudes and behaviors determined by such influences. It is important to learn what the family's cultural and religious traditions are with regard to solving problems, healthcare and healing, and where the current family members stand in relation to those traditional values. It is also important to consider the family's cultural expectations about relationships with healthcare professionals, as this will set the tone for their clinical responses.

Furthermore, class background between family members or between family members and the healthcare professional may create discomfort, which will need to be dealt with in the interview. Questions about social class pertain not just to the family's current income but also to cultural background, education, and religious and social status within their community. Once the clinician has a clear picture of the cultural and religious factors influencing a family, it is possible to raise delicate questions geared to helping families identify any behaviors that, although culturally sanctioned, may be keeping them stuck, such as a woman sacrificing her own needs to devote herself exclusively to the needs of others (see McGoldrick, Giordano, & Garcia-Preto, 2005).

Potential Problems for the Interviewer

Interviewers should always be conducting a self-assessment as the session proceeds regarding difficulties they may encounter in engaging the family members. These difficulties may be related to cultural differences, class, gender, age, race, sexual orientation, or religious, spiritual, or other beliefs. Clinicians may get caught in triangles with the family or between the family and other institutions such as the referrer, other therapists, or the therapist's work system. Clinicians should also remain mindful of how their own life cycle stage or cultural background may be an asset or a liability in engaging family members.

Inquiring About Cultural Beliefs and Experiences

We always need to conduct interviews in ways that are sufficiently congruent with the family's beliefs that they can connect with the recommended interventions. What are the family's cultural beliefs about the problem and about possible solutions? How might the interviewer respond to these beliefs in assessment and intervention?

We have found the following questions—developed over the years with many colleagues, including Ken Hardy and Tracy Laszloffy (1995) and Doug Schoeninger (in preparation)—helpful in aiding clients to understand their cultural background. Of course, the timing and context for discussing such questions depend entirely on the context of the interview.

Cultural Genorgram Questions

- What ethnic groups, religious traditions, nations, racial groups, trades, professions, communities, and other groups do you consider yourself a part of?

- When and why did you or your family come to the U.S.? To this community? How old were family members at the time? Did they and do you feel secure about your status in the U.S.? Did they (do you) have a green card? Did they and do you feel secure about your status within your community?
- What language did they (do you) speak at home? In the community? In your family of origin?
- What traumatic wounds have any of your racial or ethnic groups experienced? What burden do they carry for injuries their group committed against other groups? How have you been affected by the wounds your groups have committed, or that were committed against your groups?
- How have you been wounded by the wrongs done to your ancestors? How have you been complicit in the wrongs done by your ancestors? How can you give voice to your group's guilt, your own sorrow, or your own complicity in the harm done by your ancestors? What would reparations entail?
- What experiences have been most stressful for your family members in the U.S.?
- To whom do family members in your culture turn when in need of help?
- What are your culture's values regarding male and female roles? Education? Work and success? Family connectedness? Family caretaking? Religious practices? Have these values changed in your family over time?
- Do you still have contact with family members in your country of origin?
- Has immigration changed family members' education or social status?
- What do you feel about your cultures of origin? Do you feel you belong to the dominant U.S. culture?

These questions can guide the clinician to remind the family of their resilience through the values of their heritage, their ability to transform their lives, and their ability to work toward long-range goals that fit with their cultural values. Questions that help to locate families in their cultural context may help them access their strengths in the midst of the stress of their current situation.

Illustrations of the kinds of questions that may help families feel the strength of their heritage include:

Questions to Strengthen Connection to Cultural Heritage

- How might your grandfather, who dreamed of your immigration but never made it himself, think about the problem you are having with your children?
- Your ancestors survived being enslaved for hundreds of years. You are here because they had great strength and courage. What do you think are the strengths you got from these ancestors that may help you in dealing with your problem?
- Your great-grandmother immigrated at 21 and became a piece worker in a sweatshop but managed to support her six children and had great strength. What do you think were her dreams for you, her daughter's daughter's daughter? What do you think she would want you to do now about your current problem?
- Your father died of his alcoholism, but when he came to this country at age 18, he undoubtedly had different dreams of his future. What do you think he cared about? How do you think he felt about the parents he left behind? What do you think he would want for you now?
- Could you go to your Hungarian Social Club and volunteer?
- Are there some Latino political groups in your town that could help you fight for the resources you and your group have deserved from the U.S. for 150 years?
- How do you think the fact that you are Italian and your wife is Irish may influence the way you handle conflicts?

The concept behind this cultural clinical assessment and all these suggested questions is to look at clients as belonging to their history, to their present context, and to the future.

When we ask people to identify themselves ethnically, we are helping them to recognize the cultural continuities and discontinuities in their history and to articulate the themes of cultural identity in their families. This line of questioning, like the rest of the genogram exploration, is, of course, a therapeutic intervention in itself, because it links the individual to his or her broader historical and sociological context. Using the genogram to collect historical and contextual assessment information is a collaborative, client-centered therapeutic process. By its nature the process involves the telling of stories and emphasizes respect for the client's perspective, while encouraging the multiple views of different family members. By scanning the family system culturally and historically and assessing previous life cycle transitions, the clinician can place present issues in the context of the family's evolutionary patterns of geography, migration, and cultural change. Among the areas to cover are:

- *Sociocultural, sociopolitical, and socioeconomic factors.* Are there sociocultural factors (related to social class, ethnicity, race, finances, educational level, employment potential, legal status, etc.) that are impeding the family's functioning? What is the family's social location in terms of finances, education, and fit in their community? What has been their educational, occupational, and financial history? What has been their political history and did it cause suffering or conflicts for family members?
- *Finances.* We usually write the annual income of the immediate family members right above the birth and death dates, and any indebtedness (especially credit card debt, which is a prevalent family problem in the U.S.), expected inheritance, or financial obligations (explicit or expected) toward other family members on the side of the genogram. Debt or success may be stressors on a family. Often, especially for families that are from marginalized cultures, the first member to "make it out" of the working class may feel particular pressures from other family members: jealousy, resentment, or pressure to help others. Families from upper class backgrounds who have lost their resources may have a special sense of shame or conflict in relation to their extended family, and those struggling to meet ongoing needs are under continuous pressure and stress.

- *Cultural heritage.* What is the ethnic and racial background of family members and what impact has racism had on them? Have they lived in an ethnic enclave or community, or in a community in which they were viewed as outsiders? Have their spiritual and religious beliefs supported or minimized their acknowledgment of their ethnic heritage?
- *Belief systems, religion, and spiritual beliefs.* What are the primary beliefs that organize the family? What is their general worldview, and are they organized by particular myths, rules, spiritual beliefs, or family secrets? What is the history of the family's religious beliefs and practices, including changes in belief? What has been the impact of intrafamily religious differences or those between the family and the surrounding community? Have any family members changed religion? How did other family members react to this change?
- *Language skill and acculturation of family members.* Family members vary in how quickly they adapt, how much of their heritage they retain, and the rate at which they learn English. Knowing and speaking the language of the country of origin will preserve its culture. What languages were spoken while the children in the family were growing up? Are there differences in language skills and acculturation within the family that may have led to conflicts, power imbalances, and role reversals, especially when children are forced to translate for their parents?
- *Connections to community.* How able are family members' in maintaining friendships? How accessible are friends, neighbors, religious organizations, schools, physicians, community institutions, and other healthcare and social service resources, including therapists? When family members move away from an ethnic enclave, the stresses of adaptation are likely to be severe, even several generations after immigration. The therapist should learn about the community's ethnic network and, when relevant, encourage the rebuilding of informal social connections through family visits, letters, or through the building of new social networks.

- *Migration history*. Why did the family migrate? What were they seeking, (e.g., survival, adventure, wealth)? What were they leaving behind (e.g., religious or political persecution, poverty)? Therapists need to be as attuned to migration stresses and ethnic identity conflicts as they are to other stresses in the family's history (Hernandez & McGoldrick, 2005). Assessing such factors is crucial for determining whether a family's dysfunction is a "normal" reaction to a high degree of cultural stress or whether it goes beyond the bounds of transitional stress and requires expert intervention. The stresses of migration may at times be "buried" or forgotten. The cultural heritage before migration may have been suppressed or forgotten, but it may still influence the family's outlook, if only subtly, as they try to adapt to new situations. Many immigrant groups have been forced to abandon their ethnic heritage and thus have lost a part of their identity. The effects of this hidden history may be all the more powerful for being hidden. Families that have experienced trauma and devastation within their own society before even beginning the process of immigration will have a monumentally more difficult time adjusting to a new life than those who migrated for adventure or economic betterment. Specific areas to investigate regarding migration include:

  - *Premigration history*. What was the situation in the country of origin politically and economically?
  - *Migration history*. How traumatic was the migration itself and did it entail losses along the way beyond the loss of the culture of origin?
  - *Postmigration history and culture shock*. What experiences did the family have when they arrived in the U.S.? Did they have problems with language, immigration status, poverty? Was there loss of social status or job options? To what extent was there a shock of cultural values? Did they live in a supportive or an antagonistic community?
  - *Migration and the life cycle*. How old were family members when migration occurred? How old were the family members

who remained in the homeland? How did the age at migration influence family members? Were certain children drawn into adult status because they learned English faster than the parents or because the family had no resources to treat them as children? Did the life cycle stage at migration bring about a reversal of the parental hierarchy, because parents were less able to negotiate the new culture than their children? Were grandparents limited by their inability to learn English? How did the life cycle phase influence the family's adaptation?

Questioning About Difficult Issues of Culture and Social Location

Many of these cultural questions may be difficult to inquire about and take considerable clinical skill. But they are nevertheless highly important. In African-American families, for example, it would be virtually impossible for issues of skin color not to have had a major influence on family relationships (Boyd-Franklin, 2006). Given the racist context in which African-Americans have existed in the U.S., since our early slave history, African-American cultures have tended to internalize racist ideology about skin color, and family triangles are highly likely to have been influenced by these pernicious factors. In white families, awareness of how their social location has been influenced by race may only surface when a family member chooses a partner of another race. However, the inequities of the racial arrangements of U.S. society affect all families, just as the inequities of gender and class arrangements do. The impact of racism, white supremacy, anti-Semitism, sexism, class hierarchies, and homophobia on families in the U.S. cannot be minimized and must be part of our assessment of all families (McGoldrick & Garcia-Preto, 2005).

The Informal Kinship Network

The information net extends beyond the biological and legal structure of the family to encompass common law and cohabiting relationships, miscarriages, abortions, stillbirths, foster and adopted children, and anyone else in the informal network of the family who is an important support. Inquiries are made about friends, godparents, teachers, neighbors, parents of friends, clergy, caretakers, doctors, and so on, who are or have been important to the functioning of the family, and this information is also included on the genogram. In exploring outside supports for the family, the clinician might ask:

- To whom could you turn when in need of financial, emotional, physical, and spiritual help?
- What roles have outsiders played in your family? Who outside the family has been important in your life?
- What is your relationship to your community?
- Did you ever have a nanny, caretaker, or babysitter to whom you felt attached? What became of her or him?
- Has anyone else ever lived with your family? When? Where are they now?
- What has been your family's experience with doctors and other helping professionals or agencies?

For particular clients certain additional questions are appropriate. For example, the following questions would be important in working with gay and lesbian clients (Burke & Faber, 1997; Laird, 1996; Scrivner & Eldridge, 1995; Shernoff, 1984; Slater, 1995).

- Who was the first person you told about your sexual orientation?
- To whom on your genogram are you out?
- To whom would you most like to come out?
- Who would be especially easy or difficult to come out to?

Tracking Family Process

Tracking shifts that occurred around births, deaths, and other transitions can lead the clinician to hypotheses about the family's adaptive style. Particularly critical are untimely or traumatic deaths and the deaths of pivotal family members. We look for specific patterns of adaptation or rigidification following such transitions. Assessment of past adaptive patterns, particularly after losses and other critical transitions, may be crucial in helping a family in the current crisis. A family's past and the relationship family members have to it provide important clues about family rules, expectations, patterns of organization, strengths, resources, and sources of resilience (Walsh, 2006).

The history of specific problems should also be investigated in detail. The focus should be on how family patterns have changed at different periods: before the problem began, at the time of problem onset, at the time of first seeking help, and at present. Specific genograms can be done for each of these time periods. (Computerized genograms, generated for all nodal points in time, will be enormously helpful in this process, making it easier to show details for the key times of stress or symptom development.) Asking how family members see the future of the problem is also informative. Seeing the family in historical perspective involves linking past, present, and future and noting the family's flexibility in adapting to changes. Questions may include:

- What will happen in the family if the problem continues?
- If it goes away?
- What changes do family members imagine are possible in the future?

Difficult Questions About Individual Functioning

During the mapping on the genogram of the nuclear and extended family, the clinician also begins to make inquiries and judgments about the functioning, relationships, and roles of each person in the family. This inquiry involves clinical sensitivity and judgment. Inquiries about these issues can touch sensitive nerves in the family and should be made with care.

Assessment of individual functioning may require considerable clinical skill. Family members may function well in some areas but not in others, or may cover up their dysfunction. Often, it takes careful questioning to reveal the true level of functioning. A family member with a severe illness may show remarkable adaptive strengths and another may show fragility with little apparent stress. Questions about individual functioning may be difficult or painful for family members to answer and must be approached with sensitivity and tact. Assessing the extent of an alcohol or gambling problem, for example, may be particularly difficult not only because of the client's defensive response, but also because family members are often intimidated and fearful of exposing problems. Family members should be warned that questions may be difficult and they should let the interviewer know if there is an issue they would rather not discuss. The clinician will need to judge the degree of pressure to apply if the family resists questions that may be essential to dealing with the presenting problem. It may make much more sense to interview family members separately around sensitive issues that arouse shame or embarrassment.

Interviewers need to exercise extreme caution about when to ask questions that could put a family member in danger. For example, if violence is suspected, a wife should never be asked about her husband's behavior in his presence, as the question assumes she is free to respond, which would not be the case. It is the clinician's responsibility to make sure his or her questions do not put a client in jeopardy. Following is a list of possible questions on individual functioning.

Serious Problems
- Has anyone in the family had a serious medical or psychological problem? Been depressed? Had anxieties or fears? Lost control? Has there ever been any physical or sexual abuse?
- Are there any other problems that worry you? When did that problem begin? Did you seek help for it? If so, when? What happened? What is the status of that problem now?

Work
- Have there been any recent job changes? Unemployment?
- Do you like your job?
- Who else works in your family? Do they like their work?

Finances
- How much income does each member generate? Does this create any imbalance in family relationships? If so, how is the imbalance handled? How does the economic situation compare with that of relatives?

- Is there any expected inheritance? Are there family members you support or whom you may need to care for in the future?
- Are there any extraordinary expenses? Outstanding debts? What is the level of credit card debt?
- Who controls the money? How are spending decisions made? Are these patterns different from the ways money was handled in the families of origin?
- Does anyone have a gambling or overspending problem?

Drugs and Alcohol

- Do any family members routinely use medication? What kind and for what? Who prescribed it? What is the family's relationship with any physician?
- Do you think any members drink too much or have a drug problem? Has anyone else ever thought so? What drugs? When? What has the family attempted to do about it?
- How does the person's behavior change under the influence of the drug? How does the behavior of others change?
- Has anyone ever been stopped for an alcohol- or drug-related offense (DWI)?

Trouble With the Law

- Have any family members ever been arrested? For what? When? What was the result? What is that person's legal status now?
- Has anyone ever had his or her driver's license revoked?

Physical or Sexual Abuse

- Have you ever felt intimidated in your family? Have you or others ever been hit? Has anyone in your family ever been threatened with being hit? Have you ever threatened anyone else in your family or hit them? Have you ever been threatened in any other way within your family?
- Have you or any other family members ever been sexually molested or touched inappropriately by a member of your family or someone outside your family? By whom? Given that physical battering has been called the number-one health problem for women in the U.S. (McGoldrick, Broken Nose, & Potenza, 2005), it is critical for clinicians to take extreme care in inquiring about power relation-

ships in families. It is estimated that over the course of the life cycle, nearly 25% of women are raped or physically assaulted by an intimate partner (Tjaden & Thoennes, 2005). Couple relationships have many dimensions that may involve abuse (economic, emotional, physical and psychological power, boundaries around the couple in relation to all other connections, including work, friends, religion, family of origin, children, etc., sexuality, chores, leisure activities, and childcare). The breadth, depth, and complexity of these dimensions give us a clue as to how carefully and thoroughly the clinician must proceed with his or her inquiries, as abuse is likely to be denied or minimized.

Regarding abuse, we have found that in addition to the genogram, the Power and Control Pyramid (Figure 3.1), is an extremely useful tool for assessing both violence and psychological abuse in the multiple domains of couple and family relationships. The pyramid can be given to partners (in separate meetings) to help them consider the power dimensions of their relationship. In addition, the clinician might ask:

- Who is making the decisions?
- Who is managing the money?
- How are conflicts resolved?
- What is each partner's attitude toward violence or intimidation in marriage?

Setting Priorities for Organizing Genogram Information
One of the most difficult aspects of genogram assessment remains setting priorities for inclusion of family information on a genogram. Clinicians cannot follow every lead the genogram interview suggests. Awareness of basic genogram patterns can help the clinician set priorities. As a rule of thumb, the data are scanned for the following:

- Repetitive patterns of functioning, relationship, or symptoms across the family and over the generations. Repetitive relationship patterns of triangles, coalitions, cutoffs, conflict, and over- and underfunctioning are central to genogram interpretation.

- Coincidences of dates—for example, the death of one family member or anniversary of this death occurring at the same time as symptom onset in another, or the age of symptom onset coinciding with the age of problem development in another family member.

Figure 3.1 Power and Control Pyramid*

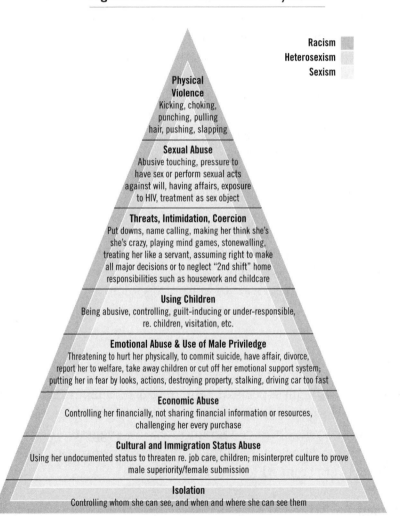

*Expanded from maps of the Domestic Abuse Intervention Project (www.duluth-model.org) and Don Coyhis of the Wellbriety Movement (www.whitebison.org).

- The impact of change and untimely life cycle transitions, particularly changes in functioning and relationships that correspond with critical family life events and untimely life cycle transitions (e.g., births, marriages, premature deaths).

Awareness of possible patterns makes the clinician more sensitive to what is missing. Such missing information about important family members or events and discrepancies in the information offered frequently reflect charged emotional issues in the family. The clinician should also be careful to note whether or not family members connect various stressor events.

Essentials of a Brief Genogram Interview

In conducting a brief genogram interview, clinicians focus on the most essential information, such as age, occupation/school grade, religion, ethnic background, migration date, and current health status of each family member. In addition, the clinician should ask questions such as, "Who outside of your immediate family is an important resource to you? Who is a stress? Who referred you to us? What other professionals have been involved in helping your family?" Wright and Leahey (1999) recommended that the clinician think of at least three key questions to ask all family members routinely, depending on their clinical context. These questions might include:

- What are family members' most pressing concerns?
- What information might family members want shared or kept from other family members?
- Who has been the greatest source of love or inspiration to family members?
- What are the greatest challenges the family members feel they are facing?
- What question would the family members most want answered by the clinician?

Wright and Leahey (1999) have had a policy of routinely recommending that the clinician commend the family on at least two strengths or resources they have observed during this brief interview. This seems an extremely good idea, especially when observations are on patterns rather than on one-time occurrences. Such commendations could include:

- Your family seems to have had a great deal of courage to face the problems you describe, in light of the resistance of others in your family to acknowledge these difficulties.
- You seem to be a family of survivors after all the problems you have struggled with: sexual abuse, violence, addiction, and mental illness.
- You seem very caring in spite of the anger and despair that you have often struggled with.

Before concluding the interview, it is also important to debrief clients in case there are issues that have distressed the family or that need further clarification. In any case, it is important for the interviewer to validate the individual or family for sharing their story. We generally do this by offering clients a copy of the graphic created and asking them to review it for accuracy. This in itself may be a major intervention, because it enables clients to see the patterns in their own family and have control over correcting the picture created. They may begin to see the systemic dimensions of their family once they see the "facts" depicted graphically. It is the goal of any genogram interview to leave the clients feeling understood and more connected to the context than when they began. We always hope that people will recognize connections between their own distress and their relationships, present and past, and that these connections will promote a sense of hope for the future solution of their distress.

4

Tracking Family Patterns Through Time and Space

 UESTIONING WHAT PLACES FAMILIES in a cultural and life cycle context is a crucial aspect of doing a genogram. We think of this process as tracking the family through time and space.

Critical Life Events

It is important to track life cycle transitions and predictable nodal life events on a genogram. These include important family transitions, job changes, entrances and exits of family members, relationship shifts, moves or migrations, losses and successes. Tracking these life events gives the clinician a sense of the historical evolution of the family and of the effect of the family history on each individual. Some of these events will have been noted as demographic data (e.g., family births and deaths). Others include romances, marriages, separations, divorces, moves, and job changes. Hopefully, genogram software will soon facilitate our keeping track of these events, making it possible to display major experiences such as birth, illness, or death, trouble with the law, job promotion, and other critical events, as well as of entry and exit of all family members in chronological order. Until we have such software, we must record critical life events on a separate family chronology to track important events.

There are certain critical life events that may be important to explore in detail, such as life cycle transitions, major traumas, and changes in relationships.

- *Births.* How did other family members react when a particular family member was born? Who attended the christening ceremony or bris? Who was named after whom and who "should have been"?

- *Deaths.* How did the family react when a particular family member died? Who took it the hardest? The easiest? Who attended the funeral? Who wasn't there who "should have been"? Were there conflicts or cutoffs or other changes over the will?
- *Moves and migration.* When and why did the family migrate to this country? How did they cope with the multiple losses of migration? How many generations of the family have lived in the U.S.? What was the context into which they came and how did they manage the adaptation to these new circumstances? How did they survive? Which members of the immigrant generation learned the language? How did language ability affect family relationships?

Family Chronologies

It is important to keep a family chronology (or list of important family events) with the genogram. A timeline of important family dates is an excellent way to track family patterns. Such a chronology, organizing all demographic information for any individual or combination of family members you wish to include, is extremely valuable. It is also useful to make a genogram for particular nodal points, as it helps to clarify what was going on at that moment, who lived together, how old family members were, and what stresses they were experiencing. Two recent developments have made the assessment of family history more important than ever: the Human Genome Project, with its resultant identification of the inherited causes of many diseases, and the establishment of national clinical medical practice guidelines based on systematic reviews of preventive interventions (Wattendorf & Hadley, 2005). It has become clear that the more accurate our information about family medical history is, the more we can do to help family members prevent illness and improve well-being.

At times it is beneficial to make a special chronology for a critical time period, particularly around symptom onset, and to track a family member's illness in relation to concurrent events or to events at the same point in the life cycle of other family members (Barth, 1993; Huygen, 1982). Thus, we would want to see if there have been major stresses in previous generations at the same point in the life cycle or when the person's parent was the same age.

An individual chronology may also be useful for tracking a particular family member's functioning, transitions, and symptoms within the context of the family. Generally each occurrence is listed with its date. When family members are unsure about dates, approximate dates should be given, preceded by a question mark (e.g., ?84 or ~84). The following chronology illustrates key dates indicated on the genogram for Ted Turner, discussed in Chapter 2 (see Color Figure 6). All the items on the chronology are shown on the genogram, but the pattern of family events gains clarity from the timeline. On the other hand, the family structure would be hard to envision without the genogram.

SHORT CHRONOLOGY FOR TED TURNER: CRITICAL EVENTS

1944   Ted, age 6, is sent away to boarding school. Feels abandoned and acts out, getting expelled.

1947   Family moves to Savannah and sends Ted (age 9) to Atlanta military school.

1953   Ted's sister, Mary Jean, age 12, is diagnosed with lupus followed by encephalitis, which leaves her with brain damage and violent seizures. Soon neither father nor son can bare her screams and she is isolated in an apartment behind the house in care of her mother.

1957   Parents separate. Conflicts over sister's care. Mother does not want her institutionalized. Sister is suffering horribly—racked with pain. Mother gets sole custody of daughter; father, who is alcoholic and abusive, gets sole custody of Ted.

1960   (Dec 15) Sister dies at age 19. Father and brother have not seen her in years.

1961   (July) Ted's daughter Laura Lee is born. He is too busy sailing to attend her birth.

1961   (July) Ted's father, Ed Turner, goes to Silver Hill, a psychiatric hospital, to withdraw from alcohol.

1962   (Sept) Ed Turner makes multimillion dollar deal of a lifetime, turning his advertising business from middling company to largest outdoor advertising business in the south.

1962 (Dec) Ed Turner goes back to alcohol detox program.

1963 (Jan) Ed Turner leaves alcohol program.

1963 (March 5) Ed Turner, age 53, shoots himself in the head with gun with which he taught Ted to shoot, following one of the many fights father and son have had over the years. Son Ted is 24.

1991 Ted Turner, age 53, suffering from depression and having felt that he might die tragically at the same age as his father, instead changes the pattern. He is stabilized by therapy and medication. He marries Jane Fonda, whose mother committed suicide on her 42nd birthday, when Jane was 17.

Clearly, a family chronology will vary in length and detail, depending on the breadth and depth of the information on demographics, functioning, relationships, and critical events available or needed for a particular assessment.

Assessing genograms also requires an understanding of how life events and changes in family functioning are interconnected. Because the genogram records many critical dates in the family's history, it is useful to the clinician for looking at coincidences of various life events and changes in family functioning. Often seemingly unconnected events that occur around the same time in a family's history are systemically related and have a profound impact on family functioning.

It is particularly helpful to track changes in a family's long-term functioning as they relate to critical family life events. We examine the genogram carefully for a pileup of stresses, the rippling impact of traumatic events, anniversary reactions, and the relationship of family experiences to social, economic, and political events. Thus, we can assess the impact of change on the family and its vulnerability to future changes.

Coincidences of Life Events

Whenever several critical family experiences occur around the same time, it is wise to request details. It is particularly important to notice the coinciding dates on the genogram, which may indicate hidden connections and reveal emotional and systemic patterns. Such "coincidences" may indicate a stressful period in the family's history. If nothing else, they pinpoint the critical periods in a family, which are likely to have left an emotional legacy. We are not talking here about one event "causing" another, but about the association of events that may be influential in the development of family patterns. Queen Elizabeth referred to the year 1992 as the "annus horribilis" due to the multiple stresses that had plagued the royal family that year: the separation of one son, Andrew, from his wife, Sarah Ferguson; the divorce of Princess Anne from Captain Mark Philips; the ongoing rumors of marital problems between Charles and Diana, who announced their separation at the end of the year; and a horrendous fire at Windsor Castle that caused $60 million dollars in damage (Color Figure 12).

In situations where there is such a pileup of stressful life events, one must be on the lookout for emotional reactivity among all family members as well as other hidden stressors influencing the family. The stress of such a pileup may show itself in physical symptoms as well: indeed, when the Queen gave her speech on the topic she had lost her voice due to a severe cold—perhaps a coincidence, or perhaps a physical indicator of the stress she was describing. It was also reported that she had difficulty sleeping for many months that year. As the Queen noted, her family's stress was compounded by stress in the country at the time. There had been months of worldwide turmoil and uncertainty, and Britain had had 3 years of severe recession, with millions unemployed and a record number of personal bankruptcies and homes repossessed.

In other situations the coincidences take place over time, perhaps on anniversaries or at the same life cycle transition. For example, Gregory Bateson's genogram (Figure 4.1) depicts a number of interesting coincidences. First, Gregory's parents were married shortly after the death of his mother's father. Second, the middle son, Martin, committed suicide on the birthday of the oldest brother, John, who had died 4 years earlier in World War I. And finally, Gregory met Margaret Mead shortly after he cut off from his mother.

Viewed systemically, these events may be more than coincidence. Gregory's parents' engagement was called off by Gregory's mother, Beat-

Figure 4.1 Bateson Family

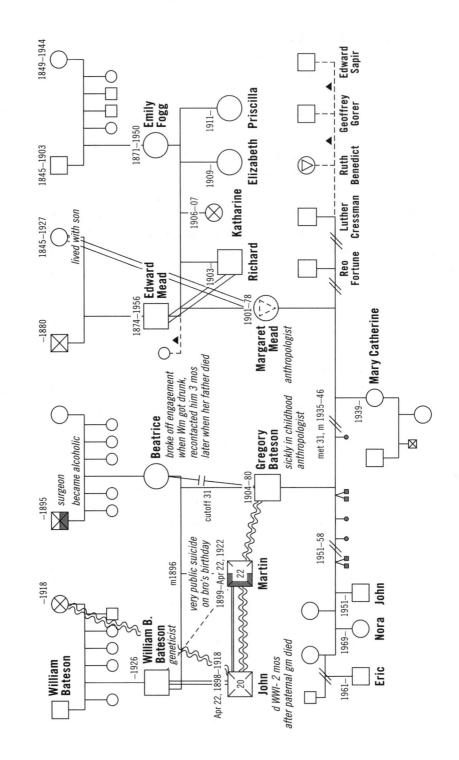

rice, when her fiancé, W. B. Bateson, got drunk. She was reacting because of her own father's alcoholism. Three months later, the alcoholic father died, and Beatrice put a notice in the newspaper, hoping to reconnect with W.B., who then recontacted her. The couple were married soon afterward. In the next generation, Gregory happened to meet and fall in love with Margaret just after becoming estranged from his mother. Margaret and her second husband were doing anthropological work in a remote area of the world at that time. We could speculate that the children in this family might similarly connect to their spouses after disconnecting, through death or cutoff, from a parent.

Gregory Bateson, the youngest of three sons of W. B. Bateson, who became a famous British geneticist, was considered the least promising of the three. Sickly in childhood, he was not a good student. The oldest son, John, was the one on whom the family's expectations fell. He and the middle brother, Martin, were only a year apart in age and were extremely close. Gregory, 5 years younger, grew up more on his own. A few days after the oldest son died in World War I, the mother wrote to Martin that "you and Gregory are left to me still and you must help me back to some of the braveness that John has taken away" (Lipset, 1980, p. 71).

Following John's death, a rift developed between Martin and the father, whose own mother had died 2 months before John—another coincidence. The father now began to pressure Martin, who was a poet, to become a zoologist. Relations between the father and his second son deteriorated. When, in addition, Martin felt rebuffed by a young woman he admired, he took a gun and shot himself in Trafalgar Square on his brother John's birthday, April 22, 1922, in what was described as "probably the most dramatic and deliberate suicide ever witnessed in London" (Lipset, 1980, p. 93). Martin's choosing to kill himself on his brother's birthday is also an example of an anniversary reaction, which is discussed later. Was he trying to give his parents a message that he could never be a replacement for his older brother?

Critical Life Changes, Transitions, and Traumas

Critical life changes, transitions, and traumas can have a dramatic impact on a family system and its members. Our own experience has led us to pay particular attention to the impact of losses (see Loss section in the bibliography). Families are much more likely to have difficulty readjusting after a loss than after other family changes. In the Bateson family, both brothers' deaths compounded each other in their impact on the youngest brother, Gregory. As Bateson's biographer noted, "Gregory had grown up unnoticed. His had been a vicarious, hand-me-down sort of youth. In part he had felt John and Martin were more able. . . . Death now made Gregory sole heir to an ambiguous intellectual heritage in the natural sciences—personified by his father—and made him a central member of his family" (Lipset, 1980, p. 90). Though his response involved fleeing his mother and his home, he seems to have developed an amazing adaptive strategy to this situation: He became one of the greatest systems thinkers of all time—fulfilling in many ways the best hopes the parents could ever have had for their son.

The Kennedy family has had more than its share of traumas and losses, as can be seen in Color Figure 13. What is most striking about this family is the extraordinary number of premature deaths or tragedies. Four of the nine Kennedy children, as well as the spouse and the fiancé of one of them, died before middle age; John had been given up for dead on at least three occasions before he was shot; Rosemary had a lobotomy in her twenties; Kathleen and her fiancé were killed taking a dangerous plane ride just after the death of her first husband in the war and a cutoff from her mother for her plan to remarry; and Ted broke his back in a plane crash (7 months after his brother John was shot) and was involved in an accident at Chappaquidick in which Mary Jo Kopechne drowned (12 months after his brother, Robert, was killed). Two grandchildren were responsible for car accidents in which someone was permanently paralyzed or seriously injured.

Often, critical life events in a family will send ripples throughout the system, having an impact on the family in many different ways. This certainly seems to be the case in the Kennedy family following the assassinations of John and Robert. In addition to Ted's accidents mentioned above, Pat separated from her husband on the day of Jack's assassination. Of the 29 grandchildren, one died flying a plane with a broken foot, one died of an overdose of drugs, one lost a leg through cancer, one died playing a dangerous skiing game, two were charged with rape, and at least four others have had drug arrests or psychiatric hospitalizations. This group includes five of the six oldest sons, perhaps suggesting the importance of sons and the pressures on the oldest in this family.

That traumatic pattern was also characteristic of Rose Kennedy's own family of origin (Color Figure 13). In her father's family only three out of 12 siblings survived in good health. The only two daughters died in infancy, as did the eldest son. Five others had severe alcohol problems and the other son had brain damage from malaria and barely functioned. On her mother's side, out of nine siblings, two sons died of childhood illnesses, one had his leg crushed by a train in childhood, two others died very early of alcoholism, and most tragic of all, the youngest daughter and her friend drowned while Rose's mother, Josie, who was only 8 herself, was supposed to be watching them. The devastating loss any family naturally would feel about the death of a child was compounded by a complex web of guilt and self-reproach that they—Josie in particular—had contributed to the death by failing to protect the children adequately.

Ted Kennedy's two life-threatening traumas both took place within the year following the death of his brothers: John in 1963 and Robert in 1968. Although such events could be totally unrelated, research has shown that stressful life events increase one's susceptibility to accidents (Holmes & Masuda, 1974; Holmes & Rahe, 1967). It probably is a coincidence, but a dreadful one, that John Kennedy was killed on November 22, the same day that both of his paternal great-grandfathers died.

Another family that experienced multiple traumatic losses at a critical time in a child's development is the Roosevelt family (Figure 4.2). The time of Eleanor's birth was a hard one for her father's family. Her paternal grandmother had died a few months earlier on Valentine's Day, and on the same night in the same house, Theodore Roosevelt's wife Alice died giving birth to a daughter Alice. Alice and Eleanor, born in the same year, in the context of similar losses, both grew up reacting differently to their early pain. Alice later said Eleanor responded by being a "do-goody," whereas she responded by showing off (Donn, 2001, p. 56). Alice grew up as a stepchild whose mother could never be mentioned and who was thought to be a bad influence on Eleanor. She eventually became deeply resentful of Eleanor for having gotten their cousin Franklin to marry her. During Eleanor's early years, her father's drinking, hospitalizations, and forced separation from the family were very traumatic for her, because she was an orphan. From childhood she was raised in her grandmother's home, with two out-of-control uncles. Her mother had died when she was 7, the middle brother when she was 9, and her father when she was 10.

Figure 4.2 Multiple Traumatic Losses in Theodore Roosevelt's Family

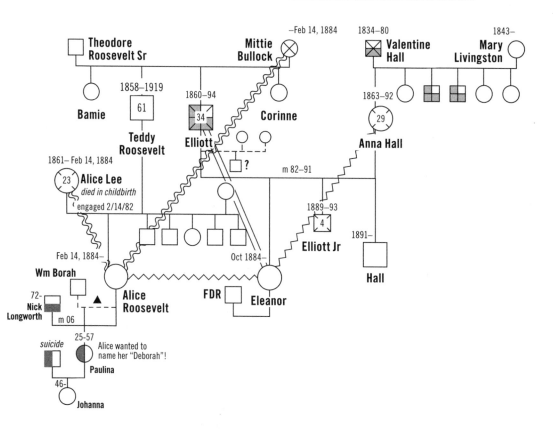

PARTIAL ROOSEVELT CHRONOLOGY

1880   (Feb 14) TR proposes to Alice Lee (it is said that she first rejected him, which left him in such despair that he attempted suicide).

1884   (Feb 14) Alice gives birth to baby, also named Alice.

1884   (Feb 14) Alice Lee Roosevelt dies at age 23.

1884	(Feb 14) TR's mother, Mittie Bulloch Roosevelt dies in same house.
1884	(Feb 16) Double funeral for Alice Lee Roosevelt & Mittie Bulloch Roosevelt (TR age 26).
1884	(summer) TR submerges grief in adventures out west and presidential politics, while his sister, Bamie, cares for Alice.
1884	(Oct) Eleanor Roosevelt born to Alice's uncle, Elliot.
1889	Eleanor's brother born.
1891	Eleanor's youngest brother, Hall, born.
1891	Eleanor's parents separate due to Elliott's alcoholism.
1891~	Elliot Roosevelt forced to leave New York. Out of touch with the family, he lives with another woman and probably has another child.
1891	Eleanor's mother Anna Hall dies (Eleanor is 7).
1893	Eleanor's brother, Elliott dies (Eleanor is 9).
1894	Eleanor's father dies of alcoholism (Eleanor is 10).
1894	Eleanor goes to live with MGM in household with two out-of-control alcoholic uncles and no one to care for her.
1904	Eleanor and Franklin are married.
1906	TR having problems as president.
1906	(Jan) Favorite son Teddy failing at Harvard.
1906	(Feb 17) Alice, age 22, marries Congressman Nick Longworth, age 34 (TR age 48).
1907	Alice's marriage is unhappy, she and husband are mostly apart. He has serious alcohol problem and many women. He is conservative Republican, whereas her father moves increasingly toward breaking from Republican party altogether.
1919	TR dies (age 61).
1923	Alice (age 39) begins affair with Senator William Borah.
1925	(Feb 14) Alice, 2 days after 41st birthday, has baby girl. Wants to name her "Deborah," but Nick opposes. Name: Paulina after St. Paul (Alice & William's favorite Bible figure).
1946	Paulina has a baby and names her Johanna.
1952	(Nov) Paulina's husband, Alex Sturm, commits suicide.
1957	(Jan 27) Paulina, age 31, commits suicide.

Seeing so many tragic events on the genogram leads us to speculate about the impact these events had on Eleanor's later development. Sometimes those born at a time of loss may be more vulnerable to later dysfunction, especially if they become the special focus of parental attention. Eleanor's experiences instead seemed to strengthen her resilience, while at the same time making her more sensitive to the tragedy of others. She later discussed having an awkward, isolated adolescence and a strong desire to have a family of her own to make up for the one she had lost. She was able to do this when she met Franklin Roosevelt. Perhaps her early experience of loss and isolation eventually propelled her to reach out to others to an extraordinary extent, as her later life of altruism to others around the world would show.

Tracking the impact of family events must occur within the context of normative expectations (Carter & McGoldrick, 2005b; Walsh, 2003). The ages of family members and family structure at the time of the event are important to consider. For instance, how children are affected by a critical event such as a loss of a parent depends on their level of emotional and cognitive development. An older child will have a different experience than a younger child. Eleanor Roosevelt, as the oldest, felt great responsibility for her younger brother after her parents died. Peter Fonda as the younger brother was very expressive of his emotional responses to his mother's suicide, whereas his older sister Jane was completely restrained, responding to the adult imperatives.

Particularly traumatic for a family is the death of an infant or a young child. In preparing the genograms of famous people, we noticed that many were born shortly before or after the death of a sibling: Beethoven, Princess Diana, Ben Franklin, Sigmund Freud, Henry Ford, Thomas Jefferson, C. G. Jung, the Wright brothers, Frida Kahlo, Franz Kafka, Gustav Mahler, Eugene O'Neill, Diego Rivera, and Harry Stack Sullivan. One might attribute this solely to the higher child mortality rates of the past or speculate that the death of a child makes the surviving child even more "special" to the parents. Or, perhaps, the child closest to the lost child feels impelled to do more for the family to make up for the loss. In any case, their siblings were less likely to have the same connection to a loss, suggesting that their "specialness" may have been influenced by their particular place in the family structure.

Finally, a "good" event can also have a powerful impact on a family. In fact, in many of the families we studied, the fame of one individual had profound repercussions for other members of the family. Not only was privacy often lost, but the children in the next generation also had a difficult legacy—a tough act to follow. Martin, the son of Sigmund Freud, said it well: "I have never had any ambition to rise to eminence. . . . I have been quite happy and content to bask in reflected glory. . . . The son of a genius remains the son of a genius, and his chances of winning human approval of anything he may do hardly exist if he attempts to make any claim to fame detached from that of his father" (Wallechinsky & Wallace, 1975, p. 948). This has not, however, stopped many from trying!

Steven Smith, the only one of the six oldest sons in the Kennedy young generation not to get into drug or behavior trouble, said of the losses of his uncles, "I had this powerful sense of the awful possibility that someone very close to me could be taken from my life. When you sense that, it can bring a sense of immediacy to what you do. You make the effort for others that you otherwise might not make, and you become very aware of trying to use your time the best way possible" (Andrews, 1998, p. 167).

Anniversary Reactions

Certain so-called coincidences can be understood as anniversary reactions; family members react to the fact that the date is the anniversary of some critical or traumatic event. For example, a family member might become depressed at the same time each year around the date when a parent or sibling died, even without making any conscious connection. This appears to have been the case in the suicide of Martin Bateson, who killed himself on his dead brother's birthday. Possibly this anniversary intensified his plight and feeling of loss to the point of suicide, without his even realizing what he was reacting to.

An event occurring on the anniversary of another event can, of course, intensify the meaning of both events. Both Thomas Jefferson and John Adams died on the 50th anniversary of the signing of the Declaration of Independence, July 4, 1826. It was almost as if both of them waited until that anniversary to die. Deaths on anniversary days undoubtedly intensify the meaning of the anniversary for the families.

One of the best documented examples of an anniversary reaction is that of George Engel (1975), a noted psychiatrist and internist who wrote in detail about his own anniversary reactions following the fatal heart attack of his twin brother. The temporal connections become evident on the genogram shown in Figure 4.3. Engel suffered a serious heart attack one year minus a day after the death of his twin, seemingly responding to the stress of the anniversary. Engel later reported experiencing another type of anniversary reaction, an anniversary of age rather than date. Engel's father died of a heart attack at the age of 58. As Engel approached this age, he found himself becoming more anxious. He repeatedly misremembered his father's age at death, fearing he would die at the same age. His experience led him to explore the psychological components of such family experiences and the mystifying way families often dissociate themselves from such emotional processes (e.g., forgetting the day or the year of significant events). Interestingly enough, the date and circumstances of the suicide of Katherine Hepburn's brother (Color Figure 17) was repeatedly misreported by her biographers for the past 80 years (Mann, 2006).

Figure 4.3 George Engel Anniversary Reactions

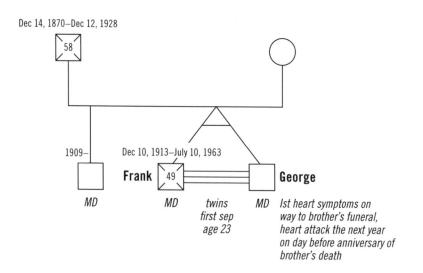

In other words, a trauma may set a family up for an anniversary reaction in the next generation of the family's life cycle. That is, as family members reach a certain point in the life cycle, they may expect the same thing to happen as happened at that point in the previous generation. For example, if a man cut off from his father when he left home, he may expect his son to cut off when he reaches young adulthood. Another example is a family in which the death of a key family member followed shortly after a marriage for two generations. That particular life cycle transition will probably become a toxic point for the next generation, with members consciously or unconsciously fearing to repeat the events yet again.

Thus, it is important to scan the genogram not only for coincidences in time but also in date, age, and point in the family life cycle. Such coincidences point to the interconnectedness of events and the impact of change on family functioning. Once these are recognized, the family can be warned of the potency of particular anniversary reactions.

Locating the Family in Historical Time: Social, Economic, and Political Events

Of course, family events do not occur in a vacuum. Family development must always be viewed against the background of its historical context—that is, against the social, economic, and political events that have influenced the well-being of the family. These include war, migration, economic depression, and so on. It is important to connect the family events that appear on the genogram to the context in which they occur (Cohler, Hosteler, & Boxer, 1998; Elder, 1977, 1986, 1992).

It is important not only to track important family events, but also to locate the family's development in historical time. For example, a suicide in 1929 might suggest certain hypotheses, such as a crisis following from the stock market crash; a marriage in 1941 might suggest other historical circumstances that would influence the couple's relationship, such as the husband's involvement in World War II. Those who had a rocky time coming of age in the late '60s or '70s, were undoubtedly influenced by the Vietnam War, whether they participated in the war or not.

Many of the tragic events in the Kennedy family, of course, took place against the backdrop of the historical and political era in which the family played such an important role. On a private level, the deaths of John F. Kennedy and his brother Robert were tremendous losses for their families, but these tragic assassinations of two important leaders were also shared by the whole nation. It is likely that this merging of the private and personal experience of the family with the public historical experience of the Vietnam era had a profound impact on the Kennedy family's adjustment to its loss, as shown by the next generation's evident difficulties with drugs, risky behavior, and acting out.

It would be impossible to understand the family of Frida Kahlo (see Color Figure 10) without knowing that she was born in Mexico near the time of the Mexican revolution. She so identified herself with her political era that she used to say she had been born in 1910, the year of the revolution, although in reality she was born 3 years earlier. But her life was fully caught up in the sociopolitical struggles of her culture and times, as her work reflects.

Scott Joplin (Figure 4.4), the first African-American composer to fully develop his compositions into an American idiom, was the first of his family's children to be born after the end of slavery (1868). If we look at the Joplin genogram we may wonder why Scott, of all his musical siblings, became the famous composer. Both parents and all of the siblings appear to have been very musical. He was extremely talented, but perhaps there were also family patterns that contributed to his special development. If we look at the genogram, we can see that he was born 7 years after the oldest son, followed in quick succession (a year apart) by two more siblings, with the younger children born at 6- and 3-year intervals. His older brother, Monroe, born in 1861, was the only one of the six Joplin children who did not have any schooling and the only one who did not become a musician. The years between Monroe and Scott's births were the years of the Civil War, so Scott was the first child born after the Civil War, which could have made his birth special for the family (even though Texas, where they lived, did not acknowledge the end of slavery until 1870). But it also seems likely that there were other pregnancies in between the two first brothers (complete sources of information are lacking). If Joplin's mother, Florence Givens, had lost children between Monroe and Scott, it could help to explain Scott's apparent special position in her heart as he would have been the first born after these losses. She not only found a way for him to play the piano as a small child in the home of a family she worked for, but also managed to buy a piano for him at the very time when her husband was leaving her for another woman. It has been suggested that Scott was triangled into his parents' relationship through his father's resentment of his mother's "overencouraging" him and that this contributed to their separation (Haskins, 1978, p. 54). In any case, Joplin had a sense of his "specialness" from early on and received considerable education, whereas his older brother apparently never went to school, though he did study music as did all the Joplin children. By the age of 16 Joplin organized a music group and before he was 25 he was "The King of Ragtime."

Figure 4.4 Scott Joplin's Family

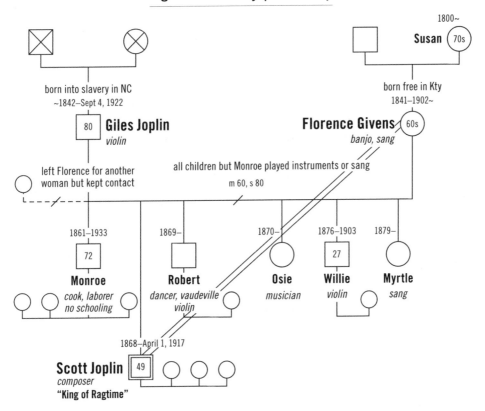

Migration is another event that has great impact on a family (see bibliography section on Migration). It is important to evaluate sibling relationships, for example, in the context of the timing of a family's migration. A family that migrates in the middle of the mother's child-bearing years may have two different sets of children, those born before and those born after the migration. The children born after the migration may have been raised in a much more hopeful context or, on the other hand, in a much more stressful one.

Maria Callas (Figure 4.5) provides an example of the stresses on a first child born after migration, where the move is compounded by many other stresses. Immigration and the subsequent stresses of dislocation appear to have had a major impact on the Callas family. Maria's Greek parents, George and Evangelica, married 2 weeks after Evangelica's disapproving father died unexpectedly in 1916. Immediately after the father's death the mother told her her daughter to marry George. The couple had first a much-loved daughter and then a son who died at age 3 of meningitis, just after which the father made sudden arrangements to move to the U.S. Coincidentally, they arrived while the country was in mourning for the death of President Harding. The husband could not initially work as a pharmacist and because they didn't know English they struggled to survive. It was in this context that Maria was born, 5 months after they immigrated. The mother was so disappointed in her being a girl and in her overall situation that she refused to relate to her for some time and the parents could not even agree on a name to give her for several years. The father struggled, but after some years had a pharmacy, until the Depression, which occurred just when Maria was starting school. Years later, Maria's sister described the insidious impact of the Depression on the family:

> What do I truly remember of the Great Crash? Did I really see people throw themselves off high buildings? . . . Of course not, but it is difficult now to disentangle real life from the endlessly repeated newsreels which brought us those images of a world gone mad. I doubt we children knew what was happening at the time. . . . As the children of the rising professional classes we were soon to be made aware that . . . many things formerly taken for granted were no longer to be relied on. . . . I suppose

Figure 4.5 Maria Callas's Family

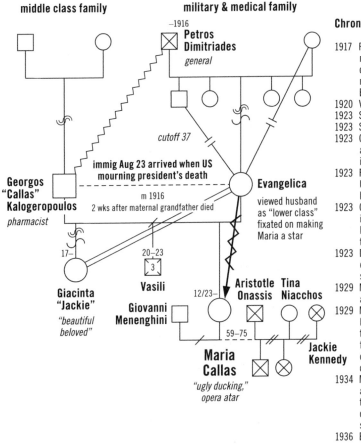

middle class family

military & medical family

–1916
Petros Dimitriades
general

Georgos "Callas" Kalogeropoulos
pharmacist

cutoff 37

immig Aug 23 arrived when US mourning president's death

m 1916
2 wks after maternal grandfather died

Evangelica
viewed husband as "lower class" fixated on making Maria a star

17–

20–23
3

Giacinta "Jackie"
"beautiful beloved"

Vasili

Giovanni Menenghini

12/23–

Aristotle Onassis

Tina Niacchos

59–75

Maria Callas
"ugly ducking," opera atar

Jackie Kennedy

Chronology

1917 Parents married only after maternal grandfather, who disapproved, died and maternal grandmother urged E to marry GC
1920 Vasily born
1923 Spring. Vasily d. meningitis
1923 Spring. E becomes pregnant
1923 GC makes secret arrangements for immigration to US
1923 Family arrives NY just when US in mourning for Pres. Harding
1923 GC has to work for minimum income as Greek teacher until he gets pharmacy license, then does okay until crash
1923 Dec Maria born, E so disappointed to have girl that she refuses to see her
1929 Maria hit by car and has anxieties from then on
1929 Maria goes to 1st grade, GC loses his pharmacy and has to rebuild, E furious with him for his "failure" and stages dramatic suicide attempt, couple's relationship is over
1934 Maria wins singing context and E decides she is her ticket to success, from then on devotes self to daughter's success
1936 E remigrates to Greece

each child thought him- or herself untouched by these strange events until one evening on returning home from school came the realization that financial disaster was upon us. . . . Now everyone was into mere survival mode and Father began to sink into debt. . . . It was the fulfillment of all [Mother's] prophesies. Father's new business had momentarily eclipsed the loss of what might have been back in Meligala—no more. We were reduced to what we had been when we first arrived. The pharmacy had to be given up . . . a smaller apartment found. When mother heard of the sale she dashed into the drugstore to confront Father as if he had been

personally responsible for the financial instability of the Western world
and when he turned his back on her and walked away she rushed to the
dangerous medicines cupboard, grabbed a handful of pills and swallowed
them. . . . Mother's self indulgent coup de theatre effectively marked the
end of their marriage. From then on they would live under the same roof
as irritable strangers. (Callas, 1989, pp 42–43)

The family went again into turmoil and eventually the mother, believing
herself superior to her husband, remigrated with the daughters to Greece,
leaving the husband in the U.S. The parents never managed to overcome
the difficulties in their relationship with Maria, who, having been
neglected in childhood by her very stressed parents, eventually became
the mother's "ticket to success" and was forced to perform to help the
mother achieve the dreams she had imagined but never been able to
realize for herself.

A different legacy seemed to play out for George Washington Blackwell, the 9th and youngest of the Blackwell family, discussed in Chapter 2
(see Figure 2.12), and the only one born after the family's migration from
England. He was the only one not bound by the family's moralistic ideals
and not involved in reform activities. Instead he was a pragmatic, financially successful businessman who became the investment manager for the
rest of the family, perhaps free to follow his own agenda because he was
born in the new country (Horn, 1980, pp. 138–139).

Erik Erikson, who will be discussed in depth in Chapter 8, changed his
name when he immigrated in 1936, perhaps in part to dissociate from his
Jewish heritage. Thirty years later, though he had become very famous as
a child theorist and therapist in the U.S., he explained to his son his
parental difficulties as a result of being an immigrant: "I left . . . too much
to Mom. This . . . had to do with my being an immigrant. She knew everything about the country, from the worth of a dollar to the needs of American children. And I honestly believed that I could not be of much use to
you" (cited in Erikson Bloland, 1999, p. 54). This touching comment,
though surely not the entire explanation of his difficulties (see Chapter 8),
indicates the profundity of the sense of inadequacy that immigrants may
have, even after many years, about "reading" the culture or negotiating it
effectively.

Complex Genograms

Because genograms can become very complex, there is no set of rules that can cover all contingencies. We want to illustrate how we have dealt with some of the common problems. First, it helps to plan ahead. Obviously, if three-fourths of the page is filled with the father's three siblings, a problem will emerge when it is discovered that the mother is the youngest of 12. It helps to get an overview of the number of siblings and marriages in the parental generation before starting. The following questions will help in anticipating complexities and planning the graphic from the start:

- How many times was each parent married?
- How many siblings did each parent have and where were each of them in the birth order?

For example, in mapping the structure of Jane Fonda's family of origin, the basic framework might look like Color Figure 4. The genogram shows Jane's parents and grandparents. Each of her parents had previous marriages and her father, Henry, had subsequent marriages. The other marriages are shown to the side of each parent and are dated to indicate the order.

Generally, the IP is the focal point of the genogram and details about others are shown as they relate to this person. The complexity of the genogram will thus depend on the depth and breadth of the information included. For example, if we were to include Jane's nuclear family, more detail on her mother's, father's, and siblings' various marriages, as well as the patterns of suicides, psychiatric hospitalizations, and traumatic events, the genogram might look something like Color Figure 5. This complex and crowded genogram reveals such important details as:

- Multiple marriages are common in this family.
- Henry Fonda's first two wives committed suicide.
- Henry Fonda separated from his second wife, Jane's mother, only a few months before she committed suicide. He had already started a relationship with his future third wife, Susan Blanchard, whom he married 8 months later, and very possibly fathered her daughter Amy, whom he officially adopted in 1953.

- During the honeymoon of Henry's third marriage, Peter Fonda shot himself and nearly died.
- Henry Fonda had two close friends who committed suicide, as did Peter's "secret love," Bridget Hayward, in 1960, 10 months after the suicide of her mother, Margaret Sullavan, Henry Fonda's first wife.
- In 1965 Peter's best friend committed suicide, his father married for the fifth time, and his sisters Pan and Jane both married for the first time.

Nevertheless, there are limits to what the genogram can show, particularly regarding complex relationships and multiple marriages. Sometimes, in order to highlight certain points, the arrangement must be reorganized. For example, the Fonda family genogram has been arranged to highlight the marriage of Henry Fonda and Frances Seymour Fonda as parents of Jane and Peter. Henry was married five times. His first wife, Margaret Sullavan, was married four times; Henry was her second husband. Margaret's third husband, Leland Hayward (who was also Henry Fonda's agent), was also married five times, including twice to the same wife. Some of the spouses were married numerous times as well. At a certain point this kind of complexity becomes impossible to depict on a genogram.

Some complex family situations may require more than one genogram. Genograms are necessarily schematic and cannot detail all the vicissitudes of a family's history. For example, the Fonda genogram does not include the following information:

- Frances Seymour Fonda was in a mental hospital when she killed herself.
- Peter's close friend, Bill Hayward, son of Henry's first wife, Margaret, was hospitalized for 4 years at the Menninger Clinic as a young adult, which had a strong influence on Peter, who feared mental illness for years.
- A woman with whom Peter had an affair (Tahlita Getty) later committed suicide as well.

- Henry Fonda's first wife, Margaret Sullavan, lived very near the Fonda family in California with her third husband, Leland Hayward, Fonda's agent. After she separated from Hayward, she moved with her children to Connecticut, where she again lived very near the Fondas.
- Peter Fonda's first wife later married his former agent.
- Jane Fonda and Brooke Hayward, Margaret's daughter, were best friends growing up and always hoped that their parents would reunite.
- Jane found out about her mother's death in a movie magazine. Peter didn't learn for 5 years that her death was a suicide. He learned this the same week that he learned that his much-loved stepmother was separating from his father. Not until 10 years later did Peter learn that his mother's death had occurred in a mental hospital.
- Henry apparently never discussed his wife's suicide with Peter or Jane.
- Henry and his mother-in-law held a private funeral for Jane's mother, which only the two of them attended. Henry went on stage that same night.
- Although Peter shot himself in the stomach during his father's honeymoon, 8 months after his mother's suicide, Henry never asked him if he was upset about his mother's death, which Peter had been told was due to a heart attack.
- During Henry Fonda's fourth honeymoon in 1957, Peter became so troubled that his boarding school asked him to leave. It was his college-age sister who had to arrange to send him to his aunt in Nebraska and who arranged for him to get psychiatric treatment.
- Just after Henry Fonda's fifth honeymoon in 1965, Peter was involved in a drug arrest. His trial ended in a hung jury. Once again, Henry never asked him if there was a connection.
- For many years Peter kept the gun given him by his friend Stormy, who committed suicide in 1965. He finally gave it to his therapist in 1972, feeling suicidal and not wanting to use it.

- Peter had certain extremely important resources growing up, including: his sister Jane, though she thought she had been very mean to him; his aunt Harriet, who saved him at several critical times; Harriet's husband, his uncle Jack, whose smile was "like Santa Claus"; his first stepmother, Susan Blanchard, with whom he has stayed close all his life; his half sister Pan, who was his godmother and a support from a distance; as well as several teachers and therapists.

It is clear that Fonda family members have been greatly influenced by suicides and remarriages and that the Hayward and Fonda families were closely intertwined. Perhaps the extraordinary strength and force of personality that Peter and Jane have shown in their careers reflect the many traumas they managed to overcome in their childhood. Furthermore, the relationship Jane and Ted Turner developed together (see Color Figure 6) might indicate another coming together (even though it did not work entirely) of resourceful people who have transformed themselves and their lives in the face of many suicides and other traumas.

Given the toxicity of suicide, the most traumatic of all deaths, the relevant facts surrounding the suicides would be critical to an understanding of the Fonda family. Such additional family information should be noted on a family chronology or, when possible, indicated on the genogram.

Multiple Marriages and Intermarriages: Richly Cross-Joined Families

Other problems arise where there are multiple intermarriages in the family (e.g., cousins or stepsiblings marrying). There comes a point when the clinician must resort to multiple pages or special notes on the genogram to clarify these complexities, although computer programs will make it much easier to include buried complexities without making the graphic too hard to read. Sometimes a genogram may be confusing because of the multiple connections between family members, as when two members of one family marry two members of another (see Freud, Chapter 8; Einstein, Figure 5.10; Kennedy, Color Figure 13; and

Roosevelt, Figure 5.8). The British Royal family genogram (Color Figure 12) provides one of the most challenging examples of this, soon becoming so complex it cannot be shown on one page. It has been said that everyone on earth is connected within "six degrees of separation"—that is, that within six connections each person becomes connected to each other. Indeed, we know that the Fondas are connected to the Adams family and to Henry the VIII, as well as to the Churchills, who are also connected to Princess Diana (see Figure 5.1). The royal families of Europe are all multiply connected and this would be impossible to indicate on one genogram. The suggestion is that the Windsors, who invented their anglicized name in 1917 to dissociate themselves from their German roots (see Color Figure 12), are connected to a great number of other families discussed in this book, including George Bush (see Color Figure 11), the Nehru family (see Figure 7.2), the Robeson family (see Figure 5.5) through Edwina Montbatten, the Bouvier family (see Figure 2.10) through Jackie's sister Lee Bouvier Radziwell's first husband Michael Canfield (which connects them to the Kennedys) and to Mia Farrow (see Color Figure 2) through Edward VII, Queen Victoria's philandering son, who was reputed to be Mia's paternal grandfather. Creating a genogram to show the British Royal family just since the time of Queen Victoria (see Color Figure 12), including all the immediate royal connections, proved quite a challenge. It also showed many other famous connections including Alexander Pushkin, David Niven, Danny Kaye, and Noel Coward.

Children Raised in Multiple Households

Genograms may become complex when children have been adopted or raised in a number of different households or when children have shifted residences many times to foster homes or to relatives or friends, as shown in Color Figure 14. This genogram shows Peter Fonda's 11 living constellations from the time he was born until he reached adulthood. It is useful to make the genogram show as much of the information on the transitions and relationships as possible. Yet many situations are very complicated. In such cases, let practicality and possibility be your guides. Sometimes the only feasible way to clarify where children were raised is to take chronological notes on each child. Genogram software will soon make it possible to track each person's location through his or her life, including the household constellation. You will be able to create a genogram for any moment in time to track the changes in detail.

Missing Information

Of key interest in developing genograms is the missing information. Why does a person know nothing about his father? Why are aunts and uncles omitted from the mother's side? What does missing information tell us about cutoffs, conflicts, or painful losses in a family? Often, filling in the missing information can lead to opening up new options for the client in terms of potential resources and clarification of the family drama that has eluded understanding. In the Fonda family, for example, in spite of scanning many biographies on Peter, Jane, and Henry, it was actually impossible to do even a minimal nuclear family genogram for either parent. In the case of their mother, this might be understandable because of her mental illness and early death, although surely her history must have profoundly affected all her siblings, and their children as well. Yet, as far as could be ascertained, Frances's father, her siblings, and Henry's siblings did not even attend her funeral, even though two of them were involved in the lives of the children! Although Henry's sister Harriet and her husband Jack played a critical role in Peter's life as mentors, guardian angels, and parental replacements when Henry and his wives were inaccessible, the other sister, Jayne, is almost never mentioned. Nevertheless, if one were trying to help Peter or Jane learn about their history, this aunt (and her husband and children, if she had them) would be key resources. Peter wrote about his inability to learn the truth of his family history, which had been "sanitized" over the generations, and which he felt blocked from discovering, though he was sure there were explanations for the mystifying experiences he had growing up. He said about going to live with his aunt Harriet at age 17, "I wanted to say good-bye to the dark, silent, booby-trapped thing that had been my 'family'" (Fonda, 1998, p.

133). Of his father's seemingly inaccessible history he said, "Things happened to him that we will never know. He was never beaten. But something happened to him that made him very quiet, very shy, and he let those qualities define his personality. They were the makeup and costume that he wore in real life. Somewhere, he found it was easier to say nothing. Easier on his heart, I mean. . . . The deeper the emotion, the deeper he hid it. I say more about our father, because I know more about him. But I'll never know enough" (p. 496). Discussing his difficulty learning his family history he said:

> Such deafening privacy extended to my mother's family, of course. All I knew of my maternal grandparents—and they were both alive until I was in my late twenties—is that my grandfather was a debilitated (and debilitating) alcoholic, who would come home some nights completely blasted, and mow the lawns, stumbling around and screaming invectives at the injustices of civilized people. My grandmother was patient to a fault with him, as she was with us during the years of our mother's gradual disappearance. . . . I doubt I would believe a story told me by any remaining elder from either side. Too much time has passed, with too much opportunity to revise and sanitize the truth, and I hardly want to bother Harriet with my questions, now that she's in her nineties. My father's autobiography, as told to someone else, was full of so much sanitation that it had little base in reality. . . . Dad was too shy, too intensely private, to truly expose the part of his history that mattered to him. (p. 116)

From a systems perspective, one might help Peter do a genogram and explore in detail the missing information (some of which could, of course, be recovered through genealogical sources), to try to break through the "sanitized" versions. Such missing information often becomes the very focus of clinical investigation, as it is precisely what has been left out of the story that is central to understanding the participants. As one of Nabokov's characters once put it: "Remember that what you are told is really three-fold, told first by the teller, retold by the listener, and concealed from them both by the dead man of the tale" (Nabokov, 1959, p. 52).

Discrepancies

Finally, there may be a problem with discrepant information. For example, what happens if three different family members give different dates for a death or conflicting descriptions of family relationships? Bill Clinton's father, Bill Blythe, was apparently a mysterious charmer; he was constantly reinventing himself. There are many discrepancies about his life (Figure 4.6). Even his birthdate is open to question. His family said he was born February 27, 1918; his military records say he was born February 21, 1917. His wife, Virginia, said she met him when he was passing through Shreveport, but military records show he had been there for 2 months before they met. He did not tell Virginia that he had married in December 1935 and filed divorce papers the following year, or that a birth certificate for a son, Henry Leon Blythe, was filed on January 17, 1938. Nor did she know that he was married again on August 11, 1938, and divorced a second time 9 months later by a judge's ruling listing "extreme cruelty and gross neglect of duty" (Maraniss, 1995). Virginia also did not know about a third marriage in 1940 to his first wife's younger sister, apparently to avoid marrying a fourth woman who claimed to be pregnant with his baby. There is even another birth certificate, filed in Kansas City in 1941, for a daughter, Sharon Lee Blythe, born to a Missouri waitress, to whom he may also have been married. (Furthermore, he may not even be the biological father of Bill Clinton. It is generally presumed that he is, but questions have been raised about whether his father wasn't still in the army in Italy when the mother conceived Bill. Clinton himself, however, considers Blythe to be his biological father.) Indeed, living with conflicts over discrepancies, as the U.S. did with President Clinton, seems to have a long history in his family.

Not only did Bill Blythe live by reinventing himself with new versions of his history, covering over the discrepancies and contradictions, but Virginia Kelley Clinton had conflicts in her workplace and community for years over her actions as a nurse anesthetist, with suits brought against her regarding the death of two patients. There were accusations and counter-charges over her behavior, and on her part over the behavior of others with whom she had worked. She held on for a very long time but was

Figure 4.6 Discrepancies Regarding Bill Clinton's Father

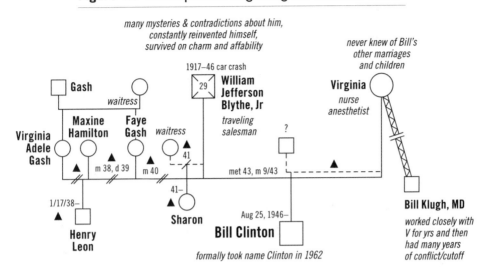

eventually pressured out of her job. The conflicts, which are very hard to get clear, caused great turmoil for many years. Virginia's father also denied that he was in the illegal liquor business with her second husband, Roger Clinton, although he was. He always denied his wife's continuous accusations of marital infidelity. The mysteries and discrepancies over the facts in their family are numerous, and yet the family remained very closely connected over the years, as discussed in Chapter 5 (see Color Figure 16).

This many discrepancies in a family is extreme, but discrepancies are common and need to be indicated somehow on a genogram, where their implications might have emotional significance for the family. Bradt (1980) long ago suggested using color-coded genograms to distinguish the source of information. Hopefully, software will soon make it easier to track discrepant information.

Such discrepancies, complex families with multiple marriages, intertwined relationships, many transitions and shifts, and multiple perspectives challenge the skill and ingenuity of the clinician trying to draw a genogram within a finite space. Improvisation and additional pages are often needed.

Ethical Genogram

Paul Peluso (2003) has proposed the use of ethical genograms, which could lead to useful genogram questions including the following:

- What are the toughest moral or ethical decisions you or members of your family have ever had to make, or should have made? How were these decisions or decision points handled?
- What kind of behavior was considered unethical? What happened when there were infractions of your family's moral code? Were there conflicts in your family over moral or ethical rules?
- Have you changed your values regarding any of the ethical rules you were taught growing up?
- How did your family's moral code compare to society's legal code? Were there people in your family who broke the law? How did others respond if this happened?
- Were there family members who transgressed the family's moral code? How did others respond if this happened? Harshly, leniently, consistently, inconsistently?
- What were the strongest family values in your family regarding ethical behavior? Honesty? Loyalty? Chastity? Fairness? Respect? Justice?

Career/Work Genograms

Gibson (2005) recommends the use of genograms in guidance programs to help children view their career aspirations in context from the time they are in elementary school. She suggested that children can begin to develop a work/career genogram for their families in 4th or 5th grade, and evolve the genogram as they move through middle and high school, hopefully using their understanding of their family's career history to develop their own aspirations. Obviously, if you are the first person in your family to embark on a path, it is very different from continuing in an already-established family path. Developing career counseling genograms with children as they grow up can help them to see their connections or their pioneering path in relation to their family heritage.

Sexual Genograms

Using sexual and cultural Genograms (Hardy & Laszloffy, 1995; Hof & Berman, 1986; McGoldrick, Loonan & Wolsifer, 2006) can be very helpful in understanding the function of symptoms, fears, and sexual relationship problems. Sexual problems evolve within the context of relationships as we move through the life cycle, and they must be considered within that context. Therapists may benefit from constructing their own sexual and cultural genogram to highlight values they bring to their therapeutic work. Onto the basic genogram framework are added particular aspects of the individual, couple, and family history that have relevance to sexual history: health and psychological history, sexual and intimate liaisons of family members beyond marital information, and themes such as avoiding discussion of sex or passing along sexualized information on family members. Constructing sexual and cultural genograms is an extremely useful way to help couples understand themselves and each other in a sexual and cultural context. It will help clients become aware of the values they have grown up with and recognize how these values influence their sexual values, behaviors, and anxieties.

Following is a list of sexual genogram questions (amplified from Hof & Berman, 1986, and McGoldrick, Loonan, & Wolsifer, 2006).

Sexual Genogram Questions

- What overt and covert messages did partners receive from their families regarding sexuality? Intimacy? Masculinity? Femininity? What might other members of the family say about these issues?
- Who was most open sexually? Emotionally? Physically? Who was most closed? How did that affect other family members?
- How was sexuality or intimacy encouraged? Discouraged? Controlled? Taught? Did previous generations differ in the messages they gave?
- Were there ways that members of your family did not conform to the sexual or intimacy mores of their religious background? What was the impact of this?
- Were there secrets in your family regarding intimacy, sex, or abuse? Incest? Other sexual abuse? Unwanted pregnancies? Extramarital

affairs? Pregnancy before marriage? Abortions? Marriage of cousins?

- What questions might you have been reluctant to ask about sex or intimacy regarding your family's genogram? Who might have answers? How could you approach people?
- How was the concept of birth control dealt with?
- How was erotic material such as books or magazines with sexual content dealt with?
- How were stronger sexual media such as pornography dealt with? How do you deal with sexual media now in your relationship?
- What were the rules about monogamy in the relationships you saw? Was attraction to other people and talking about it all right?
- Were extramarital affairs or visits to prostitutes tolerated or discussed? How are these issues dealt with now in your relationship?
- Were there family members in previous generations who had an intimate relationship you would want to emulate or not emulate?
- How do you feel your family members' sexual or intimate relationships were influenced by their ethnicity? Poverty? Success? Gender? Sexual orientation? Immigration? Language difficulties? Race?
- Have members of your family married out of their ethnic, class, or religious background? How did that affect others in the family? How do you think it affected their sexual and intimate relationship?
- How do the values of your religious or cultural background influence your own views of sexuality and intimacy? Are there ways in which they are different?
- Were there people whose pattern of sexuality or intimacy did not conform with your family's cultural or gender norms? How were they reacted to by others in the family?
- How would you want to change the messages you give the next generation regarding sexuality and intimacy from the messages you received in your family?
- How were the norms in your family similar to or different from the norms in your partner's family of origin? How do you think those differences may affect your sexual and intimate relationship?

- How do you think you have done as a couple navigating the differences? What shared values have you arrived at about sexual issues?
- How did factors such as prejudice or oppression affect your family and personal development as a sexual person?
- What were your first sexual experiences like? How did you feel about them then? How do you feel about them now?

Obviously it would be extraordinarily difficult to draw a graphic that would physically represent all the sexual information one might want to gather on a genogram. Most commonly, multigenerational patterns of affairs are obvious on genograms, but the subtler sexual issues would require special symbols and connection lines to depict. Nevertheless, such themes are important, and using a genogram format for organizing the tracking of sexual themes is the most efficient framework for assessing sexual history.

There are any number of subjects on which "themed" genograms can be created: caretaking, health and illness, education, hope and resilience, humor, work, pets and hobbies, and so on. The essential issue is that tracking family patterns over time rather than just focusing on an individual is a crucial framework for understanding human experience in the context of history.

5

Interpreting Family Structure

BY EXAMINING RELATIONAL STRUCTURE, family composition, sibling constellations, and various family configurations, clinicians can make many hypotheses about themes, roles, and relationships that can be checked out by eliciting further information about the family. The interpretive principles for evaluating genograms are based on the principles of family systems theory. For further elaboration of ideas outlined here, the reader is referred to literature on Bowen theory (see bibliography section on Assessment, Genograms, and Systems Theory) sibling constellation (see bibliography section on Siblings), McGoldrick, (1995), Harriet Lerner (1990, 1994, 1997, 2002, 2005), and the writings of other family theorists who affirm the value of understanding family history in solving current problems.

The first area to explore on a genogram is the basic family structure—that is, the structural patterns revealed by the lines and symbols on the diagram. Examining this graphic structure allows us to hypothesize about family roles, relationships, and functioning based on household composition, sibling constellation, and unusual family configurations.

Family patterns also tend to intensify when they are repetitive from one generation to another. Family members in similar structural arrangements as the previous generation are likely to repeat the patterns of that generation. For example, a mother who is the youngest of three sisters will probably find herself overidentifying with her youngest if she also has three daughters. Or, if a family has had three generations of separation and divorce, they may view divorce as almost a norm.

Household Composition

Household composition is one of the first things to notice on a genogram. Is it a traditional nuclear family household, a single-parent household, a multihousehold family, a multifamily household, an extended family household, or a household that includes outsiders?

Traditional Nuclear Family Household

The percent of U.S. households that are traditional nuclear families (a couple in their first marriage and their children) has been steadily declining, from 40% of all households in 1970 to 23% of households in 2003 (Fields, 2003). By itself, this family structure might not attract the clinician's attention. However, if the family is under severe stress or there is serious marital conflict, the clinician will want to explore what factors and strengths have helped to keep the family together and what additional resources may be needed or accessible, as such structures tend to be less flexible under stress than more extended family units. In addition, nuclear family structures can be expected to have certain predictable parent-child triangles, such as mothers joining with children in relation to the father, one parent allying with a child against the other parent or against another child, parents joining in relation to a "sick" or "bad" child, or siblings joining together in relation to fighting parents.

Single-Parent Households

A single-parent household, in which only one parent is raising children, may be formed by a single parent's bearing or adopting children, or after the death, divorce, separation, or desertion of one of the parents. Seeing a single-parent structure on the genogram should cue the clinician to explore the reasons for single parenthood, the difficulties in raising children alone, economic problems, and available resources, such as extended family, godparents, and friends.

Color Figure 15 shows the first years of Bill Clinton's life with his mother, Virginia, who was 23 when he was born and living as a single parent with her own parents. Newly widowed, with no real job skills and no money, she had few resources. Luckily, her parents were available, although the most common triangle of such three-generational households soon developed: The parent feels like an outsider living in the grandparents' household, while the grandparents tend to develop a tight relationship with the child. As Clinton's mother (Clinton-Kelley, 1994) put it:

> Mother, meanwhile, was totally involved in showing me how mothering was done. She meant well, but I felt like a lowly student nurse again . . . while . . . my mother played God. . . . When mother wasn't monopolizing him, I would take him out for a spin in his carriage. (pp. 61–63)

Virginia decided to spend the next year in New Orleans to finish school, leaving Bill at home with her parents. The relationship problems intensified when she returned and was living at home again:

> Mother increasingly rubbed me the wrong way. I was 25, 26, even 27, and still living with my parents. It was a blessing, of course, that I had somebody to take care of Bill during the day. But there's always a price to be paid for such a service. Mother had already grown incredibly attached to Bill while I was in anesthetist school, and now, with me working, she still held sway over him. She would dress him and feed him and walk him and buy him things. Nothing was too fine or too expensive for her beloved grandson. (pp. 77–78)

Such problems are predictable in single-parent structures, and clinicians should inquire about such typical patterns whenever they see them on a genogram. Also of interest would be the impact on the family (particularly on the children) of the loss of the other parent and associated relational patterns and triangles. In Bill Clinton's case, he said he was happily unaware of the triangles in his early childhood:

> I was in the care of my grandparents. They were incredibly conscientious about me. They loved me very much, sadly, much better than they were able to love each other or, in my grandmother's case, to love my mother. Of course, I was blissfully unaware of all this at the time. I just knew I was loved. Later, when I became interested in children growing up in

hard circumstances . . . I came to realize how fortunate I had been. For all their own demons, my grandparents and my mother always made me feel I was the most important person in the world to them. (Clinton, 2005, pp. 9-10)

Of his lost father, Bill Blythe, he said:

All my life I have been hungry to fill in the blanks. Clinging eagerly to every photo or story or scrap of paper that would tell me more of the man who gave me life . . . Whatever the facts . . . given the life I've led, I could hardly be surprised that my father was more complicated than the idealized pictures I had lived with for nearly half a century. . . . My father left me with the feeling that I had to live for two people, and that if I did it well enough, somehow I could make up for the life he should have had. And his memory infused me, at a younger age than most, with a sense of my own mortality. The knowledge that I, too, could die young drove me both to try to drain the most out of every moment of life and to get on with the next big challenge. Even when I wasn't sure where I was going, I was always in a hurry. (Clinton, 2005, pp. 5–7)

Often single-parent households are part of larger multihousehold networks, sometimes called binuclear families (Ahrons, 1998) or multinuclear families, in which children are part of several different family structures at the same time. Such families require children to develop complex adaptive skills to deal with the different contexts they must negotiate in each home.

Remarried Families

When one or both parents remarry following a divorce or death, bringing a stepparent into the household, a remarried family is formed. The children of the previous marriages may all live in the same household, they may be divided among households, or they may move back and forth between households.

Remarried families have to deal with particular issues, such as custody, visitation, jealousy, favoritism, loyalty conflict, and stepparent or stepsibling problems. The clinician should explore the impact of the divorce and remarriage on each family member. The relational patterns and triangles inherent in this type of family are reflected in Bill Clinton's family (Color Figure 16). His father, William Jefferson Blythe, Jr., had been married several times before marrying Clinton's mother, Virginia Cassidy, who learned of these previous marriages only many years later, when she was already dying herself.

It can be a challenge to map the fluctuating structure and living arrangements in such families. Virginia Cassidy married again in 1950, when Bill was 4. Her second husband, Roger Clinton, had also been married before. Virginia Cassidy later divorced Clinton, but then remarried him a few months later. In midlife Bill Clinton became aware that he had two other half siblings from Bill Blythe's earlier relationships. He has met with his half brother, but not with his sister (Clinton, 2005).

Extended Family Networks

Ethnic groups vary tremendously in their definitions of family (McGoldrick, Giordano, & Garcia-Preto, 2005). It is important to attend to structures that include godparents or other kinship networks and to assess how the relationship patterns may be affected by these structures. Aunts, uncles, cousins, foster children, and housekeepers may be part of the household. Babysitters, close friends, or other "outsiders," who are especially important to the family, often become members of the informal extended kinship network and should be included in the genogram, as we have illustrated for the Clinton's housekeeper/caretaker Cora Walker, who worked for the family from 1953 on and whose daughter Maye then cared for Virginia Clinton until she died in 1994. We have also included Bill Clinton's friends from earliest elementary school, Vince Foster, Mac McLarty, and Joe Purvis, who came with him 50 years later to the White House.

A nuclear family may live with grandparents. This is particularly common for single parents, where a mother might live with her mother for aid and support, as Virginia Blythe Clinton did. With a three-generational household the clinician should explore issues around cross-generational boundaries, alliances, and conflicts, particularly reflected in issues of parenting. In the case of Virginia Clinton, she had always adored her father but found her mother overpowering.

The clinician should explore the roles and relationships of extended family members living in the household. Relationship issues will vary according to the individual's role and structural position in the family. A spouse's parent, brother, sister, aunt, uncle, or cousin may seem like an intruder to the other spouse; a foster or adopted child is likely to become involved in predictable triangles as the "special one" or the "problem one," depending on the child's own qualities and those of the family. It is important to consider the reverberations in both the immediate and extended family caused by the entry of an extended family member or other person into the household.

Sibling Constellation

The importance of birth position, gender, and number of years in age from other siblings has long been discussed in the literature, although there has not always been agreement on the role sibling constellation plays in development (see Siblings bibliography section). Many factors influence sibling patterns, including timing of a child's birth, sibling position, ethnicity, and life circumstances. In addition, under certain circumstances, such as family disruption, siblings may become each other's main protector and resource. When Bill Clinton's parents divorced in 1962, Bill, who had never been adopted by his stepfather, decided to change his name officially. The change was not to connect with his abusive, alcoholic stepfather, whom his mother was just leaving, but in order to have the same name as his young half brother, to whom he felt a deep loyalty and sense of protection.

At present, sibling patterns are undergoing significant changes, primarily because of the different childbearing, childrearing, and family structural patterns that have followed the increased availability of birth control, the women's movement, the entry of more women into the workforce, and changing family structures.

Sibling experiences vary greatly. An important factor is the amount of time brothers and sisters spend together when young. Two children who are close in age, particularly if they are of the same gender, generally spend a lot of time together. They share their parents' attention and are often raised as a pair. Siblings born farther apart obviously spend less time with each other and have fewer shared experiences; they grow up in the family at different points in its evolution and in many ways are like only children, as they have gone through each phase of development separately (Toman, 1976). Jung (see Color Figure 7) is an example of a functional only child for this reason. Because his older brother died before he was born and his sister was born 9 years later, Jung's experience was probably more that of an only child than of a sibling.

In today's world of frequent divorce and remarriage, families often have a combination of siblings, stepsiblings, and half siblings, who may live in different households and only come together occasionally. There are also more only children, whose closest siblinglike relationships are with their playmates. In addition, more often than in previous generations, there are two-child families, where relationships tend to be more intense than when there are multiple siblings. Clearly, the more time siblings have with one another, the more intense their relationships are likely to be. In large sibling groups, subgroups tend to form according to sex and distance in age. Two brothers born 18 months apart may form a dyad, and their two younger sisters born 5 and 7 years later may form a second subsystem.

Siblings often come to rely on each other, especially when parents are unavailable or unable to provide for their nurturing needs. From early childhood Jane and Peter Fonda had to fend much for themselves. They experienced the early emotional loss of both parents, their father because he was distant by personality and because he was usually away working, their mother because she was mentally ill; then came their mother's very traumatic suicide, and they were shifted into multiple living situations before adulthood. As often happens for siblings in such traumatic circumstances, they became for each other the anchor in a painful and unstable world. From earliest childhood, Peter said, his father was away most of the time "and forgot or didn't notice that our mother increasingly spent time in her bedroom with the curtains drawn. . . . Jane and I pulled together. . . . We began to carve holes in the wall between our rooms so we could talk at night. We had (still have) our very secret word that we could whisper into our little holes" (Fonda, 1998, pp. 14–15). "Moving a family, uprooting and relocating, no matter how close or great the distance is one of the most stressful things in life. . . . I felt that Jane and I had been sent into exile from our Paradise, hauled along on some unspoken crusade of our parents" (p. 35). "Jane became my savior. And though she says she hated me and treated me meanly, she was there for me at every critical moment. Sister and brother, brother and sister" (p. 39).

It was Jane who was there for him when at age 10 he shot and injured himself while his father was away on his third honeymoon. It was Jane, then just starting college, who came for him when at 16 he was expelled from prep school and had no other guardian. He said of her, "I really didn't have anyone else but Jane. She meant everything to me" (p. 54). And many years later: "I needed her approval as much as I needed anything. Jane had always been just slightly below Dad on the need-of-approval scale and as we were closer and more in touch with each other, her blessing was the more important one" (pp. 292–293).

At one crisis in her life, when she was over 50, Jane made Peter promise to spend 5 days alone with her. She said she needed to talk about their childhood together, to know all the little details he remembered, so she could try to put the crazy, broken pieces of the puzzle of their early life together, and she feared she might lose him before she could do it (p. 474).

Birth Order

Sibling position can have particular relevance for a person's emotional position in the family of origin and future relations with a spouse and children. An oldest child is more likely to be overresponsible, conscientious, and parental, whereas the youngest is more likely to be childlike and carefree. Jane Fonda, being 2 years older than Peter, was always the responsible child, following in her father's footsteps into acting at an early age, whereas Peter for many years played the role of rebel against authority. Often, oldest children feel special and particularly responsible for maintaining the family's welfare or carrying on the family tradition. They may feel they have a heroic mission to fulfill in life. In addition, sometimes the oldest will resent younger siblings, feeling they are an intrusion on his or her earlier exclusive possession of the parents' love and attention. Middle children may feel caught in between or have a need to find their niche and define themselves as different (Sulloway, 1996). Birth order can also profoundly influence later experiences with spouses, friends, and colleagues, though, of course, it does not guarantee a particular type of personality. There are many other factors that influence sibling roles, such as temperament, disability, physical appearance, ethnicity, intelligence, talent, gender, sexual orientation, and the timing of each birth in relation to other family experiences—deaths, moves, illnesses, and changes in financial status.

Twins

The ultimate shared sibling experience is between identical twins. Twins and other multiple births are becoming more common. About one person in 50 is a twin, although about one in eight pregnancies begins as twins (Wright, 1995). They have a special relationship that is exclusive of the rest of the family. The grip twins hold on our imagination perhaps relates to the fact that their very existence challenges our sense of uniqueness (Wright, 1995). They have been known to develop their own language and maintain an uncanny, almost telepathic sense of each other. When one twin dies the other may experience lifelong guilt. Even fraternal twins often have remarkable similarities because of their shared life experiences.

The major challenge for twins is to develop individual identities. Because they do not have their own unique sibling position, there is a tendency for others to lump twins together and they may have to go to extremes to distinguish themselves from each other.

Different Roles for Brothers and Sisters

Brothers and sisters generally have very different roles in families. Sisters of sisters tend to have very different sibling patterns than sisters of brothers. Indeed, the research indicates that, because of society's preference for boys, the segregation of boys and girls in their socialization is quite extreme from early childhood (Maccoby, 1990). In coed situations boys tend to ignore or mistreat girls, whose wishes do not get equal attention. If a brother is older, he is often favored and catered to. If the brother is younger, he may be envied and resented by the sister for his special status.

The example of Princess Diana, although particular to her family's situation, also reflects general gender problems, which exist the world over (Figure 5.1). She was the third daughter in a family whose status depended on producing a son who would become, on the death of his

Figure 5.1   Princess Diana's Family

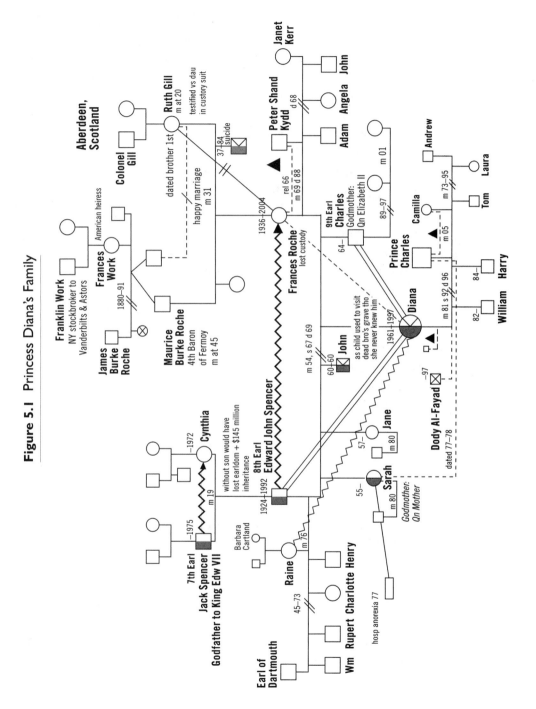

father, the seventh Earl Spencer of Althorp, inheriting an estate worth about $140 million dollars. The parents were desperate for a son, as they would have to leave the family home if they did not have one. The one son they had, born the year before Diana, was deformed and died soon after birth. When Diana was born, the parents were so disappointed that they did not bother to register her birth, and she is the only one of her siblings who did not have a royal godparent. As Diana said, "I was a disappointment. My parents were hoping for a boy. They were so sure I'd be a boy they hadn't even thought of a [girl's] name for me." (Campbell, 1998, p. 1). Although she was finally given the name of the one ancestor who almost married into the royal family, her position probably led to both her sense of inadequacy and her carefully cultivated aura of being special. Throughout her childhood, she frequently visited her dead brother's grave, though she had never known him. As the third girl in a family that required a son and had just lost one, she would definitely need to be "different" to find a niche, and different she became. Her position was greatly alleviated, of course, when her younger brother was born 3 years later. Indeed, he became, not surprisingly, her favorite (the more so because the parents divorced soon after) and the two of them became each other's primary refuge, as we have just seen with Jane and Peter Fonda.

In early childhood, sisters are often caretakers of one another and of their brothers, as well as rivals and competitors for parental attention. Parents may, with the best of intentions, convey very different messages to their sons than to their daughters. Here, for example, is a description by Jackie Robinson, the remarkably versatile Brooklyn Dodger first baseman who integrated baseball, of his daughter, Sharon, the middle child with two brothers (Figure 5.2), and the role of his wife, Rachel, who had had the same sibling constellation.

> She was just such an ideal and perfect child in our eyes and in the opinion of virtually everyone who came in touch with her that she sometimes seemed a little too good to be true. While fathers may be crazy about their sons, there is something extraordinarily special about a daughter. It's still the same—our relationship—perhaps even deeper. . . . Rachel had been brought up with the same family pattern—a girl in the middle

of two boys. She was the busy, loving, but not necessarily always happy, mainstay of her family, who took care of her younger brother. With a kind of grim amusement, I recall our assumption that Sharon was strong enough to cope well with whatever confronted her. We took her development for granted for many years. She rarely signaled distress or called attention to her problems by being dramatic. (Robinson, 1972, p. 242)

Figure 5.2 Jackie Robinson's Family

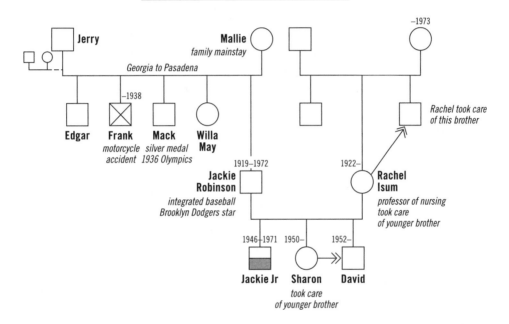

Sharon herself fell into many of the typical sister behaviors, in spite of both parents' efforts to the contrary and in spite of the fact that her mother was a highly dynamic and successful woman and role model of strength. She later wrote:

At times Jackie [her older brother] would hold me down and tickle me until I cried. Despite all this, I easily fell into the role of my brother's protector. . . . In spite of my mother's warnings to the contrary, I was running up and down the hill in our backyard fetching water and food for my brothers, while they sat on the bank of the lake fishing. (Robinson, 1996, p. 88)

There are many reasons for the complexity of sister relationships: the familial bonds, the length of these relationships, the caretaking responsibilities sisters tend to be given, and their competitiveness for male attention and approval. There is also a special intricacy and intimacy in sister relationships. Our society has generally denied the importance of these relationships. In most of our legends and stories a man stands between sisters, who compete for his attention (Bernikow, 1980). Mothers are, of course, hardly mentioned at all, unless divisively, as in *Cinderella*. Older sisters in literature are usually depicted as evil, whereas the youngest is the infantilized baby and favorite, "Daddy's girl," receiving his love and wealth in return for her loyalty and willingness to be his "love object." The influence of this negative mythology on how women in families see each other is an important issue in clinical assessment. Conflict between women should never be accepted at face value, but should be assessed in terms of who benefits when women cannot be each others' allies (McGoldrick, 1989).

It is also important to assess sibling gender roles (and all other gender roles) in relation to culture. In many cultures daughters are more likely to be raised to take care of others, including their brothers. Some groups, such as Irish and African-American families, may, for various historical reasons, overprotect their sons and underprotect their daughters (Watson, 1998). Other groups have less specific expectations. Anglos, for example, may believe in brothers and sisters having equal chores. In any case, it is essential to notice how gender roles influence sibling patterns.

Unlike oldest sons, who typically have an unacknowledged feeling of entitlement, oldest daughters often have feelings of ambivalence and guilt about their responsibilities. Whatever they do, they may feel that it is not quite enough and that they can never let up in their efforts to caretake and to make the family work right.

The Oldest Child

In general, oldest children are likely to be the overresponsible and conscientious ones in the family. They make good leaders because they have experienced authority over and responsibility for younger siblings. Being the firstborn can be a mixed blessing. As the answer to parents' dreams and the beginning of a new family, the firstborn may receive an intensity of attention denied to the children that follow. But the burden may at times be heavy. Oldest children tend to assume responsibility for others, working hard to elevate the group to an elite position.

George Washington (Figure 5.3) is an outstanding example of this. He grew up as an oldest, although he had two much older half brothers (whom he did not get to know until adolescence). One of them, Lawrence, became his guardian after his father died. Washington's leadership ability was a major factor in the formation of the United States. At the age of 20 Washington joined the Virginia Militia, quickly distinguishing himself to become commander in chief of all Virginia forces by the age of 23. He had a seemingly miraculous ability to lead his men into battle and emerge unscathed. A brilliant leader, he kept a single-minded focus on his objec-

Figure 5.3 Washington Family

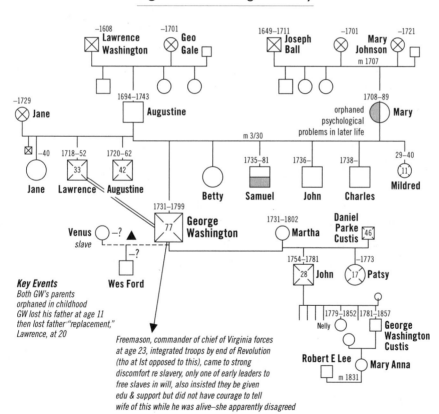

Key Events
*Both GW's parents
orphaned in childhood
GW lost his father at age 11
then lost father "replacement,"
Lawrence, at 20*

*Freemason, commander of chief of Virginia forces
at age 23, integrated troops by end of Revolution
(tho at 1st opposed to this), came to strong
discomfort re slavery, only one of early leaders to
free slaves in will, also insisted they be given
edu & support but did not have courage to tell
wife of this while he was alive–she apparently disagreed*

tives and his obligation to support his men and accomplish his goal, regardless of the personal sacrifices involved, just as he was supportive of his younger siblings and many other family members throughout his life.

Another typical oldest was Che Guevara, the responsible oldest of five children (Figure 5.4). Che, like George Washington, was a natural leader. It is, perhaps, no wonder that Che became a hero of the guerrilla revolutions in Cuba and South America. He was carrying out the role of the oldest, adhering to his parents' socialist and revolutionary values. His father, Ernesto Guevara Lynch, had been deeply entrenched in the politics of the time, befriending Spanish exiles after the Spanish Civil War and founding his town's Comite de Ayuda a la Republica, part of a national solidarity network with Republican Spain. Che's mother, Celia Guevara de la Serna, was also a revolutionary. She ran a bohemian household, filled with books and newspapers, where her children were encouraged to speak freely. Che grew up surrounded by people emotionally involved with the Spanish Republican cause. As the first born son and a fragile child (he suffered attacks of asthma throughout childhood), Che grew up especially close to his mother, who tutored him at home. From earliest childhood he revealed a personality that echoed his mother's in many ways—decisive, opinionated, radical, and independent, with strong intuitive loyalties to other people (Anderson, 1997, p. 17).

The oldest daughter often has a similar sense of responsibility, conscientiousness, caretaking, and leadership as her male counterpart. However, daughters generally do not receive the same privileges, and families generally do not have the same expectations for them to excel. Thus, oldest daughters are often saddled with the responsibilities of the oldest child without the privileges or enhanced self-esteem. When siblings are all female, oldest sisters may have certain privileges and expectations urged on them that would otherwise go to sons, such as was the fate of Katherine Hepburn's suffrage-leader mother, the oldest of three daughters, who ended up having to take her sisters with her when she went to college.

When a boy follows an oldest girl in the family line up, he may become a functional oldest, as was the case with Thomas Jefferson (see Color Figure 18) and John Quincy Adams (see Figure 2.13).

Figure 5.4 Che Guevera

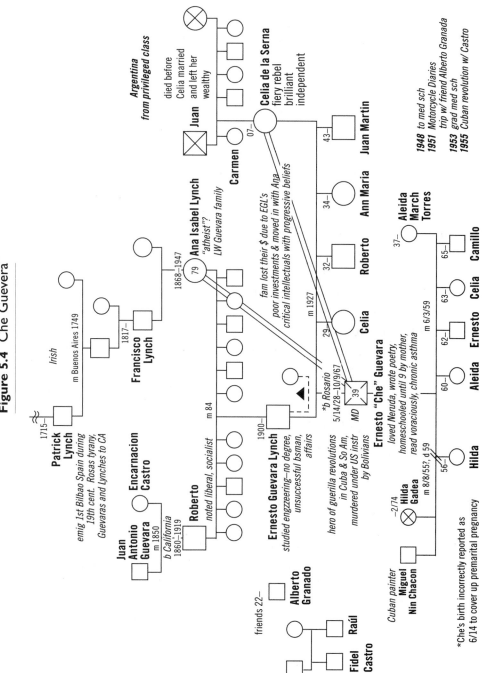

Argentina from privileged class

died before Celia married and left her wealthy

Juan   Celia de la Serna
fiery rebel
brilliant
independent

Carmen

07–

Juan Martin

43–

Ann Maria

34–

Roberto

32–

Celia

29–

1948 to med sch
1951 Motorcycle Diaries
         trip w/ friend Alberto Granada
1953 grad med sch
1955 Cuban revolution w/ Castro

Irish

m Buenos Aires 1749

Patrick
Lynch
emig 1st Bilbao Spain during
19th cent. Rosas tyrany,
Guevaras and Lynches to CA

1715–

Juan
Antonio
Guevara
m 1850
b California
1860–1919

Encarnacion
Castro

Roberto
noted liberal, socialist

Francisco
Lynch

1817–

Ana Isabel Lynch
"atheist"?
LW Guevara family

1868–1947

79

m 84

m 1927

fam lost their $ due to EGL's
poor investments & moved in with Ana
critical intellectuals with progressive beliefs

Ernesto Guevara Lynch
studied engzzeering–no degree,
unsuccessful bsman,
affairs

1900–

hero of guerilla revolutions
in Cuba & So Am,
murdered under US instr
by Bolivians

*b Rosario
5/14/28–10/9/67
MD   39

Ernesto "Che" Guevara
loved Neruda, wrote poetry,
homeschooled until 9 by mother,
read voraciously, chronic asthma

Aleida
March
Torres

37–

Camillo

65–

Celia

63–

Ernesto

62–

Aleida

60–

m 6/3/59

Hilda

56–

Hilda
Gadea
m 8/8/55?, d 59

–2/74

Cuban painter
Miguel
Nin Chacon

*Che's birth incorrectly reported as
6/14 to cover up premarital pregnancy

friends 22–

Alberto
Granado

Fidel
Castro

Raúl

A younger child may also be thrust into the oldest role by a sibling's illness or disability. Katherine Hepburn (Color Figure 17) became the oldest surviving child in the family when she was 13, after her older brother, then 15, hung himself. She had become the functional oldest years earlier, when she was given the role of caretaker for this brother, who had suffered from depression and various other problems in childhood. Several other factors may have influenced this role reversal, including many other suicides of men in her family and the heroism of the women who survived and reinvented themselves in the face of their losses. Indeed, Katherine Hepburn's mother, Kit Houghton, whose own father had killed himself when she was only 13, had been left an orphan 2 years later when her mother died as well, having struggled to ensure that her daughters would be able to have an education and thus not be dependent on men for their survival. Kit Houghton managed to wage a legal battle with her uncle and go to Bryn Mawr at 16, while supporting two younger sisters until they too began college!

The Youngest Child

The youngest child often has a sense of specialness, which allows self-indulgence without the overburdening sense of responsibility that comes with being the oldest. This sense may be more intense when there are several siblings. The younger of two probably has more a sense of "pairing" and twinship—unless there is a considerable age difference—than the youngest of ten. Freed from convention and determined to do things his or her own way, the youngest child can sometimes make remarkable creative leaps, leading to inventions and innovations, as in the examples of Thomas Edison, Benjamin Franklin, Marie Curie, Paolo Freire, and Paul Robeson (for more detailed discussion of these families, see McGoldrick, 1995; Sulloway, 1996).

Given their special position as the center of attention, youngest children may think they can accomplish anything. The youngest may feel more carefree and content to have fun rather than achieve. Less plagued by self-doubt than their older brothers and sisters, they are often extremely creative and willing to try what others would not even dare to consider. They can also be spoiled and self-absorbed, and their sense of entitlement may lead at times to frustration and disappointment. In addition, the youngest often has a period as an only child after the older siblings have left home. This can be an opportunity to enjoy the sole attention of parents, but it can also lead to feelings of abandonment by the siblings.

Other general characteristics of youngest children are readily apparent. Because the youngest has older siblings who have often served as caretakers, he or she may remain the "baby," a focus of attention for all who came before, expecting others to be helpful and supportive. Youngest children may feel freer to deviate from convention. Youngests may even feel compelled to escape from being the "baby," which may cause a rebellion, as with Edison and Franklin, who both ran away in adolescence.

A younger sister tends to be protected, showered with affection, and handed a blueprint for life. She may either be spoiled (more so if there are older brothers) and have special privileges or, if she is from a large family, frustrated by always having to wait her turn. Her parents may have simply run out of energy with her. She may feel resentful of being bossed around and never taken quite seriously. If she is the only girl, the youngest may be more like the princess, and yet the servant to elders, becoming, perhaps, the confidante to her brothers in adult life and the one to replace the parents in holding the family together.

Paul Robeson (Figure 5.5), a brilliant and creative youngest, was the multitalented star in his family, the more extraordinary because the family was African-American, living in a racist society. An outstanding athlete in every sport, Phi Beta Kappa and valedictorian of his college class, a lawyer turned world-famous singer, actor, and then political speaker, Robeson was deeply aware of the importance of each of his siblings in his life. He said everyone lavished an extra measure of affection on him and saw him as some kind of "child of destiny . . . linked to the longed-for better days to come" (Robeson, 1988, p. 16). This is a common role for a youngest, especially when the family has experienced hard times.

The Middle Child

The middle child in a family is "in between," having neither the position of the first as the standard-bearer nor the last as the "baby." Middle children thus run the risk of getting lost in the family, especially if all the siblings are of the same sex. On the other hand, middle children may

Figure 5.5 Paul Robeson

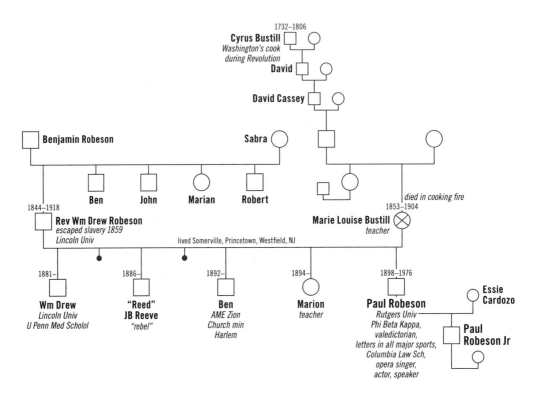

develop into the best negotiators, more even-tempered and mellow than their more driven older siblings and less self-indulgent than the youngest. They may even relish their invisibility.

Martin Luther King (Figure 5.6) is an example of the best a middle child can be in terms of ability to play multiple roles and bring others together. His brilliant ideas of nonviolent group resistance are a good fit with his middle sibling position, as a sibling in the middle does not have might on his or her side and the power of joining forces is a natural idea for a middle child. Unlike the youngest, who would be unlikely to make a good leader, middle children may become outstanding collaborative leaders because they can draw together multiple factions through collaboration and mediation.

Middle children are under less pressure to take responsibility, but they need to try harder to make a mark in general, because they have no special role. In the Robeson family there were three middle children, who all

Figure 5.6 Martin Luther King's Family

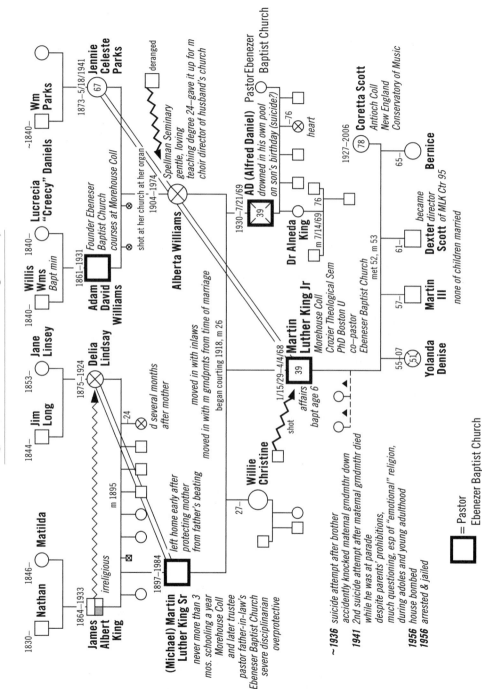

played out variations of the middle child role. The oldest brother, William Drew, was named for the father and followed in his footsteps, attending the same college, Lincoln University, before going to medical school. The second oldest, Reed, also brilliant but too overtly angry to survive easily as an African-American in their community, became the "lost" middle child; Paul believed he learned the quality of toughness from this brother. The third son, Ben, an outstanding athlete and even-tempered role model for Paul, became a successful minister like their father. The fourth child and only daughter, Marion, became a teacher like their mother and was noted for her warm spirit. For Paul, Ben, and Marion—those closest to him in age—were the most important mentors, "reserved in speech, strong in character, living up to their principles, and always selflessly devoted to their younger brother" (Robeson, 1988, p. 13). This support was all the more important because the children's mother died tragically in a fire when Paul was only 5. Both Ben and Marion were willing to do without the limelight and to facilitate the relationships of others, typical characteristics of middle children.

There were lessons also from Reed, who carried a little bag of stones for self-protection, should he encounter a dangerous situation. Robeson admired this "rough" second oldest brother and learned from him a quick response to racial insults and abuse. Paul had a special feeling for this brother, who did not live up to the father's high expectations of the Robeson children. He later wrote:

> He won no honors in classroom, pulpit or platform. Yet I remember him with love. Restless, rebellious, scoffing at conventions, defiant of the white man's law. I've known many Negroes like Reed. I see them every day. Blindly, in their own reckless manner, they seek a way out for them-selves; alone, they pound with their fists and fury against walls that only the shoulders of many can topple. . . . When . . . everything will be different. . . . the fiery ones like Reed will be able to live out their lives in peace and no one will have cause to frown upon them. (Robeson, 1988, p. 14)

Although Reverend Robeson disapproved of Reed's carefree and undisci-plined ways and eventually turned him out for his scrapes with the law,

Paul saw Reed as having taught him to stand up for himself. Reed, like many middle children, may have expressed feelings that others did not have the courage to express, in his case the rage against racism. In the famous biographical play about Robeson, he says there was one conversation he and his father could never finish—about this brother Reed. Remembering the night his father turned Reed out, fearing he would set a bad example for his younger brother, Paul imagines getting together with his father and brother Ben to go looking for Reed and bring him home. He imagines defending Reed to his father:

> Aw Pop, don't change the subject. . . . Reed was not a bad influence. Only horrible thing he said to me was, "Kid, you talk too much." All he ever told me to do was to stand up and be a man. "Don't take low from anybody, and if they hit you, hit 'em back harder." I know what the Bible says, Pop, but Reed was your son too! You always said you saw yourself in me. Pop, you were in all your sons. (Dean, 1989, p. 298)

This dramatization expresses eloquently the varied roles different siblings take in a family and how much it matters if one is cut off, even though some in the family may not recognize these effects.

Not surprisingly, middle children may show characteristics of either the oldest or the youngest, or both combined. A middle child, unless he or she is the only girl or only boy, has to struggle for a role in the family. Although the child may escape certain intensities directed at the oldest or the youngest, he or she may have to struggle to be noticed. Alfred Adler (Figure 5.7) is another good example of a middle child. Adler was one of the first to theorize about the importance of the sibling constellation for family development, and it is clear many of his ideas derived from his personal experience.

> According to Adler, each one of the children in a family is born and grows up with a specific perspective according to its position in relation to the other siblings. From the outset, the position of the oldest brother is better than that of the younger ones. He is made to feel that he is the stronger, the wiser, the most responsible. That is why he values the concept of authority and tradition and is conservative in his views. The youngest brother, on the other hand, is always in danger of remaining the spoiled

Figure 5.7 Alfred Adler's Family

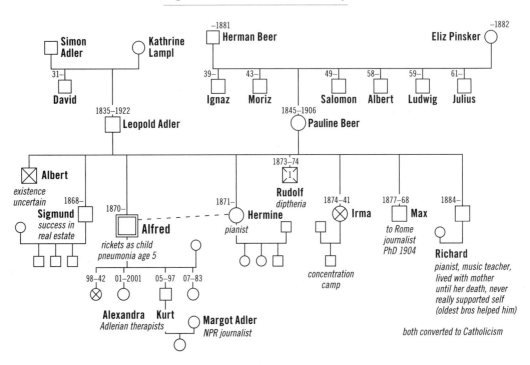

and cowardly family baby. Whereas the oldest will take his father's profession, the youngest may easily become an artist, or then, as the result of overcompensation, he will develop tremendous ambition and strive to be the savior of the entire family. The second child in a family is under perpetual pressure from both sides, striving to outmatch his older brother and fearing to be overtaken by the younger one. As for the only child, he is even more disposed to be spoiled and pampered than the youngest one. His parents' preoccupation with his health may cause him to become anxious and timorous. Such patterns are subject to modifications according to the distance between siblings and according to the proportion of boys and girls and their respective position in the family. If the oldest brother is closely followed by a sister, there comes a time when he will fear being outdistanced by the girl who will mature more rapidly than he. Among many other possible situations are those of the only girl in a family of boys, and of the only boy among a constellation of girls (a particularly unfavorable situation, according to Adler). (Ellenberger, 1970, pp. 613–614)

This appears to fit with Adler's own family experience. Adler, himself sickly as a child (he had rickets, nearly died of pneumonia at age 5, and was twice hit by moving vehicles), felt he grew up in the shadow of his older brother, Sigmund(!), who became a successful businessman, following in their father's footsteps. As can be seen on the genogram, Alfred was followed closely by his sister, Hermine, with whom he apparently had little relationship in adulthood; it is very possible that he did grow up in fear of being outdistanced by her. When Alfred was 4, the third little brother died in bed next to him. The fourth brother, Max, seems to have been "born to rebel" (Sulloway, 1996) and was apparently very envious of Adler; he distanced from the family by moving to Rome and converting to Catholicism. Richard, a typical youngest, seems to have been spoiled and never quite able to take care of himself. He lived with his mother until her death, aspiring to be an artist and musician, and then had trouble supporting himself, living at times with Adler and receiving support from him and from the oldest brother, Sigmund. Even Adler's own children, who became well known Adlerians themselves, steeped in their father's theories about the importance of siblings, did not know the full story of their father's siblings and even less about their grandparents (personal communication, Kurt & Alexandra Adler, 1984).

Missing information is always of interest on a genogram. In Adler's case, in spite of his explicit belief about the importance of sibling relationships for determining behavior, his biographers have given only sketchy and conflicting information about his own sibling constellation (see bibliography section on Adler). We know even less about the sibling or family patterns of Adler's parents, a fact that is also true for Freud, Horney, and Jung, in spite of the great interest in their work and in their psychological makeup. Clearly, biographers have yet to take a systemic view of history (McGoldrick, 1995).

The Only Child
Only children may have the seriousness and sense of responsibility of the oldest and the conviction of specialness and entitlement of the youngest. At the same time they tend to be more oriented toward adults, seeking their love and approval, and in return expecting their undivided attention.

Their major challenge is how to get along "up close and personal" with others their own age. They tend to be more socially independent, less oriented toward peer relationships, more adultlike in behavior at an earlier age, and perhaps more anxious at times as a result of the attention and protectiveness of their parents. They often maintain very close attachments to their parents throughout their lives but find it more difficult to relate intimately with friends and spouses.

Indira Gandhi, the second Prime Minister of India, is an example of an only child (see Figure 7.2). She grew up quite isolated and lived primarily in the presence of older people, early becoming her father's confidante. She clearly had the sense of mission and responsibility of an oldest, but as a leader she was autocratic and led a rather isolated existence, keeping her own counsel. Both her father and paternal grandfather were functional only children. Her father, Jawaharlal Nehru, was 11 years older than his next sibling, and the grandfather, Motilal Nehru, also a leader of India, was many years younger than his siblings. He was raised in the home of his adult brother because their father had died before Motilal was born. The illnesses of both Jawaharlal's mother and Indira's mother undoubtedly compounded both father and daughter's independent roles as only children and their connections to each other.

Sibling Position and Couples

Sibling relationships often pave the way for couple relationships—for sharing, interdependence, and mutuality—just as they can predispose partners to jealousy, power struggles, and rivalry. Because siblings are generally one's earliest peer relationships, couples are likely to be most comfortable in relationships that reproduce the familiar sibling patterns of birth order and gender. Generally speaking, couples seem to do better when the partners complement their original sibling pattern—for example, when an oldest pairs with a youngest, rather than two oldests marrying each other. If a wife has grown up as the oldest of many siblings and the caretaker, she might be attracted to a dominant oldest, who offers to take over management of responsibilities. But as time goes along, she may come to resent his assertion of authority, because by experience she is more comfortable making decisions for herself.

All things being equal (and they seldom are in life!), the ideal couple relationship based on sibling position would be a husband who was the older brother of a younger sister and a wife who was the younger sister of an older brother. Of course, the complementarity of caretaker and someone who needs caretaking, or leader and follower, is no guarantee of intimacy or a happy marriage, but it may ensure familiarity.

In addition to complementary birth order, it seems to help in coupling if one has had siblings of the opposite sex. The most difficult coupling might be the youngest sister of many sisters who marries the youngest brother of many brothers, as neither would have much experience of the opposite sex in a close way, and they might both play "the spoiled child," waiting for a caretaker.

Eleanor Roosevelt, an oldest, and her cousin Franklin, an only child (Figure 5.8), are a good example of two strong-willed spouses whose marriage seems to have survived because of their ability to evolve separate spheres. Leaders in their own separate worlds, they came to live apart except for holidays. Early in the marriage, Eleanor generally subordinated herself to Franklin and to his powerful mother, Sara Delano, who played a major role in their lives. However, as Eleanor became more self-confident and developed interests of her own, she began to show the determination of an oldest. The crisis came when Eleanor discovered letters revealing Franklin's affair with Lucy Mercer. Apparently it was Franklin's mother who negotiated a contract between them for Eleanor to return to the marriage. (This contract is the only document in the entire Roosevelt archive that is not open to the public.) Because oldests and only children are generally oriented to parents, Sara may have been the only one who could have kept them from separating—and she did.

The Roosevelts remained married but lived separate lives, with politics as their common ground. After Franklin's paralysis due to polio, Eleanor became essential to his political career. She nevertheless had her own intimate relationships, her own political views and activities, and her own living space in a separate house at Hyde Park, which she shared with her friends.

Richard Burton and Elizabeth Taylor (Figure 5.9), who married and divorced each other twice, provide a dramatic example of two youngest

Figure 5.8 Eleanor and Franklin Roosevelt

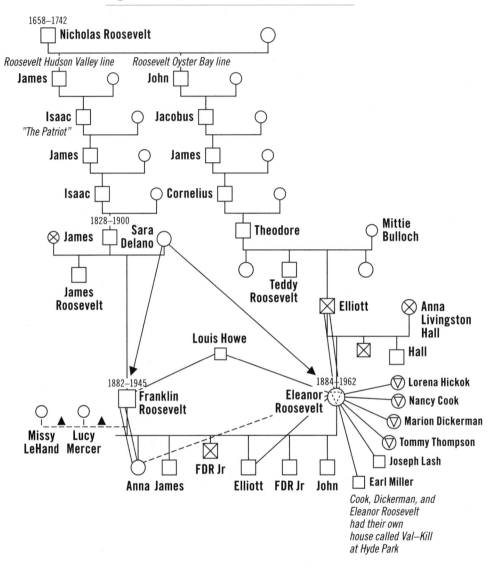

children who competed to be "junior," both seeking a caretaker. Burton was the second youngest of 13 children, but was treated like a youngest, as he was reared apart from his younger brother. In very large families several of the younger children will often have the characteristics of a youngest. Elizabeth Taylor was the younger of two, with an older brother

Figure 5.9 Burton/Taylor (Marriage of Two Younger Siblings)

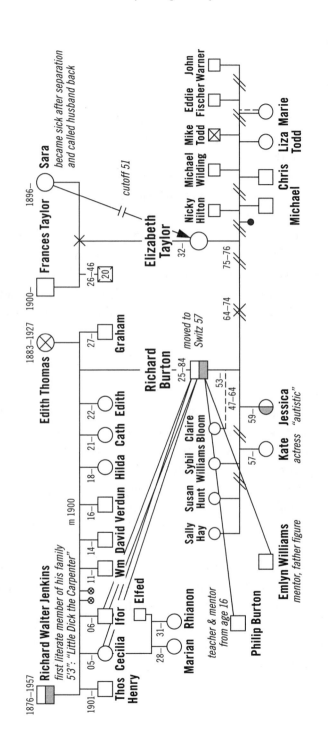

whose needs were often sacrificed to her stardom, which, of course, solid-ified her special position. Burton and Taylor were known for their histri-onic love quarrels, each outdoing the other in their demanding and childish behavior.

There are, of course, many other possible sibling pairings in marriage. Only children may tend to marry each other, but this has the particular difficulty that neither has the experience of intimate sharing that one does with a brother or sister. They may try either to fuse into one or to seek more separateness than other spouses. Middle children may be their most flexible partners, as they have experiences with multiple roles.

Of course, spouses from complementary sibling constellations may have problems, in which case it is important to check the particular family more closely. A case in point is Margaret Mead, an oldest, who married Gregory Bateson, a youngest (see Figure 4.1). Their sibling positions seem clearly reflected in their personality styles. Although Bateson was a youngest, he was forced to take over the legacies of his two older brothers after their death. Mead and Bateson's daughter, Catherine, described their differing styles:

> Margaret's approach must have been based on early success in dealing with problems, perhaps related to the experience of being an older child and amplified by years of successfully organizing the younger ones. Gregory's experience was that of a younger child with relatively little capacity for changing what went on around him. Instead he would seek understanding. Indeed, he had a kind of abhorrence for the effort to solve problems, whether they were medical or political. (Bateson, 1984, p. 176)

Mead's and Bateson's respective sibling positions and problem-solving styles did not lead, however, to a complementary helper/helped relation-ship, but to struggle and disappointment in the other. Margaret's role as the senior partner was emphasized by the fact that she was 3 years older than Gregory. (Her mother, also an oldest, had been similarly 3 years older than her husband.) Catherine Bateson described her parents' relationship:

In the marriage she was the one who set the patterns, for Gregory lacked this fascination with pervasive elaboration. . . . His life was full of loose ends and unstitched edges, while for Margaret each thread became an occasion for embroidery. (p. 27)

It was Gregory, more than anyone else, who lashed back at her for trying to manage his life. . . . She would see a problem and her imagination would leap to a solution. (p. 111)

[He] began with his rebellion against Margaret, a rebellion shot through with resentment against his family and especially against his mother. (p. 160)

It may well be that the suicide of his brother Martin in 1922, which followed on heavy-handed parental attempts at guidance and led to a period of increasing efforts to shape Gregory's choices as well, was an ingredient in his anxiety about problem solving and indeed about any effort to act in the world. (p. 176)

This description of Bateson reflects well his position as a youngest, waiting to be taken care of, yet rebellious against the one (Margaret, an oldest) who does it. As discussed in Chapter 4, the expectations of his sibling position were changed by the traumatic deaths of his two older brothers, thrusting him at age 18 into the position of only child and replacement for the loss endured by his family. The shift in Gregory's sibling position in early adult life may thus have contributed to the incompatibility between him and Margaret, even though their birth positions were complementary.

There is some similarity between Gregory, whose role as the only surviving child in his family intensified to the point of a toxic cutoff from his mother, and Margaret Mead's father, an only child who was doted on by his mother from the time of his father's death when he was 6. Whereas the intensity in adolescence of his mother's pressure led Bateson to cut off his mother, Edward Mead's closeness to his mother from early childhood led him to bring her into his marriage household, where she lived for the rest of her life.

Sibling Position and Parenting

A parent may overidentify with a child of the same sex and sibling position. One father who was an oldest of five felt that he had been burdened as a child with too much responsibility, while his younger brothers and sister "got away with murder." When his own children came along, he spoiled the oldest and tried to make the younger ones toe the line. A mother may find it difficult to sympathize with a youngest daughter if she felt envious of her younger sister. Parents may also identify with one particular child because of a resemblance to another family member.

Intergenerational problems related to sibling position may arise when the identification is so strong that parents perpetuate their old family patterns, as when a mother who hated being bossed around by her older brother is always accusing her son of tormenting his younger sister. In other situations, the parents' own experience is so different that they may misread their children; a parent who was an only child may assume that normal sibling fights are a sign of children's pathology.

Sibling Relationships in Adult Life

Sibling relationships can be an important connection in adult life, especially in the later years. However, if negative feelings persist, the care of an aging parent may bring on particular difficulty. At such times, siblings, who may have been apart for years, have to work together in new and unfamiliar ways. The child who has remained closest to the parents, usually a daughter, often gets most of these caretaking responsibilities, which may bring long-buried jealousies and resentments to the surface.

Once both parents have died, siblings are truly independent for the first time. This is when estrangement can become complete, particularly if old rivalries continue. Strong feelings can be fueled by all the old unresolved issues and conflicts. But the better relationships the siblings have, the less likely it is that this or other traumatic family events will lead to a parting of ways.

Other Factors Influencing Sibling Constellation

It is important not to take the hypotheses about sibling constellations too literally. The usual sibling constellation predictions may be influenced by a number of other factors that affect whether or not people fit the characterizations. For example, how the sibling pattern fits into the constellation of cousins may modify or intensify certain sibling patterns. For example, the role of Woody Allen as older brother of a younger sister was probably intensified by the fact that all his cousins in his large extended family, in addition to his mother's five sisters, were female. Indeed, throughout his high school years he shared a room with a female first cousin to whom he had always been close. Such a pattern probably intensifies to an extreme a family pattern where the older brother of a younger sister is viewed as special and highly valued.

Jackie Bouvier Kennedy (see Figure 2.10) is another example of a family where it is essential to know how the sibling constellation is embedded in the cousin constellation. Jackie was the older sister of a younger sister, with whom she always had an intensely close, but also competitive, relationship. She was also a halfsibling and stepsibling of many children to whom she became connected through her mother's second marriage. In addition, she was part of an extended family of cousins on her father's side, who spent much time together in the formative summers of her childhood. In this constellation she was one of three cousins born in the same year. Jackie had a special preference for several older male cousins, above all her cousin Michel, 9 years older, whom she even remembered in her will. Michel's special role in the family was intensified when his mother divorced his alcoholic father, an event that created great distress throughout the entire family because they felt they were losing the sole male Bouvier of that generation. This sense of the fragility of the male line had begun in the previous generation, when there were only four males out of 12 children and only one of these lived to marry and have children himself. Five of the siblings never married, though they lived a long time. "Aunt and uncle power" can thus also influence a sibling constellation in the next generation, giving special extra care and attention to certain nieces or nephews, which may intensify sibling patterns. Aunts and uncles can play an important role in conveying the strong sense of their own unfulfilled dreams or of family legacies to children of the next generation.

Other experiences in a family's history may also modify sibling patterns. For example, Richard Burton (see Figure 5.9) grew up in a complex family situation after the early death of his mother. His oldest sister, Cis (Cecilia), 19 years older than he, had recently married, and she became the primary mother figure for him and for many of the other siblings. However, as Burton put it, "Cis was wonderful, but she was not my mother" (Bragg, 1990, p. 69).

> His father had been replaced by an elder brother [Ifor], then by a teacher [Philip Burton], and then by another dominating man [Emlyn Williams] . . . his younger sisters were his nieces [Cis's daughters], his older sisters more like aunts, the brothers like uncles, the cousins like brothers, the real aunts like mothers . . . he had many alternative worlds. . . . Complexity, elaboration, alternatives, parallel lives, that was the way it had always been; that was his "norm." (Bragg, 1990, p. 69)

Thus, we must always explore sibling constellation, like any single factor in family life, within the context of the complexity of multiple family patterns. Out of temperament or necessity, siblings may often play nonsibling roles and nonsiblings may play sibling roles, as they did for Burton. Indeed, the empirical research on sibling constellations is at best inconclusive, because there are so many other factors that can change or modify the influence of sibling position. Nevertheless, an awareness of sibling constellation can provide clinically useful normalizing explanations of people's roles in their family, as well as indicate other factors to explore when the typical patterns are not found. In addition, adult siblings, often ignored by clinicians, can be extremely important resources in therapy and healthcare.

Timing of each sibling's birth in the family's history. Sometimes, when a child is born at a critical point in a family history, there are special expectations for that child, in addition to those typical of his or her sibling position. These expectations may exaggerate a sibling position characterization (as with the oldest who acts super-responsible) or modify the usual sibling roles (as with a middle or youngest who functions as an oldest or only child). Particularly critical are family deaths and transitions. A child born around the time one of the grandparents dies may play a special role in the family, as illustrated by Sigmund Freud, who was not only born at the start of a remarried family, but also just 3 months after his paternal grandfather's death.

The child's characteristics. A child with special characteristics may also shift the expected sibling patterns in a family. For example, children may become functional oldests if they are particularly talented or if the oldest is sickly, as appears to have happened with Katherine Hepburn in relation to her oldest brother (see Color Figure 17). An older child may also be treated as a youngest if he or she has special problems (such as a psychological or physical disability).

The family's "program" for the child. Parents may have a particular agenda for a specific child, such as expecting him or her to be the responsible one or the "baby," regardless of that child's position in the family. Children who resemble a certain family member may be expected to be like that person or to take on that person's role. Children's temperaments may be at odds with their sibling position. Noteworthy is the situation where children cannot fulfill the sibling position role that is structurally ordained for them. Some children struggle valiantly against family expectations—the oldest, who refuses to take on the responsibility of the caretaker or family standard bearer, or the youngest, who strives to be a leader. And, of course, cultures differ tremendously in the expected roles of birth order and gender. Asian cultures, for example, tend to have highly stratified expectations for children, depending on their birth order and gender, whereas Jewish and Anglo families tend to be relatively democratic. In some families, the child most comfortable with the responsibility—not necessarily the oldest child—becomes the leader.

Naming patterns of siblings are often significant signals of family "programming." For example, Gregory Bateson, named for one of his father's heroes, Gregor Mendel, though the youngest son, was perhaps being "programmed" to aim at great accomplishments as a natural scientist. On the other hand, John Quincy Adams (see Figure 2.13) broke a four-generation family tradition of naming the oldest son John by naming his first son George Washington Adams, after a man to whom his father was not close. Although names or nicknames may give hints on the genogram about the family's "programming," the clinician needs to look for other indications. For example, the Kennedy family's history (see Color Figure 13) suggests that the males were programmed to run for political office. As is well-known, the oldest son of Joseph P. Kennedy was slated by his father to run for president but died before he could. Later, his three brothers all ran for president and two of his brothers-in-law ran for vice-president or governor. Not surprisingly, a number of the members of the next generation have also run for office.

Of course, other times names reflect different circumstances. Ossie Davis was named Raiford Chatman Davis for his paternal grandfather (Davis & Dee, 2000), but when the county clerk asked for the name and the mother said "R.C. Davis," he thought she said "Ossie Davis." Because he was white and she was black in the racist context of deep Georgia, she could not challenge him, so Ossie it was from that time on!

The child's sibling position in relation to that of the parent. The child's position in the family may be particularly highlighted if it repeats the position of the same-sexed parent. Thus, a man who is the oldest son of an oldest son may have certain specific expectations placed on him that do not apply to his younger brother. If a man's relationship with his own father was charged, there is a good chance that in the next generation the relationship with his son in the same ordinal position may also turn sour. This is more likely, of course, in cultures with strong rules governing sibling functioning in relation to birth order (McGoldrick & Watson, 2005).

Unusual Family Configurations

As the clinician scans the genogram, sometimes certain structural configurations will "jump out," suggesting critical family themes or problems. The genogram of Elizabeth Blackwell, the first woman physician in the U.S., discussed in Chapter 2 (see Figure 2.12), illustrates several of these patterns: (a) the preponderance of successful professional women; (b) the fact that none of Samuel Blackwell's five sisters ever married, nor did any of his five daughters and only a few of the 12 women in the fourth generation; and (c) the frequency of adopting children, even by the unmarried Blackwell women.

This configuration opens for exploration the role of gender in this family of extraordinary feminists (several of them men!) and successful women. It would be fascinating to know the rules and attitudes in the family that influenced this pattern. Some of these patterns have been suggested by Horn (1983), who said that the family viewed marriage nega-tively and actively discouraged the daughters from marrying. Two of Eliz-abeth's three sisters-in-law, Lucy Stone, the famous suffragette, and Antoinette Brown, the first woman minister in the U.S., had become best friends in college at Oberlin. They had resolved never to marry but to adopt and raise children; however, when they met the extraordinary Blackwell brothers, they changed their minds. Of the five Blackwell sisters, four were very successful (Elizabeth and Emily as physicians, Anna as a writer, and Ellen as an artist), and the fifth, Marion, was an invalid. Similarly, of the five daughters of their brother Samuel, four were very successful (two became physicians, one became a minister, and one became an artist) and the fifth was also an invalid. This reveals a pattern of complementarity common in families where siblings or partners are polar opposites. One is forced to wonder whether deeper forces are at play in some families, where one person seems to take on a role for the others—maybe to absorb certain negative energy, which is lived out through sickness or anger, while others are freed for creativity and achievement.

Thomas Jefferson, the third president of the United States, has an extraordinarily convoluted genogram involving marriages and liaisons from within the same few families, slave and white (Color Figure 18). Such configurations were a common occurrence in the era of slavery; white slave owners frequently fathered children with their slaves and then denied this parentage, making it very difficult for African-Americans to know their history (Pinderhughes, 1998). The cutoffs and conflicts produced by this exploitation of African-Americans, as well as by the systematic effort to suppress the cultural and family history of African-Americans throughout our history, has been a shameful part of our national heritage. Facing this history is an important part of healing and changing such patterns of exploitation. Making sense of this interracial configuration is a challenge. As Pinderhughes (1998) has said:

> The invisibility of African-Americans in the recorded history of the United States has led to a pervasive ignorance for everyone, Black or white, about African-Americans and their contributions to the building

of our country. . . . With no power to affect the writing of American history and few resources to disseminate our story, it has remained invisible or distorted by negative stereotypes, and we have until recently remained unable or unwilling to challenge the distortions, untruths, and omissions that have been accepted about our past. . . . But we are coming to realize that knowledge of the past, even if painful, can nourish a people's strength. This realization has stimulated us to unseal these memories and reclaim the truth, no matter how cruel and shocking, so that the festering wound can begin to heal and so that we can better cope with the present and build the future. (p. 170)

Historians have been extremely reluctant to face the truth of this history in families like that of Thomas Jefferson, in which there were many interconnected secret affairs and relationships. Jefferson's white family, along with numerous white historians, went to great lengths to cover up this part of the family history. Historians have only recently been forced at long last to confront their own racism by the DNA tests performed on descendants of Jefferson and Hemings. It is often necessary to reassess carefully the history we have been told in order to understand the truth of the relationships on our genograms.

Indeed, Jefferson's father-in-law had a long secret relationship with his slave Betty Hemings, by whom he had six children, and the indications are that Jefferson later had a 38-year secret relationship and seven children with Betty's daughter, Sally Hemings, who was the half-sister of his wife, Martha Wayles. Jefferson's daughters both married cousins; Martha married a cousin on her paternal grandmother's side, and Maria married her maternal first cousin. In addition, Martha Jefferson's first husband was the younger brother of her stepmother's first husband.

Another example of an unusual family configuration would be a family in which two siblings married siblings from another family, such as the Freud/Bernays family (see Figure 8.4). Sigmund married Martha Bernays, and his sister Anna married Martha's brother Eli. The two couples were very competitive for years.

Albert Einstein (Figure 5.10) left his first wife to marry a woman who was doubly related to him already. She was his first cousin on his mother's

Figure 5.10   Einstein Family

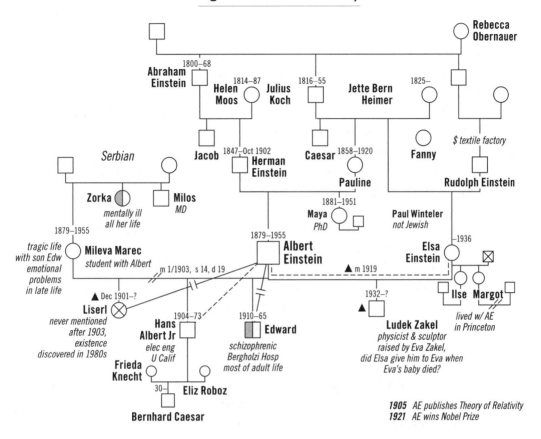

side and his second cousin on his father's side. He and his first wife Mileva also had a mysterious first child, Liserl, born in 1901 (before their marriage in 1903), who was never mentioned for almost 100 years! Concealing information, particularly about births, liaisons, and traumatic deaths, often intensifies its impact on a family. The discovery of Liserl's existence has led to much speculation about what happened to her and why her existence was kept a secret. Recently another possible child of Einstein has emerged. This man, now in his sixties, bears a remarkable resemblance to Einstein and has spent his life as a physicist. Apparently Einstein's second wife may have given up this child in infancy.

Could it be that in both the Einstein and Jefferson families the secrecy and cutoff and the closely cross-joined family members show a parallel process of fusion? We might wonder about the Freud family along the same lines, given the secrecy they kept about Freud's father's first two wives and other issues (see Chapter 8), and then perhaps the fusion reflected in Sigmund and Anna's marrying two siblings. Finally, there is the fact that both Sigmund and his son Martin's had affairs with their wives' sisters.

The unusual connections seen in the graphic configurations of the Jefferson, Freud/Bernays, and Einstein families might lead to a number of speculations about triangles set up by these intrafamily marriages, as well as about possible family expectations influencing members against marrying outside the group. In Jefferson's case, we know that his wife elicited from him a deathbed promise that he would not remarry. He himself, having lost his wife and four children, was protective with his two surviving daughters and apparently encouraged them, as well as many of his slaves, to marry within the family (Brodie, 1974, p. 47). He was especially close to his daughter Martha, and perhaps not surprisingly, he had many problems relating to her husband, Thomas Mann Randolph, and felt closer to his other son-in-law, Jack Eppes, the son of his wife's sister, Elizabeth. Randolph, in fact, became very jealous of Eppes, sensing Jefferson's preference.

Unusual family configurations on the genogram should also be clues for the clinician about other patterns such as multiple remarriages in each generation or structural contrasts (e.g., one spouse coming from a large family and the other an only child), which might suggest family imbalance, and so on.

Children Growing Up in Multiple Families: Foster Care, Adoption, and Orphanage Experiences

Many children grow up in multiple settings, because their parents divorce, die, remarry, or have special circumstances, that require the child to live for a while or even permanently in a different place. Clinicians have often failed to make full use of genograms in such circumstances to track children through the life cycle, taking into account the multiple family contexts to which they belong. We believe that genograms can be a particularly useful tool for tracking children in multiple contexts. The many different family constellations children may live in are otherwise extremely hard to keep in mind. The more clear clinicians are in tracking this history, however complex, the better able they will be to validate the child's actual experience and multiple forms of belonging. Such maps can begin to make order out of the multiple household changes children may go through when sudden transitions or shifts in placement are necessary because of illness, trauma, or other loss.

Dr. Fernando Colon, a family therapist in Ann Arbor, Michigan, has for many years been one of the strongest advocates of the relevance of family history for children who have lived in foster care. Colon grew up in several foster homes after the loss of his mother. As an adult he put much effort into exploring his own genogram (Colon, 1973, 1998; Colon-Lopez, 2005) and helping others to think contextually about child placement and foster care (Colon, 1978). He has made very clear the importance of the genogram of the foster family for understanding a child through the life cycle. Colon himself still has ongoing connections with the biological grandchildren of his third foster mother. They shared holidays and frequent other visits with their grandmother, his foster mother. They have much in common through this shared history, a history that is so often not acknowledged in our foster care system and in our society at large. One of the most powerful aspects of genograms is the way in which they can steer us to the rich possibilities of complex kin relationships, which continue throughout life to be sources of connection and life support. It is not just our shared history that matters, but also current connections that strengthen us and can enrich our future.

Colon-Lopez has published his full story (2005) with illustrative pictures and genograms. He grew up mostly in foster homes from earliest infancy. Colon had experience in virtually every sibling constellation during his childhood years, a factor that probably increased his flexibility in dealing with multiple relationships as an adult. He was the youngest of three, the oldest of three, the middle of three, the older of two, the younger of two, and, rarely, an only child, although, as the one child who remained with his third foster family until he graduated from high school, his position there was a special one. At the same time, the three foster brothers who stayed for long periods of time (4 years each), not surprisingly had more significance for him, especially as they were all close to Colon in age. Less evident from the ages alone was the extremely special relationship that he and his foster mother had with his brother Johnny, who was severely retarded and lived in the family for only 4 months. Both Colon and his foster mother became very attached to Johnny, and Colon remembers clearly how hard Johnny had tried to learn to say Colon's name, Fernando, and how he and his mother cried when they had to let Johnny go.

Although the foster care system at that time operated on the principle that children were never to have contact with other family once they moved to a new home, Colon's foster mother did not believe in that sort of cutting off of the past and made great efforts to reverse that process of cutoff. In the early days of placement, one of his foster brothers, Kenneth, was especially depressed. Kenneth was one of five brothers, and despite the regulations, the foster mother took him to see his brothers, after which he began to adjust to his new situation. Colon remains connected to his foster mother's grandchildren, in addition to his close, ongoing connections with family members on both sides of his biological family.

Whether relationships have been good or bad, beneficial or injurious, they are not to be dismissed. And most of the time they are not all positive or all negative, but rather some of each. Organizing family data on genograms has enabled people to put many fragments of their lives back together in a meaningful whole. As an adult, Colon undertook a remarkable endeavor to find and reconnect with his family in Puerto Rico and in the U.S., which has continued over the past 30 years. Though his father had told him his biological mother had died, he found the town where she lived and went there, finding out that she had spent years in a mental hospital and he had missed her by only a few years, but that he was related to almost everyone in the town.

His experience is an awesome lesson to anyone who is unable to see beyond the cutoffs that may occur in a family. In our view, *no* relationship should ever be discarded because you never know who may be connected to that cutoff. We urge people never to cut off, even when there has been abuse, but rather to keep the lines of communication open in case the person should become willing to deal with the issues and reconnect. Colon, by making creative use of his genogram, has stayed connected to his foster family and reconnected richly and rewardingly with his families of origin a whole generation later (Colon-Lopez, 2005).

The accepted practice of severing family ties—be they biological or through adoptive, foster, or divorced and remarried families—is, in our view, a tremendous tragedy. It has often led to therapists' being drawn in to replace other relationships in a person's natural system. As Fernando Colon's own family demonstrates so well, such cutoffs leave us depressed, bereft, and weakened. A cutoff of one person tends to lead to multiple cutoffs of other family members and to the loss of many potentially rich relationships. It weakens the entire fabric of one's life. Doing the genogram can counter this tendency to oversimplify and cut off by making clear the enormity of the losses, as one scans the numerous people involved.

As Colon's story shows, connections with others who have grown up in the same foster family may last a lifetime, and reconnections at later life cycle stages may be particularly meaningful. The same is, of course, true for orphanage experiences, as the touching memoir of John Folwarski (1998) illustrates. Folwarski calculated that he had approximately 3,000 siblings—that is, 3,000 other children in one generation shared the same home (St. Hedwig's Orphanage in Chicago) and the same foster parents and grandparents—the nuns and priests who ran the home. Figure 5.11 shows Folwarski's diagram for the family as he experienced it during the years he grew up (1937–1950).

As adults, many of his "siblings" have come together to share memories, have reconnected with some of their teacher/mothers, and have strengthened their sense of family through a realization that their genogram has real meaning for them all. Indeed, Folwarski described the experience of creating and looking at the diagram itself as having a powerful meaning for him in terms of validating his history. This is one more illustration of the importance of creating genogram maps—to bear witness to the truth and complexity of people's lives, no matter how traumatic their experiences may have been.

Figure 5.11 St. Hedwig's Orphanage Family

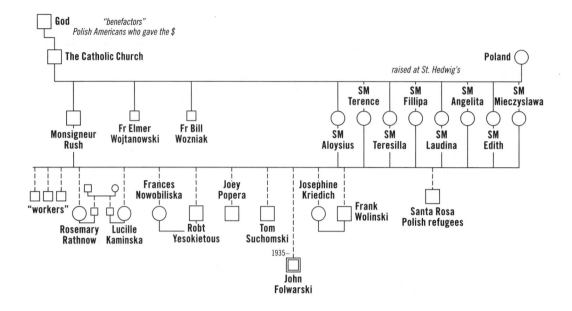

Assessing Family Patterns and Functioning

R EADING THE GENOGRAM FOR PATTERNS of balance and imbalance in family structure, roles, functioning, and resources allows the clinician to develop hypotheses about how the family is adapting to stress. Balance and imbalance speak to the functional whole of a family system. Family systems are not homogeneous; contrasting characteristics are usually present in the same family. In well-functioning families, such characteristics usually balance one another. We have already seen, for example, the complementary fit of oldest and youngest, where the oldest child's tendency to be caretaker balances the tendency of the youngest to let others assume that role.

The clinician detects patterns of balance and imbalance by looking for contrasts and characteristics that "stick out," and then asking: How do these contrasts and idiosyncrasies fit into the total functional whole? What balances have been achieved and what stresses are present in the system due to a lack of balance? For example, if one person is doing poorly in a family in which everyone else is doing well, one might ask what role the dysfunction plays in the total system.

The Family Structure

Sometimes, differences in family structure may be seen over a number of generations. For example, there may be a multigenerational contrast in the family structure for the two spouses, creating a graphically lopsided genogram: One spouse may come from a large family and have countless aunts and uncles whereas the other is an only child of two only children. This could lead to both balance and imbalance. On the one hand, each spouse may be attracted to the experience of the other. One likes the privacy of a small family and the other the diversity of a large family. On the other hand, the imbalance between the large number of relatives on one side and the paucity on the other may create problems. One spouse may be used to playing to a crowd and engaging in multiple relationships whereas the other needs a more exclusive, private relationship. Another structural issue involving balance occurs when one spouse comes from a family where divorce and remarriage are common and the other comes from a long line of intact households. Seeing this structural contrast on the genogram might cue the clinician to explore the spouses' different expectations about marriage.

Roles

In well-functioning families, members take a variety of different roles: caretaker, dependent, provider, spokesperson, and so on. Sometimes it will be evident from the genogram that there are too many people for one particular role. An only child raised by a single parent, grandparents, and aunts and uncles would be an example. The opposite situation may occur when a single family member is in the position of caring for an inordinate number of family members, as Ted Kennedy did after his brothers' deaths (see Color Figure 13). Being the sole surviving male member of his generation, Ted has had a special role in the two fatherless households, as well as responsibility for his own family. A clinician seeing this family would want to explore what balance has been worked out and what other resources have been brought in to help take care of the many children involved.

In modern marriages role allocation is seldom based solely on gender and is often shared. Thus, both parents may be caretakers, providers, and spokespeople for the family. However, this balance is not achieved automatically or easily, and it may be an area of conflict, particularly for dual-career families.

Level and Style of Functioning

Family members operate with different styles and at different levels of functioning. Often these patterns are balanced, so that the functions of different family members all fit together. Again, we scan the genogram for contrasts and idiosyncrasies in functioning, which may help to explain how the system functions as a whole.

Any newly formed family needs to fit together different styles and ways of relating to the world. The result may be more or less complementary and growth-enhancing for the offspring. Certain balances in families may also lead to or allow dysfunction in a family system. For example, we often see on a genogram a complementary pattern of alcoholics married to spouses who are overfunctioners (Bepko & Krestan, 1985; Steinglass, Bennett, Wolin, & Reiss, 1987), as in Figure 6.1.

Figure 6.1 Alcohol Problems (Over- and Underfunctioning)

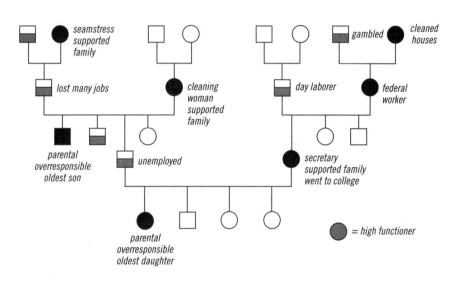

Here, the nondrinking spouse is pressed to become overresponsible in order to balance an underresponsible alcoholic partner. Because alcoholic behavior by its nature leads to underresponsibility, the other partner takes up the slack; otherwise children must fill in, taking on adult roles. The willingness of the partner to be a caretaker and of the other to be taken care of may stabilize the relationship. At times the whole family may become organized in this complementary way around the dysfunction of one member.

Sometimes, when there is dysfunction in one area, the family will find ways to compensate for common difficulties. This seems to have been the case with the family of Alexander Graham Bell, the inventor of the telephone (Figure 6.2). Both Bell's mother and wife were almost totally deaf. Three generations of males in the family—Bell himself, his father and uncle, and his grandfather—all specialized in speech projection and elocution. Bell's grandfather wrote a classic text on phonetic speech, and both Bell's father and uncle devoted themselves to teaching their father's methods. The family was a highly inventive one. When Alexander was a young teenager, his father suggested that he and his brother develop a talking machine. The instrument they developed replicated the mechanics of speech so well that it annoyed a neighbor, who thought he heard a baby crying. Some members specialized in speech and hearing, compensating for those who spoke with difficulty because they could not hear at all.

Figure 6.2 Alexander Graham Bell's Family

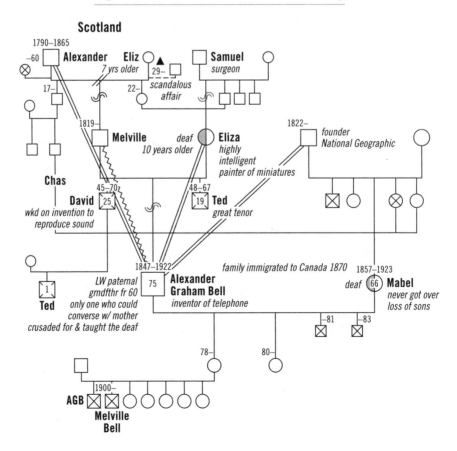

In analyzing possible patterns of functioning in families, it is essential to determine whether there is a fit or a balance in the system. Do extreme contrasts between family members maintain the stability of the system or are they pushing the family toward a different equilibrium? At times a system breaks down, not because of the dysfunction of one or two members, but because of the burnout of caretakers who previously created a balanced fit in the system. In the case of chronic illness, family members are frequently able to mobilize themselves for support of the dysfunctional person in the short term but are unable to maintain such behavior over the long term.

Caretaking Genograms

To understand the politics of caretaking around loss, it is useful to create a "caretaking genogram" to indicate which family members have needed long-term caretaking before death and who has done that caretaking. We consider this issue so important that we have developed a symbol (single line with a double arrow) to indicate the primary caretaker and others who take caretaking responsibility for family members in need.

For example, in my own family (MM), virtually every member of my parents' and grandparents' generations required long-term caretaking (Figure 6.3), and virtually all of it was done by women. My mother cared for my father for 10 years after a massive stroke, my aunt cared for her husband for the 20 years that he was slowly dying of emphysema, my paternal grandmother and aunt cared for my grandfather for the year that he was dying of cancer, and my aunt cared for my grandmother for several years until her death. That same aunt, who had cared for her husband and both parents for so many years, lived to be 100, being cared for at home by a group of women caretakers. These home caretakers were all women of color, illustrating the politics of caretaking, which is generally an undervalued job in our society. It is for this reason in particular that we need to pay attention to caretaking patterns in clinical genograms.

Families themselves may not mention caretaking issues, because we have all been socialized not to appreciate the caretaking requirements of family life. Because caretaking is not valued work within our society, it often goes unnoticed and is done by those with the least power and

Figure 6.3 Caretaking Genogram

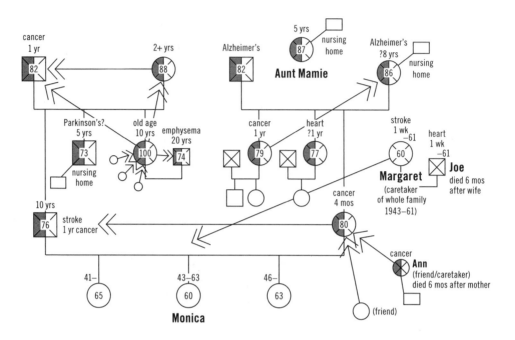

status—women, and, at the least rewarded level, women of color. At the same time, it has long been known that one of the primary reasons families seek help is not just the appearance of a symptomatic family member, but also the burnout of the caretaker, who is no longer able to manage the task. Thus intervention may require assessment of the whole genogram to tap into sources of resilience and resources that can be utilized to help the family get back on track.

One can also use genograms to show how required caretaking has affected a family at particular moments in time (Color Figure 19). In my family, there have been a number of different points in the life cycle when caretaking issues were primary. As can be seen from this diagram, the losses were not untimely, so the effect on the children was minimized, but the strain on women was extensive, possibly affecting triangles elsewhere in the system. It is obvious to me now that the first period of caretaking in my mother's life (1957–1966) was a time of great strain in our relationship. Both grandmothers were in very bad shape for a long while. My mother's negative relationship with both her mother and her mother-in-law meant that she was blocked from helping them in their last years. I realize now that during the second major caretaking period (1969–1979), not only did her role change but also her power in the system. She became an effective leader for us all, where previously her leadership skill had been seriously circumscribed by her role as "wife" to her husband. During that earlier time, she had much responsibility without much power. When she became my father's caretaker, she had responsibility, but for the first time, she had control of her own money. In spite of her financial and personal burdens, she became more loving and less defensive. It was only by exploring these caretaking patterns, in relation to gender, power, and the life cycle, that I could make sense of many of the dynamics in my own family.

Doing these caretaking genograms for my own family has greatly increased my sensitivity about future caretaking. Thinking about who we need to care for as well as who may be there to care for us may make us more thoughtful in our interpersonal relationships. Walsh (1998) recommends that we foster caregiving as a team approach, involving both male and female family members and encouraging siblings to share the burdens and blessings of caretaking.

In many cultures it is daughters-in-law who, having the least power in the family structure, do the caretaking of mothers-in-law, and the politics of gender contribute to the conflicts so often found in these relationships. In our society such problematic relationships are usually most pronounced in families of Asian heritage, where daughters were traditionally raised to leave their families of origin at marriage and become incorporated into their husbands' families, leaving wives with marginal status. In the dominant society of the U.S. it is more often daughters than daughters-in-law who have this caretaking responsibility. However, challenging such skewed expectations may be essential for preserving sibling relationships, which have been shown to be a primary resource throughout adult life. When the daughter has been overburdened with caretaking of aging parents, a family session or strategic coaching of the daughter to challenge the rules may do a great deal to rebalance family relationships more functionally and equitably.

For example, Arlene Adams (Figure 6.4) had been frustrated for a year as she made the 3-hour weekend trek to care for her mother, who was

Figure 6.4 Arlene Adams

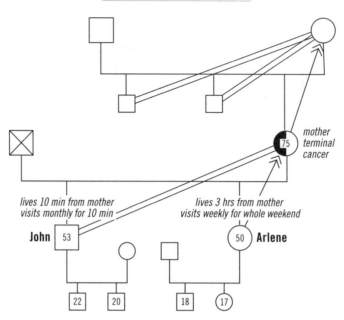

dying of cancer, whereas the brother, John, who lived 10 minutes away, rarely managed to see his mother more than once a month. When Arlene would arrive, her mother would recount with great pride what John and his two sons had been up to over the past week, which the mother learned in weekly phone calls from John's wife. Meanwhile the mother never asked Arlene anything about her own life or her children and seemed oblivious to the extreme sacrifice she made to spend the weekend with her each week.

Over time Arlene was able to transform her irritation and frustration about her role as second-class citizen in her family in relation to her brother. She sought occasions to talk with her mother and brother by letter and finally in person about their family roles since childhood. With her mother she was able to discuss her sense that her mother had played second fiddle to her own brothers with the maternal grandparents, which had troubled Arlene for many years. Although initially resistant to this insight, Arlene's mother was soon saving up examples to tell her on the weekend of instances she remembered when her parents had put her brothers first. Mother and daughter were drawn closer by this sharing.

Tracking Resilience

Tracking families' resilience (Walsh, 2006) in the face of loss, trauma, and dysfunction is extremely relevant to genogram assessment. It is the family's resilience that enables it to survive. It is important to focus on such resourcefulness and to underline it. Mexican artist Frida Kahlo (see Color Figure 9) provides a remarkable example of such resilience. Her artwork reflected her incredible ability to transform the trauma and pain she experienced into something creative and life-enriching. Her resilience and the resilience of her family are evident in many aspects of their history. For example, she first became ill at age 6 with polio, which left her right leg weaker and smaller. At 18 she experienced a traumatic bus accident, in which she was impaled on a metal pipe that went completely through her pelvis and fractured her spine. The accident left her with chronic pain for the rest of her life, in spite of numerous operations. Coincidentally, her father had suffered a fall at the same age, which left him with brain damage and seizures, changing the course of his life and dashing his hopes of university study. His accident became a factor in his emigration to Mexico the next year, where he changed his name from Wilhelm Kahl to Guillermo Kahlo. In Mexico he became a noted photographer, although he suffered ongoing sequelae from the accident. Frida, who became his favorite child, discovered an outlet in art following her accident. She had earlier held her father's hopes of becoming a scholar and physician. Instead, she became an artist, as her father had done before her, and her maternal grandfather before that.

Both Kahlo's parents experienced severe traumas early in life. Her mother, a brilliant and attractive woman of Spanish, Mexican, and Indian background, had been in love with a German, who committed suicide in her presence. All her life she kept a book of his letters and, though she married Guillermo Kahlo and had four daughters and a son with him, she never seemed to have been able to live up to her potential. Guillermo Kahlo himself, who had so much promise when he began school at the University of Nuremberg, was unable to continue his studies after his accident. His mother died at about the same time. His father remarried very soon after, and disliking the stepmother, Kahlo soon decided to emigrate to Mexico. There he married and had three daughters, though the second died within a few days. Then his wife died tragically in childbirth with the third daughter. Kahlo met his second wife the same night. This wife agreed to marry him only if he sent his two daughters away to a convent school. This second wife also encouraged Kahlo to go into business as a photographer with her father. Unfortunately, Kahlo seems never to have come to terms with his earlier traumas. Over the years he became bitter and withdrawn in spite of his obvious abilities and early efforts to reinvent himself. It was his favorite daughter, Frida, who demonstrated the most remarkable ability to transform traumatic experiences into hope and art, in spite of much more severe disabilities.

Family Resources

Family members often differ in resources such as money, health, vigor, skills, meaningful work, and support systems. When extreme differences in these areas appear on the genogram, it is important to explore how the system handles the imbalance. When such differences appear in couple relationships, they may compound the power imbalances that always exist between men and women or, of course, may counter such imbalances if it is the woman who has the money, health, work advantage, or social status.

In the genogram shown in Color Figure 20 the spouses differ in class and occupational background. Immediate questions arise:

- How do the spouses handle their differences in socioeconomic class and cultural background?
- How do they handle their different levels of income and expectations about their standard of living?
- Is there an important imbalance in some other area? Is there a difference in values?
- What is the impact of spouses' coming into a marriage with very different financial resources? Different educational and job status? Different social class standing?
- What is the impact on siblings of having different financial resources, different educational and job status, and different social class standing?

Of course, other family members' reactions are important to assess as well. How did the two different families feel about the marriage? Was there approval or disapproval for the match? The genogram alerts the clinician to possible issues on these dimensions.

Differences in resources may also become problematic when one sibling becomes more successful than the others. For example, if one sibling in a family becomes highly successful and all others are less so in terms of finances or social status, there may be an imbalance; an unsuccessful sibling may not be able to meet family expectations, and may in turn resent the achiever for both the success and the lack of support. When resources (emotional as well as financial) are lacking, siblings may have conflict or cutoff, particularly around the caretaking of a parent or an ill sibling. Families may get caught up in struggles over who did more for the person in need. When most siblings are doing well and only one sibling or one parent is in need, it may be easier to develop a satisfactory balance of resources without unduly taxing any one member. In some cases a very wealthy sibling may end up contributing financially but not with time or emotional caretaking, which also contributes to a sense of imbalance in the family. Geographic distance of siblings from each other or from parents may also create imbalances, especially if only one sibling lives close enough to do the caretaking for a needy parent. He, or more likely she, may burn out and become resentful. Siblings who are not married or who do not have children may also be inequitably expected to do the caretaking for parents (especially for a single parent). All such imbalances in sibling responsibility for parents should be explored and inequities challenged, because they can otherwise have far-reaching negative effects on family relationships.

7

Relational Patterns and Triangles

THE GENOGRAM ALLOWS THE CLINICIAN TO DETECT intense relationships in a family and, given the family's structure and position in the life cycle, to hypothesize about the important relationships and boundary patterns of that family. Understanding triangular patterns where two family members join against a third is essential in planning clinical intervention. "Detriangling" is an important process through which family members are coached to free themselves from rigid triangular patterns. The complexity of family relationships is infinite. In addition, relationships naturally change over time. In spite of such complexity, the genogram can often suggest relational patterns to be further explored.

The smallest human system is, of course, a two-person system. Genograms can be analyzed in terms of dyadic relationships, with relationship lines depicting these patterns in at least a crude way as "close," "fused," "hostile," "conflictual," "distant," "cut-off," and so on. Repeated dyadic patterns can then be tracked throughout the system. But these dyadic patterns typically form into three-person relationships where two are joined in relation to the third.

If we focus simply on the dyadic relationships in a genogram, we might see that in each generation all sons have conflictual relationships with their fathers and close relationships with their mothers, whereas daughters have the opposite—distant or conflictual relationships with their mothers and close relationships with their fathers. Meanwhile, all the couples have distant or conflictual relationships. Surely these relationships are intertwined. The closeness of mother and son relates to the distance between father and son, and the couple problems are related to the parent-child alliances. In other words, there is a complementary pattern of marital distance; intergenerational coalitions and conflicts go together. The prediction may be made that the son and daughter in the third generation who are caught in cross-generational alliances and conflicts with their parents and with each other will repeat this pattern of distant marriages and alliances and conflicts with their children unless they work to change it.

Dyadic relationships tend to be linked and function together. It helps to look at the family system as a set of interlocking triangles. From this perspective a father's closeness to his daughter may be a function of his distance from his wife and may play a role in the mother's conflict with her daughter. The same could be hypothesized for any threesome in this system: that the functioning of any two tends to be bound up with the interrelationships of the three in a predictable way. The subject of triangles is one of the most important in systems theory (Bowen, 1978; Caplow, 1968; Carter & McGoldrick, 2005b; Fogarty, 1975; Guerin, Fogarty, Fay, & Kautto, 1996; Kerr & Bowen, 1988).

Triangles

Although it would be impossible in this short book to explain all the complexities of systemic thinking that underlie the interpretation of relational patterns on genograms, we offer a number of common relational configurations to help in interpreting genograms. The genogram is a valuable tool for inferring possible triangles based on partial knowledge of family relationships.

Our primary focus is on triangles, or sets of three relationships in which the functioning of each is dependent on and influences the other two. The formation of triangles in families involves two people functioning in relation to a third. This usually serves to reduce tension in the initial dyad. For example, two family members may join in "helping" a third, who is viewed as needy or the "victim," or they may gang up against the third, who is viewed as "the villain." It is the collusion of the two in relation to the third that is the defining characteristic of a triangle (Bowen, 1978). The behavior of any one member of a triangle is a function of the behavior of the other two.

Any triangle tends to be part of a larger systemic pattern as well. Thus, a child's tantrum with an overburdened mother is not only a function of the relationship between mother and child, but also probably a function of the relationship between the mother and father, or between those two and an overinvolved paternal grandfather, or between one or several adults and a precocious older sibling, to mention just a few of the possibilities. In Bowen's conceptual framework, healthy development involves differentiation or maturity, which refers to a person's functioning independently in each relationship and not automatically falling into a pattern of relating to one person based on that person's relationship with a third person.

When there is high tension in a system, it is common for two people to relieve stress by forming a triangle with a third. Differentiation means reaching the point of relating on an individualized basis to each person rather than on the basis of the relationship that person has to someone else. Thus, a daughter would be able to have a close relationship with her mother, even if her father, to whom she is also close, is in conflict with her mother. This must be distinguished from two children who may join together to gain power in dealing with an intimidating parent. Such a coalition would be different from a triangle, because the two would intentionally join to strengthen their position, not to make their individual functioning dependent on each other's relationship with the overpowering parent.

Parent-Child Triangles

Two parents may resolve tension by joining together to focus on their child. Regardless of the specific emotional pattern displayed (anger, love, clinging dependency), it is the joining together of the two people in relation to a third that defines triangular relationships. Genograms are an extremely handy tool for recognizing such triangles, because structural patterns, life cycle information, and specific data on dyadic relationships help to make obvious the threesomes who are likely to become triangulated. Just because three people are relating, does not necessarily make them a triangle. Triangulation refers to the interdependent functioning of the threesome. The functioning of each depends on the other two. If one person in a triad chooses to side with another in one conversation, this is not necessarily a triangle. However, if this relational pattern occurs regularly, it probably is.

Often sibling rivalry really reflects triangles, as shown in the genogram of Eugene O'Neill (Figure 7.1). The brothers Jamie and Eugene had an intense and competitive relationship throughout their lives (Jamie died at age 45). Seeing this on the genogram would suggest possible tension between the parents, the conflict in the second generation both deflecting and reflecting conflict in the previous generation. In fact, the O'Neill parents had a difficult and tense relationship throughout their marriage. Perhaps the tension between the brothers was exacerbated by the fact that Jamie was blamed for the death of the middle brother, Edmund, whom he had unwittingly exposed to measles. Eugene was blamed for the mother's addiction to morphine, which began at the time of his birth. The sibling conflict undoubtedly not only reflected the parental conflict but also served as a distraction from the parents' individual problems.

Figure 7.1 O'Neill Family Relationships and Triangles

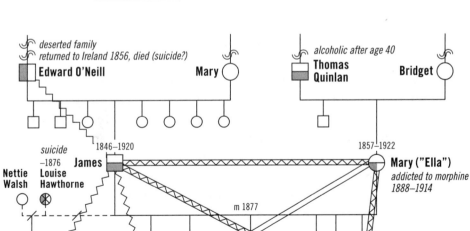

A very common triangular pattern occurs when one parent draws a child into a collusion against the other parent, who becomes an outsider. Expressed systemically, this could also be described as distancing and pressing the other parent and child to handle things on their own; in any case, a child may thus have a fused relationship with one parent and a conflictual relationship with the other.

Incidentally, a son having an extremely close relationship with his mother is not in and of itself a problem and certainly not necessarily a damaging experience. We found it to be common in many of the famous people we have investigated, including Bill Clinton, Franklin Roosevelt, Harry Truman, Frank Lloyd Wright, Douglas MacArthur, Jimmy Carter, Che Guevara, and many others.

However, when people's close and conflicted or distant relationships are interconnected in triangles, the dysfunctional implications are real. Many times, given the patriarchal arrangements in which family relationships have been embedded, these triangles reflect problems in the larger system as well, as the example of the Nehru family illustrates (Figure 7.2).

Jawaharlal Nehru described a triangle in which he felt caught between his parents as he grew up. As a small child he had stolen a pen from his father and the whole family had been involved in searching for it:

> The pen was discovered and my guilt proclaimed to the world. Father was very angry and he gave me a tremendous thrashing. Almost blind with pain and mortification at my disgrace I rushed to my mother and for several days various creams and ointments were applied to my aching and quivering little body. I do not remember bearing any ill-will towards my father because of this punishment. . . . My admiration and affection for him remained as strong as ever, but fear formed a part of them. Not so with my mother. I had no fear of her, for I knew that she would condone everything I did, and because of her excessive and indiscriminating love for me I tried to dominate over her a little. (cited in Ali, 1985, p. 8)

Over the years he often enlisted his mother as his ally in the many struggles he waged against his father, especially for more money when he was studying in England (Wolpert, 1996, p. 8). Nehru's biographer, Tarik

Figure 7.2 Nehru-Gandhi Family

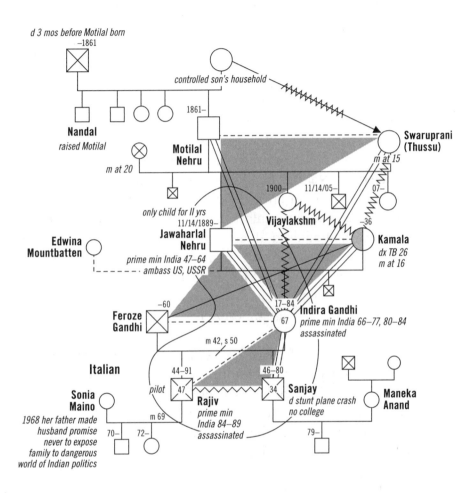

Ali, explained this triangle in terms of the patriarchal gender arrangements of their context. He said Nehru's father adored his only son:

The violence inflicted on the young boy was . . . part of an older tapestry. The family reproduces in its own unique fashion the relations of authority that exist in society as a whole. The subordination of women is the most notorious aspect of this process, but there is another, equally crucial dimension: the ritual socialization of men. . . . The father-son relationship enshrines and symbolizes male domination. Violence is always there, lurking in the background, sometimes hidden, sometimes openly practiced. The bruises inflicted are often visible. Even when the actual pain has gone, the suppressed anger and resentment can stay with the victim for the rest of his life. The effects naturally vary from one individual to another. Jawaharlal's attachment to his father was genuine, but it could not have been free of ambiguity. (p. 9)

This triangle was played out again in Nehru's relationship with his daughter, Indira. As a child, Indira was extremely close to her mother, who was disrespected by Nehru's family and not protected by her husband. Kamala taught her daughter not to trust men and to become independent. However, she developed tuberculosis by the time Indira was 11 and died before Indira reached adulthood, and Indira and Nehru turned to each other in a closeness that ended only with his death. Indira married Feroze Gandhi and had two sons but left her husband, whom her father had not approved of in the first place, and went with her sons to live with her father when her sons were young. Feroze had always feared his wife would leave him for her famous family. Then in the third generation, Indira became extremely close to her younger son, Sanjay, and to her older son, Rajiv, only after Sanjay's death. In all three generations the couple bond was weak, leaving family members vulnerable to intergenerational triangling for many generations. And, of course, we haven't even mentioned the numerous triangles with the daughters-in-law (Rajiv's Italian wife Sonia and Sanjay's Sikh wife, Maneka Anand, whose father's death many even have implicated Sanjay), nor Nehru's very long love affair with Edwina Mountbatten, a member of the British Royal Family and the wife of Prince Philip's uncle (see Color Figure 12).

The genogram of Eleanor Roosevelt presents an example of another type of parent-child triangle (Figure 7.3). Although both parents died by the time she was 11, Eleanor remembered having a special relationship with her father, while feeling her mother was harsh and insensitive to his predicament. The father was an irresponsible alcoholic, and her mother had him committed to an asylum and separated from him, but to Eleanor he was the hero and her mother the villain. This triangle, in which

Figure 7.3 Eleanor Roosevelt Triangles

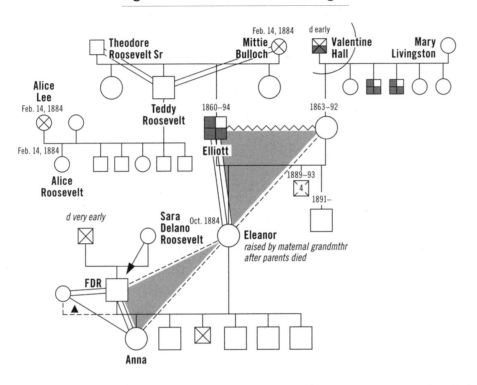

Eleanor took her father's side against her mother, is common when parents are in severe conflict. Children tend to get caught in loyalty conflicts between them. The child may attempt to placate or mediate between them—a precarious position indeed. This type of parent-child triangle is extremely common in cases of divorce and remarriage (discussed later). In the next generation, this triangle was repeated with Eleanor's daughter Anna, an oldest like Eleanor, who preferred her father, Franklin, and saw Eleanor as overly harsh. Throughout her adolescence she had a stormy relationship with Eleanor, which did not change until her father contracted polio. Eleanor felt the ultimate betrayal in her daughter Anna's entertaining FDR and his girlfriend behind Eleanor's back at the White House and at Camp David. Fortunately, in later life Eleanor and Anna reversed this pattern of mother-daughter cutoff and became very close (McGoldrick, 1995).

Common Couple Triangles

A couple may triangle not just children but also other people, animals (the family dog, for example), or things (such as TV or alcohol). Color Figure 21 shows a genogram of a family at the beginning of therapy. The husband's primary connections were with work, the financial markets, and television. What was not known until much later because of the husband's denial was his connection to alcohol (shown here as a secret affinity). Because of the denial of both the husband and his wife, the therapist did not know for a full year that he was highly dependent on alcohol. The presenting problem was that the husband felt unable to relate to his wife, who wanted the relationship but under the surface was intensely angry with the husband. Both of them were more connected elsewhere than to each other and had been for many years. Neither spouse, who were both of Anglo heritage, was aware of the intense cutoff they each had from their highly dysfunctional families of origin. Both described their backgrounds as "normal." The wife was focused on her children and on keeping the family home and had good connections to her friends. The husband had very little connection to his children, who were eager to have a relationship with him. In the course of therapy both spouses began exploring their problematic relationship with each other in relation to their genogram and were offered the challenge to deal with the genogram cutoffs.

As is evident in Color Figure 21 both spouses made considerable change in their family of origin relationships. In addition, the husband began to connect with his children and to shift his relationships with alcohol and the financial markets. The wife reconnected with her brother and his ex-wife and began to travel, which had always been a passion of hers. These changes did not resolve the couple's conflict, but they did shift it so that the husband was able to begin to approach his wife and she was less focused on her anger at him. This example is typical of a systemic effort to work with a couple on viewing all their relationships in context rather than just focusing on what they are frustrated about with each other. Both partners had triangulated with others to resolve the anxiety they did not feel they could handle with each other, which was a replication of issues both had earlier felt unable to deal with in their families of origin. Such detriangulating is a major focus of systemic therapy, which explores couples relationships in context rather than focusing primarily on the couple's relationship with each other without regard for how this intersects with their other relationships.

Perhaps the most common couple triangle is the in-law triangle. Classically, this involves a favorite son, his mother, and his wife. The in-law triangle may play itself out in a variety of ways. The spouses may divert their own conflicts by focusing on what is wrong with the husband's mother. Or the wife may blame the mother-in-law for her husband's inadequacies, while the mother-in-law blames the daughter-in-law for keeping her "darling boy" away. The husband may enjoy letting his mother and his wife do battle; he probably has difficulty dealing with both of them. Of course, in-law triangles can occur between two spouses and any of their parents, but the wife often takes a more central and involved emotional role and thus becomes the focus of stress in this situation. Also, in certain cultures, such as Asian, where wives traditionally lived with and were subject to the control of their mothers-in-law, such triangles are greatly intensified.

Another common couple triangle involves an affair. Clearly, an extramarital relationship has implications for a marriage and can become a major area of concern even if the marriage survives. The affair may relieve some of the tension of a conflictual relationship by giving one of the partners an outlet or it may divert the couple from underlying problems. The triangulated affair may be ongoing or in the past, as with Eugene O'Neill's father, James, who had two affairs preceding his marriage (see Figure 7.1). The first woman committed suicide when James broke off the relationship. The second relationship, with Nettie Walsh, resulted in a paternity suit when she claimed that James was the father of her son. The scandal surrounding the paternity suit remained an issue throughout James and Ella's marriage.

Wilhelm Reich, one of Freud's followers, spent his life focused on sexuality as the core dynamic of human development. His genogram (Color Figure 22) illustrates the triangles of an affair that led to family tragedy. Wilhelm discovered his mother having an affair with his tutor and told his father, who then confronted the wife. She committed suicide in response. Perhaps Reich's later professional promotion of guilt-free sexuality in all its forms was an attempt to make up for the disastrous results of his part in that family's triangles. Sadly, in the next generation, Reich's son experienced a similar trauma at the same age. The FBI came seeking Reich and his son was forced to say where he was. Reich was taken to prison, where, unfortunately, he died soon after.

Triangulating occurs with things other than people as well. A spouse's investment outside the family may be in work, hobbies, alcohol, pets, the Internet, and so on, but the impact is the same. It often happens that the closer the husband gets to the job, the alcohol, or the Internet, the more negative the wife becomes toward both him and the object of his "affection." The more negative the wife becomes, the closer the husband moves toward the triangulated thing. When this happens, it should be noted on the genogram. Peter Fonda was extremely attached to his dog, especially after his mother's suicide, when he felt very much alone, because his father was gone and his grandmother had come to live with them. She, however, was very bothered by the dog and one day had it put to sleep while Peter was away (Figure 7.4). He never forgave her.

Figure 7.4 Peter Fonda Triangulation With Dog and Grandmother

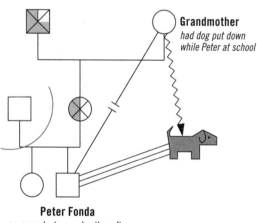

Peter Fonda
*never spoke to grandmother after
she had dog killed*

Undoubtedly this triangle reflected other family triangles the grand-mother could not deal with. The dog probably became a scapegoat for the frustrations she was suffering, including her daughter's mental illness and suicide, being left alone (by her dead alcoholic husband and by Henry Fonda) to deal with the aftermath of the suicide and care for the children, and her other son-in-law's alcoholism. As pets often do, the dog himself was probably reacting to the stresses that had taken place in the family and may have been difficult for the grandmother to handle. Thus do triangles focus multiple stresses in particular nodal relationships and interactions in a family.

Triangles in Divorced and Remarried Families

When separation or divorce appears on a genogram, certain relational patterns are predictable. For example, children may idealize the missing parent, blaming the custodial parent for the loss of the other, as Eleanor Roosevelt did (see Figure 7.3). Children may become caught between the warring parents, one siding with one and another with the other. And in-laws are likely to side with their own child against the spouse.

When one or both parents remarry, there are additional triangles to explore (McGoldrick & Carter, 2005b). Perhaps one of the reasons such triangles are so easy to identify on the genograms of remarried families is that the structure of the family, rather than the personalities of the partic-ipants, usually defines the situation. This makes the triangles rather predictable. Children are basically never prepared to lose a parent, whether by death or divorce. Parents are not replaceable. And no parent ever ceases to matter, no matter how many years ago he or she died or disappeared. Thus, the insider-outsider structural pattern in remarried families is endemic to the situation and tends to create triangles. How children respond to new stepparents depends on many factors, including their gender and life cycle stage at the time of the divorce (McGoldrick & Carter, 2005b), but certain triangles are highly predictable. For example, Henry Fonda's remarriage to Susan Blanchard after his previous wife's suicide (Color Figure 4) seems to have elicited a very different reaction from Peter, who was 10, than from Jane, who was 13. Peter still very much needed a mother. Jane was beginning adolescence and breaking away was more predictable for her. When Fonda reseparated four years later, when Peter was 14 and Jane 17 and going off to college, Peter was heartbroken at the possibility of losing his second mother; his father argued that it would be insensitive to him and his new bride for Peter to see his stepmother. Peter retorted that *he* hadn't divorced Susan and would see her whenever he wanted (Fonda, 1998, p. 84). We can easily see the patterns of interlocking triangles that get set in motion by the changing structures of remarried families (Figure 7.5).

Figure 7.5 Fonda Family Divorce and Remarriage Triangle (1955)

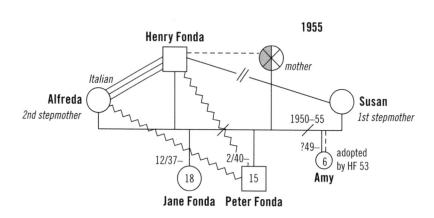

The genograms shown in Figure 7.6 demonstrate some of the predictable triangles in remarried families. One common triangle involves the children in a family with a biological father and a stepmother with whom they do not get along. This is not surprising. The stepmother can never replace the biological mother and the child's alliance will almost always be with the biological parent rather than the stepparent, except in cases like that of Peter Fonda, who had already lost his mother and was still a child, desperately needing a connection. For the custodial father in a remarriage, the new wife generally offers hope after his loss. For the child she is a threat: She might take the remaining parent away.

Different types of triangles are common in this situation. One involves the children, the biological father, and the stepmother, with hostility between the children and the new wife (the "wicked" stepmother). The stepmother often feels threatened that her spouse gives more attention to his children than he does to her, and the husband is usually caught in a loyalty conflict between his wife and his children. This situation thus creates an unstable triangle for him, because it is hard to stay connected to others who are at war. The structure here shows clearly how he is likely to flounder. But the structure also indicates the solution: The father must position himself to strengthen his connection first to his children, because the new marriage follows his prior commitment to his children.

A second common triangle, usually interlocking with the first, involves the children, the stepmother, and the biological mother. The children may resent the stepmother's efforts to replace their biological mother. The new wife feels unaccepted in her own home and the biological mother may feel threatened by the new wife. It is not uncommon for overt conflict to occur between the mother and stepmother in this triangle. Indeed, interlocking triangles involving the husband, his ex-wife, and his new wife are very common. There is tension between the new couple and the ex-wife, with the ex-wife on the outside. Two types of triangles are likely here. The new couple may band together against the ex-spouse, seeing her as the cause of all their problems, or the new wife and the ex-wife may have overt conflicts, with the husband perhaps even encouraging his new wife to fight the old battles for him.

Of course, triangles also occur with a biological mother, her children, and a stepfather. However, because our culture places greater expectations on motherhood than on fatherhood, stepmothers generally have the most difficult experience (McGoldrick & Carter, 2005b).

The structure, as in other situations, implies the solution: The step-parent needs to avoid seeking a central position in the children's lives that would promote a loyalty conflict for them in relation to their own parent. The stepparent should stay in a more distant position in relation to the children, fostering instead their connection to their mother and to their father, as shown in the last genogram pictured in Figure 7.6. The other requirement to keep this set of relationships in balance is for the divorced parents to maintain a working partnership that allows children to stay loyal to both parents—obviously not an easy task for many families!

Figure 7.6 Genograms of Typical Triangles in Divorced and Remarried Families

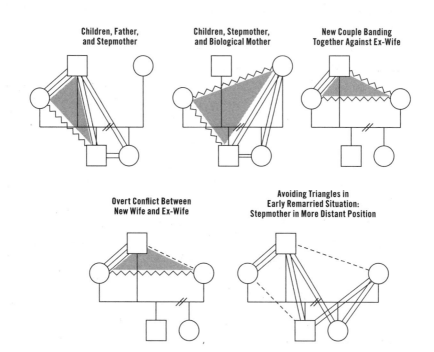

The aftermath of such triangles in remarried families can be seen in the genogram of Eugene O'Neill (McGoldrick, 1995), who, after his divorces, had a poor relationship with the children from his second marriage as well as his first (Figure 7.7). O'Neill separated from his second wife, Agnes, when their youngest child, Oona, was only 3. In bitter disillusionment, he cut off not only his wife, Agnes, but the children as well, refusing even to mention their names. He resented the "exorbitant" alimony payments he was expected to pay, and Agnes was extremely jealous of his third wife, Carlotta. When Oona grew up and married Charlie Chaplin, O'Neill refused to have any involvement with her ever again. This may have been compounded by other interlocking triangles.

Color Figure I Rodriguez Family Experiences and Relationships

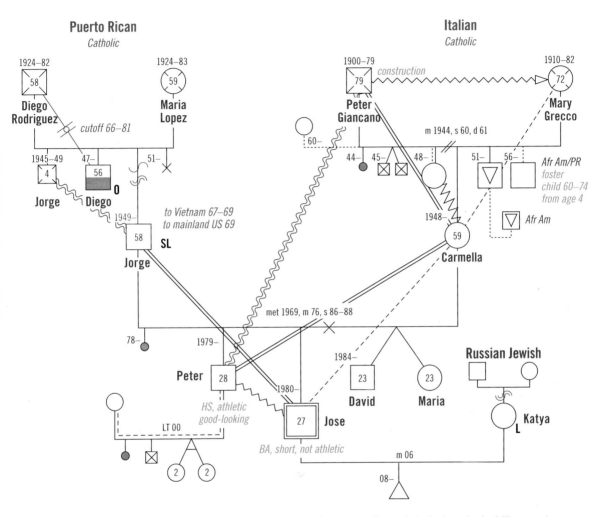

Blue = names
Green = location, cultural & religious background
Teal blue = about person

Red = cutoff, psychological or physical illness or trauma
Purple = other important information

Color Figure 2 Mia Farrow's Biological and Adopted Children

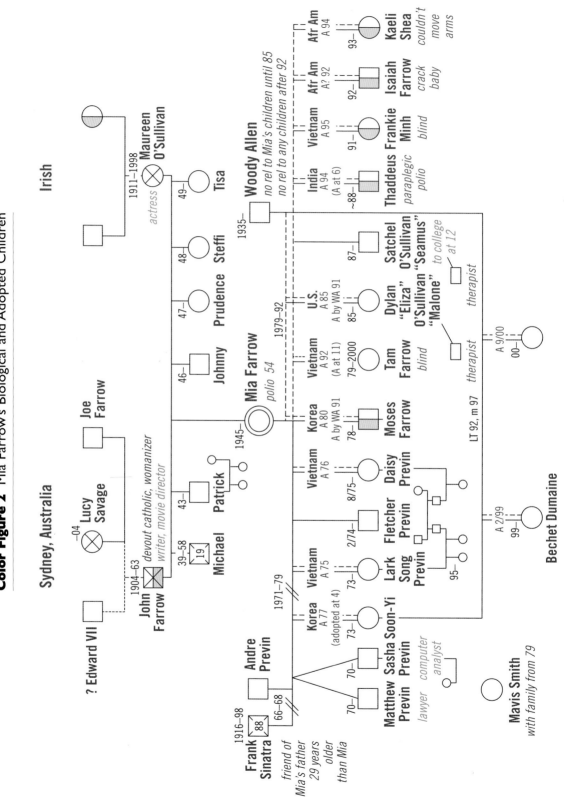

Color Figure 3 Louis Armstrong Living Situations

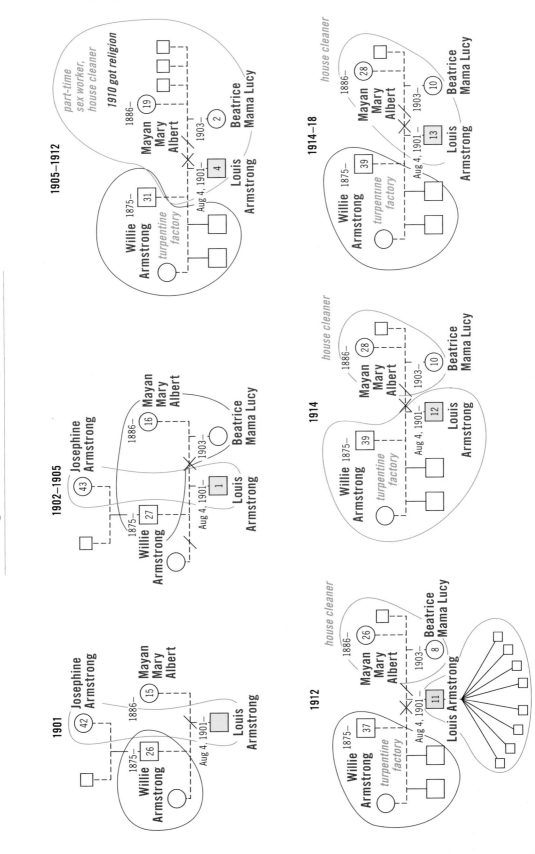

Color Figure 4 Fonda Family Demographics

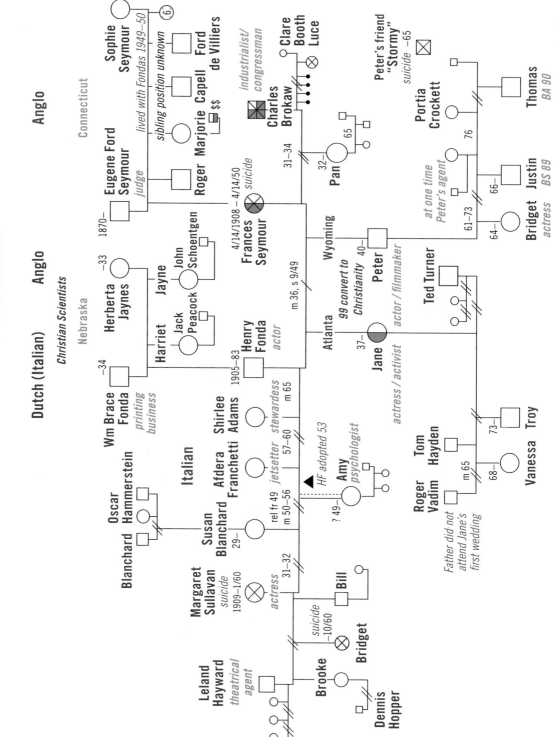

Color Figure 5 Fonda Family Functioning

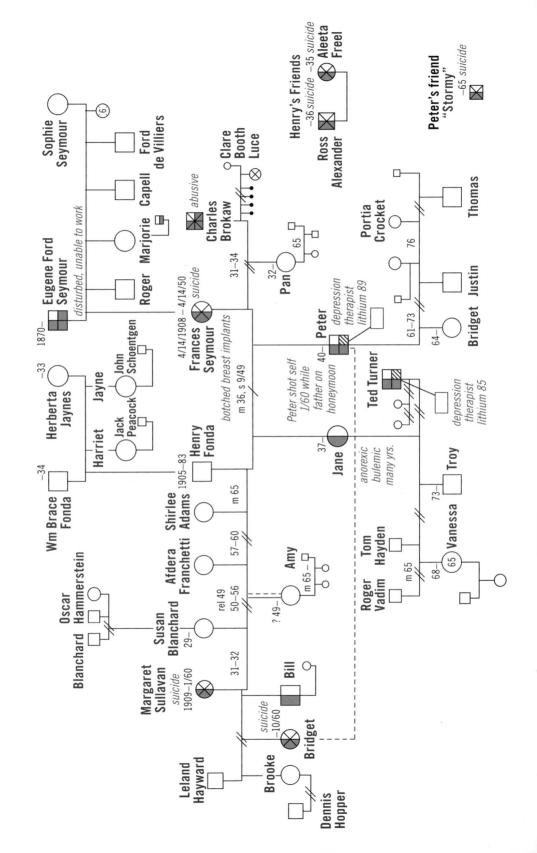

Color Figure 6 Turner Family Functioning

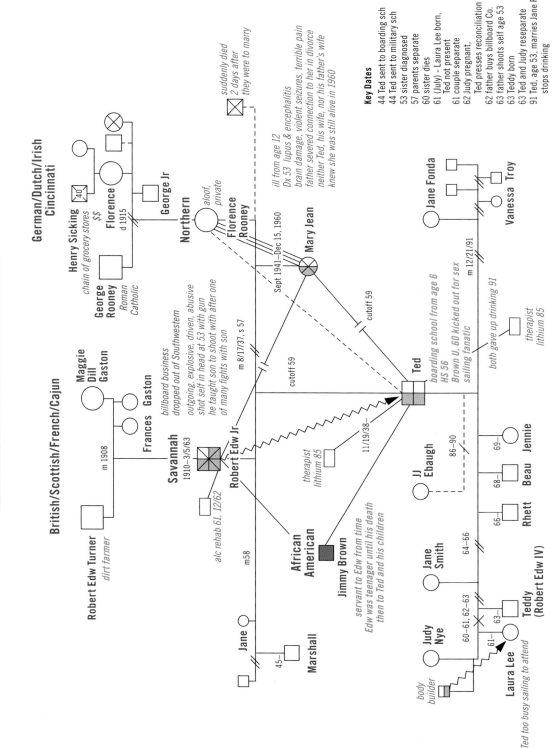

British/Scottish/French/Cajun

German/Dutch/Irish
Cincinnati

Robert Edw Turner
dirt farmer

Maggie Dill Gaston

m 1908

Frances Gaston

Savannah
1910–3/5/63

Robert Edw Jr
*billboard business
dropped out of Southwestern

outgoing, explosive, driven, abusive
shot self in head at 53 with gun
he taught son to shoot with after one
of many fights with son*

alc rehab 61, 12/62

m 8/17/37, s 57

Henry Sicking
*chain of grocery stores
$$*

Florence
d 1915

George Rooney
Roman Catholic

George Jr

Northern
aloof, private

Florence Rooney

Sept 1941–Dec 15, 1960

Mary Jean

*suddenly died
2 days after
they were to marry*

*ill from age 12
Dx 53 lupus & encephalitis
brain damage, violent seizures, terrible pain
father severed connection to her in divorce
neither Ted, his wife, nor his father's wife
knew she was still alive in 1960*

cutoff 59

cutoff 59

Jane

45–

Marshall

African American

Jimmy Brown

*servant to Edw from time
Edw was teenager until his death
then to Ted and his children*

therapist
lithium 85

11/19/38–

JJ Ebaugh

86–90

Ted
*boarding school from age 6
HS 56
Brown U, 60 kicked out for sex
sailing fanatic*

both gave up drinking 91

m 12/21/91

Jane Fonda

Vanessa   Troy

therapist
lithium 85

body builder

Judy Nye

60–61, 62–63

63

Teddy
(Robert Edw IV)

61–

Laura Lee

Ted too busy sailing to attend

Jane Smith

64–66

66–

Rhett

68–

Beau

69–

Jennie

Key Dates
44 Ted sent to boarding sch
44 Ted sent to military sch
53 sister diagnosed
57 parents separate
60 sister dies
61 (July) – Laura Lee born,
    Ted not present
61 couple separate
62 Judy pregnant,
    Ted presses reconciliation
62 father buys billboard Co.
63 father shoots self age 53
63 Teddy born
63 Ted and Judy reseparate
91 Ted, age 53, marries Jane Fonda,
    stops drinking

Color Figure 7 Jung Family

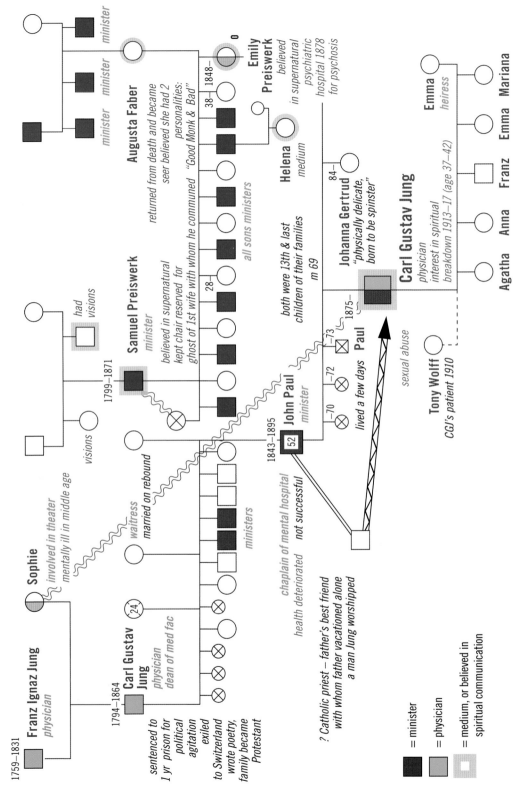

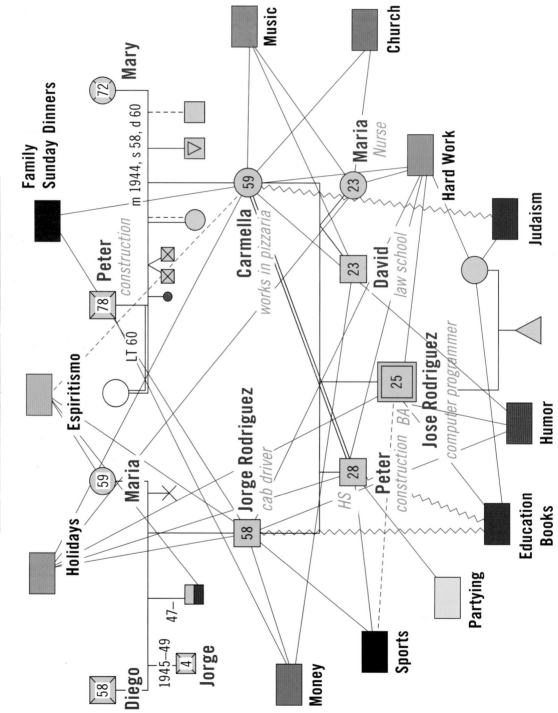

Color Figure 8 Rodriguez Family Contextual Connections

Color Figure 9 Genogram by Frida Kahlo; "My Family," 1951. © Frida Kahlo Museum, Mexico City (Greenberg, 1997).

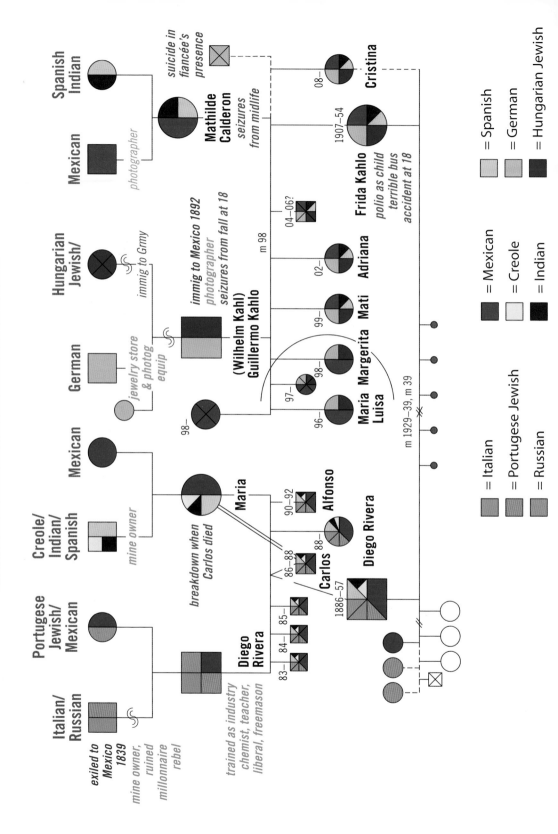

Color Figure 10 Cultural Genogram: Kahlo-Rivera Family

Spanish Indian

Mexican — *photographer*

Hungarian Jewish/ — *immig to Gmy*

German — *jewelry store & photog equip*

(Wilhelm Kahl) Guillermo Kahlo
immig to Mexico 1892
photographer
seizures from fall at 18

Mathilde Calderon
seizures from midlife

suicide in fiancée's presence

Cristina 08–

Frida Kahlo 1907–54
polio as child
terrible bus accident at 18

m 98

04–06?

Adriana 02–

Mati 99–

Maria Luisa 96– **Margerita** 98– 97–

m 1929–39, m 39

98–

Mexican

Creole/ Indian/ Spanish — *mine owner*

Maria
breakdown when Carlos died

Diego Rivera

Portugese Jewish/Mexican

Diego Rivera 83– 84– 85–

trained as industry chemist, teacher, liberal, freemason

Italian/ Russian
exiled to Mexico 1839
mine owner, ruined millonnaire rebel

Carlos 86–88

Alfonso 90–92

88–

Diego Rivera 1886–1957

Legend:

= Spanish
= German
= Hungarian Jewish

= Mexican
= Creole
= Indian

= Italian
= Portugese Jewish
= Russian

Color Figure 11 George W. Bush

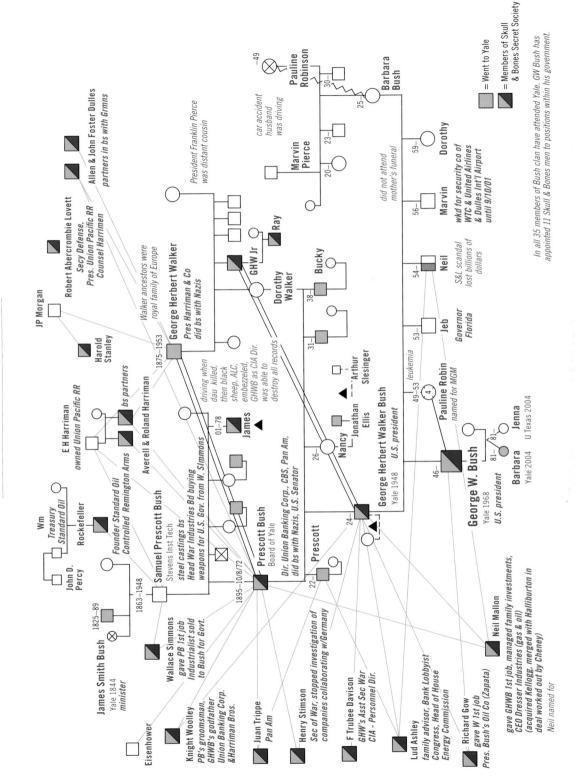

In all 35 members of Bush clan have attended Yale. GW Bush has appointed 11 Skull & Bones men to positions within his government.

= Went to Yale

= Members of Skull & Bones Secret Society

Color Figure 12 British Royal Family (Windsors)

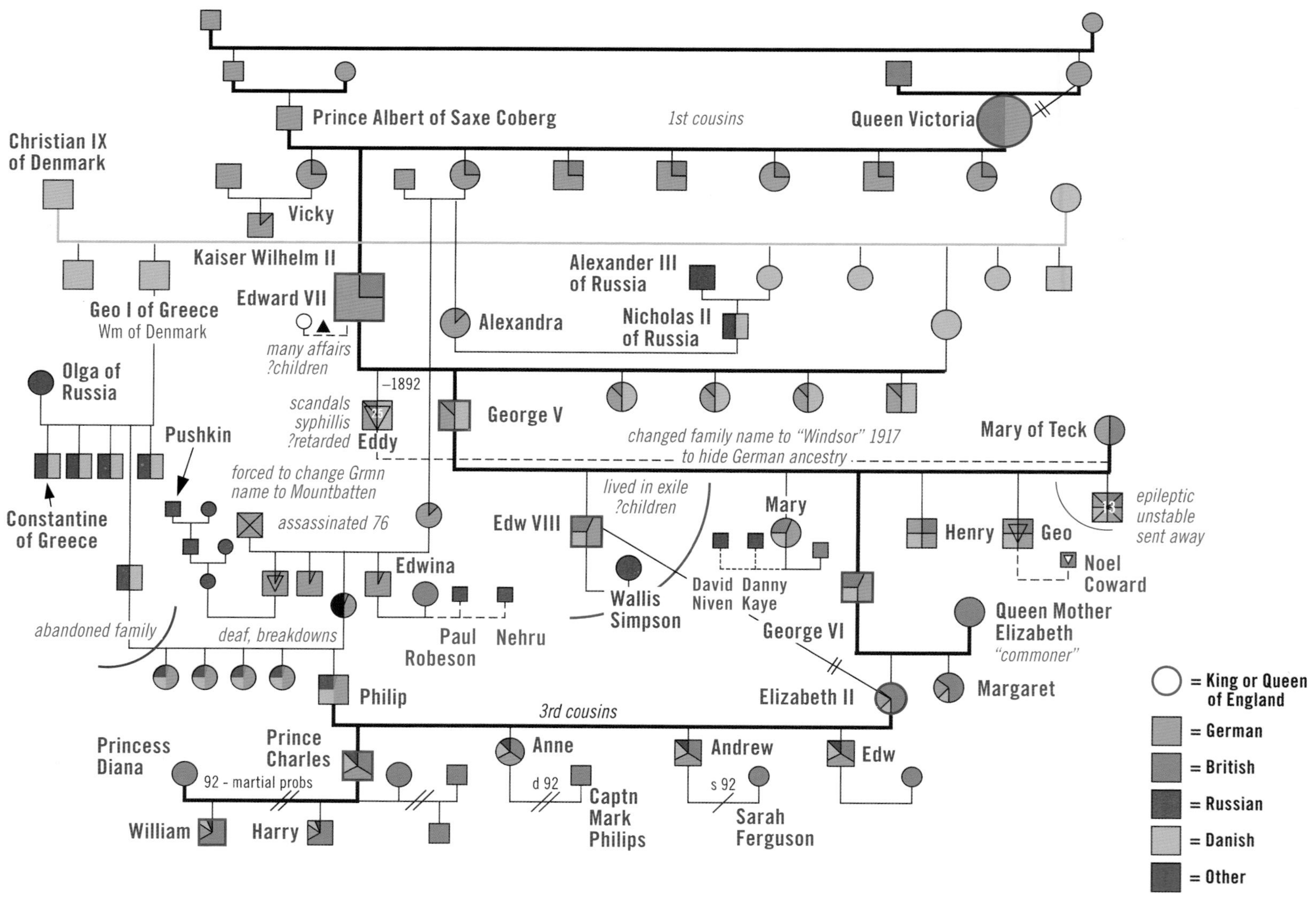

Color Figure 13 Kennedy Family

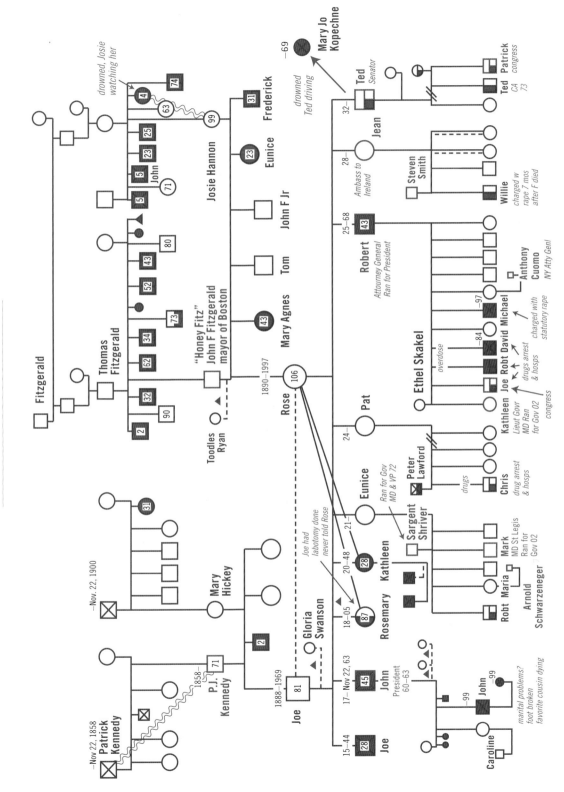

Color Figure 14 Peter Fonda's Living Situations Before Adulthood

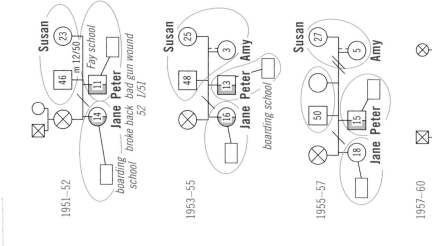

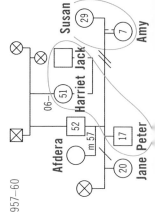

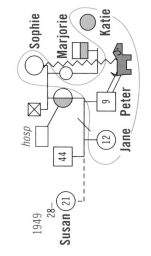

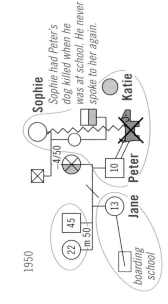

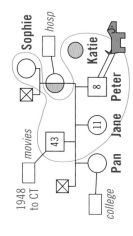

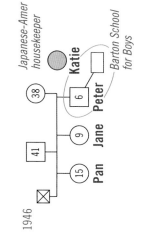

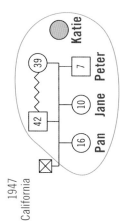

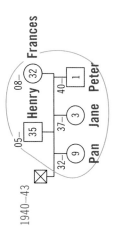

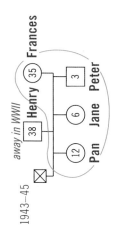

Color Figure 15 Bill Clinton's Living Changes

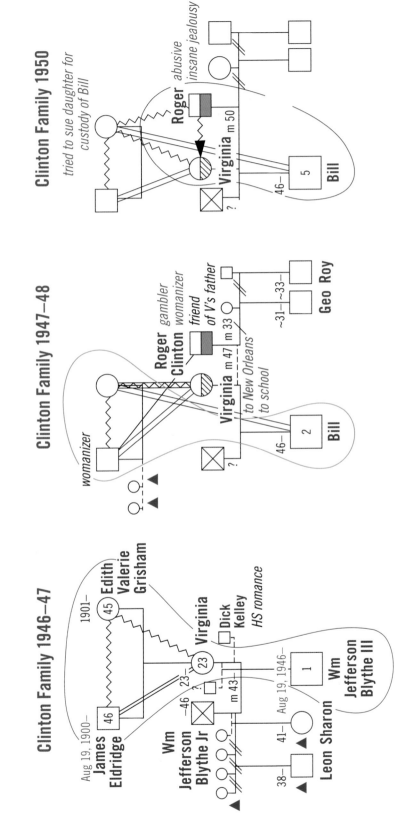

Clinton Family 1946–47

Clinton Family 1947–48

Clinton Family 1950

Color Figure 16 Bill Clinton's Family

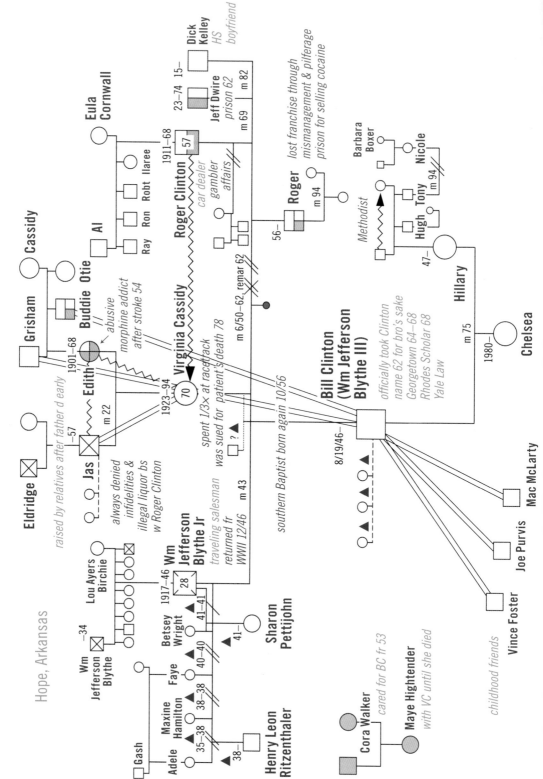

Color Figure 17 Hepburn Family

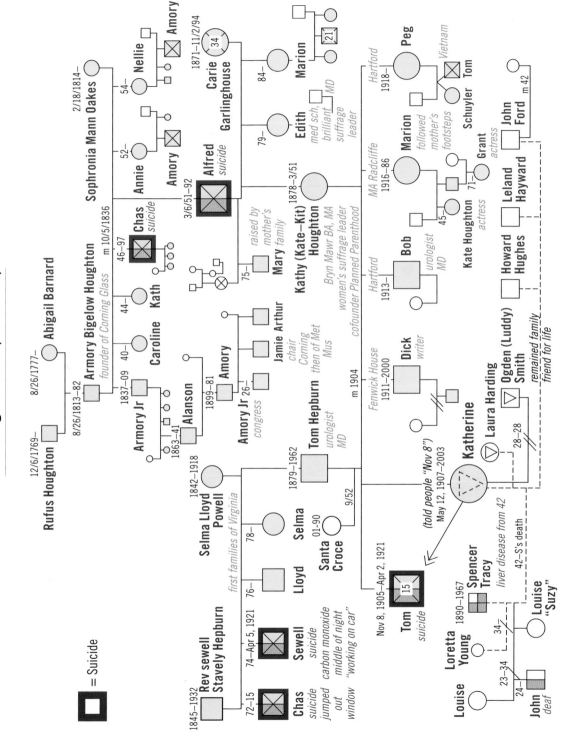

Color Figure 18 Jefferson Family

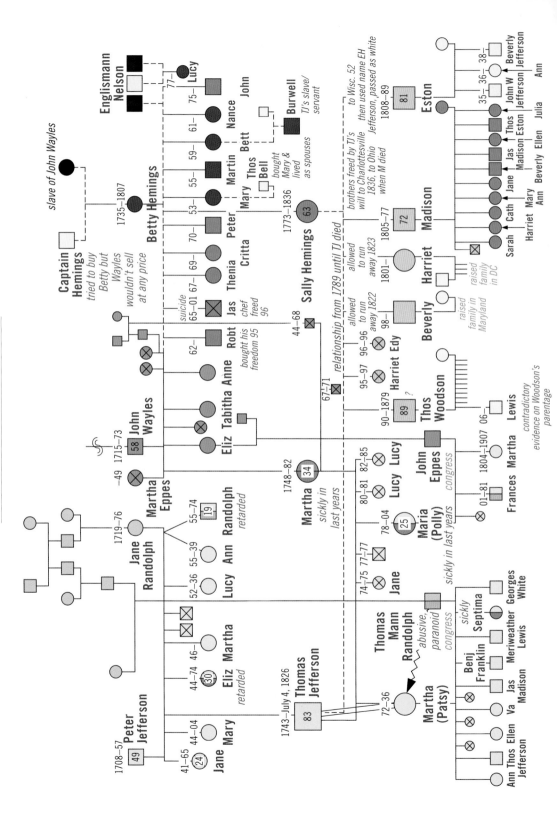

Color Figure 19 Caretaking Genogram Over Time

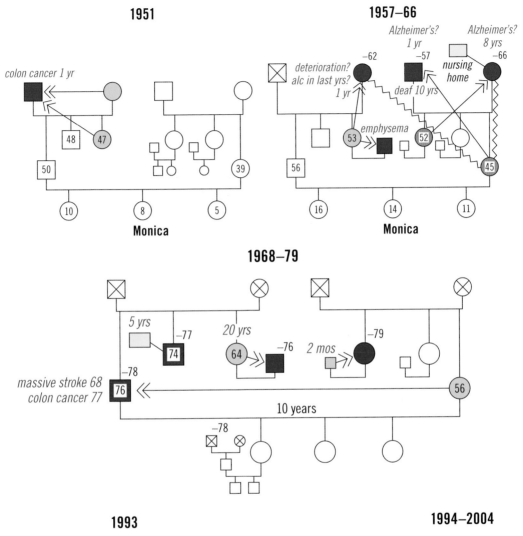

1951

colon cancer 1 yr

10 8 5
Monica

1957–66

Alzheimer's? 1 yr *Alzheimer's? 8 yrs*

deterioration? alc in last yrs? 1 yr *nursing home*

emphysema *deaf 10 yrs*

16 14 11
Monica

1968–79

5 yrs –77 *20 yrs* –76 *2 mos* –79

massive stroke 68 colon cancer 77 –78 56

10 years

–78

1993

–78

hospice

cancer 91 again 93 3 mos *college friend*

52 50 47 73
Monica

40-yr Friend d 6 mos later

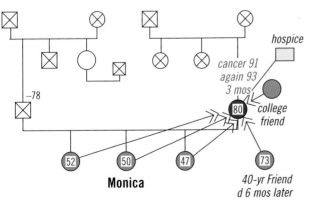

1994–2004

–04

100

Monica

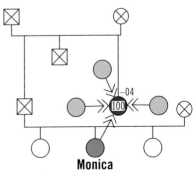

● = caretakee ◯ = primary caretaker (family) ◯ = secondary caretaker ◯ = primary caretaker (woman of color)

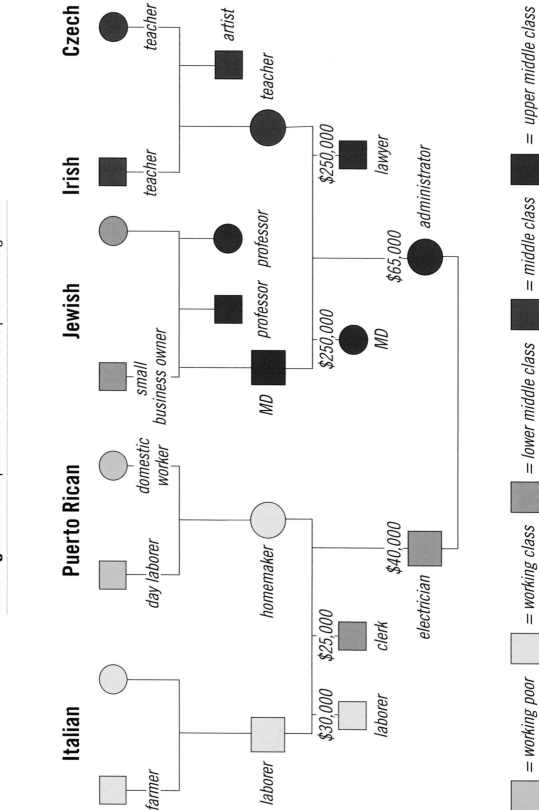

Color Figure 20 Couples With Different Occupational Backgrounds

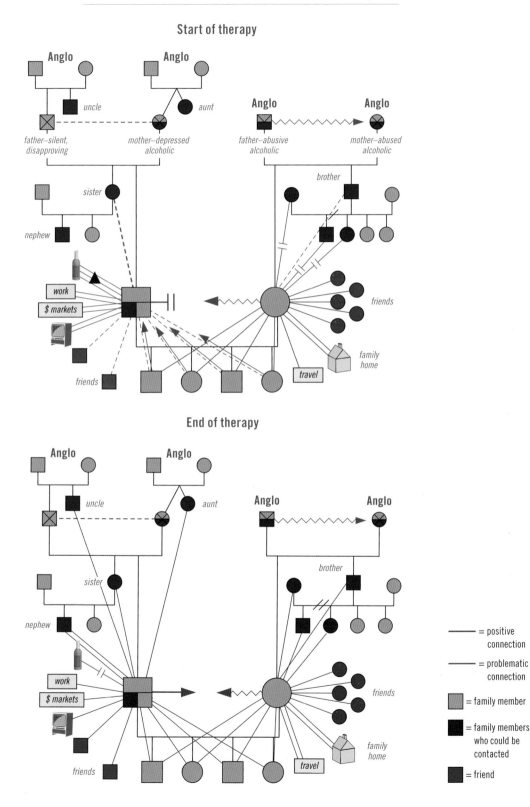

Color Figure 21 Couple at Start and End of Therapy

Color Figure 22 Reich Family Triangles

1908

*jealous of wife,
violent to son*

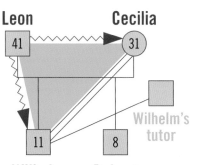

Leon 41 — Cecilia 31
Wilhelm 11 — Robert 8
Wilhelm's tutor

Wilhelm   **Robert**
*Wilhelm close to mother
but not to abusive father.*

1909

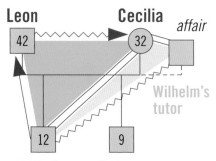

Leon 42 — Cecilia 32
affair
Wilhelm 12 — Robert 9
Wilhelm's tutor

Wilhelm   **Robert**
*Mad at mother for not
protecting him, Wilhelm
tells father of her affair.*

1910 and onwards

*sons saw his death
as "indirect" suicide*   *suicide*

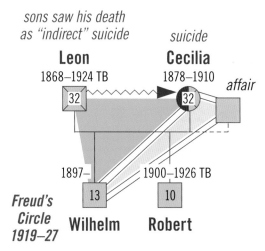

Leon 1868–1924 TB   32
Cecilia 1878–1910   32
affair
*Freud's
Circle
1919–27*
1897–   13   1900–1926 TB   10

Wilhelm   **Robert**

*Father abusively confronts
mother, who kills herself.
Rest of Reich's life he focused
on theory that guilt-free sexual
expression is the cure of all
neuroses.*

1956

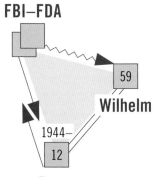

FBI–FDA
59
Wilhelm
1944–   12

Peter
*When Reich's son was about
same age as father had been,
FDA & FBI persecuted Reich for
his ideas. Burned all his books.
Came to arrest him, and asked
Peter his whereabouts.
Peter later feared he had given
father away. Reich died in prison.
His books are still in print!*

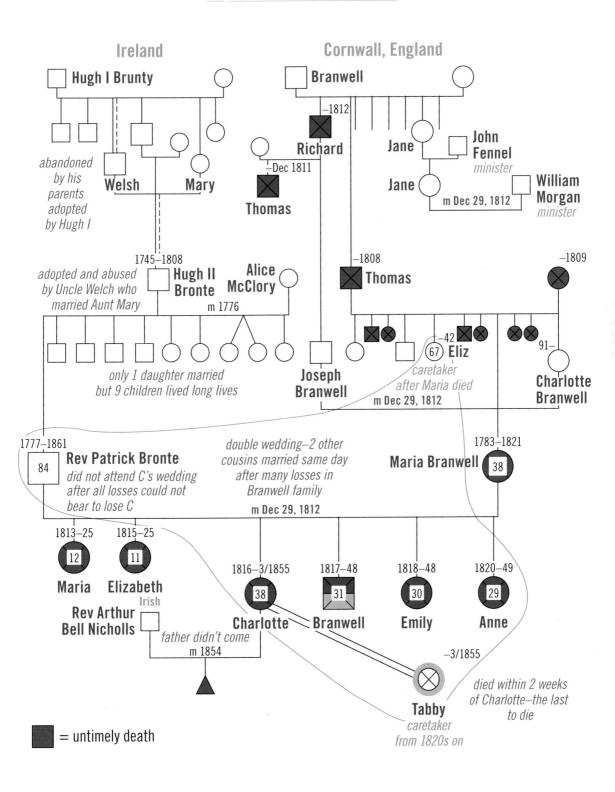

Ireland

Cornwall, England

Hugh I Brunty

Branwell
−1812

abandoned by his parents adopted by Hugh I

Welsh   Mary

Richard

Thomas
−Dec 1811

Jane

Jane

John Fennel
minister

William Morgan
minister
m Dec 29, 1812

adopted and abused by Uncle Welch who married Aunt Mary

1745−1808
Hugh II Bronte   Alice McClory
m 1776

−1808 Thomas

−1809

only 1 daughter married but 9 children lived long lives

Joseph Branwell

−42
67 Eliz
caretaker after Maria died
m Dec 29, 1812

91−

Charlotte Branwell

1777−1861
84 Rev Patrick Bronte
did not attend C's wedding after all losses could not bear to lose C

double wedding−2 other cousins married same day after many losses in Branwell family

m Dec 29, 1812

1783−1821
Maria Branwell 38

1813−25
12 Maria

1815−25
11 Elizabeth

Rev Arthur
Bell Nicholls
Irish
father didn't come
m 1854

1816−3/1855
38 Charlotte

1817−48
31 Branwell

1818−48
30 Emily

1820−49
29 Anne

−3/1855

Tabby
caretaker from 1820s on

died within 2 weeks of Charlotte−the last to die

■ = untimely death

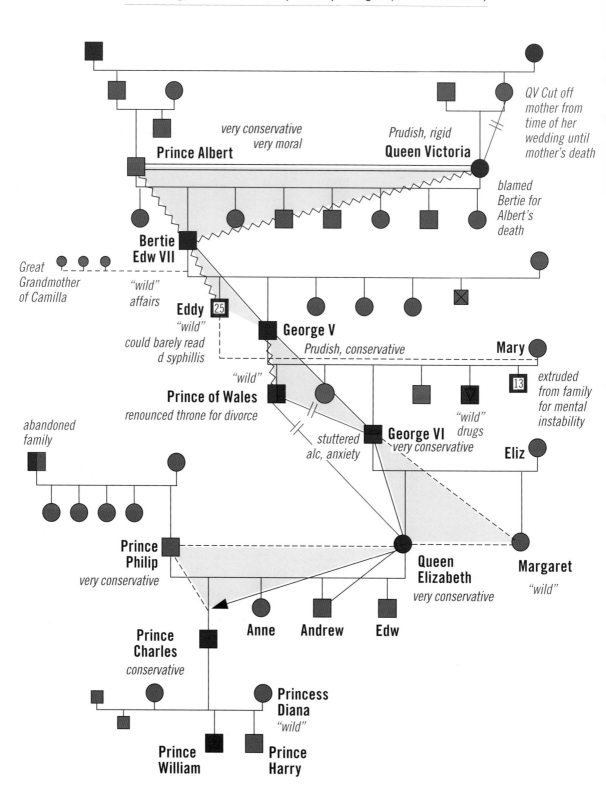

Color Figure 24 British Royal Family Triangles (Past Generations)

QV Cut off mother from time of her wedding until mother's death

very conservative
very moral

Prince Albert

Prudish, rigid
Queen Victoria

blamed Bertie for Albert's death

Bertie Edw VII

Great Grandmother of Camilla

"wild" affairs

Eddy 25
"wild" could barely read d syphillis

George V
Prudish, conservative

Mary 13
extruded from family for mental instability

"wild"

Prince of Wales
renounced throne for divorce

George VI
very conservative

"wild" drugs

stuttered
alc, anxiety

Eliz

abandoned family

Prince Philip
very conservative

Queen Elizabeth
very conservative

Margaret
"wild"

Anne **Andrew** **Edw**

Prince Charles
conservative

Princess Diana
"wild"

Prince William **Prince Harry**

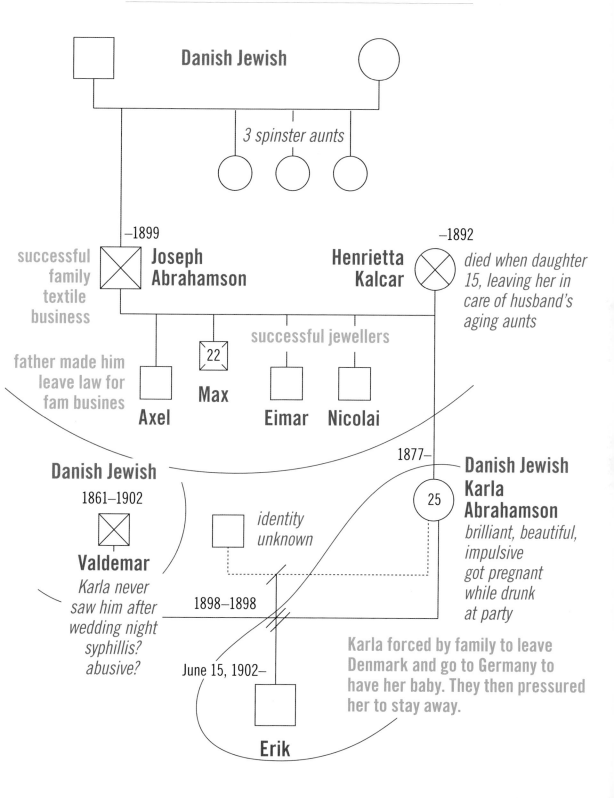

Danish Jewish

3 spinster aunts

successful
family
textile
business

−1899

**Joseph
Abrahamson**

−1892

**Henrietta
Kalcar**

*died when daughter
15, leaving her in
care of husband's
aging aunts*

successful jewellers

father made him
leave law for
fam busines

22

Axel

Max

Eimar   **Nicolai**

Danish Jewish

1877−

**Danish Jewish
Karla
Abrahamson**

*brilliant, beautiful,
impulsive
got pregnant
while drunk
at party*

1861–1902

Valdemar

*Karla never
saw him after
wedding night
syphillis?
abusive?*

25

*identity
unknown*

1898–1898

June 15, 1902−

Karla forced by family to leave
Denmark and go to Germany to
have her baby. They then pressured
her to stay away.

Erik

Color Figure 26 Erik Erikson's Family

1917 (Erik's Adolescence)

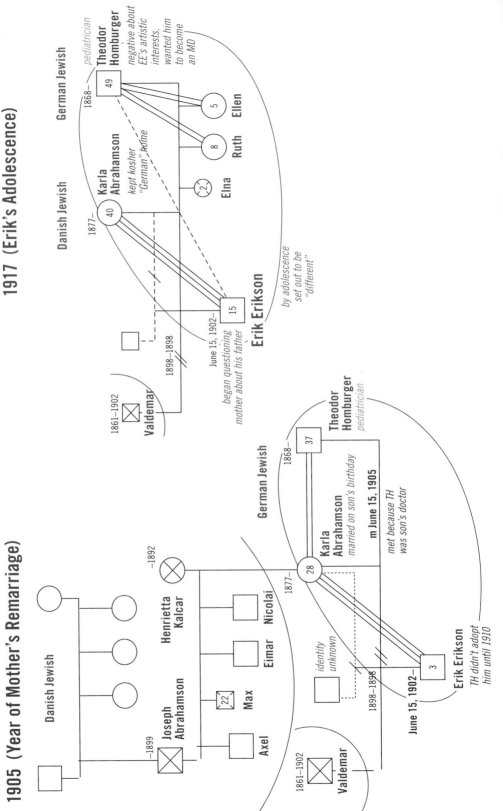

1905 (Year of Mother's Remarriage)

Color Figure 27 Erik Erikson's Family (1944)

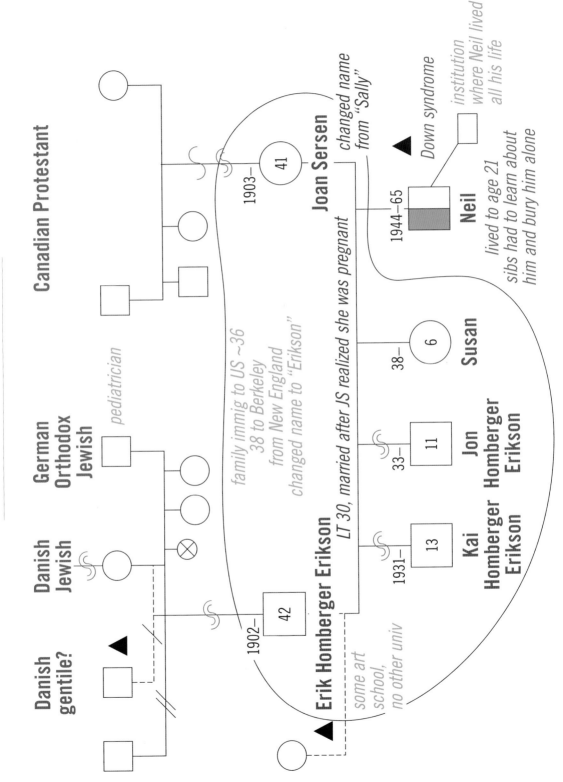

Canadian Protestant

German Orthodox Jewish

Danish Jewish

Danish gentile?

pediatrician

family immig to US ~36
38 to Berkeley
from New England
changed name to "Erikson"

changed name
from "Sally"

Joan Sersen

1903–

41

1944–65

Neil

Down syndrome

institution
where Neil lived
all his life

lived to age 21
sibs had to learn about
him and bury him alone

Erik Homberger Erikson
LT 30, married after JS realized she was pregnant

1902–

42

some art
school,
no other univ

1931–

13

Kai
Homberger
Erikson

33–

11

Jon
Homberger
Erikson

38–

6

Susan

Color Figure 28 Freud Family (1939)

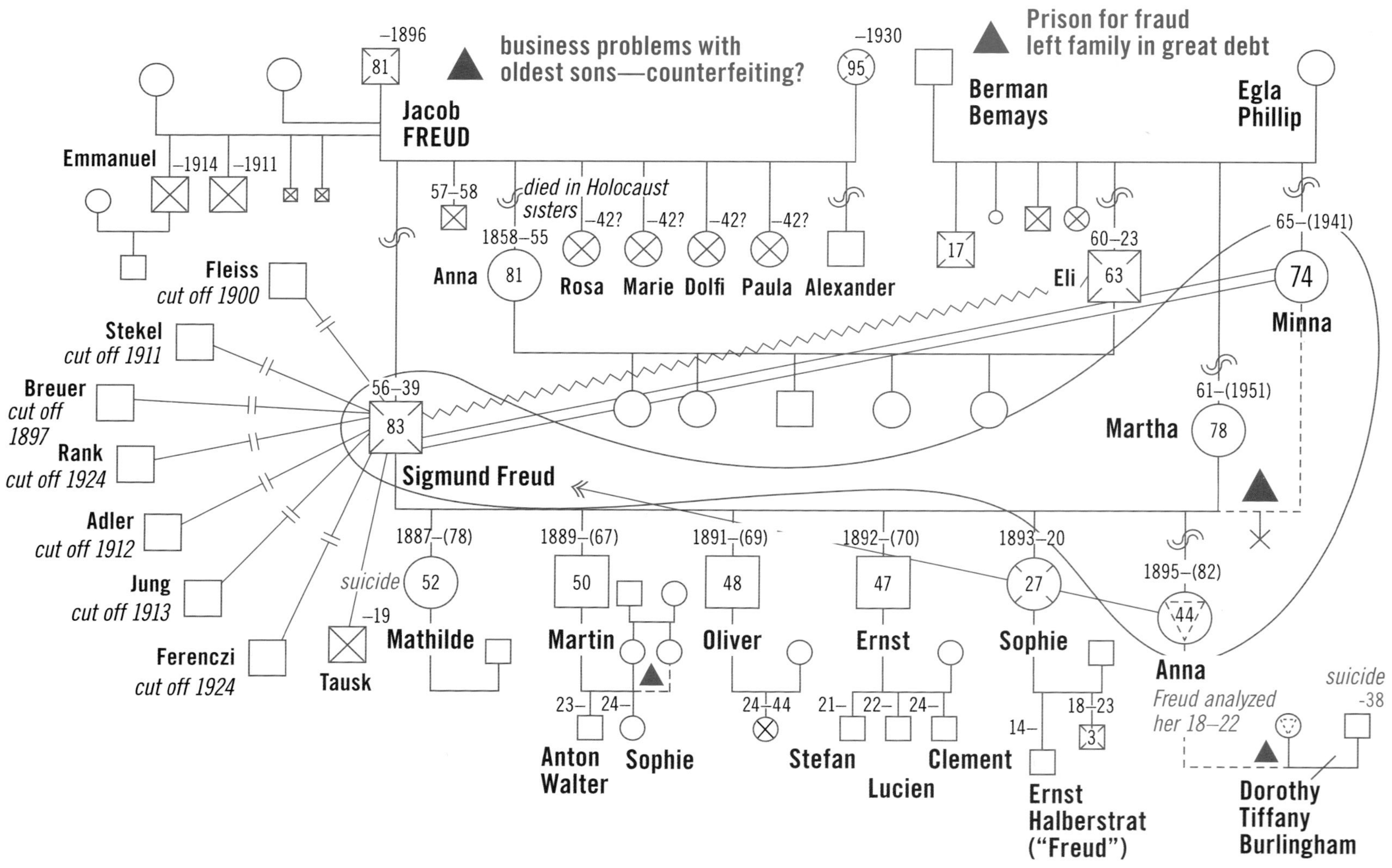

Color Figure 29 Family Play Genogram: Jenny

Color Figure 30 Family Play Genogram for Single-Parent Father

Color Figure 31 Family Play Genogram: Alexis

Color Figure 32 Family Play Genogram: Noguci

It seems that Agnes herself may have had a sexual relationship with Chaplin, who had also been a very good friend of Carlotta (Gelb & Gelb, 1987). Triangles may multiply quickly in remarried families!

Figure 7.7 Eugene O'Neill Remarried Triangles

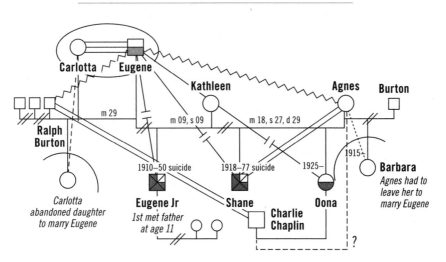

Finally, in-laws are usually not neutral on the subject of remarriage. For example, there may be a great deal of tension between the husband's mother and his new wife. Thus, the grandparent generation often gets involved in remarried triangles, intensifying the process by joining with their adult child, especially against the ex-spouse, whom they may blame for the divorce.

Triangles in Families with Foster or Adopted Children

Parent/child triangles are particularly common when one or more of the children is a foster or adopted child. Tension between the parents—perhaps because of their failure to conceive a child together—may be present before the child was adopted. This may lead the couple to focus intensely and negatively on the adopted child, who may be treated as an outsider, serving to distract the family from other concerns.

In many ways, families with foster or adopted children are like remarried families in that there are two families involved: the caretaking family and the biological family. This is true whether the biological parents are known or not, because people can triangulate a memory or idea as well as actual people. For example, consider Figure 7.8, which shows interlocking triangles. In this case, two sons were adopted from different families. When the older son, Brad, became a father, he decided to reconnect with his biological parents. His biological mother had contacted him when he was in college but his adoptive parents were so upset about it that he refused to see her again. He changed his mind seven years later when his son was born. He had also recently met with his father and half sister, but his parents again became extremely angry, saying his contact was a betrayal of all they had done for him. This activated an interlocking triangle between Brad, "the bad brother," and Bob, "the good brother," who had no interest in contact with his biological family.

Figure 7.8 Triangle of Adoptees and Biological and Adoptive Parents

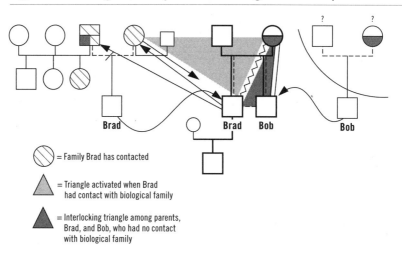

An adoptive child may fantasize that his or her biological parents would be more loving, generous, and so on. The adoptive parents may also participate in fantasized triangles of blaming the biological parents in absentia for their difficulties with the adoptive child (bad genes). If there are biological children as well, triangles between the foster/adopted and biological children are common.

Multigenerational Triangles

As mentioned earlier, triangles can cross many generations. Probably the most common three-generational triangle is when a grandparent and grandchild ally against the parents. Seeing this on a genogram suggests a hypothesis of a triangle where a parent is an ineffectual outsider to a cross-generational alliance. Such multigenerational triangles are common when one parent is absent and the other, usually the mother, shares a household with the grandparents, as happened in Bill Clinton's family (see Color Figure 15). The mother may lose power as the grandparents take over child-rearing responsibilities or as a grandparent-grandchild alliance forms against her.

Relationships Outside the Family

There also tends to be a correlation between the level of intensity of relationships within a family and a family's relationships with outsiders; the more closed the system is to relationships outside the family, the greater the intensity of relationships within it. Thus, if one sees on the genogram patterns of fused relationships or intense triangles in the immediate family, one might investigate the family's boundary with the outside world. For example, the fusion between Eugene O'Neill and his third wife, Carlotta (see Figure 7.7), was intensified by their equally intense cutoff from their children, their extended families, and all others in the outside world.

The Brontë family (Color Figure 23) developed a similar pattern of fusion and cutoff, probably similarly influenced by loss. Charlotte was the only one of all the children who had any ongoing relationships outside the immediate family. The other three siblings who lived to adulthood all died within a 9-month period, one after another, almost as though their fusion made it impossible for them to live without each other. First the alcoholic and drug-addicted son died a miserable death in the household. From the day of his funeral the second youngest sister, Emily, never left the house again and died soon afterwards, and the youngest sister, Anna, followed soon after that. Such a genogram raises questions about the reason for the strong boundaries around the family. None of the siblings except Charlotte ever left home for more than a brief period. They became ill whenever they went away. The two sisters who died in childhood developed their fatal illnesses during their first period away from home and died within a short period of each other. Indeed, when Charlotte first told her father she wanted to marry, he became enraged and fired her fiancé, who was his curate, later allowing the marriage only if they promised never to leave him (McGoldrick, 1995). When she did marry and become pregnant she and her lifelong caretaker, Tabby, died within 2 weeks.

Triangles Over Time

It helps to track family triangles over time to better understand family process. Consider the British royal family in the last generation (Figure 7.9). When he was young, Prince Charles was apparently very close to his mother, if not to his father. Then he met Camilla, a sophisticated woman 2 years older than he who reportedly said, "My great-great-grandmother was your great-great-grandfather's [Edward VII] mistress. So how about it?" His mother was apparently extremely negative about the relationship and at the time Charles felt he could not risk alienating her, so he gave Camilla up to preserve his relationship with his mother. It was not until 6 years later, when Charles was 29, that he met a new prospect, Diana, the 16-year-old younger sister of a woman he was dating. His mother approved and the couple was married. But once they were married, Diana became unhappy and symptomatic—depressed and bulimic. Her dreams were not coming true. Charles was also unhappy and went to his mother for support, but she seems not to have helped and conveyed that he still wasn't handling his situation. He was now having serious marital problems. Meanwhile, Diana went to therapy and her therapist conveyed that she was stuck with a very difficult family and situation. Diana began to feel better. She became involved with affairs, friends, philanthropic work, and the media. Meanwhile, Charles remet Camilla.

Before long the whole world became involved in their relationship, mostly on the side of Diana. When Diana soon afterwards became engaged and then died tragically, the negative triangulating against her stopped. (This is extremely common when someone dies an untimely

Figure 7.9 British Royal Family Triangles

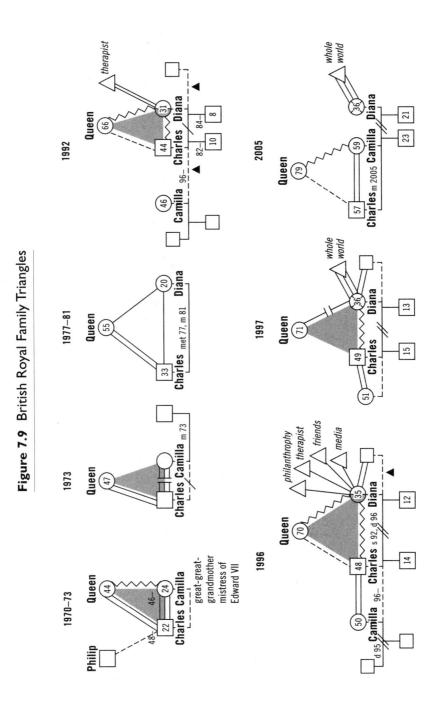

death. They become glorified.) It took Charles another 8 years to finally marry the woman he had loved for 30 years; he was, apparently, no longer concerned about his mother's continuing disapproval.

If we look back in the royal family to triangles in previous generations, other triangles played out for similarly long periods of time. Queen Victoria, Charles's great-great-great grandmother, was alienated from her mother from the time of her wedding until her mother's death. Charles's mother was cut off for 30 years from her uncle, who had abdicated because he wanted to marry a divorced woman. Thus do triangulating patterns often continue over long periods in families, though the participants may change places. The precedents of such triangles have an extraordinarily long history within the royal family, and the followup of what will happen over time with Charles's marriage and with his children, as with every family, remains to be seen.

Actually, going back to the generation of Queen Victoria, we see a similar pattern in each generation over the heir to the throne (Color Figure 24). Victoria was so well known for the rigidity of her standards and rules that the very term "victorian" refers to these high standards. Her oldest son, Bertie, who did not become king until he was in his fifties, was known since his youth for his love of the wild life. His oldest son, having gotten into a dissipated life from his youth, died at 25, which many said was fortunate because he would have been incapable of ruling. The throne was left to his very conservative, prudish younger brother, King George V. George would not even meet with anyone who was divorced. King George's oldest son again preferred life on the wild side, to the extent that he abdicated to marry the twice divorced Wallis Simpson, and the conservative George VI replaced him, again taking the position never to let him come back home with his wife. Thus, there were significant triangles in every generation with either a good son and a bad son or a good parent and a bad parent; the triangles that Diana and Charles became involved in were part of a very long story.

8

Tracking Individuals and Families Through the Life Cycle

C LINICAL ASSESSMENT REQUIRES US TO THINK of life cycle development as we gather genogram information (McGoldrick & Carter, 2005a). The genogram captures the family as it evolves over time. All human beings must define and redefine themselves as they move through their lives in the context of their changing relationships. Because genograms depict individuals in this evolutionary context, they enable us to assess people as they move through life. They are an extremely valuable instrument for tracking human development, which would be difficult to assess without a mapping tool of this breadth and depth. Genograms and family chronologies are useful tools for assessing families in life cycle perspective, tracking the spiral of family evolution as generations move through time in their development from birth to death (see the Family Life Cycle section in the bibliography). Family evolution is like a musical composition, in which the meaning of individual notes depends on their rhythmic and harmonic relationship with each other and with the memories of past melodies, as well as those anticipated but not yet written. Genograms can elucidate the family life cycle, which can in turn aid in the interpretation of the genogram. Both the patterns that typically occur at various phases of the life cycle and the issues to be predicted when life events are "off schedule" are relevant to understanding family developmental process.

The Life Cycle of Erik Erikson

The genogram of one of the most famous human development theorists, Erik Erikson, provides an interesting illustration of the value of this tool for understanding people in life cycle context. Though Erikson was preoccupied with the concept of identity all his life, he never had the opportunity to learn his own identity. He and others made many efforts to discover his father's identity, but he also held back from learning the truth. He eventually invented his own last name "Erikson" as if to say, "Erik, son of myself." Many said his name change hid the Jewish part of his identity, and even the German part of his background (he had been raised from birth in Germany), emphasizing a Scandinavian connection with a father he had never known and a culture where he had never lived.

Erikson's widely accepted theory of human development appears to reflect some of the particularities and weaknesses of his own family and cultural situation that played out over his life cycle (Carter & McGoldrick, 2005; Friedman, 1999). Erikson's model describes eight stages, each with a theme contrasting healthy and dysfunctional patterns:

1. **Infancy**:   Trust vs. mistrust
2. **Early childhood**:   Autonomy vs. shame and doubt
3. **Play age**:   Initiative vs. guilt
4. **School age**:   Industry vs. inferiority
5. **Adolescence**:   Identity vs. identity diffusion (described as a sense of identity apart from one's family)
6. **Young adult**:   Intimacy vs. isolation
7. **Midlife**:   Generativity vs. self-absorption
8. **Mature age**:   Integrity vs. despair

Although Erikson's first stage focuses primarily on an interpersonal task, mother-child trust versus mistrust, the following stages until young adulthood focus entirely on the ability to manage for oneself, rather than on the development of interpersonal relationships or communication *in relation* to one's family. The skill of "intimacy" in young adulthood will surely be difficult to achieve if one has been focusing on initiative, autonomy, industry, and identity apart from family for the previous 20 years. Furthermore, the values that are considered dysfunctional in healthy development—shame, doubt, guilt, a sense of inferiority, and identity diffusion—are actually essential to a healthy interpersonal ability for intimacy. Closeness requires the recognition that we:

- Don't know everything (a healthy sense of interdependence and inferiority)
- Will at times do the wrong thing (causing shame and guilt, which can motivate us to change our behavior)
- Will need to leave room for doubt in our ideas and actions in order to learn from others, and
- Will need to have an interdependent sense of our identity in relation to our families and others, not just *apart from* them.

Many have critiqued Erikson's scheme as meant only for men, but even for men his stages posit an ideal that is incompatible with intimacy. If all one's developmental energy has been focused on autonomous striving, one would not have developed interpersonal skills necessary for mature intimacy and interdependence.

Erikson's genogram (Color Figure 25) may help us understand the limitations of his schema. Erikson said the primary issue in the first 2 years of life was developing a trusting relationship with one's mother. It has been said that Erikson's mother, a Danish Jew, became pregnant with Erickson after getting drunk at a party given by her brothers, and that she was either asleep or too drunk to recognize what happened when someone had intercourse with her (Friedman, 1999). She discovered she was pregnant while on a trip to Germany and was told by her family, supposedly to avoid disgrace and scandal, not to return to Denmark but rather to have the baby where she was. Her family then urged her to remain in Germany to raise him. It is not clear whether Erickson's mother knew who the father was. In any case, she never told her son the truth and he was obsessed with this question throughout his life. As Erikson's daughter later wrote:

> My father never knew . . . even who his father was. One of the saddest things about that, from my point of view, is that his mother refused throughout her life to tell him the identity of this all-important person. Her stated reason was that she had promised the man she married when my father was three that she would never divulge this information. But her explanation conveys a greater concern for someone else's wishes than for my father's aching need to know. (Erikson Boland, 1999, pp. 56–57)

The maternal family basically extruded Erikson's mother until 3 years later, in 1905, when she married a German Jewish pediatrician, Theodor Homburger, on her son's 3rd birthday—again, an act that did not respect his need for his own identity (Color Figure 26). Homburger required of Karla only one promise: that Erik be told he was his biological father, which Erikson never believed. He later said "[I] felt all along . . . doubt in my identity . . . all through my childhood years. . . . I was quietly convinced that I came from a different background" (Friedman, 1999, p. 33). Homburger's apparant ambivalence about taking on this relationship revealed itself in his taking 5 years to complete the adoption papers to make Erik legally his son. Erikson's closest childhood friend, Peter Blos, said that "adoption was the great theme of Erikson's existence" (Friedman, 1999, p. 28). Erikson later created a woodcut of himself, his mother, and her new husband on their honeymoon, which they took with him; it showed him miserable and alone while they embraced in the background. Obviously, in his view he had lost his beloved mother to her new husband and was not happy about it. It is perhaps not surprising that Erikson's theory of human development placed so much emphasis on autonomy and individuation rather than on interconnection. His mother was forced to manage on her own without the support of her family just as she became his parent, and he had to accept losing her to her new husband and learn to manage for himself from early childhood, as the woodcut shows. It is probably not surprising that, for the rest of his childhood, Erikson focused on autonomy, initiative, and industry as the stepchild in a remarried family where three half sisters would follow over the next several years.

In the years of his childhood (Color Figure 26), Erikson remained close to his mother but did not become particularly close to his sisters, who were 7 and 10 years younger than he. (The sister closest in age to him had died at age 2.) The family was required to speak German in the home, which created a lifelong feeling of regret in Erik, as he forgot how to speak Danish. As he grew up, he repeatedly questioned his mother about his paternity. She finally acknowledged that Homburger wasn't his father and at 14 told him he was the son of her first husband, but he sensed this wasn't true either. He talked constantly with his friend Peter Blos of the characteristics he thought his father might have. Throughout his life his mother gave him a variety of different stories, but never the truth. He said of the search, "if my father hadn't cared enough about me to want me . . . why should I look him up now" (Friedman, 1999, p. 39), but he could not stop wondering, even though he feared knowing the truth.

Later in Erikson's life he seemed to repeat the secret keeping that his mother and stepfather had forced on him. His theory describes the phase of "generativity" as occurring after the phase of childrearing, a task others would see as our most generative! Erikson and his wife Joan developed this part of the theory at a difficult time in their lives, following the birth of their fourth child, Neil, who was born with Down syndrome in 1944 (Color Figure 27).

Erik and Joan Erikson made the decision to keep the existence of their fourth child, Neil, a secret. He was put in an institution and they decided to tell their other children he had died, although, in fact, he lived to the age of 21. They rarely visited him. When he died, they did not attend the funeral and left their other children alone to handle his burial. One cannot help wondering if this terrible secret of their family history did not influence the parents' ideas about the life cycle—in particular, their concept that generativity does not refer to the period of the life cycle when one is bearing and raising children, but rather to the midlife period instead. The Eriksons apparently characterized Neil as "a developmental aberration and wished that he had never been born" (Friedman, 1999, p. 22). Their sad story is not just about their personal failure to deal with the truth of their family's history, but also reflects our society's pressure for success. This often leaves families with disabled children to feel invalidated, alone, abandoned, and possibly pressured to lie about their lives in order to preserve an image of normality. The Eriksons' dreadful story reveals society's insidious pressure on families to distort their lives with lies and secrecy regarding any experiences that lie outside society's life cycle norms. Their story should surely lead us to question the assumptions of "normality" laid out by Erikson in the years when he was living a lie, pretending that he had a "perfect" family of five while secretly extruding the 6th member, who didn't fit in. Erikson was a leading theorist about children and his views of human development are still the most widely taught. The limits of his theory make clear the value of assessing families in life cycle context and especially of tracking the power of secrets in families. Secrets may distort family process for generations and lead to imbalances in functioning between the external picture presented to the world and the internal realities of family relationships.

Indeed, genograms can be very helpful in tracking the specific nodal points in a family's history. Genogram software will soon be able to help us track families through the life cycle, offering a snapshot of particular moments in time to help us understand these nodal points, such as the time when Erikson was born, the point of remarriage, or the time when his son Neil was born.

For example, we do not really know what was going on in Karla's family when she became pregnant with Erik, though this moment would be most interesting to understand. Were there stresses in her family that led them to extrude her when she became pregnant rather than supporting her and her baby? What might have influenced her to become drunk and pregnant at a young age? Karla's mother had died when she was 15 and her father and older brothers appear not to have wanted to care for her themselves; they left her to the father's aging sisters. The father died when she was 21. That same year she married and was traumatically abandoned on her honeymoon; her older brother Axel had to go to Rome to get her. Axel himself had had to give up his legal studies because of the father's pressure to join his business, so the family, though successful, seems to have been under some emotional pressure. If Karla had indeed become pregnant at a party given by the older brothers, it would appear to implicate them in her pregnancy. Did they indirectly contribute to her being abused and then blame her for shaming the family?

How did the parents die and what was the impact of their early loss on Karla and on the brothers? Did the brothers feel their own social status was threatened for some reason other than their sister's pregnancy? Or did they mistreat her because of gender-related imbalances of power in their family, which would have been typical at that time? Were the three "spinster" aunts the ones who made the decision to pay her to stay out of sight or did the brothers make this decision? And did their stresses continue over the next few years, leading them not to let her come back even after the baby was born, leaving her alone with her child in a foreign country?

At the point of remarriage (see Color Figure 26) we can see that Erikson, by 3, was too old not to know that Homberger was not his father.

If we look at the later moment of decision to keep the secret about Neil in 1944, we can imagine the tragic difficulty the family must have experienced as the immigrant parents of three other children, making their dreadful decision to keep Neil's existence a secret. The reality of the war going on and the fact that Erikson was a half Jewish immigrant could have figured into the decision. Genograms for a given moment in a family's history can highlight the stresses on them at that point by showing who lived in the home and how old they were then, allowing you to track details of family history around key points in time.

It is very interesting that Erikson's daughter Sue, who struggled all her life with her father's difficulty with intimacy, came to the conclusion that mature development requires one to be capable of having "authentic interpersonal encounters" in which you are "acceptable for who you are" (Erikson Boland, 1999, p. 61). She herself pointed out the disadvantage of having to live a life where shame, doubt, guilt, a sense of inferiority, and identity diffusion were viewed as indicating developmental failure. She said her mother had told her neither she nor Erikson could seek help because of his public reputation. His theory made him unable to admit inadequacy and thus be open to receiving help when needed. Sue said:

> When you have created a public image that denies your private experience of yourself—one that is, in important ways, the reverse of the shameful self—the contrast between the two creates feelings of personal fraudulence. I think my father suffered terribly because he could not in his intimate relationships be what his image suggested he would be. . . . My longing to connect with my father was thwarted by his need to avoid feelings of inadequacy—by the defenses he had developed early on to ward off shame and depression." (Erikson Boland, 1999, p. 61)

In using the example of her father, she makes very clear how essential these issues are for a healthy interpersonal ability for intimacy—to know that you don't know everything (inferiority), to know that you will make mistakes (guilt), to be able to doubt your ideas and actions, and to have a sense of your identity in relation to your family and others, not just apart from them. By contrast, Erikson's mother, Karla, was forced to survive completely on her own, and he in turn was forced to grow up without these normal developmental assets.

As we have seen with the Erikson family, the genogram of critical points in the life cycle can help us understand the future evolution of the family. The genogram can track family patterns as people move through each phase of the family life cycle. Different configurations on the genogram suggest possible triangles and issues that may be relevant at each phase.

Families progress through a series of milestones, transitions, or nodal points in their development, which may include leaving home, forming a couple, the birth of children, child rearing, launching, and retirement. At each nodal point in the life cycle the family must reorganize itself in order to move on successfully to the next phase. These transitions can be very difficult for some families, who have trouble adapting to new circumstances and who tend to rigidify at transition points. Regardless of the presenting problem, clinicians should always assess whether it reflects difficulties the family is having handling life cycle transitions. The ages and dates on the genogram suggest what life cycle transitions the family is adapting to and whether life cycle events occur within normative expectations. There are normative expectations for the timing of each phase of the family life cycle, such as the likely ages of family members at each transition point. Although these norms are ever-changing and must not be regarded as fixed, when events happen outside this range of expectations, the clinician should consider the possibility that the family is experiencing some difficulty negotiating a life cycle transition.

Thus, it is important to scan the genogram for family members whose ages differ greatly from the norm for their life cycle phase. The dates on the genogram of births, deaths, leaving home, marriage, separation, and divorce are all helpful in this regard. For example, the fact that none of the children in a family left home or married for the first time until their forties might indicate some problems in leaving home and forming intimate relationships. Or one might ask a couple in which the husband is 27 and the wife 47 how they happened to get together and how this pairing might fit with various patterns in their families of origin and in their community. A woman who has her first child at 43, a man who becomes a father at age 70, or a family in which three the sons died before middle age—all suggest systems where deviations in the normative pattern of the life cycle deserve further exploration.

In all cultures, there is generally a preferable life cycle timing for couples to marry. In our society, those who marry before their 20s or after their mid-30s are at greater risk for divorce, although this normative time frame for first marriage has become dramatically later in the past few years. Couples are increasingly marrying in their late twenties or even their mid-thirties. The possibility of preserving sperm and eggs is expanding the life cycle options for childbirth as well.

The time between meeting, engagement, and marriage, and between separation, divorce, and remarriage is also of interest. A short interval between life events does not allow much time for family members to deal with the emotional shifts involved (McGoldrick & Carter, 2005b). For example, Henry Fonda's remarriage 8 months after his second wife committed suicide (see Figure 2.7) would suggest unresolved emotional issues and at least the possibility of an affair. In fact, Henry had begun a relationship with his future wife the year before. It even appears possible that she became pregnant and had a child at that time by Fonda, whom he adopted a few years later. Rushing into the new marriage suggests the importance to Henry of putting the previous marriage behind him. One would also wonder how the family, particularly the children, adjusted to such rapid family changes. In light of this, the fact that Henry never discussed Frances's suicide with his children makes it all the more apparent that he did not process his grief or trauma alone or with his children before trying to move on.

The Life Cycle of Freud's Family

Tracking family history over the life cycle is a pivotal pathway toward understanding any person or family. Clinically it is particularly useful for clients to do the genograms for their family from a life cycle perspective in order to understand their family legacies. Considering Freud's place as our psychological ancestor, his legacies may shed important light on our own heritage. Actually, however, Freud, like many other people who are embarrassed or pained by aspects of their background, preferred to downplay his family history, so it takes some digging to uncover. Nevertheless, the genogram of the Freud family can help us to see him in life cycle context.

Courtship and Marriage of Freud's Parents: The Joining of Families
Because the life cycle is circular and repetitive, we can start at any point to tell the story of a family. With the Freud family, we might begin a few years before the birth of Sigmund, at the time of his parents' courtship.

A genogram of the time of marriage or remarriage shows the coming together of two separate families, indicating where each spouse is in his or her own family life cycle. To start a new family, both partners must come to terms with their families of origin. The genogram gives clues to the role and connectedness of each spouse in his or her own family of origin. If one spouse feels competitive with the other's family of origin (as happened with Freud) or if parents do not approve of their child's marital choice, in-law triangles are likely to develop. The genogram also shows the previous relationships that may affect or interfere with the marital bond. Unfortunately, we know virtually nothing of the in-law relationships in this generation of the Freud family.

CHRONOLOGY OF THE FREUD FAMILY AT TIME OF JACOB AND AMALIA'S MARRIAGE

1832   Jacob Freud, age 16, marries Sally Kanner.

1833   (April) Jacob and Sally's first child, Emanuel, is born.

1834   Jacob and Sally's second child, Philipp, is born.

1835? Third child is born. Gender, date of birth, and date and cause of death are unknown.

1837? Fourth child is born. Gender, date of birth, and date and cause of death are unknown.

1852   Jacob's first wife, Sally Kanner, is recorded as alive. Did they divorce? Did she die by end of year?

1852   Jacob Freud marries a second time, to Rebecca. Two entries list Jacob's wife as Rebecca aged 31 and 32 (Krüll, 1986).

1852   (October–December) Rebecca dies (?)

1853   (December) Jacob, who appears to have business problems, hands over his business to son Emanuel. It is unclear what work Jacob did after this point in his life. (His son will also have career issues at midlife.)

1854   (or earlier) Emanuel marries Maria.

1854   (or slightly earlier) Amalia's father loses his fortune and is disgraced.

1855   (July 29) Jacob and Amalia are married. Jacob is listed as widower since 1852.

1855   (August 13) Emanuel's first son (later Sigmund's nephew), John, is born.

As can be seen in this chronology and in the genogram of the Freud family in 1855 (Figure 8.1), the marriage of Jacob Freud and Amalia Nathanson, the daughter of a man he had been in business with 10 years earlier (before both men had serious business problems), had a number of atypical aspects. Jacob, who was 40, was marrying for the third time. Amalia was just 20. In fact, she was even younger than Jacob's sons from his first marriage. Virtually nothing is known about Jacob's first wife, Sally Kanner, or the two children from that first marriage who died; even less is known about Jacob's second wife, Rebecca. We do not know what happened to either wife, whether the couple divorced or the wives died. In addition, Jacob's first marriage took place when he was only 16, suggesting the possibility of an unexpected pregnancy (Anzieu, 1986). The second marriage is even more mysterious. Rebecca was never mentioned by any family member and we know of her existence only from public records. She appears to have married Jacob in 1852. Jacob's sons Emanuel and Philipp were grown and would obviously have known her. Surely Amalia would at least have known of her existence, as they all lived in the same town and Jacob had worked with her father; yet, if anyone ever did mention her to Freud, he never told anyone else. Was there something about her of which the family was ashamed? Mental illness? Suicide? In any case, Jacob and Amalia obviously began their new family in the shadow of Jacob's earlier marriages and the loss of two of his first four children.

Figure 8.1 Freud/Nathansohn Family (1855)

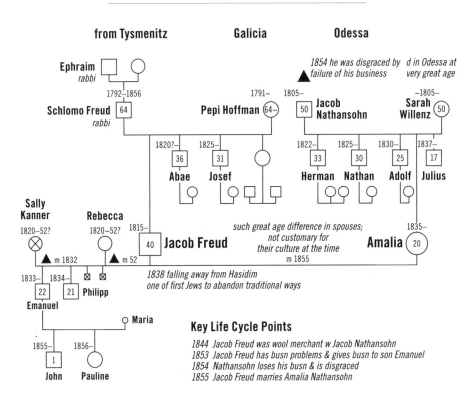

Key Life Cycle Points

1844 Jacob Freud was wool merchant w Jacob Nathansohn
1853 Jacob Freud has busn problems & gives busn to son Emanuel
1854 Nathansohn loses his busn & is disgraced
1855 Jacob Freud marries Amalia Nathansohn

When examining a genogram, it is particularly important to note the ages of family members as they move through the life cycle. With any newly married couple, it is important to note the spouses' positions within the life cycles of their respective families. Jacob was already a grandfather, whereas Amalia, 20 years younger and a peer of his sons, was at the young adult phase. How did these two happen to marry? We know that such age differences were not the custom at this time and place (Krüll, 1986). One wonders what led Amalia to agree to marry a man so much older, with grown sons and two previous marriages. Perhaps her father's recent loss of his fortune and being disgraced may explain her need to settle for an older man (Swales, 1986). In any case, Amalia was a vivacious young woman, one of the youngest in her family. Jacob, for his part, had done fairly well in his thirties as a traveling salesman with his maternal grandfather, but he seemingly came to a standstill in midlife. One would predict, upon seeing these differences in experience and expectation on a genogram, that this might be a problematic life cycle transition for the next generation. Unresolved issues in earlier phases of the life cycle tend to lead to more difficult transitions and complexities in later life cycle stages. Thus, it is likely that, with Jacob's previous marriages, his mysterious past, the discrepancies in their ages and expectations, as well as their financial precariousness, Jacob and Amalia entered their marriage with many complex issues unresolved.

There are at least two predictable triangles in the genogram of a remarried family: (1) that involving the two new spouses and the previous spouse (or the memory of the previous spouse), and (2) that involving the two new spouses and the children of the previous marriage. We know nothing of Amalia's relationship with Jacob's previous wives. Nor do we know details of her relationship with Emanuel and Philipp. We do know from comments Freud made in his adult life that in his fantasy his mother and Philipp were lovers, and that within 3 years of the marriage Jacob helped to arrange for his sons to emigrate to England, which he may have done partly to put them at a safe distance from his wife.

The Transition to Parenthood and Family With Young Children

A genogram of the early parenting years often reveals stressors that could make this phase difficult. By providing a quick map of the sibling constellation, the genogram may reveal the particular circumstances surrounding the birth of a child and how those circumstances may have contributed to a child's special position in that family. Additionally, the genogram will show the typical mother-father-child triangles of this period.

CHRONOLOGY OF THE FREUD FAMILY, 1856–59

1856   (Feb 21) Schlomo Freud, Jacob's father, dies. (Jacob is 40 and his wife is 6 months pregnant with her first child, Sigmund. Later Jacob will die when Sigmund is 40!)

1856   (May 6) Sigmund is born to Jacob and Amalia in Freiberg, Moravia (now Pribor, in the Czech Republic).

1857   (Oct) Sigmund's brother Julius is born.

1858   (March) Amalia's 20-year-old brother, Julius Nathansohn, dies of tuberculosis.

1858   (April 15) Sigmund's brother Julius dies.

1858   Wilhelm Fleiss, for many years Sigmund Freud's closest friend and "brother," is born. Sigmund identified Fleiss with his brother Julius.

1858   (Dec) Sigmund's sister Anna is born.

1859   (Jan) Sigmund's nursemaid is reported and jailed for theft by Sigmund's half brother Philipp during Amalia's confinement with Anna.

1859   (Aug) Sigmund's half brothers, Emanuel and Philipp, emigrate with their families, including Sigmund's nephew, John, to whom he is very attached.

1859   (Aug) Freud family moves from Freiberg to Leipzig, apparently because of economic reversals.

Sigmund was born in 1856 in Freiberg, Moravia. As can be seen from the genogram of the Freud family for 1859 (Figure 8.2) and the chronology, much was going on in the family around the time of his birth. His specialness for his father may have been intensified by the death of Jacob's father less than three months before Sigmund was born. Sigmund was named for this grandfather, Schlomo, a rabbi. Sigmund was, perhaps, raised to follow in his footsteps to become a kind of rabbi—a teacher and intellectual leader. Sigmund's family role was obviously also influenced by his innate brilliance. Another factor accounting for his special role was probably that he was born at the high point in the family's hopes. Shortly afterward the family had to migrate twice and Jacob suffered significant business failures, from which he seems never to have entirely recovered. Sigmund's younger sisters, particularly Anna and Dolfi, may have borne the brunt of these negative changes on the family.

Figure 8.2 Freud Family (1859)

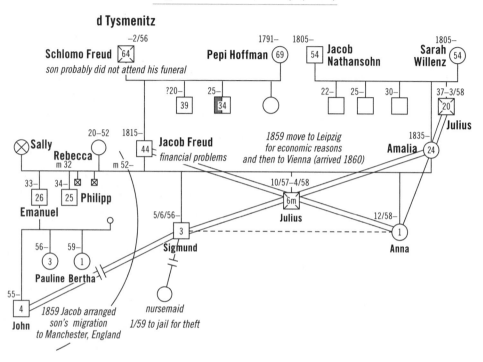

Equally important, Sigmund's brother Julius, born when Sigmund was 17 months old, lived for only 6 months. The death of a child tends to intensify parental feelings about the surviving children. The child nearest in age, especially a child of the same sex, often becomes a replacement for the lost child. Thus, Sigmund may have become even more important to his mother after the death of her second son. The loss of this infant would itself have been intensified by the fact that, exactly a month before his death, Amalia's youngest brother, also named Julius, died at the age of 20 from pulmonary tuberculosis (Krüll, 1986). Undoubtedly she knew that her brother was dying when she named her son for him 6 months earlier. The naming is especially interesting, as it goes against the Jewish custom of naming a baby in honor of someone who has already died. Is the emotional imperative somehow more powerful here than the cultural custom, which had been followed for Sigmund? In later life Sigmund said that he had welcomed this brother with "ill wishes and real infantile jealousy, and his death left the germ of guilt in me" (cited in Krüll, 1986, p. 135).

The oldest sometimes resents the later born, feeling threatened or displaced by the new arrival. From a very early age, Sigmund may have seen his sister Anna as an intrusion, and she may have resented his special position and privileges in the family. She was conceived the month before the loss of the second child, Julius. Discovering she was pregnant at virtually the same moment she experienced the tragic death of her baby must have been intensely difficult for Amalia. Sigmund's sibling rivalry with his sister Anna may have been compounded by family ambivalence about her as the first child born after a lost son. These feelings of rivalry can linger into adulthood. Sigmund's relationship with his sister Anna seems never to have been very close and they were alienated as adults.

The first phase of this new family, of which Sigmund was the first child, finally concluded with a splitting and emigration of part of the family. We do not know really know why the Freud family left Freiberg. When Sigmund was 3, his stepbrothers and their families emigrated to England, and Jacob moved his family first to Leipzig, and then to Vienna, probably in part because of economic reversals. It is possible they had been involved in a counterfeiting scheme, which made escape a necessity (Swales, 1986). Emanuel and Philipp may also have been reminders to Amalia of Jacob's earlier family. And, as mentioned, maybe the possibility of an extramarital relationship between Amalia and Philipp led Jacob to want them at a distance. In any case, Jacob and Amalia shared a nursemaid with Emanuel and his wife, and the children played well together, so their family's departure was a significant loss.

Another complicating factor in terms of the sibling constellation can be seen on the genogram. For the first 3 years of his life, Sigmund was raised almost as a younger brother to his nephew John, who was a year or so older than he. Sigmund commented on the importance of this relationship to Ernest Jones (1953):

Until the end of my third year we had been inseparable; we had loved each other and fought each other and. . . . this childish relationship has determined all my later feelings in intercourse with persons my own age. (p. 8)

Another loss for Sigmund was the nursemaid, who was dismissed for stealing, while Amalia was confined for the birth of Anna. Thus, within a period of only 3 years, Sigmund experienced a multitude of losses: the death of his brother, the dismissal of the nursemaid, the emigration of his stepbrothers and their children, the birth of his sister (which took his mother away), and finally the uprooting of his whole family. The Freuds were never to be financially stable again.

CHRONOLOGY OF THE FREUD FAMILY, 1860s AND 1870s

1860   Freud family settles in Vienna.
1860   (March) Sigmund's sister Rosa is born.
1861   (March) Sigmund's sister Marie (Mitzi) is born.
1862   (July) Sigmund's sister Dolfi is born.
1863   (May) Sigmund's sister Paula is born.
1865   (July 20) Uncle Joseph Freud arrested for counterfeiting.
1865   (Oct) Maternal grandfather (Jacob Nathansohn) dies.
1866   (Feb) Uncle Joseph Freud sent to prison for 10 years.
1866   (April) Sigmund's brother Alexander, named by Sigmund, is born.
1868   Sigmund enters gymnasium.
1873   Sigmund enters medical school.

Sigmund was the first of eight children (Figure 8.3). The genogram shows the family until the year Sigmund finished gymnasium and began medical school.

It is the birth of the first child, more than the marriage itself, that most profoundly marks the transition to a new family. For the new spouse, the child tends to signify greater legitimization and power of the current family in relation to the family of origin. Sigmund definitely seemed to

Figure 8.3 Freud Family (1873)

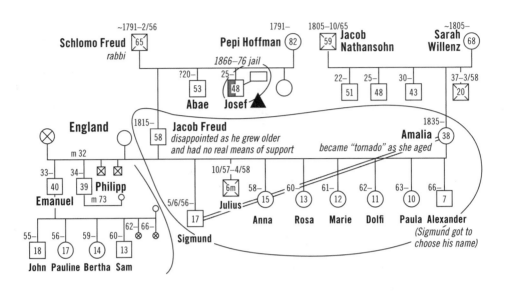

have a special place in his mother's heart. He had an intense relationship with her and she always referred to him as her "Golden Sigi." By all accounts he was the center of the household. There is a well-known family story that when his sister Anna wanted to play the piano, their mother bought one, but got rid of it immediately when Sigmund complained that the noise bothered him. His sister received no further piano lessons. Sigmund's special position is further indicated by the fact that the family gave him the privilege of naming his younger brother, Alexander, born when Sigmund was 10. (In his own marriage, Sigmund named every one of the six children, all for his male heroes or their female relatives!) The Freuds' cultural preference for sons further exalted Sigmund's position in his family.

Family With Adolescents

Once children reach adolescence, the task is to prepare the family for a qualitative change in the relationships between the generations, as the children are no longer so dependent on their parents. During this period two common triangles are likely to develop, the first involving the adolescents, their peers, and their parents, and the second involving the adolescents, their parents, and their grandparents. As adolescents are seeking their identity and emerging into their sexual and creative potential, parents are often struggling with the realization of their own limitations in terms of both work and relationships, which may add to the intensity of intergenerational conflicts.

We have little specific information on family events during the years of Freud's adolescence, but the genogram suggests a family with many child-rearing burdens, as there were seven children, all still in the home. We may wonder also whether the discrepancy in age between Jacob and Amalia might have been felt even more at this stage of the life cycle. Jacob, in his fifties, may have been feeling his age. Sigmund later described his father as having been rather grouchy and disappointed in his older sons Emanuel and Philipp. In contrast, Amalia, 20 years younger, was still energetic, attractive, and youthful. We do not know whether these differences in age, energy level, and outlook led to tension or conflict between Jacob and Amalia, but, given her devotion to Sigmund and the demands of a large household, it is likely that her energies were more focused on her children than on her spouse. Sigmund later reported that he felt as though he had to make up for his father's emotional absence. Jacob's brother Joseph was jailed during this period for counterfeiting, the pain and humiliation of which, Sigmund later said, turned his father's hair gray. It appears that Jacob was implicated in the scheme—or at least Emanuel and Philipp were, which, as mentioned earlier, may have accounted for their earlier move to England (Krüll, 1986; Swales, 1986).

It is during adolescence that children begin to have interests outside the family, both in school and with friends. Sigmund did very well in school and was at the top of his gymnasium class for 6 of his 8 years there. His success with his peers was less spectacular. By all accounts he was a shy, serious young man who focused more on his studies than on socializing. The genogram will sometimes indicate important peers in a child's life and whether family boundaries easily expand to embrace outsiders. We know of Sigmund having only one close friend at school, Eduard Silberstein, with whom he corresponded and formed a "secret society." At

16, he had a crush on a friend's sister, Gisela Fluss, but never expressed his feelings to her. Perhaps he was responding to a mandate from his family to excel in school and to succeed in life and thereby justify his special position in his family and make up for their other disappointments in the older half brothers and in Jacob, who never seems to have made a real living in Vienna.

Family at Midlife: Launching Children and Moving On

The launching phase, when children leave home to be on their own, in the past usually blended into marriage, as children often did not leave home until they married. Now most go through an increasingly lengthy period of being a single adult. This phase, the cornerstone of the modern family life cycle, is crucial for all the other phases that are to follow. The short-circuiting of this phase, or its prolongation, may affect all future life cycle transitions. The genogram often reveals the duration of the launching phase, as well as factors that may contribute to a delay of launching.

The information that we have on the Freud family during the launching phase is quite scanty. As has already been mentioned, Sigmund held an almost exalted position in his family. Sometimes this can lead to difficulties in launching, when a young adult is hesitant to leave such a favored position and the parents are unwilling to let their special child go. This was true for Sigmund, who lived with his parents until he was 30, when he married Martha Bernays and they moved to an apartment together. As was customary, one other daughter, Dolfi, never married and remained at home to be the parental caretaker, as Sigmund's daughter Anna did in the next generation.

One interesting fact from the perspective of the life cycle is how long it took Sigmund to complete his medical studies. He took 8 years to get his degree and did not practice for quite a few years after that. This was unusual in those days, particularly for students who were not independently wealthy. Perhaps he was hesitant to finish and move on to the next phase—supporting himself. Or perhaps he felt that his mother needed him to stay with her. In any case, he, apparently, did not think seriously about supporting himself until he wanted to marry Martha. When a delay in moving on to the next phase is indicated by the genogram, as in

Freud's case with his prolonged time as a student and his lengthy engagement, the clinician should explore the impediments to moving on in the life cycle. In this case they appear to have been both financial and emotional.

CHRONOLOGY OF THE FREUD AND BERNAYS FAMILIES, 1880S

1855   Bernays's oldest son, Isaac, born.

1856   Bernays have miscarriage of second child.

1856   Bernays have a second son.

1857   Bernays have a daughter, who died at 2.

1859   Bernays's second son dies at age 3.

1859   Bernays's baby daughter dies at age 2.

1860   Bernays's son Eli born (who will eventually marry Freud's sister Anna).

1861   Bernays's daughter Martha born (who will eventually marry Freud).

1865   Bernays's youngest daughter Minna is born (who will eventually have an affair with Freud).

1867   Berman Bernays, the father, goes bankrupt and is arrested for fraud.

1868   Berman goes to prison.

1872   Martha's oldest brother, Isaac, who already had many problems, dies at 17.

1873   Sigmund enters medical school.

1879   Berman dies, leaving the family in great debt.

1881   Sigmund completes medical school after 8 years.

1882   (April) Sigmund meets Martha Bernays.

1882   (April) Sigmund destroys his papers and letters just after meeting Martha.

1882   Eli meets Anna.

1882   (June 17) Sigmund and Martha Bernays become secretly engaged.

1883   Minna, Martha's sister, becomes engaged to Ignaz Schonberg, close friend of Sigmund. Ignaz has tuberculosis.

1883   (June) Martha and Minna move with their mother to Hamburg, a move arranged by Eli, probably because of the debts and subsequent embarrassment. Sigmund is very upset by the distance and blames Eli for it.

1883   (Sept) Sigmund's friend, Nathan Weiss, commits suicide.

1883   (Oct) Eli, Martha's brother, marries Sigmund's sister, Anna. Sigmund does not attend or even mention the wedding in letters to Martha.

1884   (July 18) Sigmund becomes involved with cocaine and recommends it to others. He publishes cocaine paper. Evidence suggests that Freud went on using and recommending the use of cocaine until the mid-1890s (Isbister, 1985).

1884   Jacob Freud has business problems.

1885   (April) Sigmund destroys all of his papers again.

1885   (June) Ignaz Schonberg breaks his engagement to Minna.

1886   Schonberg dies of tuberculosis.

1886   (Sept 14) Sigmund and Martha are married, enabled by a gift of money from Martha's aunt.

1887   (Oct) Sigmund and Martha's first child, Mathilda, is born (named for colleague Breuer's wife).

1887   Sigmund meets Wilhelm Fleiss, who becomes his most important and intimate friend until their break in 1904 over an accusation of plagiarism.

Marriage, The Next Generation

Having gone through several transitions of the Freud family life cycle, we come to the next phase: the marriage of Sigmund Freud and Martha Bernays. A genogram of the time of marriage will often provide valuable clues to the difficulties and issues involved in the joining together of two family traditions in a new family.

If we look at the genogram (Figure 8.4) and chronology of the family of Martha Bernays, we see certain striking parallels with the Freud family.

The Bernays, like the Freuds, had to deal with the death of young children, and the oldest surviving son, Eli, was very similar to Sigmund, the oldest surviving son of younger sisters. In 1867, when the children were not even teenagers, the father was arrested and jailed briefly for fraud, bringing disgrace to the family, very similar to the shame Sigmund and his family experienced when their uncle and perhaps father and half brothers were involved in counterfeiting. There may also be a parallel in the previous generation with Freud's maternal grandfather, whose business failed, leaving the family with a sense of ruin and disgrace when Amalia was 18. Similarly, when Martha Bernays was 18, her father, having earlier disgraced the family, died of a heart attack, leaving the family in great debt. Like the Freud family, with Jacob's apparent unemployment in his later years, it is not clear how the Bernays family survived. Martha's older brother, Eli, who took over the running of the family, eventually fled Vienna to avoid bankruptcy and the payment of debts owed to friends. Martha's mother moved with her daughters to Hamburg, which infuriated Sigmund, who had met Martha in 1882 and was secretly engaged 2 months later. We might speculate that the similarities of disgrace and secrets in the background of Sigmund and Martha may have been part of their attraction to one another.

What is immediately apparent from the genogram is the unusual double connection between the Freuds and Bernays in Sigmund's generation. Such unusual configurations often suggest complicated relationships between the two families, as well as possible triangles. The oldest son in each family married the oldest daughter of the other family. As mentioned earlier, Sigmund and his sister Anna never got along. Perhaps Sigmund felt ordinary sibling rivalry of an oldest child with a younger sister. Or perhaps he associated Anna's birth with the losses of his brother Julius, his uncle Julius, his nursemaid, his half brothers, and his cousins. Whatever the reasons, Sigmund seemed to resent the fact that Eli, unlike himself, had the money to marry Anna. Indeed, it appears that Eli's control of a small legacy from Martha's family was at least part of the reason that Sigmund and Martha could not marry sooner (Young-Bruehl, 1988). It was perhaps for these reasons that Sigmund *did not even attend their wedding*. In fact, he did not even mention it in his letters to Martha,

Figure 8.4 Freud Family (1884)

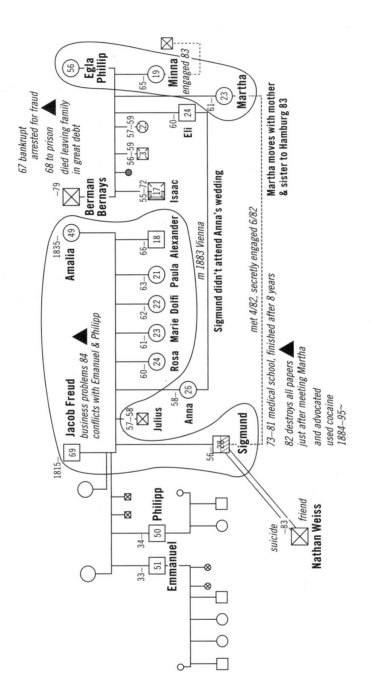

although he wrote to her almost daily and shortly after the wedding discussed the possibility of attending the wedding of one of her cousins, certainly a much less important family event.

Sigmund's negative feelings toward his sister and brother-in-law seemed to intensify later when the couple moved to New York and the less educated Eli became very wealthy whereas the highly educated Sigmund had to struggle to support his family. Triangles were created around the polarization of Eli and Anna's family having money but having materialistic values, whereas Freud and his side of the family eschewed money but thought of themselves intellectually superior.

Triangles emerging at this life cycle stage often involve one partner and the family of the other, and, indeed, such triangling was prominent in this case. Even before their marriage there were difficulties between Sigmund and Martha regarding their families. Both came from families with financial problems, and financial concerns stood in the way of their marrying for more than 5 years. Sigmund blamed Eli for Martha's moving with her mother and sister to Hamburg the year after they were engaged, which meant they had to go for long periods without seeing each other. Freud felt threatened by Martha's relationship to her family of origin and was demanding, possessive, and overtly jealous of her loyalty to her brother Eli. He wrote to her:

> Are you already thinking of the day you are to leave? It is no more than a fortnight now, must not be more or else, yes, or else my egotism will rise up against Mama and Eli-Fritz. And I will make such a din that everyone will hear and you understand, no matter how your filial feelings may rebel against it. From now on you are but a guest in your family like a jewel that I have pawned and that I am going to redeem as soon as I am rich. For has it not been laid down since time immemorial that the woman shall leave father and mother and follow the man she had chosen? (letter to Martha, 8/14/1882, Freud, 1960, p. 23)

Sigmund even threatened to break off their engagement if Martha did not give up her loyalty to her brother, writing to her:

You have only an Either-Or. If you can't be fond enough of me to renounce your family for my sake, then you must lose me, wreck your life and not get much yourself out of your family. (cited in Appignanesi & Forrester, 1992, p. 31)

Nevertheless, throughout their marriage, Martha did maintain contact with other members of her family and remained true to their faith, Orthodox Judaism, despite her husband's rejection of religion. After many years of marriage, she said that Sigmund's refusal to let her light the Sabbath lights from the first Friday night after her marriage was one of the most upsetting experiences of her life (Appignanesi & Forrester, 1992). As soon as Sigmund died, Martha, who was then 68 years old, began again to light the candles every Friday night.

Parenthood, the Next Generation

CHRONOLOGY OF THE FREUD FAMILY, AROUND 1896

1887   First daughter, Mathilda, born (named for wife of colleague, Breuer).

1889   First son, Martin, born. Sigmund named him for his mentor, Charcot.

1891   (Feb) Oliver, the third child, is born (named for Sigmund's hero Oliver Cromwell).

1892   Beginning of Sigmund's estrangement from colleague Breuer.

1892   (April) Ernst, the fourth child, is born (named for Sigmund's teacher Ernst Brucke).

1892   Eli Bernays, Martha's brother, goes to America.

1893   Eli returns to take his wife, Sigmund's sister Anna, and their family to the U.S. (Two daughters, Lucy and Hella, stay with Sigmund's family for a year.) Sigmund gives Eli some money for the trip.

1893   Sophie, Sigmund's fifth child, is born and named for the niece of his teacher Hammerschlag.

1894   Sigmund is having heart problems, but does not tell his wife that he fears dying. He tries to give up smoking. He suffers depression, fatigue, and financial problems.

1895   (Feb) The "Emma Eckstein episode" begins. Sigmund has his friend Fleiss operate on his patient and Fleiss makes a mistake, leaving gauze in the wound, which almost kills her.

1895   (March) Anna is conceived.

1895   Still depressed and having cardiac symptoms, Sigmund treats himself with cocaine. He starts smoking after giving it up for over a year. Fleiss performs a nasal operation on him.

1895   Sigmund decides to begin self-analysis.

1895   Sigmund begins *Interpretation of Dreams*.

1895   (Dec) Anna, the sixth and last child, is born, named for Sigmund's teacher Samuel Hammerschlag's daughter, a young widow and patient of Sigmund's (Anzieu, 1986). Sigmund connects the expansion of his practice with Anna's birth.

1895   (Dec) Martha's sister Minna moves in with the Freud family after having lived with them part-time before that.

1896   Sigmund develops extremely negative feelings about friend and colleague Breuer.

1896   (April) Sigmund writes of migraines, nasal secretions, fears of dying.

1896   (May) Sigmund writes clearest account of seduction theory: belief that women's anxieties are based on actual childhood sexual abuse. His presentation scandalizes his audience.

1896   Medical community isolates Sigmund for his ideas.

1896   Sigmund calls Emma Eckstein's hemorrhages "hysterical."

1896   (Oct 23) Jacob Freud dies. (Sigmund is 40 at the time.) Jacob had been very ill for a month or so. Because Martha was away on her first trip in 10 years to visit her mother, only Minna is there to console Sigmund over the loss of his father.

1897   (Jan) Sigmund is passed over for a university promotion.

1897   (Feb) Sigmund is informed that he will finally be proposed for the title of professor.

1897   (March) Sigmund's disgraced Uncle Joseph dies.

1897   (March) Daughter Mathilda has a very bad case of diphtheria.

1897   (May) Sigmund is again passed over for promotion—becomes anxious.

1897   (May) Sigmund has incestuous dream about daughter Mathilda.

1897   (July) Sigmund takes the first of at least 17 vacations with Minna.

1897   (Sept) Sigmund renounces belief in "seduction theory" (he had thought that his father had an inappropriate sexual relationship with Sigmund's sister Anna). In despondence he feels need for self-analysis; outlines "Oedipal theory."

1897   (Oct 15) Sigmund develops ideas of Oedipus complex.

1898   Sigmund, 42, and Minna, 33, take a 2-week vacation together, registering as a married couple (Blumenthal, 2006).

1899   Sigmund publishes *Interpretation of Dreams*.

1900   End of Sigmund's self-analysis.

1900   Trip with Fleiss ends in falling out that would turn out to be permanent.

1900   Trip with Minna in Italy. Did Minna become pregnant by Sigmund and have an abortion at a clinic? They travel together extensively from September 12, 1900, through mid-February, 1901 (Swales, 1982). Jones said she was treated for tuberculosis, but there is no other mention of her having that illness.

The early years of a family with young children are always eventful, though often difficult for marriages, with so much of the spouses' energy necessarily taken up with their children and work. As can be seen in the chronology and Figure 8.5, Sigmund and Martha married and had six children within 8 years. While Martha handled virtually all parenting responsibilities, Sigmund struggled to enlarge his medical practice and began some of his most creative intellectual work. When a family is in this phase, the clinician should be alert to child-rearing pressures and normative strains in the marriage.

The birth of the last child may be an important turning point in family life. It seems that Martha became very preoccupied with raising her six children, while Sigmund, who was not very involved with the children, became involved with his sister-in-law, Minna, whom he had described in May 1894 in a letter to his friend Fliess as "otherwise my closest confi-

Figure 8.5 Freud Family Immediate Household (1896)

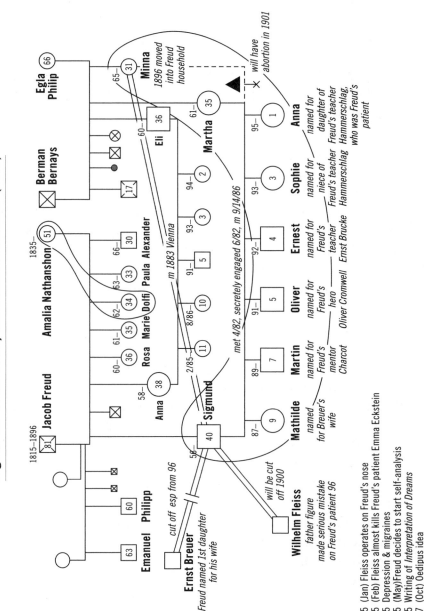

1895 (Jan) Fleiss operates on Freud's nose
1895 (Feb) Fleiss almost kills Freud's patient Emma Eckstein
1895 Depression & migraines
1895 (May)Freud decides to start self-analysis
1895 Writing of *Interpretation of Dreams*
1897 (Oct) Oedipus idea

dante" (Masson, 1985, p. 73). Minna began living in the Freud household the same month that his last and favorite child, Anna, was born. Fourteen years earlier she had been engaged to Sigmund's close friend, Ignaz Schonberg, who had broken off the relationship shortly before his death from tuberculosis. Sigmund's view in that early period was that he and Minna were alike because they were both wild, passionate people who wanted their own way, whereas Ignaz and Martha were good-natured and adaptable (Jones, 1955).

Minna had never married. When other relatives appear as household members on a genogram, we should speculate about the possibility of triangles involving the spouses and the children. Sigmund and Minna had an extremely close relationship in every way. Minna's bedroom in the Freud household could be entered only through the master bedroom (Eissler, 1978). Minna and Sigmund took many vacations alone together (Swales, 1986), ostensibly because they both enjoyed traveling and had so much in common, whereas Martha did not enjoy the same pursuits, at least not at Sigmund's pace (Freeman & Strean, 1981). Minna was much more interested than Martha in discussing Sigmund's ideas. Indeed, Martha said of psychoanalysis: "If I didn't realize how seriously my husband takes his treatments, I should think of psychoanalysis as a form of pornography" (Appignanesi & Forrester, 1992, p. 45). Sigmund and Minna began vacationing together as husband and wife (Blumenthal, 2006; Swales 1986) and Minna later told Jung that she and Sigmund had an affair. There is evidence that she became pregnant and had an abortion in 1901 (Swales, 1986). We know nothing about Martha's attitude toward her husband's relationship with her sister. Interestingly, Sigmund's oldest son, Martin, repeated this pattern and had an extramarital relationship with his wife's sister (Freud, 1988).

Repeating his father's changes at midlife, Sigmund experienced a major life crisis during this phase of the life cycle. In Freud's case it led to his greatest intellectual discoveries and his major formulation, and then recantation, of the seduction theory (Masson, 1992). During these years Sigmund also showed symptoms of depression and "pseudo" cardiac problems. He complained of lethargy, migraines, and various other somatic and emotional concerns. He was clearly in a great deal of distress. He began his famous self-analysis and constructed the edifice of a new theory, which led to the publication of his most famous work, *The Interpretation of Dreams*.

A look at the genogram may elucidate why this was such a turbulent, but productive, time in Sigmund's life. In December 1895, Anna, the last child, was born. Martha, worn out by five pregnancies in 7 years, had been surprised and unhappy to learn that she was pregnant for the sixth time. It seems that after this last child Sigmund and Martha decided not to have another. Sex between the couple apparently diminished considerably from this point (Anzieu, 1986; Roazen, 1993). Anna was conceived exactly at the time of one of Freud's most explosive professional consultations. He referred his patient Emma Eckstein to his friend Wilhelm Fleiss, who believed in operating on people's noses to cure them of sexual problems, which Fleiss thought resulted from masturbation. Fleiss made a mistake during the operation and left gauze in the wound, which almost killed the woman. Freud, whose relations with Fleiss had been extremely intense, experienced a profound sense of disillusionment and distress over this situation.

Often the last child has a special position in the family. This was true of Anna, who was, by the way, named not for Freud's sister but for the daughter of his friend and beloved teacher, Samuel Hammerschlag. This young woman, Anna Hammerschlag Lichtheim, was herself a patient and friend of the Freuds (Krüll, 1986). Anna Freud apparently felt that she was not the preferred child and spent an enormous amount of effort all her life trying to win her father's approval. She, rather than his wife, took care of him when he was ill. He became her analyst, beginning in 1918, when she was 23. She went in his stead to his own mother's funeral for him! She alone among his children never married, devoted herself to her father, and chose to carry on his work.

In 1896, less than a year after Anna was born, Sigmund's father died, a loss Sigmund said was the most significant and upsetting event in a man's life. At the time of his father's death, Martha was away visiting her mother for the first time in many years, and Minna was the only one there to console him, which may have contributed to the affair they then began. The death of a parent marks a critical point in the life cycle and it is not uncommon for people to begin an affair in the wake of a loss. He wrote shortly after his father's death:

> By one of those obscure paths behind official consciousness, the death of the old man has affected me profoundly. . . . His life had been over a long time before he died, but his death seems to have aroused in me memories of all the early days. I now feel quite uprooted. (Masson, 1985, letter of November 2, 1886)

In addition to the loss, a parent's death is a painful reminder of one's own mortality and of the passing of the mantle of tradition and responsibility to the next generation. Now Sigmund had his mother to support as well. In addition, his disgraced uncle Joseph and one of Martha's uncles had died that year.

About this time Sigmund adopted his friend Fleiss as a father figure in his self-analysis, which seems to have reflected his own midlife crisis, perhaps precipitated by a number of events in the family and his own life cycle. In addition to the loss of his father, the birth of his last child, and his affair with Minna, he was having career problems and he had just turned 40. He was struggling to support a large family. Just as the midlife period for Freud's father was marked by a new love relationship, occupational shift, and migration, Sigmund's crisis seemed to involve changing intimate relationships and career upheaval. He was able to resolve it more positively than his father with the consolidation of his career, the publication of his book, his appointment as a professor, and his growing recognition as the founder of a new theory.

Family in Later Life

As members age, families must come to terms with the mortality of the older generation. As each generation moves up a level in the developmental hierarchy, all relationships must be reordered (Shields, King, & Wynne, 1995; Walsh, 1998). There are special problems for women, who are more often the caretakers (Dolfi and Anna) and who tend to outlive their spouses (Freud's mother, Amalia, and wife, Martha). When the last parent dies, the relationships between siblings become independent for the first time. Often the genogram will reveal which child was delegated to become the caretaker of the aging parents, as well as common triangles among siblings over the management of these responsibilities. Sibling conflicts and cutoffs at this point usually reflect triangles with parents that have persisted from much earlier life cycle phases, especially with regard to who was the favored sibling in childhood.

Of course, the particular dynamics of sisters living together and one having an affair with the other's husband would add a major level of complexity to the relationship. We know nothing of Martha's relationship with Minna as the years went on, or even of the level of complicity she may have had in her sister's affair with her husband. She certainly knew they were very close and travelled together frequently, and she must have been part of the sleeping arrangements in their home. As far as is known, the sisters were always cordial, but if one were working clinically, this would be an area for investigation, as it would be for the next generation when Freud's son Martin has an affair with his wife's sister. Such betrayal can seep into relationships years later, involving people who were not even aware of or involved in the original secret and betrayal.

CHRONOLOGY OF THE FREUD FAMILY, AFTER 1900

1902   (March 5) Sigmund becomes Professor Extraordinary.

1909   Daughter Mathilda marries.

1911   Death of half brother Philipp.

1911   Cutoff with Alfred Adler. Sigmund called it "the disgraceful defection of Adler, a gifted thinker but a malicious paranoiac" (letter of Aug 20, 1912 to James Jackson Putnam, quoted in Kerr, 1993, p. 416).

1912   Cutoff with follower William Stekel.

1913   Cutoff with Carl Jung.

1913   Daughter Sophie marries.

1914   First grandchild is born (Ernst Halberstadt, who later became an analyst and changed his name to Ernest Freud).

1914   Death of half brother Emanuel.

1918	Sigmund begins analysis of his daughter Anna, which seems to have lasted at least until 1922.
1919	Important follower, Victor Tausk, commits suicide.
1920	Daughter Sophie contracts pneumonia and dies.
1923	(May) Sigmund is diagnosed with cancer and has first operation.
1923	(June 19) Favorite grandson, Sophie's son, dies of tuberculosis. Sigmund weeps for the first time. He never gets over the loss, which follows so shortly on his own illness.
1923	(Oct 4) Sigmund has a second cancer operation.
1923	(Oct 11) Sigmund undergoes a third operation. Over next 16 years he will undergo more than 33 operations.
1923	Eli dies in New York. Sigmund writes bitterly about his money and suggests that maybe now his sister Anna will do something for her four indigent sisters.
1924	Break with follower Otto Rank.
1924	Rift with Ferenczi.
1926	Theodore Reik is prosecuted for "quackery."
1930	Sigmund's mother, Amalia, dies.
1938	Family is finally able to emigrate.
1939	Sigmund Freud dies in London.

Sigmund's father died in 1896. Amalia was left to be cared for by her children for the next 34 years. Sigmund and his youngest brother, Alexander, took financial responsibility for their mother and sisters, although it was the middle daughter, Dolfi, who remained at home, unmarried, with their mother. Sigmund also lived a long time, to the age of 83 (Color Figure 28), and was cared for by his daughter Anna. Anna became her father's main follower and intellectual heir. Although Martha Freud was still alive (she lived until 1951), it was Anna who became his primary caretaker through his many operations for jaw cancer. For Anna, as for Dolfi in the previous generation, this meant that she was never able to leave home. She was 44 at the time of her father's death. He had been unwilling to function without her for many years. Though she had been briefly in love with her first cousin, Edward Bernays, in 1913, she later said it was good that the relationship had not worked out because, as he was her double cousin, it would have been double incest. She had early dreamt that her father was the king and she the princess and people were trying to separate them by means of political intrigues. She resolved on becoming partners with Dorothy Burlingham, an American mother of four children, who was the youngest of eight daughters of the glass millionaire Louis Comfort Tiffany. Though Dorothy never officially divorced, she and Anna lived and vacationed together for the rest of their lives. Together they ran a war nursery, a psychoanalytic training institute, and a world-famous children's clinic. (Dorothy's husband committed suicide in 1938, having tried in vain to convince her to return to him.)

The genogram may be helpful for understanding or predicting the reactions of family members to key events at different stages of the cycle. For example, Sigmund had a very strong reaction to the death of his 3-year-old grandson in 1923, shortly after he himself was diagnosed with cancer:

> He was indeed an enchanting little fellow, and I myself was aware of never having loved a human being, certainly never a child, so much. . . . I find this loss very hard to bear. I don't think I have ever experienced such grief, perhaps my own sickness contributes to the shock. I worked out of sheer necessity; fundamentally everything has lost its meaning for me. (in Freud, 1960, June 11, 1923)

A month later he wrote that he was suffering from the first real depression of his life (Jones, 1955, p. 92), and 3 years later he wrote to his son-in-law that since this child's death he had not been able to enjoy life:

> I have spent some of the blackest days of my life in sorrowing about the child. At last I have taken hold of myself and can think of him quietly and talk of him without tears. But the comforts of reason have done nothing to help; the only consolation for me is that at my age I would not have seen much of him.

Sigmund's words suggest he was struggling to come to terms with his own mortality. This was particularly difficult not only because his grandson's death was so untimely but also because his daughter, Sophie, the child's mother, had died 3 years earlier at the age of 27.

Contrast this grandson's death with Sigmund's reaction to the death of his own mother 7 years later, in 1930:

> On the surface I can detect only two things: an increase in personal freedom, since it was always a terrifying thought that she might come to hear of my death; and secondly the satisfaction that at least she has achieved the deliverance for which she had earned a right after such a long life. No grief otherwise, such as my ten years younger brother is painfully experiencing. I was not at the funeral. Again Anna represented me as at Frankfort. Her value to me can hardly be heightened. This event has affected me in a curious manner. . . . No pain, no grief, which is probably to be explained by the circumstances, the great age, and the end of the pity we had felt at her helplessness. With that a feeling of liberation, of release, which I think I can understand. I was not allowed to die as long as she was alive, and now I may. Somehow the values of life have notably changed in the deeper layers. (quoted in Jones, 1955, p. 152)

In this case Sigmund, at 74, was more reconciled, through his years of struggling with cancer, with his own eventual death. He was relieved that the sequential order of the life cycle would be honored: the death of parents first, the death of children second. The untimely or traumatic loss of a family member is typically extremely difficult for families to mourn, and therapists are urged to pay especially careful attention to untimely deaths on a genogram and to be alert to dysfunctional patterns that develop in response to such losses (McGoldrick & Walsh, 2004; Walsh & McGoldrick, 2004).

9

Clinical Uses of the Genogram

W E HAVE ONLY BEGUN TO TAP THE CLINICAL POTENTIAL of the genogram. Genograms have been used in many different ways by different therapists—to engage families, to reframe and detoxify family issues, to unblock the system, to clarify family patterns, and to connect families to their history and thus empower them and free them for their future. They also serve as a psychoeducational tool to help families understand their patterns and learn to research their family process. Creating genograms on paper as three-dimensional maps provides a unique chronicle that is in itself a remarkable therapeutic intervention that allows families to view themselves systemically.

Over the past few years there has been a burgeoning of literature on clinical applications of the genogram (see bibliography). A wide range of uses and modifications have been proposed: family sculpting of genograms (Papp, Silverstein, & Carter, 1973; Satir, 1988), cultural genograms (Congress, 1994; Hardy & Laszloffy, 1995), gendergrams (White & Tyson-Rawson, 1995), sexual genograms (Hof & Berman, 1986), genogrids emphasizing the social network developed to facilitate work with lesbians (Burke & Faber, 1997), family play genograms (see Chapter 10), and genograms with many age groups, different symptoms, and life situations (see bibliography). This chapter offers a few suggestions to inspire readers about the rich clinical potential of genograms.

Genogram Interviewing to Engage Families

The genogram interview provides a practical way of engaging the whole family in a systemic approach to treatment (Alexander & Clark, 1998;

Weber & Levine, 1995). We prefer to involve as many relevant family members as possible, so that both the clinician and the family members can see the problem in its familial context.

Genogram interviewing shows interest in the whole family system. The process of mapping family information on the genogram implies that a larger picture of the situation is needed to understand the problem. It conveys a major systemic assumption: that all family members are involved in whatever happens to any member. It also suggests the ongoing connectedness of the family, to both the past and the future.

Equally important, the genogram interview facilitates building rapport with family members by exploring their relationships around key family traditions and issues of specific concern to the family. Genogram questioning goes to the heart of family experiences: birth, love, illness and death, conflict and cutoff. Its structure provides an orienting framework for discussion of the full range of family experiences and for tracking and bringing into focus difficult issues such as illness, loss, and emotionally charged relationships.

Genograms can provide almost instant access to complex, emotionally loaded family material. However, the structure of the genogram interview allows the clinician to elicit such information in a relatively nonthreatening way. Also, the genogram framework helps both the clinician and the family to organize family experiences in ways that can lessen the toxicity of even the most painful traumas by allowing a context for the experiences over time and space and by allowing memory and survival narratives to overcome pain, shame, secrecy, and silence. Casual, matter-of-fact interviewing to complete a family genogram often leads to straightforward giving of information. Even the most guarded person, quite unresponsive to open-ended questions, may be willing to discuss his or her family in this structured format. There is also something impressive about not just gathering information but also displaying it to the family in an organized, graphic way. Cognitive understanding of symptomatic behavior as it relates to emotionally charged relationships can increase the family members' sense of mastery over their situation. Doing a family's genogram becomes a collaborative task that empowers family members, as they are the experts on their own history and the therapist is only the recorder and witness of it. On the other hand, creating a genogram offers the clinician the opportunity to give something back to the family, namely the graphic map of their story. For many families the richness of their history is an important affirmation, no matter what painful elements there may be.

Some clinicians display the genogram to the family on a blackboard, on large notepads, or on a computer. Genograms seem to possess a certain mystique and thus may become an important "hook" for some families. Wachtel (1982) has argued that their power is akin to that of psychological tests, which add weight and credibility to a clinician's inferences about family patterns. I (MM) often give to clients at the end of their first session a printout of the computer-generated genogram that I make during the session. This invites clients' participation in the assessment, as I ask them to correct the genogram for us before the next meeting. They are often amazed and fascinated to see how much information about their history can be organized on a small page in this way.

Dealing With Resistance in the Genogram Interview

When people come in with a problem, they may have a limited view of what is wrong and what needs to be changed. Their view is often a rigid, nonsystemic view based on the belief that only one person, the symptomatic one, needs to change. Any effort to move directly to other problematic areas in the family will often be blocked by vehement denial of other family difficulties. One cannot simply set out to gather all the genogram information in the initial session and ignore the family's agenda for the appointment. Such a single-minded approach would surely alienate the family from treatment. Gathering information for the genogram should be part of a more general and gradual approach of joining with the family and seeking clues about the current problem.

Resistance is often sparked as clinicians touch on painful memories and feelings related to the information being gathered. For instance, if it comes out that a brother died in a car accident, a grandparent committed suicide, or a child was born out of wedlock, various members may seek to redirect the session. "Why open up old wounds," they may ask, "when we know that Joe here is the problem?"

Sometimes, seemingly innocuous questions may provoke an intense reaction. For instance, one client burst into tears after being asked how many siblings he had. The question had stirred up memories of his favorite brother, who had died in a drowning accident. Ostensibly simple questions may also unearth family secrets (Imber Black, 1993, 1998). A question such as "How long have you been married?" may lead to embarrassment or concealment if the couple conceived their first child before marriage. Even questions of geography such as "Where does your son live?" may be sensitive for a parent whose son is in jail, in a psychiatric hospital, or totally out of contact with the parent.

The family's initial concealment of information may often be overcome by careful, sensitive exploration of the situation. Resistance can show up in various ways. It may be direct and vehement, or it may be subterranean, with family members becoming bored, restless, or disruptive (Wachtel, 1982). When meeting repeated resistance to discussion of family history, the clinician may find that focusing on the resistant person for a while proves productive. Allow the person to feel heard. Let him or her know you're still aware of and concerned with the presenting problem. Be reassuring to him or her about where you're going. Let the family know how doing a genogram will help you better understand their present situation and therefore be of assistance.

Sometimes family members are so resistant that you have to forego the genogram interview altogether for a bit. In these instances, as you refocus on the presenting problem, you can still seek to make connections between it and past events and patterns whenever possible. These connections help to remind people of their belonging to something larger than themselves. Constantly demonstrating the relevance of the larger family context to the family members' immediate concerns helps them realize they are not alone. Eventually a family's resistance and concealment of information may be overcome as they begin to see the connections between their concerns and historical family patterns. You can often return to organized questioning for the genogram in subsequent sessions.

The following case of the Rogers family (Figure 9.1), offers an example of a family that began therapy with intense resistance to questioning about their genogram. (Edited segments of this case are available

Figure 9.1 Rogers Family (1994)

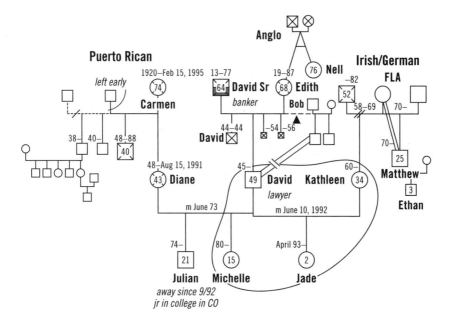

on the videotape *The Legacy of Unresolved Loss*, McGoldrick, 1996, available from www.MulticulturalFamily.org or www.Psychotherapy.net). Their reluctance was gradually overcome through linking the presenting problem to family history on the genogram. In the end, the family members themselves became "researchers" of their own genogram.

Kathleen Rogers, the second wife of David Rogers, made the initial appointment for the family in 1995. The guidance counselor of her 15-year-old stepdaughter, Michelle, referred them for therapy because Michelle had been cutting high school classes and acting out. David, 49, was an attorney from a well-off family of British ancestry. He was resistant and distant although on the surface pleasant and outwardly cooperative. His first wife, Diane, of Puerto Rican background, had died in 1991 of leukemia after a 2-year illness. In their 18-year marriage, they had had two children, Julian, 21, and Michelle, 15. Ten months after Diane's death, David married Kathleen, 14 years his junior, a woman of Irish-German background who had never been married before. She was now a full-time homemaker and mother of a 2-year-old, Jade. Kathleen's parents divorced in 1969, when she was 9. Her mother remarried the next year and had a son, Matthew, who became the favored child. Thus Kathleen, like her stepdaughter, felt "on the outside" of a reconfigured family in her generation. Kathleen was basically out of contact with everyone in her family of origin at the start of therapy. She had never even seen her 3-year-old nephew, Ethan. Her father, who had a bar in Brooklyn, died in 1982 of a heart attack.

Michelle was the one with most contact with the Puerto Rican side of her family. She had gone with her mother and brother to Puerto Rico during the summers for many years and, when she was 11, she went alone, ostensibly to help her ailing maternal grandmother, Carmen, but really their intention was to protect Michelle from the "sadness" of her mother's illness and death. Her brother, Julian, was allowed to stay home because the father thought that at age 17 he could better handle his mother's grave condition.

In the initial session the parents were clear that they wanted to solve Michelle's problem: her acting out in school, hanging out with the "wrong" friends, and having a "chip on her shoulder." Neither parent believed that the presenting problem had any connection to unresolved mourning for her mother or to the recent death of her maternal grandmother, Carmen, which had coincided with Michelle's behavioral change. Indeed, I (MM) learned in the course of therapy that Michelle was not brought home from Puerto Rico for her mother's funeral in 1991, nor was she told about her grandmother's death until it was mentioned casually days later. When I tried to gather genogram information during the first session, the father became actively hostile and said I was wasting their time. He considered information about his own family completely irrelevant, including the fact that his father died of sclerosis of the liver (which he did not think was related to alcohol abuse) or that his name, David, had first been given to an older son, who died in infancy. Kathleen was even more negative about questions regarding her family, whose constellation was almost identical to the current family pattern.

Gradually, I was able to help the father listen to his daughter Michelle's feelings of closeness to both her mother and grandmother and review the family genogram history with both his daughter and son, who returned from college for a session in which he expressed pain that the mother's death had never been discussed and that the father had remarried so quickly. David was asked to take his children to their mother's grave for the first time, and gradually he began to confront other losses in his own life, which he had also suppressed. Initially he had presented his own childhood as happy and uneventful, but eventually it came out that his parents had almost cut him off when he "married down" to a Puerto Rican. After months of therapy he finally agreed to try to learn more about his history from his only living relative, his Aunt Nell. He made a trip to his hometown to visit this aunt, his mother's identical twin sister, whom he had not seen since his mother's funeral 8 years earlier. He appeared at the next session more animated than ever before, carrying his mother's photograph albums and diaries, lent to him by his aunt. Through this information he was able to get in touch with his parents' difficulties and some of his own childhood pain for the first time. He uncovered two "secrets"—one about his father's drinking and the other about an affair his mother apparently had with the father's best friend. When the affair came to light, relations between the two families, who had been very close for years, abruptly ended, resulting in the loss of David's best childhood friend as well as his father's only real friendship. As David learned about his history, he began to connect with his feelings on a deeper level and to become more responsive to both his daughter and his second wife, who previously had to bear all the feelings in the family without any of the power necessary to make things change.

In this case it was possible to press on, in spite of the family's resistance, to get the basic genogram information, and then to proceed through the family member (Michelle) who most realized its relevance, to make connections for others. Occasionally family members are so resistant to discussions of genogram information that we have to leave the subject until we find some way of engaging them. In situations when we have eventually succeeded in building a relationship with the family, we find that the resistance comes specifically from anxiety and fears about family experiences embedded in the genogram—for example, the stigma of a parent who committed suicide or was in a mental hospital.

Of course, there are times when people's discussion of their history becomes an avoidance of taking appropriate action in the present, and this must be challenged, as when a parent tries to sidestep the immediate needs of children or to avoid dealing with alcohol or drug abuse by sidetracking discussion to the genogram (or anything else, for that matter!).

The genogram can be useful in working with such rigid systems. The genogram interview organizes questioning around key family life experiences: birth, marriage, life transitions, illness, and death. Collecting information on these events can open up a rigid family system and help clients get in touch with paralyzing blocked emotional and interpersonal issues.

For example, the Carusos, an Italian family, were referred for consultation by their lawyer, who hoped the referral would influence the court case of the oldest of their three sons, John, who had been arrested for selling drugs (Figure 9.2).

Initially the family presented a united front: They were a close, loving family whose son had come under the influence of "bad friends." They denied the seriousness of his crime, offered little factual information, and minimized any relationship problems, but they said they were willing to

Figure 9.2 Caruso Family

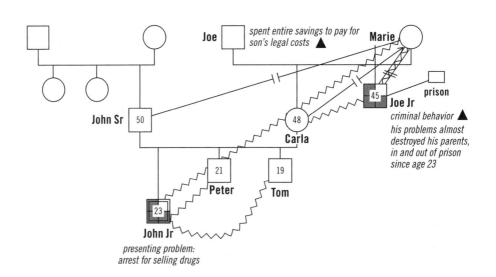

do anything to help. Few connections were apparent in gathering the basic genogram information until we got to the question of the whereabouts of the maternal uncle. The mother, Carla Caruso said that she did not know where her brother was but then admitted that he was in jail and had many previous arrests. This led to questioning about the maternal grandmother's reaction to John's problem, at which point the family's united front began to break down. The parents reluctantly admitted that they had stopped talking to the maternal grandmother since John's arrest because of her "insensitive" response: "Let him rot in jail." Carla's parents had taken a second mortgage on their house to pay their son's bail and legal fees. Carla said she had always, until then, been very close to her mother, but now viewed her mother as "disloyal." Further detailed questioning about the family history led to the information that Carla's brother had first been arrested at age 23 (John's present age). The maternal grandfather had, against the grandmother's wishes, spent all the family savings repeatedly bailing his son out of trouble, and she was now very bitter that her son had brought almost total ruin on her family. It was only through discussing the details of the uncle's criminal behavior, a family secret that John and his brothers did not know, that the family's "cool" about their present situation was broken. Carla talked about her pain in watching her own mother's agony over the years, as well as her own fury at her brother for the shame he had brought on the family. She was desperately afraid of reliving her parents' experience but feared that discussing the matter with her mother would confirm that the family was "doomed" to repeat the past, so she had stopped talking to her mother. As we spoke, John's brothers opened up for the first time in the interview, expressing their resentment toward their brother for putting the family in the terrible position of having to decide whether to put their life savings on the line or let him go to jail. The father, who had been the most adamant in denying any family difficulties, talked about his sense of betrayal and failure that his son had so cut him off. It was only through the leverage of the previous family experiences that the family's present conflicts became evident.

In their attempt to avoid dealing with painful past experiences and unresolved emotional issues, families often rigidify their relationships and view of themselves. Calm, nonthreatening, "research" questions often open up these matters, so that family members can begin to relate to one another in ways that open up new possibilities for the family. The genogram interview is especially useful for engaging obsessive, unresponsive, or uninvolved clients. Obsessive clients who may otherwise dwell on the endless details often come quickly to emotionally loaded and significant material during a genogram interview. Unresponsive family members may find themselves more engaged as their family story is revealed.

Probably the issue around which families become blocked more often than any other is loss (see Loss section in bibliography). Norman and Betty Paul (1986) led the way in the use of genograms to unblock the family system by focusing on losses in the multigenerational family. The meaning of symptoms is expanded by involving the clients in an explanation of deaths or life-threatening experiences in either the immediate or extended family. In the Pauls' view, the distortion and "forgetting" in family members' perceptions that occur around loss are among the most important influences on symptom development. They routinely sent genogram forms to prospective clients to be completed before the first session; this provides important information about how the clients orient themselves to their original family. In the first session the Pauls would carefully track the dates of birth and death and the causes of death of family members for the past three generations. In their experience, clients usually indicate some degree of mystification about doing their genograms, until they begin to see the hidden connections.

The Pauls' (1986) in-depth study of one such couple in *A Marital Puzzle* illustrated a case in which the husband was asked to bring genogram information to the first therapy session. He left off the chart the fact that both of his parents had died, although he was specifically asked for it; when questioned, he said he did not remember exactly when they had died. The Pauls' therapeutic model focused attention on the importance of rediscovering such dissociated family experiences. Some years ago we developed family forms that asked for genogram information in multiple ways, including asking for the dates of death of the grandparents in three different sections. The respondents frequently gave different dates each time, indicating how charged the issue of death is.

Clarifying Family Patterns

Clarifying family patterns is at the heart of genogram usage. As we collect information to complete the genogram, we are constantly constructing and revising hypotheses based on our ongoing understanding of the family. We usually discuss our observations with the family and offer these observations as tentative hypotheses that the family may elaborate or revise as we jointly explore the family history.

The Caruso family discussed earlier illustrates how the genogram can become a guide to understanding patterns for both family and therapist, clarifying the present dilemma in ways that open up possibilities for alternative behavior in the future. From the genogram, we could see a pattern of repetition of criminal behavior. Then, as the connection was made between the son's and the uncle's criminal behavior and the possibility of the family history being repeated was pointed out, the family began to look at the son's behavior within the family context and to explore the legacy and conflicts that were perpetuating the behavior. They could also concentrate their efforts on changing the pattern.

Clarifying genogram patterns serves an important educational function for family members, allowing them to see their lives and behavior as connected to family history. In addition, dysfunctional behavior is often eliminated once the family patterns that underlie it are clarified.

Reframing and Detoxifying Family Issues

Families develop their own particular ways of viewing themselves. When there are many problems, family members' perspectives may often rigidify and become resistant to change. Genograms are an important tool for reframing behavior, relationships, and time connections in the family, as well as for "detoxifying" and normalizing the family's perception of itself. Suggesting alternative interpretations of the family's experience points the way to new possibilities in the future.

The genogram interview allows the clinician many opportunities to normalize the family members' understanding of their situation. Simply bringing up an issue or putting it in a more normative perspective can often "detoxify" it. Using information gathered on the genogram, the clinician can also actively reframe the meaning of behavior in the family system, enabling family members to see themselves in a different way (Bowen, 1978; Carter & McGoldrick, 2005b; Gerson, Hoffman, Sauls, & Ulrichi, 1995; Shellenberger & Hoffman, 1998). The family structure suggests normative expectations for behavior and relationships (e.g., "It's not surprising you're so responsible because oldest children commonly are," or, "Usually two youngest who marry tend to wait for each other to take care of them. How did it go with you?"). Similarly, an understanding of life cycle fit can provide a normalizing experience (e.g., "People who marry as late as you did may be pretty set in their ways. Was that true for you?"). Pattern repetition and the coincidence of events show the larger context of problematic behavior (e.g., "Perhaps your feelings had something to do with all the stressful events that were occurring at the time?"). And relational patterns and family balance help demonstrate the interdependency of family members (e.g., "Most people react that way when they are the 'odd person out,'" or, "Usually, when one person takes on more than her share of responsibility, the other person takes on less").

Bowen was a master at detoxifying reactive responses with genogram questioning. Here is an example, in the following excerpt of an interview by Bowen of a man who felt intimidated by his "domineering, possessive mother":

Bowen: What are the problems of being the only child of an only-child mother?

Client: My mother was a very domineering woman who never wanted to let go of anything she possessed, including me.

Bowen: Well, if you're the only one, wouldn't that be sort of predictable? Often in a relationship like that, people can with some accuracy know what the other thinks. . . . In other words, you're describing a sort of an intense relationship, and not too unusual with a mother and an only son, especially a mother who doesn't have a husband, and your mother was an only. How would you characterize your mother's relationship with her mother?

Here Bowen used discussion of the family structure to normalize a mother's behavior and the special mother-child bond of an only child. Bowen therapy is characterized throughout by such tracking, detoxifying, and reframing of multigenerational family patterns.

Using Genograms to Design Interventions

Family therapists with a Bowen systemic approach have been using genograms for many years as the primary tool for assessment and for designing therapeutic interventions. More recently, therapists with different approaches have come to use the genogram for recordkeeping, assessing families, and designing strategic interventions.

Wachtel (1982) suggested using the genogram as a "quasi-projective technique" in family therapy, revealing unarticulated fears, wishes, and values of the individuals in the family. She described using about four hour-long sessions to complete a genogram on a marital couple. After getting the basic "factual data," she would ask the spouses for a list of adjectives to describe each family member, and then for stories to illustrate the adjectives used. Keeping track of the conceptions the spouses have about various family members and how these conceptions are passed down from one generation to another, she could then investigate the spouses' conception of the relationships between people, commenting throughout "on emerging family issues, patterns, and assumptions and their possible relevance to the current situation" (Wachtel, p. 342). Differences of opinion become grist for the mill of therapy, and spouses are urged to seek missing genogram information between sessions.

Clinicians employing a strategic approach have come to use the genogram not only for recordkeeping and family assessment, but also as a map for designing strategic interventions. Pointing out why a family needs to be the way it is and what problems could arise through change sometimes paradoxically leads to change. Genogram patterns are used in this therapeutic model first to convey a positive understanding of the present dysfunctional situation, thus paradoxically challenging the rigidity of the present stabilization. As change does occur, genogram information is again used to reinforce emerging patterns and to underline the normative evolution of the family.

The use of genograms in therapy can be an important way to counter the invalidation that recent immigrants and families of color experience in most institutional settings, allowing families respectful acknowledgment of their history and helping them translate adaptive strategies they used in other contexts to solve current problems (Boyd-Franklin, 2006; Hines, 2005; McGoldrick, Giordano, & Garcia-Preto, 2005). In general, in our "solution focused" society, the history of oppressed groups gets suppressed as a way of keeping the dominant groups in place. As Morales (p. 13) said, "Memory, individual and collective, is a significant site of social struggle. . . . The stories of the abused are full of dangerous, subversive revelations that undermine the whole fabric of inequality." Thus, helping families tell their personal and cultural stories is an important part of both personal and social liberation from the constraints of oppression.

For example, we worked with a client, Ahmed, and his Muslim family, who had immigrated from Jordan to the U.S. in 1978 (Figure 9.3). Ahmed was a steady worker as a machinist, but he had a history of abusing his wife and daughters. The family members were living separately—the daughters in a foster home, the mother in the family apartment, and the father with his brother—after several restraining orders had been placed on him.

The treatment program in which Ahmed was involved worked at multiple levels to support him as a person to take responsibility for his behavior (Almeida, Messineo, Woods, & Font, 1998). To foster Ahmed's support system, we explored his history through his genogram, an exploration we did in part with his brother, Mohamed, with whom he had been staying. The discussion focused on his place within his family and his family's traumatic history. Initially both brothers seemed to experience the genogram questioning as a waste of time, in part because there was such a large family—13 siblings, 14 aunts and uncles, and 35 nieces and nephews to talk about. But as they got into the discussion of family members, the people on their genogram and their significance became "real," particularly for Ahmed, who had had many experiences of loss. Not only did it turn out that his birth was surrounded by the loss of three siblings, but the

Figure 9.3 Ahmed's Family

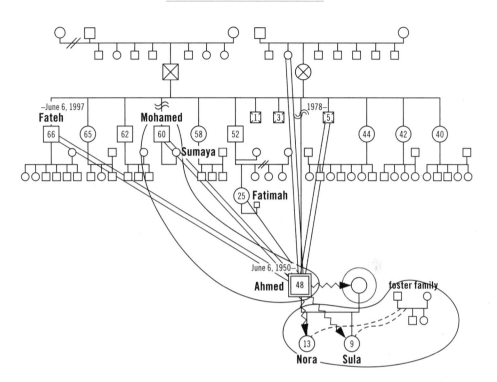

oldest brother, Fateh, had died the previous year on Ahmed's birthday, while visiting, "because his heart was so big from loving that it burst." Doing the genogram also brought Ahmed to tears when he remembered how he had loved the brother closest to him in age who had died in childhood of polio. These critical aspects of Ahmed's "belonging" in his history became threads in his treatment, helping him to feel his own resourcefulness as he sought the inner strength to do the right thing for his wife and children, with the support of others in his treatment community (Almeida et al., 1998). Indeed, during that session we learned that one of their nieces, Fatimah, a practicing Muslim and a feminist, was living in a neighboring town. She became an important resource and ally in the therapy, bridging relationships between Ahmed, his wife, and his daughters.

Using Genograms to Transform Current Relationships

A major therapeutic task is to empower clients to bear witness to their own and each other's losses and to develop a sense of survivorship, meaning, mastery, and continuity. Families often need help in expanding their view of themselves and their history in context—to see the continuity of their experience with their ancestors, as well as current family and community, and realize their connection to those who will come after them. Many forces at work in our society deprive people of their sense of continuity. Reversing this puts not just the death, but also their whole lives, in better perspective, strengthening them for their shared future.

We have found that relatively simple interventions aimed at connecting family members in the present and with their past losses may make a considerable difference to their sense of themselves and therefore to their resourcefulness in managing their future. The Chen family brought this home to us in a striking way (Figure 9.4).

They were referred because Mark, the 14-year-old son, had been involved with drugs and was "acting out" at school. The school had previ-

Figure 9.4 Chen Family

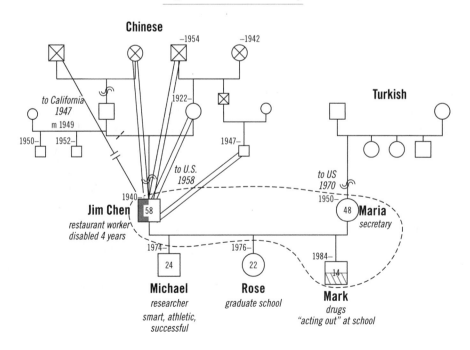

ously referred the family to various drug treatment facilities several times. They described the parents as noncompliant with therapy and unable to set effective limits on their son, who was seen as a very bad influence in the school system.

Mr. Chen, a 58-year-old restaurant worker who had been disabled 4 years ago with a back injury, immigrated from China at the age of 18. He met his wife, who immigrated from Turkey at age 20, in the U.S. The couple had very successfully raised their two older children, who were close in age and much older than Mark. The oldest, Michael, finished college at age 19 and was doing professional research at a nearby university. Their daughter, Rose, was in graduate school in a nearby city. Mark was 10 when the father hurt his back and became disabled and unable to function as a restaurant worker. Since that time the father had felt a powerful sense of inadequacy as a parent, a role about which he had a deep sense of responsibility.

Inquiring about the family's history in relation to the son's drug abuse and acting out, we became convinced that the parents had, in fact, complied with all that had been requested of them but had not connected to Al-Anon or other programs they were referred to because they could not make any sense of the concept of "detachment" from their son regarding his drug abuse; they felt the school was blaming them for failing to do something they didn't know how to do. They had been taking Mark for regular drug screenings, and he had been clean for over a month, but the school was still negative to him and wanted him to leave the school.

When we began to do the family's genogram, the father became very tearful about his own father, who had died the year before he married. Taking this into consideration, we decided to construct a ritual based on the family's genogram history to empower them in the present in relation to their survival history. We were not sure how the father's pain over his own father's death was connected to the present situation, but his obvious emotion about his father made clear that there was some connection. The father, mother, and Mark were all asked to write letters to the dead grandfather, in the hope that this could bring relationship patterns from the genogram into the present relationships. The following week all three read their letters, excerpted here:

The Father's Letter

Dear Father:

I think about writing to you all the time. I often think of you in the dim light of evening, which brings me back my memories of my childhood. Many kids have their golden childhood years. I never enjoyed what I experienced. Instead there was war, hunger and loneliness. I didn't have a chance to attend school. Worst of all, no father to guide me. All these memories will remain forever in my heart and mind. They cause me such grief, all I can do is cry. My heart is bound by a rope that chokes it. I feel such heartache. There are so many questions that I want to ask you. You are a husband and a father. Have you yet fulfilled your duty to your wife and your children? When I was in China we sent you many letters, but never once did we receive word from you. My mother took care of me, when I was a child. She worked hard and made little money, but she did the best she could to raise me. I heard from my uncle that she had a chance to remarry, but, because I was so young, she didn't want me to have a stepfather. My mother was bound by tradition, which would never allow her to remarry, so you ruined her whole life.

You had a farm in which you took special care of all the seedlings and vegetables and they grew. You took care that all the buds growing in the greenhouse were strong enough, before you took them out to plant them. When you planted them out in the field, you made sure there were no weeds, before you planted your vegetables. You fertilized, watered and cared for your vegetables very, very carefully. You worried that they would not grow.

I also am your seed. How come you didn't take such good care of me? I wanted to go to school—to have a good education, just as you took care of vegetables, which need fertilizer and water. You make sure that vegetables grow with no weeds to block their growing. I too needed this type of nourishment in the farm of education. Do you agree with me? You never gave me a chance to have a decent education. When I came to the United States, I told you all of this. But your heart was made of iron. You said to me: "You are 18 years old. I have brought you here so you could provide for your mother and your nephew." From such a young age I carried such a heavy burden to take care of my family alone. Do you believe that the way you treat your family is right? Do you feel ashamed of yourself? It's a quiet night. Please think about it. I have very little left to say, so I shall end here. I wish you good health. At last I can tell you that now I am married, with three children of my own. I am a good husband and a good father, not only to provide my family with food and shelter but I also to make sure that my children get as much from their education as they can. I love my children and there's nothing I would not do for any one of them.

Your son,

Jim Chen

Mark's Letter

Dear Grandfather:

How are you? All I can say is that you were pretty "beeped" up, but I can't really hate you for treating my father like that. I can't really say that I like you either, since I have never met you in my life. But from what I have heard of you, I guess you didn't care about my dad, your son. Well, I have to go.

Peace,

your grandson

The Wife's Letter

Dear Father-in-Law:

I didn't meet you because you were dead before I married your son. But I know all about you and how you treated my husband and my mother-in-law. I feel hurt for them, especially for Jimmy. I can imagine how sad he felt through that period of time. Even though he did not have a normal childhood like other kids had, because of you, he always told me that he forgives you. He has always believed in forgiveness, love, and peace. You caused him and his family much pain; he worked to help his mother, sister-in-law, and nephew, so they could live well. He always told me that he never regretted that. He never saw them as a burden. After we married he still sent his aunt money for her needs as well as for our nephew. How could you as a father treat your son like this? But Jimmy was lucky. He had wonderful uncles and a wonderful grandfather. Jimmy used his grandfather to learn the most from. Today Jimmy is not like you, but like his wonderful grandfather. He always remembers his grandfather with love—he was very firm, but at the same time treated him with affection and love. My husband treats his children just like his grandfather. I am proud of him and I tell my children how lucky they are. They have a wonderful father who is always there for them and any of their needs.

Prior to reading the letter the son had been bored, turning in his chair, uninterested in the conversation. Following the letters, we were able to mobilize the family to work with us and the school to keep the son engaged, involved at home, and participating in school without further disruption.

In this case the genogram helped to empower a nuclear family in relation to their history, which had become disrupted and cut off. Rituals that enable family members to come together to bear witness to their history, however painful, can be a great resource and source of resilience.

Interventions in Family Medicine

The following illustrations show how a genogram can be used in medical treatment. The first illustrates the importance of gathering information in the initial interview.

A 28-year-old chemical engineer, Ty Anderson, sought help at a local family practice center for stomach pains in August 2007 (Figure 9.5). As was done for all new patients prior to the doctor-patient encounter, the nurse drew a genogram for Anderson. Working from the genogram, the doctor began her assessment by trying to put the patient's stomach pain in context. She noted that this was a particularly difficult time for Mr. Anderson and hypothesized that recent family events might have had a stressful impact on him and his family. The patient and his second wife, Rita, were in the midst of several major transitions. They had moved 6 months earlier and were expecting their first child in 5 months. In addi-

Figure 9.5 Ty Anderson (2007)

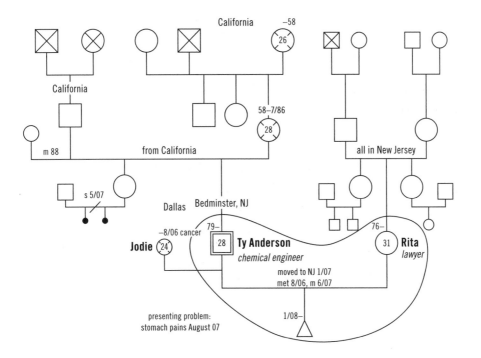

tion, the patient's sister and her husband had recently separated, an event that would probably reverberate throughout the family system.

The genogram reflects a number of temporal connections, anniversary reactions, and repetitive patterns that might exacerbate the stress of the upcoming events for Mr. Anderson. His first wife had died of cancer in August 2006, and thus he might be having an anniversary reaction. There is a repetitive pattern of early female death: His mother, his maternal grandmother, and his first wife all died in their twenties, which might make him acutely sensitive to the physical vulnerability of women. It seemed likely that he would be particularly worried about his wife's upcoming childbirth, especially because his maternal grandmother had died in childbirth and his sister had two miscarriages before her recent separation. Because Mr. Anderson and his mother occupied similar sibling positions (both were youngests), the physician speculated that he might have identified with his mother and might now fear dying himself, as he was the same age as she was when she died. The physician also noted the timing of the couple's marriage. Mr. Anderson met his current wife a week after his first wife's funeral and they were married within a year. Given the short transition period, the physician wondered whether Mr. Anderson had dealt with his grief related to his first wife's death and hypothesized a hidden triangle in which the present wife was in some ways the outsider to the unresolved relationship with his first wife.

Finally, looking at the level of support in the family, it was evident that Mr. Anderson had no family in the area, whereas his wife's parents and all her siblings were nearby, which, perhaps, left the couple with an imbalance in emotional resources. During a brief discussion of these family factors, Mr. Anderson was able to admit his fears about the pregnancy, as well as continuing thoughts of his first wife, about which he felt guilty. He accepted a referral for consultation with a family therapist. Physical examination did indicate that he was suffering from gastroesophageal reflux, probably exacerbated by his emotional state. Medication was prescribed. The patient was asked to bring his wife along to his followup visit 2 weeks later. By that time he had gone for the consultation with the family therapist and his symptoms had disappeared. He and his wife were apparently doing a good deal of talking about his past experiences and he was feeling much better psychologically as well as physically.

In this case the genogram interview identified a number of psychosocial stressors that needed to be dealt with and the referral began the process, easing the pressure on Mr. Anderson and his family. The genogram allowed the physician the opportunity to practice preventive healthcare.

The next example illustrates a more complex case, in which the response to genogram information was less immediate.

Dan Rogoski, a 49-year-old insurance salesman, went to see his physician complaining of heart palpitations. The doctor could find no evidence of any organic dysfunction, so he checked the genogram in the patient's chart. He could see from the genogram that the patient's father died of a heart attack, his mother suffered multiple heart attacks and strokes, and he had a sick sister and a deceased brother. The doctor decided he needed to find out more about Mr. Rogoski's family history and asked more questions to fill in the genogram (Figure 9.6).

The physician noted from the genogram inquiry a number of family events that might be affecting the patient. Rogoski's son, Erik, who had many behavioral and drug problems before joining the navy, was due to return home shortly; perhaps he was worried about this son's problems starting again. His ex-wife's mother had recently died, which would be likely to increase her distress and could lead to an increase in her drinking, which was already out of hand. This, in turn, would probably add stress to both sons, who would be living with her. Mr. Rogoski's sister, who suffered from multiple sclerosis, was also deteriorating. She lived with their mother, who had just turned 68 and might soon be unable to care for the sister. As the only healthy sibling, Mr. Rogoski felt responsible for his sister's care. He might also fear his own vulnerability to disease, because of the illness of both siblings.

The physician noted also that Dan was now the same age as his father when he had died of a heart attack. His youngest son was 20, the age he

Figure 9.6 Rogoski Family (2006)

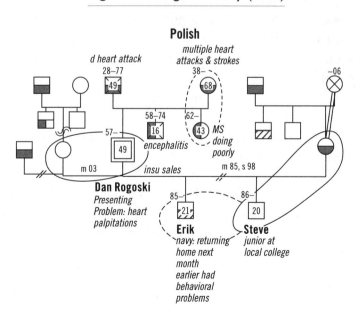

had been at the time the father died. Perhaps Dan feared that history would repeat itself.

Finally, there was the pattern of drinking in the family. Both of his parents had drinking problems, as did his son, his first wife, and the families of both of his wives. Based on this history, it was possible that Mr. Rogoski had a drinking problem or that someone in his family thought he did.

From the genogram information, the physician was able to ask Mr. Rogoski about each of these areas of concern: his son's coming home, his ex-wife, his sister's dysfunction, his being the same age as his father when he died, and his drinking. Although the patient admitted to some general concern in each of these areas except drinking, he was sure they had no bearing on his physical state, saying he never let things like that get to him. As for the drinking, he admitted, when asked, that his wife thought he drank too much, but that was just because her father and her first husband were alcoholics and she was too sensitive. This answer, of course, raised more questions about the extent and nature of his drinking and about his relationship with his wife. Although physical findings were negative, the physician decided, on the basis of the information gathered here and the patient's response, to request a follow-up visit with both Mr. and Mrs. Rogoski 2 weeks later, "just to see how the heart was doing."

At the follow-up meeting the family stresses were reviewed and Mrs. Rogoski confirmed her worries about her husband's anxiety and drinking. The doctor mentioned the possibility of their going to AA or Al-Anon or to therapy, but the idea was immediately rejected by both spouses. However, a month later Mrs. Rogoski called back, saying that she felt the tension had not diminished and she would now like the name of a therapist they could consult. The doctor again suggested that she could attend Al-Anon, but she refused, although she did take the name of a local therapist. At medical follow-up 6 months later, Mr. Rogoski proudly announced that he had celebrated his 50th birthday and felt very relieved and healthy. He said he had been trying to deal with his ex-wife about their son Erik, who seemed not to be getting on his feet after leaving the navy and was drinking too much.

Although neither Mr. Rogoski nor his wife responded immediately to the doctor's observations about the family situation, the genogram helped the doctor to assess the family stress and relationship factors and gradually he became an important resource for the spouses at a later point when they could respond. They will undoubtedly need to turn to him again in the future. Having the genogram in the chart will make it easier for him to keep track of ongoing changes, particularly for the son Erik, for Mr. Rogoski's sister as she needs more support, as the conflicts between Mr. Rogoski and his ex-wife abate or continue, and if tension with the present wife over alcohol abuse resurfaces.

There are indications that when one member of a family is in distress, others will react as well (Huygen, 1982; Widmer Cadoret & North, 1980). In this case, by recognizing the multiple stresses Mr. Rogoski was experiencing, the physician became aware of the need to bring in Mrs. Rogoski as well, to evaluate her response and ability to support her husband and to at least plant the seed that other help was available for them if they should want to use it. This probably made it easier for Mrs. Rogoski to seek the referral later, as her doctor was already familiar with the situation and had himself suggested a source of help for them.

Genogram assessment in medical practice can suggest which family patterns are repeating, so that preventive measures can be taken; what resources the patient has to help with an illness; what problems there may be in medical compliance; what family stresses may be intensifying the difficulty; and what further psychosocial intervention might be needed, such as including others in follow-up medical visits or making outside referrals.

Family Patterns, Significant Events, Concurrent Life Stresses, and Cultural Issues

The Montessinos-Nolan family genogram (Figure 9.7) illustrates a family in which there were extremes of success and failure, health and illness, and serious triangulating for several generations. The family sought help because they (especially the mother) had concluded that behavior of the middle daughter, Barbara, was out of control. The genogram was created over the first couple of sessions and included a family sculpting to illustrate the alliances and triangles. This provided a quick visual map of many family factors that might be playing a role in the current stress.

Figure 9.7 Montessinos-Nolan Family (2003)

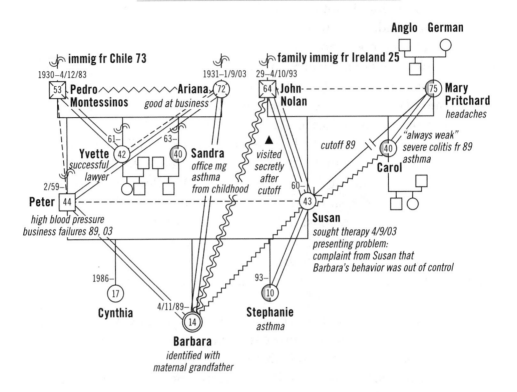

NONCOMPLEMENTARY SIBLING POSITIONS OF THE PARENTS

- Both Peter and Susan were oldest children who appeared to be in a struggle for control (as is typical in marriages of two oldest siblings; see Chapter 5).

ANNIVERSARY REACTIONS

- Both grandfathers' deaths occurred within a day of Barbara's birthday (the paternal grandfather before she was born and the maternal grandfather when she was 4), which coincided also with the time when the family applied for treatment. The maternal grandfather had been very close to Susan from her birth, visiting her on the sly after his wife refused to talk to the family at all.
- Peter's family migrated from Chile when he was 14, the same age that Barbara was now.

- Susan's cutoff with her mother and the illness of her sister Carol both occurred the same year as Barbara's birth.
- In addition to all these stresses, Peter's business failed the year Barbara was born, and he had again just lost his job.

MULTIGENERATIONAL TRIANGLES
- In the immediate family, Barbara had a close relationship with her father and a hostile relationship with her mother. The parents had a distant relationship.
- The mother in her own family of origin also had a close relationship with her father, was cut off from her mother, and had parents who were distant.
- The father in his family of origin had a close relationship with his mother and a distant relationship with his father, and the parents' relationship was hostile.
- Peter's middle sister, Yvette, appears in a parallel but converse triangle: close to her father and distant from her mother, which would make it likely that she would have conflicts with her brother, although so far the siblings had remained very close.

THE CONCURRENCE OF LIFE STRESS EVENTS
- Barbara was very close to her paternal grandmother, who had died 3 months earlier.
- Peter had recently lost his job, and he also had a business failure the year Barbara was born.
- The oldest daughter, Cynthia, was leaving for college in the fall, which would put more stress on the rest of the family.

AN IMBALANCE BETWEEN OVERFUNCTIONERS
AND UNDERFUNCTIONERS
- Peter's sister Yvette was a very successful lawyer (a high functioner) and she was his father's favorite, whereas Peter had repeated business failures and was currently unemployed (an underfunctioner).
- Cynthia was a high functioner. Is it possible that there was an imbalance, with Barbara becoming the dysfunctional middle sister and the youngest, Stephanie, having repeated asthma problems?

- The mother, Susan, was always healthy and successful, whereas her younger sister, Carol, was reportedly always viewed as vulnerable and overprotected by the mother, even before she got colitis.

PATTERNS
- The youngest daughters in the family all had asthma: Peter's youngest sister suffered from it since childhood, as did Carol and Stephanie.
- Susan's younger sister, Carol, had severe colitis and her symptoms began in 1989, the same year that Susan and her mother had a falling out and cut off from each other, after which the father secretly visited the family and remained close.
- The middle daughter, Barbara, had always been identified by the family with her maternal grandfather. She had dreams in which he appeared to her, and the family believed she was his reincarnation (they did not speak of this until late in the therapy, though they had acknowledged they identified her with him).

FINANCES
- Peter had recently lost his job and was currently unemployed, and Susan earned a small salary as a substitute teacher. If Peter did not find a position soon, they would have to borrow money to live.
- Cynthia was planning to leave for college in the next few months and this was going to be a major expense for the family.

CULTURAL ISSUES, RESPONSIBILITY TO FAMILY
- Peter's family of origin was Chilean. Peter valued interdependence and taking responsibility for your extended family, a Latino family value. Susan's family of origin was of British, German, and Irish descent, third- and fourth-generation in the United States. Susan valued independence and taking responsibility for your children only through college, an American family value. These cultural differences were a source of stress in their relationship.
- Peter wanted to spend more time with his sisters' families and he wanted his daughters to be close to their cousins. Susan preferred to

spend their free time doing things together as a nuclear family and thought their marriage would be better if Peter spent more time alone with her and their daughters. Susan saw Peter's attachment to his family of origin as a way for him to distance himself from her.

- Susan had been cut off from her mother since 1989. This worried Peter because his mother-in-law was elderly and ill. He wanted Susan to make peace with her mother. Since the death of his own mother, he was even more adamant that they reconcile with Susan's mother. Peter saw Susan's lack of empathy for her mother as "cold." This was a source of stress in their marriage.

The process of collecting information using a genogram is therapeutic in itself. Often the conversation about repetition of family patterns, significant events, and concurrent life stresses that occurs while doing the genogram will encourage a dialogue that helps families to see multiple possibilities and outcomes. When Susan applied for treatment for her daughter, Barbara, she was focused on Barbara's "out of control" behavior. Through the telling of their stories, Susan and Peter saw that Barbara's bad behavior was a manifestation, or symptom, of the family stresses related to finances, anxiety about Cynthia's leaving for college, multigenerational triangles, and cultural differences.

As Susan discovered that she and Peter were repeating the patterns from their families of origin, she began to see the problem in a new way. She wanted to develop a good relationship with her daughter. She did not want a repetition of her relationship with her mother. When Susan and Peter realized they were repeating family patterns of behavior in their triangle with Barbara, they were able to work together to change their relationship. As Susan and Peter came together, Barbara's position changed. Because she could no longer depend on her father as an ally in her conflicts with her mother, she and her mother became better at managing their relationship with each other directly.

Although Susan had described her relationship with Peter as distant, they really loved each other and were committed to their marriage. Acknowledging their cultural differences helped them to view their disagreements in a less threatening, more benign way. When Susan saw

Peter's attachment to his sisters as a cultural value she realized that he was not avoiding her. At the same time, when Peter understood Susan's independence as a cultural value he recognized that she was not "cold." When they began to confer more as parents, and to agree on how to raise their children, they grew closer and their marriage improved.

One final case may illustrate the power of hidden genogram information to transform a client's experience of himself (Figure 9.8). Frank Petrucci was a successful 50-year-old Italian-Irish businessman, recently married for the third time. He had abandoned his previous children, Sophia and Ophelia, when he left his wives. In his third family, he took on the responsibility of three sons who had lost their father, a successful and powerful lawyer who had died after several years of a debilitating disease. Frank was very happy with his new wife and sons but found himself withdrawing from the very intimacy he sought, which led his wife, Christine, to frustration and anger. When asked about his family of origin, Frank did not want to talk about it. He admitted that he had grown up in an often disrupted context, moving frequently as his mother moved from one relationship to another. She had married seven times before he was 24. He had been cut off from his own father from age 7, when his mother packed him up and took him 1,000 miles away. In the following years he vaguely remembered being "captured" back and forth by each parent, as they fought their bitter battles with each other. His mother was abusive and alcoholic and from an early age Frank had to take care not only of himself, but often also of her. Once, he remembered, his father tried to reconnect, but when he took out a picture of his son by his second wife, Frank got up in fury and left.

It took many months in therapy to move Frank from anger to curiosity about his genogram. Finally, he discovered through some detective work that his father had died the year before. He decided to go back to his hometown and see the house where he was born and his father's grave. Arriving at the house, he found a young African-American woman living there. When he introduced himself, she gave a shocked response that her name was Lucy Petrucci. It turned out she was one of seven children of Frank's half brother, Don, who had married an African-American woman. Their youngest child and only son was also named Frank Petrucci. Lucy

Figure 9.8 Petrucci Family

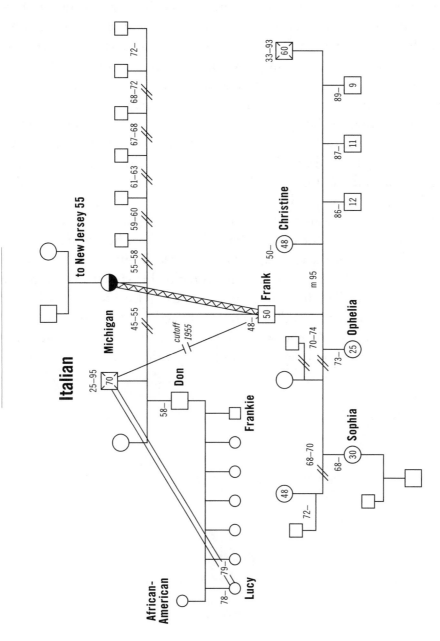

was the oldest, and she had been the closest to the grandfather, Frank's father, who lived with the family until he died. That night the family took Frank out and, as he later described it, he experienced a love and connection he had never even realized he needed. His newly discovered niece, Lucy, was able to fill him in on much of the history of his father that he had never known; she had been closest to Frank, Sr. in his last years and was the last one to speak to him the night he died. His newly found half brother shared recollections of their father's longing for Frank over the years and his pain when Frank rejected him the one time he had tried to connect. He shocked Frank by telling him that the father had repeatedly taken him to the old neighborhoods where he had lived with Frank as a small boy. He was particularly surprised to feel so close to this Black family, as he had been a strong racist for as long as he could remember. His reconnection made him profoundly aware that he had lost a lot more than just his father when the cutoff occurred in his childhood. And the reconnection affected more than just Frank—his family shared in it, and it helped him rethink his connections to the children he had left behind as well. It also "miraculously," as he thought, facilitated a shift in his relationship with his wife. As she said, "one reconnection can't change a whole life, but somehow he now seems a softer, gentler, Frankie."

10

Family Play Genograms
Coauthored with Eliana Gil, Ph.D.

O NE TECHNIQUE FOR MAKING THE GENOGRAM come to life is doing a family play genogram. In this technique family members choose from an array of miniature people, animals, and objects to represent each family member. The exercise brings out interesting information about family members' views of each other, as well as of long-dead family members. The discussion they have about the miniatures each has chosen draws on family members' creativity, fantasy, and imagination and helps to clarify family history and expand their view of relationships and conflicts. Sometimes family stories, rumors, or legends influence symbolic representations based on hearsay rather than first-hand knowledge. Such views can be explored and expanded with family play genograms, which allow members to create new combined narratives based on what each has heard about extended family members.

Family members young and old can use the miniatures as a jumping-off point for sharing secret or familiar understandings of family history. As with family sculpting, where participants are asked to visualize and physically demonstrate how relationships would be different in the future if the family were to come to terms with its experiences, the family play genogram exercise may include setting up imaginary genograms that take members into a hoped-for future when their relationships with each other and their history could be different. Introducing the element of metaphor into the discussion of the actual facts of the genogram history often gives family members greater flexibility in imagining possibilities for change, even while acknowledging that the content of their history cannot be changed.

Family play genograms are a natural expansion of the assessment and therapeutic benefits of the genogram. Developed by Eliana Gil, play genograms combine the structure of genograms with the playful use of miniature items (of people, animals, and objects of all sorts) to allow children and adults to create imaginative genograms that can serve as a revealing assessment and intervention tool with children. Play genograms also have transformative possibilities for family relationships in therapy. Like other forms of play therapy, they allow family members to express their inner experience—by expressing their own thoughts, feelings, and fantasies about themselves and other members of their family—within the construction of a miniaturized world. Miniatures provide graphic but playfully small representations that may indicate how families are both connected and separate or different. Play genograms can be used with an individual, even a small child as young as 5 or with an aging great-grandmother of 85. They can also be used with multiple family members to understand each person's view of the relationships. The genogram is usually drawn with the person or family on a large sheet of easel paper or poster board (3 x 4 feet). Family members are asked to include not only biological and legally related family members, but also anyone who has been important in the family's life, including friends and pets. Once this drawing is complete, clients are asked to choose an item from a selection of miniatures to represent each person on the genogram, including themselves. They are then asked to place their items in the circles or squares of the genogram drawing. Family members are given as long as they want to make their basic choices and then asked to share their thoughts about the choices they have made. Small children are often more comfortable choosing each item separately, and parents may help them to place the item near the right family member. When working with a young child, the therapist may prompt the child as he or she goes along to facilitate therapeutic conversation. The clinician may give reluctant children examples of concrete and abstract choices to encourage them to explore possibilities. Some people choose more than one miniature to represent a family member. This may reflect ambivalence or the complexity of a relationship. When working with children in foster care or other family situations where children have had multiple caretakers, it is helpful to construct a series of genograms on the same sheet of paper, and it may make sense to give a sequence of instructions in order to pace the interview and to help process the information before the genogram gets too crowded.

For example, family members may be asked to pick an item for each family member in their current household, including the pets. They may then share information about their choices. From this beginning, children in foster care may depict previous family constellations, whereas other family members may choose items to represent different segments of the extended family. Clients may include friends, therapists, teachers, pets, or other important relationships, both past and present. This helps children to reference and prioritize their world and gives the clinician a complex yet easily visible assessment. Family members take turns discussing their choices, which facilitates their elaboration of the meaning of the items they have picked for different family members. Clinicians observe the selection process for the type of interactions family members have while making their choices. The interactions among family members will inform the clinician about the family's patterns of relating beyond their verbal interactions. Encouraging family members to make their choices at the same time will yield a broader range of assessment information. Conflicts about specific miniatures are more likely to arise when the family is engaged in the activity together, and as conflicts arise the clinician can observe the family's style and patterns of problem solving. When everyone has made choices, family members are encouraged to look at the family play genogram and to make comments and ask questions. Rather than asking family members why they chose a particular object, it may help to invite a more open dialogue in which family members volunteer a broad range of information about the items and the relationship between the items and the people in the family.

The first person to speak tends to set the tone for the type of information that will be provided. Thus, it may help if the clinician asks expansive questions to promote a dialogue among the family members, such as, "Tell me a little more about that."

The symbolic nature of the miniatures makes them a fascinating tool for drawing out unrecognized family characteristics and patterns in a creative and fanciful format. Even difficult relationships may be humorously reflected in ways that can reveal the individual's resilience. One client, who had experienced a great many traumatic stresses in her life, chose a rather small male figure for her ex-husband. When discussing her choice, she said that at one time her husband had loomed very large, but these days he played a much smaller role in her life and she thought the silly little figure reflected this change. This same woman chose an American Indian doll with little babies all over it to represent herself, saying she felt that for many years her life had been focused on raising her children. Her choice of the item was an excellent reflection of the burden and stress she felt, while at the same time she laughed as she discussed its meaning. Somehow the humor in the play and the smallness of the miniature allowed her to express her feelings with a humorous appreciation for herself and her situation. Her teenage daughter chose to represent the mother as "walking teeth"—a miniature wind-up mouth that can walk on its little feet. The daughter had recently been feeling great resentment toward her mother, but somehow the translation into the walking teeth expressed both the daughter's frustration that her mother "talked too much" and the silliness of that aspect of their interaction. Through their choices they learned a great deal about each other's perceptions of themselves and their relationships as well as about their shared and different perceptions of the extended family. Sharing their perceptions in the context of the family play genogram gave a lightness to their discussion, which had become charged and overfocused on the conflicts they were having with each other. The exercise allowed them to see themselves in a much larger context and to find many points of connection.

Once family members have each told their story about the items they have chosen, it is helpful for the therapist to ask permission to take a photograph of the family play genogram. The individual or family may take the photograph home to facilitate additional conversation, and the clinician can keep a copy of the pictures to recreate play genograms at a later time for a continuation of the therapeutic dialogue. The play genogram technique is just one of the many ways that the genogram can facilitate therapy.

Using Play Genograms to Invite, Engage, and Enliven the Therapeutic Encounter

The family play genogram technique often bypasses client resistance and can elicit candid disclosures revealing perceptions of self and others. One of the reasons this occurs is because the narratives individuals have developed about themselves, their families, and their childhoods have become rigid and self-reinforcing, leading to the exclusion of certain information.

Cocreating genograms with families in therapy has long been accepted as an important way of gathering and organizing information about families, especially about family composition, cross-generational patterns of achievement and dysfunction, and relational issues between family members (emotional distance, closeness, or cutoffs). Genograms help both the clinician and the family gain a broader understanding of the client's family system and history, as well as organize, reflect, and gain new insights about family patterns and significant life events.

Play allows for active engagement with fantasy, akin to visualization. In the process of playing, clients are able to achieve a variety of positive outcomes, including externalizing the problem (which sometimes is more difficult in verbal therapy). Many individuals feel cultural and personal restrictions about speaking of their problems. They may have feelings of disloyalty, discomfort with therapy, and a fear of exaggerating a problem, making it more important through disclosure, or of being seen as vulnerable or weak. Play allows them a smoother transition into difficult emotional material.

Once symbols are utilized to communicate to oneself and others, different processes become possible. When problems feel overwhelming to a client, "miniaturizing" them may help clients begin to manage them. Some of the other processes that occur during play therapy include projection and working through. Projection occurs when clients infuse objects with emotions or personality traits; it creates a safe enough distance in which to begin to acknowledge, understand, or address personal issues.

A Play Genogram Session With Jenny

Such reluctance to explore family issues occurred with Jenny, who had lived in foster care for several years (Figure 10.1). Her biological mother had been in treatment for substance abuse and had recently been sent to prison for several years for selling drugs. Jenny's foster family had agreed

Figure 10.1 Jenny

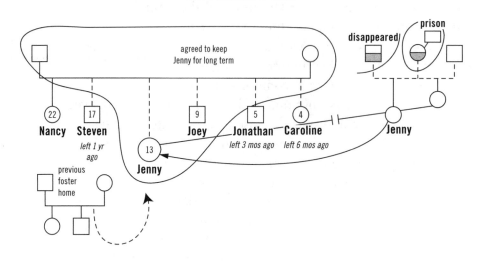

to keep her in long-term placement, but she was depressed and easily angered. She was getting into trouble in school, arguing with classmates and neglecting her schoolwork. She refused to participate in individual therapy because, as she said, "talking about things" was useless; it wouldn't change anything. However, she agreed to family therapy with her 9-year-old foster brother, Joey, the only other foster child currently living in the home.

We (SP and children) drew the family's genogram on a large sheet of paper, starting with Jenny and Joey, the foster parents, and their biological daughter, Nancy. Jenny and Joey were asked to add anyone they wished to include in the genogram. They added three other foster children who had previously lived in the home with them (Steven, Jonathan, and Caroline). Next they were asked to choose the miniatures that best showed their thoughts and feelings about everyone in the family, including themselves.

During the process of making their selections, Jenny and Joey talked about their choices for the other foster children who had lived with them. They agreed on Alice in Wonderland for Nancy, "because she's pretty," a wizard for Steven, who had left the previous year, "because he was smart," and Humpty Dumpty for Jonathan because he was "cute and round."

They chose a clown for Caroline because she had a cloth clown that she took to bed with her. They wondered if she still liked to sleep with it (Color Figure 29).

When they were finished choosing the miniatures, they were asked to tell about their choices. Jenny said she had chosen the Little Mermaid for herself because she felt like she was "under water" and that no one understood her. She went on to say that if the mermaid came out of water to live on dry land she would die. The metaphor facilitated a therapeutic conversation that would probably not have been possible if Jenny were speaking directly about her own feelings, because she believed talking about things was useless. But through the Little Mermaid, she shared a profound expression of her existential dilemma in a relatively safe play situation.

Joey chose a fierce figure carrying a weapon, stating that if he had that weapon he would always win. Clearly, having some way to protect himself was important to him. Both children expressed their feelings about their fears, losses, and feelings of abandonment. They also spoke about their strengths. Joey had chosen the Cinderella figure to represent Jenny, saying that Cinderella is "pretty and nice." For their foster mother Joey picked a bride and Jenny chose a powerful female figure with a weapon. Jenny described her foster mother as "a strong lady." For their foster father Joey chose a groom and Jenny chose Bullwinkle. Jenny said that her foster father was funny and easy-going, like the cartoon character.

At 13 years old Jenny was able to use metaphors in her choice of miniatures to represent her feelings for each person. Joey's selections were more concrete, as would be expected for a 9-year-old. The play genogram is a good tool for working with children and families at various developmental levels. In future sessions Jenny and Joey were able to process their feelings in a nonthreatening way by referring to the figures in the play genogram, talking, for example, about how the Little Mermaid could be safe and about Cinderella's strengths. We used the metaphor of the mermaid and being "in the water" to further the discussion about Jenny's sense of alienation from other family members. We began to focus on what it would be like to be "out" of the water—that is, if she were better understood by others. We noted that if she were out of the water, she would be joining all the other earth creatures in her play genogram. When we asked Jenny what it would be like for her on solid ground instead of water, she remarked that she would then have legs and wouldn't be a half fish anymore. "If I had legs, I could get places on my own, and maybe there would be places that I would like to visit. I might also like to play or run and maybe I would even learn to drive if I had legs." She realized that legs gave her a sense of control and mobility, allowing her to feel more ready to take action on her own behalf. We then talked a little about being understood and I asked her to make a list of all the things she would want to understand and then who she was most eager to be understood by. This was a very fruitful discussion that allowed her to recognize her own holding back more clearly.

Materials Used for Family Play Genograms

The miniatures used in family play genograms are limited only by the therapist's imagination. At our institute (www.MulticulturalFamily.org) we use and sell small portable kits of miniature items that can be bought in a dollar store or craft store, including buttons, stones, and all kinds of animals and figures 1 to 2 inches in diameter. We have also used stickers and genogram collages to allow children to make family play genograms that they can take home. It is only a matter of time before a family play genogram program will be available on the Internet, allowing family members to choose items and place them on their genogram, as they can now place family pictures of individuals on genograms created with GenoPro.

The most common items for family play genograms are 2- to 3-inch figures, trees, animals, and so on that can be bought from official play therapy sites on the Internet or in toy stores or craft stores. We recommend that therapists attend to the cultural and ethnic background of clients and have available items that reflect diverse interests and cultures. Skin color of human figures is an obvious issue. It would, of course, be much harder for families of color to relate to a set of figures that have pink skin. Muslim families may resist depicting family members in human form and may prefer more symbolic representation. Another important cultural consideration is to provide items that represent multiple human environments—urban and rural, mountainous and desert. We also keep clay and paper available and encourage clients to make their own miniatures when they cannot find an appropriate one among the selection available.

Additional Family Play Genogram Exercises

Depending on the clinical situation, the therapist's and family's imagination are the only limit for what can be done using family play genogram items. For specific cases any of the following might prove useful:

- Doing a genogram of the family at a particular time in the past that was traumatic or difficult, such as a time of loss, adolescent intergenerational conflict, or cutoff.
- Doing a genogram that represents resources and sources of resilience; asking participants to pick items to represent people who have been particularly meaningful in their lives.
- Contextualizing a serious conflict in the immediate family by exploring specific relationships in the extended family.
- Conducting imaginary conversations among the miniatures chosen. For example, the therapist might ask a family: If the hummingbird and the horse (items representing the beloved grandfather who had just died) could have a conversation about the family, what might they say about Taisha's problem now? If the praying mantis (an 11-year-old boy's choice for his mother, who had lost custody due to accusations of abuse) could speak to the eagle figure (the boy's choice for himself), what do you think she might say? And then what would he say? And what might he say to the chameleon who became an eagle (his sister) or to the little bear cub (his baby brother)?
- Having a discussion about selections the family members made but then discarded.
- Asking family members to move their miniatures. For example, having the adolescent figure turn around to ask a parental figure a specific question.

• Having the client take the physical posture of his/her chosen miniature and explore how that feels.

In one family the mother had lost custody of the three adolescent daughters and a youngest son, and the father was overwhelmed by his parenting task. I (MM) asked the children to choose items to represent each parent, and the father to represent each child, and each of them to represent one other person whom they viewed as a resource. The children chose a dragon, a cobra, a man's bust split into dark and light, and a lobster for the mother, indicating the difficulties they had trusting and dealing with her, but they were unwilling to elaborate much on their choices, especially the youngest ones. For the father they chose a businessman, a computer, a rock representing peace on it, and a clock because he was always hurrying them to be on time. For himself the father chose an eagle with spread wings because he said he felt he was always having to hover over them. The youngest son chose a car to represent himself, whereas the daughters represented their interests in sports and fashion. The father chose a young woman with roller skates, a guitar, and a loving dog for the three girls and a small boy for his son. When they finished discussing their immediate family, they described the miniatures they chose for the person who might be able to help them in their current situation (Color Figure 30).

The father, who at first said there was no one he could think of, chose a squeaking nun for his half sister, 15 years his senior, who had been a mother figure for him when he and his younger brother were children and their mother became ill. The three adolescent daughters all chose family friends—parents of their own friends to whom they felt attached (represented by a monkey with a baby, a kangaroo, and a wizard)—whereas the youngest son chose his dog, which made the others laugh because they all agreed this was their best, most loving resource! The specifics that came out in creating the family play genogram enabled the family to acknowledge resources they could draw on for help and simultaneously provided them with an opportunity to share stories of good times with these extended "kin," which helped them feel more connected to each other. Several weeks after that session a crisis arose due to the father's having to go out of town. He was able to take advantage of all these resources to work out a support structure for the children. Initially he could not imagine asking his sister for help, but, although she was surprised by his call, she was more than happy to help.

The Case of Alexis: Child Sexual Abuse in a Remarried Family

Alexis was a 14-year-old Dominican-American girl who was sexually abused by her stepfather over a period of 3 years, from the time Alexis was 10 years old until she was 13 (Figure 10.2). The abuse finally stopped when she told her school counselor about it. Her stepfather was arrested, he admitted to the sexual abuse, and he was incarcerated. Alexis began acting out by staying out late, smoking cigarettes and marijuana, and cutting school. She remained in therapy for 6 months but refused to discuss the sexual abuse, saying that she had already spoken about it, it was in the past, and she did not have any feelings about it anymore.

Figure 10.2 Alexis

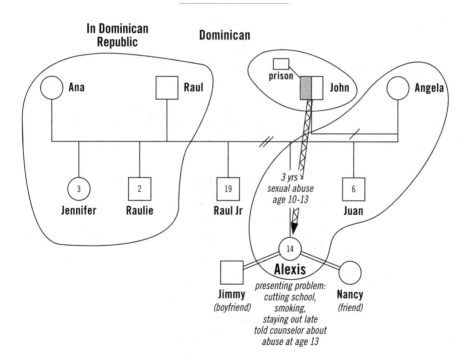

In therapy I (SP) constructed a genogram with Alexis of her immediate family, where she was the middle child with two brothers, and asked her to add anyone she wished to include (Figure 10.2). She decided to add her biological father Raul's new family (his wife Ana and their two children, Jennifer and Raulie), her best friend, Nancy, and her boyfriend, Jimmy. Next Alexis was asked to choose miniatures to show her thoughts and feelings about everyone in the family, including herself (Color Figure 31).

Alexis placed her biological father looking toward the two young children from his second marriage and away from Alexis's part of the family. She chose the smallest female figure to represent herself, and she chose a queen to represent her mother. She chose an ominous figure with a weapon for her stepfather. These were all compelling visual representations of her feelings about herself and her parents. I did not share my observations, but rather asked Alexis to tell me about her genogram.

"I chose this figure for my father because he has darker skin and he is very handsome." Then she described all of the figures representing the children, stating why she chose each one. She said that she chose the Cinderella figure for her best friend "because she is pretty," and the "light-skinned guy" for her boyfriend because he was handsome and had light skin. She pointed to the small girl and baby miniatures representing her half siblings and talked about how much fun she had with them when she visited her father in the Dominican Republic a year ago. For her older brother Alexis chose the cartoon figure Bart Simpson because, as she described it, he was "always in trouble in high school. He can't get away with anything." Interestingly, she did not choose a miniature for her father's second wife.

Alexis had not yet talked about the figures she chose for her mother and her stepfather. I pointed to the figures and asked, "Tell me about these." This opened up the conversation.

"I chose this ugly guy for my stepfather because he looks mean and scary." She went on to say she hoped he would stay in jail and she worried that he might get out and come back into their home. She also talked about the figure she had chosen for her mother, stating that her mother had complete power over her. I asked to her say more about this, and she replied by expressing feelings of fear, anger, and powerlessness. She talked about her biological father's role, saying that if he had been there for her "none of this would have happened." Placing her father's miniature looking away from her family and toward his younger children from his second marriage was a powerful visual representation of her feelings of abandonment.

The play genogram opened up the possibility for Alexis to talk about her feelings regarding the sexual abuse, even though she thought she had nothing more to say about it. She also discussed her ambivalence about her mother's power in various ways. Her mother had been powerless when her stepfather was abusing her. Now her mother had power because she knew what had happened and she had filed for divorce. Alexis said that she felt sometimes her mother had too much power over her because she set limits. On the other hand, she said her mother was using her power for good, because she wanted the best for her children.

We took a picture of the play genogram for the file. In future sessions Alexis used this play experience to discuss how the queen became powerful when she gained knowledge and the "ugly guy" seemed to shrink as the queen's power grew. In the process she recognized that her own figure seemed small and she wondered if her new knowledge increased her power.

The Nogucis: A Family of Outsiders

The Noguci family (Figure 10.3) sought help for their 14-year-old son, Brandon, who was refusing to go to school, staying up or out all night and sleeping all day, and destroying furniture when confronted by his parents about his refusal to obey even the most minimal rules. The father, Koji, was a graphic designer who had come to the U.S. from Japan to study art. The mother, Terry, was an art teacher from a working class Irish background. The two had met in college.

Koji and Terry came in believing that they were not good parents. They had been told what to do about their son—namely, to set firmer limits—but they had not been able to do it, and they therefore felt like failures. They were angry at each other and at the school, as well as at their son. They seemed unable to have any sustained conversation as a couple; their only attempts at conversation were about Brandon.

Figure 10.3　Noguci Family

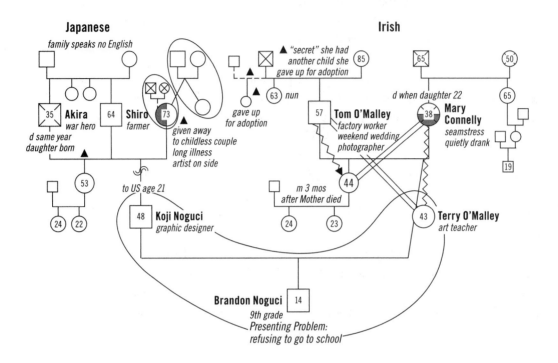

Although the parents were compliant about giving genogram information, they were not engaged in the story of their history and were
extremely defensive about being asked to participate in therapy. They
strongly resisted thinking systemically, perhaps because they were deeply
cut off from their own families of origin and did not want to identify with
them. This seemed to leave them totally lost about how to relate to their
son. Brandon was also stuck between being a child and moving toward
adulthood. He could not negotiate the passage to adulthood because his
parents never clarified boundaries, leaving it unclear which generation he
belonged to. Whenever the therapist tried to focus on the parents' setting
limits or on their relationship with each other, they withdrew or seemed
annoyed. Brandon was generally nonresponsive in the therapy, whether
with his parents or alone. In an attempt to engage him in a nonverbal
medium, the therapist asked him to make a sand tray world using miniatures. In an eloquent expression of his stuckness, Brandon was unable to

make a single choice to include in the sand tray, until his parents joined the session. At that point, encouraged by his father, he reluctantly contributed a few figures.

The following week the therapist decided to do a family play genogram, hoping to connect the family members to their history. The family's genogram was drawn on a large piece of paper. Each family member in turn picked a figure for him- or herself and then for each other (Figures 10.4 and Color Figure 32). There was much discussion, inquiry, and laughter about the choices. Brandon insisted on including two of the same miniatures he had contributed to the family sand tray the previous week. This was the first indication of "belonging" and continuity since the therapy had begun. Terry's choices for her parents led to her first open exploration of the struggle she had in figuring out her place in her family. She chose a rolling pin for her mother and went on to talk about how she belonged to her father and her sister belonged to her mother, a "very

Figure 10.4 Noguci Family With Family Play Figures

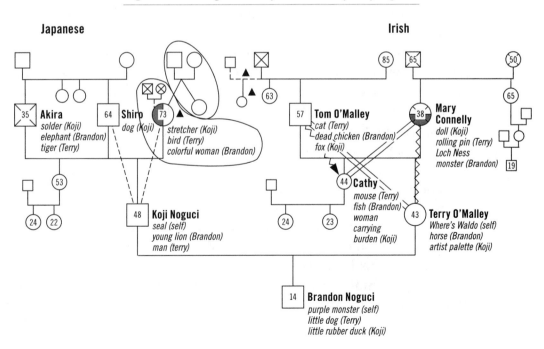

boring housewife." Her complex feelings for her parents and sister had been compounded by her mother's death, followed by her sister's marriage, just when Terry was on the verge of leaving home. She had felt abandoned by her sister and guilty that her father had always favored her. When Brandon asked her why she chose a cat for her father and a mouse for her sister, she said, with some feeling, that although she had loved her father, she recognized that he had always been cruel to her sister.

Exploration of Koji's side of the genogram led to an interesting discussion of why he had also distanced from his family. Koji had chosen a soldier to play his uncle, Akira, who was also his mother's first husband; a dog to represent his father, Shiro; and a stretcher bed to represent his mother. Terry's mystification about these choices led Koji to explain several experiences he had hardly remembered himself until now. He had grown up not knowing his family history. At age 8 he asked his older sister why their father's picture was kept on the altar with the pictures of all the dead relatives. The sister laughed and told the parents, who were also amused that he had confused his father, Shiro, with his uncle Akira, a military hero who had died in the war. Koji felt humiliated by being laughed at and took the experience to mean he was an "outsider" in his family and could not ask the true history. Not until he was an adult and leaving for America did his mother, by then quite ill with heart disease and arthritis, tell him how grateful she had felt to his father, Shiro, who was 9 years younger than she, for agreeing to marry her and take her little daughter from the first marriage. Otherwise, she told him, she would have had nowhere to go. She told him also that, as a twin, she had been given away by her parents to be raised by an older childless couple, whereas her twin sister had been raised by their parents. She had cared for the couple, but both of them had been frail and died soon after her marriage to Akira.

Koji said he had chosen the stretcher for his mother because she was always ill. Brandon had chosen an attractively decorated woman figure and placed her on the bed to be his grandmother. Koji said he had chosen the dog to be his father because he always thought of his father as weak. After what his mother told him, he felt perhaps his father had never been able to replace his older brother. Being a farmer, with less education than his brother, he took the responsibility for his brother's wife but could never really take the place of his brother, who had died a war hero, so he too felt like an outsider.

Koji grew up feeling he did not belong in his family. He did not understand his history and could not ask about it. He was the child of two parents who both probably felt they were outsiders compared to their more desirable siblings. Perhaps when he became involved with Terry, who herself had an impaired sense of belonging in her family, they complemented each other's difficulty being at the center of a family. Through the creation of the family play genogram, both parents were able to begin to tell their stories to each other, and Brandon was able to participate and even give to his parents a newfound sense of connectedness.

As the three of them shared the meanings of the figures they had chosen to represent themselves, each other, and the extended family, they seemed to join for the first time in being a family who could surmount their difficult history and find a way of belonging with each other. Both parents laughed about the miniatures they had chosen for themselves. Terry's Where's Waldo was seen as someone who has an idea where he's going but is hard for others to find. The others agreed that this was true about her. Koji said he thought at times he was slippery like a seal but that he had also chosen the animal because of its power and ability to swim fast. We noticed that the parents had chosen more effective miniatures for the other parent than they had chosen for themselves (Koji chose an artist's palette for his wife and she chose a man for him). The symbols became a way of talking about the roles they were playing in relation to the roles they wanted to play. The parents had chosen symbols for Brandon (the duck and the little dog) that suggested someone who needs protection. Even Brandon's choice for himself, the purple monster, seemed to be making a joke of intimidation. In a follow-up discussion with Koji about his role, we wondered if he might not find some position that would be between the symbols of soldier and dog that he had chosen to represent his father and his uncle and the symbols he and his wife and son had offered (seal, lion cub, man). Their choices in the family play genogram seemed to make clear that the parents needed to take a stronger, more protective role with their son and had been hampered by their history in doing this. Both Brandon and Terry seemed in a way to be suggesting solutions to Koji's ineffective symbol of his mother (the stretcher). Brandon put a colorful woman in the bed and Terry had suggested the bird, who was both colorful and liked to sing. Koji was reminded that his mother had a beautiful voice and loved to sing when she was young. There seemed a similar suggestion about Terry's mother. Terry had represented her with a rolling pin, reflecting her constrained role as housewife, whereas Brandon's choice of the Loch Ness monster might suggest a power that goes beyond death and beyond what can be seen.

This session became a key experience we could refer back to with a kind of shorthand to encourage Terry and Koji to take a stronger position in relation to their son, labeling him as a "play monster" rather than a real monster, who, like a little duck, needed to be taught to swim. Soon after this session both parents were able to follow through on limits for Brandon, to the extent that they insisted he have consequences and go to court to appear before a judge for his truancy. When the judge gave a strong message that it was either school or jail until he was 16, Brandon began going to school.

Combining play, imagination, and creativity with the genogram history often has the effect of opening up families to their history on a deeper level. Perhaps the element of play lowers their defenses and resistance; perhaps, as with Koji, the choice of miniatures can lead to making unconscious connections with deep childhood feelings one could not describe in words. In this case, the family play genogram provided a structure within which Brandon's parents could share stories of their experiences in their families of origin. Just as Brandon needed clear and definite limit setting, the parents needed the concrete and nonthreatening structure of the play genogram to confront their history and change their present.

11

Using Genograms for Family Research

ALTHOUGH THE GENOGRAM IS ALMOST AS OLD AS the fields of family therapy and family medicine, focus on its enormous possibilities as a research tool has been slow in coming. This is remarkable, given the potential of genograms for tracking and maintaining so much family information in a simple graphic format, and given the fact that it is a tool so widely used by clinicians for mapping their patients' context.

We are at a crossroads of understanding the potential of genograms for research. We know now that clinicians find genograms helpful for thinking systemically and for mapping family patterns and "making sense" of client problems in context. Publications since the last edition of this book make clear that the genogram is an effective and ever more widely used clinical tool. The application of genograms has been expanding to a widening range of clinical situations (Altshuler, 1999; Campbell et al., 2002; Daughhetee, 2001; Dunn & Dawes, 1999; Dunn & Levitt, 2000; Foster, Jurkovic, Ferdinand, & Meadows, 2002; Frame, 2000a, 2000b, 2001; Gibson, 2005; Gordon, Staples, Blyta, & Bytyqi, 2004; Granello, Hothersall, & Osborne, 2000; Hockley, 2000; Hodge, 2000, 2001, 2005a, 2005b; Malott & Magnuson, 2004; Massey & Dunn, 1999; Niederhauser & Arnold, 2004; Olsen, Dudley-Brown, & McMullen, 2004; Rogers, 1994a; Rogers & Durkin, 1984; Wimbush & Peters, 2000; Wright & Leahy, 1999, 2000; Zide & Gray, 2000).

Furthermore, new software programs specifically designed for clinical work have encouraged the new computer-savvy generation of therapists to use the graphics in their clinical work and in teaching. Nevertheless, we appear to have hardly begun to realize the research potential of genograms. Even the standardization of genogram symbols and notation is a process still in its early developmental stage.

The literature affirms that clinicians who use genograms find them a useful clinical tool, and much of the research on the clinical usefulness of the family genogram comes from the field of family medicine. Genograms have been viewed as a way to sensitize physicians to relevant psychosocial issues of their patients; to enhance evaluation, diagnosis, and care of patients; to provide a framework for assessment and interaction with particular patients (e.g., the elderly) at a critical time in the healthcare process (e.g., diagnosis of a serious illness); and to prevent problems or intervene with families to address them (Alexander & Clark, 1998; Baird & Grant, 1998; Bannerman, 1986; Campbell et al., 2002; Christie-Seely, 1986; Crouch, 1989; Crouch & Davis, 1987; Dumas, Katerndahl, & Burge, 1995; Garrett, Klinkman, & Post, 1987; Like, Rogers, & McGoldrick, 1988; Mullins & Christie-Seely, 1984; Olsen, Dudley-Brown, & McMullen, 2004; Shellenberger, Shurden, & Treadwell, 1988; Sproul & Gallagher, 1982; Troncale, 1983; Wright & Leahy, 1999, 2000; Zide & Gray, 2000).

Research has demonstrated that family has a powerful influence on health and illness and that marital and family relationships have as significant an influence on health outcomes as biological factors (Campbell et al., 2002). The value of family history in assessing risk for common diseases is becoming increasingly realized (Wattendorf & Hadley, 2005). The Human Genome Project and the resultant identification of the inherited causes of many diseases and the establishment of national clinical practice guidelines based on systemic reviews of preventive interventions make such an assessment even more obvious (Wattendorf & Hadley, 2005). With the advances in genetic research, detailed genograms showing family demographics, the history of serious illness, relationships, and genetic risks will soon become essential components of every patient's healthcare evaluation (Campbell et al., 2002).

Scherger (2005) has written a call to arms about the current crisis in family medicine and the need to redesign the field to allow family physicians to truly offer family-oriented care, for which attention to genogram information would be a major part. Scherger argues powerfully for using new information technologies to help track and deal with families in a contextual way as the only serious possibility for providing appropriate care to families in our society. But we will have to develop the technologies to address families systemically and help physicians to use genograms to reorient our health care system away from the current morass of paperwork and insurance industry-driven impediments to service.

Reliability Research in Family Medicine

Historically, there were a number of studies done in family medicine on subjects such as the impact of a screening family genogram on first encounters in primary care (Rogers, 1994b; Rogers & Cohn, 1987), reading and interpreting genograms (Like et al., 1988), completion and reliability of the self-administered genogram (Rogers, 1990), prediction of health risk from family genograms (Rogers, Rohrbaugh, & McGoldrick, 1992), and how experts read family genograms (Rohrbaugh, Rogers, & McGoldrick, 1992).

Like and colleagues (1988) studied reading and interpreting genograms by examining the usefulness of the genogram as a data-gathering and assessment tool. Six information categories that could be used for generating and testing clinical hypotheses were outlined (Table 11.1): (1) family structure, (2) life cycle issues, (3) pattern repetition across generations, (4) life experiences, (5) family relationship patterns, and (6) a balance or imbalance in family relationships. Three clinical case vignettes were offered to demonstrate how physicians could read and interpret genograms systemically. These vignettes illustrated how physicians could learn to read and interpret genograms in a systemic fashion using the six interpretive categories. The study showed that genograms provide a rich source of data and can be used in the clinical problem-solving process familiar to physicians.

In a related study, Rogers, Rohrbaugh, and McGoldrick (1992) evaluated the efficacy of genograms for predicting health risk in comparison to predictions made using demographic and chart review data. Six family physicians who had substantial experience reading and interpreting genograms were asked to evaluate 20 actual patient cases and make three

Table 11.1
Genogram Information Categories for Clinical Practice

Category 1. Family Structure
- Composition of family or household (e.g., intact nuclear family, single-parent household, remarried family, three-generational household, household with extended or nonfamily members)
- Sibling constellation (e.g., birth order, siblings' gender, distance in age between siblings, other factors influencing sibling patterns such as timing of each child's birth in family history, child's characteristics, family's "program" for the child, parental attitudes and biases regarding sex differences)
- Unusual family configurations (e.g. consanguineous marriage, multiple marriages)

Category 2. Family Life Cycle
- Present family life cycle stage (e.g., launching young adult, the new couple, the family with young children, the family with adolescents, the family with elderly members)
- Family life cycle transitions or developmental crises
- Family life cycle events that are "off time" (e.g., early death, delayed launching, spouses of very different ages, late child-bearing)

Category 3. Pattern Repetition in Families Across Generations
- Repeated patterns of illness (e.g., specific diseases, symptoms)
- Repeated patterns of functioning (e.g., somatization, denial, substance abuse)
- Repeated patterns of relationships (e.g., enmeshment, conflicts, cutoffs)
- Repeated structural patterns (e.g., divorce, remarriage)

Category 4. Life Experiences
- Recent life stressors (e.g., marriage, pregnancy, acute illness)
- Chronic life stressors (e.g., chronic illness, poverty, racism)

- Coincidences or recurring significant dates, ages, and temporal life events (e.g., anniversaries, holidays)
- Cultural, social, economic, political, or environmental forces (e.g., ethnicity, migration, natural disasters, warfare)

Category 5. Family Relational Patterns
- Type of relationships in the family (e.g., cutoffs, conflicts, distant, fused, enmeshed)
- Triangles (e.g., parent-child triangles, couple triangles, divorce-and-remarried-family triangles, triangles in families with foster or adopted children, multigenerational triangles)
- Types of relationships with nonfamily members

Category 6. Family Balance or Imbalance
- Balance or imbalance in family structure
- Balance or imbalance in family roles
- Balance or imbalance in level or style of functioning
- Balance or imbalance in resources

predictions. The experts were more confident in their predictions when they had genogram data compared to having demographic data only. Although genograms were not demonstrated to be more accurate than standard clinical chart review for predicting short-term health outcomes, they may be more efficient in drawing physicians' attention to key problems and issues.

Rohrbaugh, Rogers, and McGoldrick (1992) also examined expert decision making and interjudge reliability of physicians and family therapists who read family medicine genograms. The experts agreed on the relative importance of major categories in general (medical condition of patient and family members, household composition, present life-cycle stage, repeated patterns of functioning over generations, sibling constellation, and traumatic illness and life events), but there was less agreement on what was most important in each particular genogram. This might reflect ambiguities in the information classification scheme and the fact that genograms display a broad, variable range of family information subject to interpretation from different theoretical perspectives. If the categories were made explicit and more precise, higher levels of rater reliability might occur. Apart from the category scheme, another problem may be that interjudge reliability requires a shared explanatory framework. The family therapists (who mostly worked together and used a Bowen systems framework) had highest rater agreement for emotional cutoff, conflictual relationships, and repeated relationship patterns over generations—all categories having special significance in Bowen's theory. Other theories used by experts for interpreting genograms include genetic theory (a primary framework for physicians, family stress, and social support theory common in medicine) and life cycle theory (taught in medicine and family therapy). Finally, genograms constructed by a research assistant might not be as good a measure as genograms constructed interactively by a skilled clinician around a presenting complaint or a reported malfunction in the family.

Subsequently, Rogers (1994a) examined whether physicians using family genogram information could identify patients at risk for anxiety or depression and found that genograms were indeed useful. Rogers outlined four characteristics of the family genogram that made it useful for stratifying patients' risk for emotional problems such as anxiety or depression: (1) family structure, (2) family demographics, (3) family life events, and (4) family social and health problems. He concluded that physicians could indeed use the basic family information recorded on family genograms to stratify their patients' risk for anxiety and depression.

Family medicine researchers Jolly and colleagues (1980) found that family practice residents could elicit and record most of the "relevant" family information during a 16-minute genogram interview and that the information thus gathered could be read correctly from the genogram by different physicians with a high degree of accuracy. The sample was small and homogeneous, and the "relevant" data were limited to objective information sought by physicians; however, the results are suggestive of good inter-rater reliability of the measure. The test-retest reliability of the genogram data has also been assessed by Rogers and Holloway (1990), who investigated the completion rate and reliability of a self-administered genogram for family practice patients. They found a high degree of test-retest reliability with assessments completed two times, 3 months apart. The reliability of the tool in a family practice setting is likely to be enhanced further by the refinement of the categories used for data collection and use of a computerized program.

Reliability Research in Family Therapy

Surprisingly less research on the reliability of the genogram has accumulated in the field of family therapy. In an effort to ascertain the reliability of family therapists' use of the genogram, Coupland, Serovich, and Glenn (1995) used fictitious scenarios and asked 17 doctoral students in marriage and family therapy training programs to record genogram information. Students were found to be highly accurate in recording family members' names and symbols, moderately accurate in recording occupations, medical issues, and personal issues, and, interestingly, much less accurate in recording dates and ages. The authors suggested that either students find recording some information on a genogram to be irrelevant or that students are not trained in genogram construction. Ongoing supervision, including evaluation and critiques of genograms, was their recommended solution to the recording problem. In a related study, Coupland and Serovich (1999) used a standardized questionnaire based on the genogram standardization design of McGoldrick and Gerson (1985) and compared a therapist-administered genogram (TAGE) to a self-administered genogram (SAGE) to assess whether the TAGE increased the therapeutic alliance. The sample consisted of 17 couples seeking therapy in two large southwestern universities; five students in the marriage and family therapy programs were recruited to be therapist participants. The standardized questionnaire bolsters reliability, as the format, symbols, and categories of information recorded on the SAGE were identical to those on the TAGE. However, Coupland and Serovich found no significant difference in the level of therapeutic alliance between the TAGE and the SAGE. They asserted that perhaps the time limit of only five sessions was not sufficient to build and measure therapeutic alliance, and further that it was likely that neither the couples nor the therapists were particularly motivated to use the genogram. There was no tangible incentive for the time and effort of participating in the research over the five sessions, and the motivation of the therapists may have been further reduced by the requirement that they implement a specified treatment intervention for the purpose of research when they may not have believed the intervention was appropriate to their therapeutic perspective or the needs of the couple.

This highlights a problem that we have encountered consistently in researching genograms, when the efforts of the researchers are limited by financial resources, which filters down to constraints on time, training, and availability of therapists who are able to make the commitment required for the research. The fact that we have not yet been able to demonstrate the power of the genogram does not mean that it is not demonstrable. We do not yet know the possibilities, and we hope that the new computerized genogram programs will encourage many researchers to explore those possibilities.

Although we support efforts to increase reliability and believe standardization of the genogram makes it more reliable and valid, we also believe that it is important to maintain the flexibility of branching to different topics, hearing the impressions of different family members, exploring different themes and hypotheses, and dealing with whatever psychometric complexities this process presents.

Research on Clinical Usefulness

Rogers and Cohn (1987; Rogers, 1994b) designed what seems to be the first experimental randomized controlled trial using the family genogram to determine the influence of screening genograms on patients' initial visits to primary care physicians. They found that the genograms captured more information about family structure, major life events, repetitive illnesses, and family relationships than did the physicians on their own. The protocol they used for patients was easy to follow and they provided step-by-step instructions for the self-administered genogram, resulting in genograms typically being completed in 20 minutes. Patients' first visits with their physicians were systematically observed by one of the investigators and two data collection forms were completed. One form recorded the patient's chief complaint and the inquiry about the patients' context (e.g., whether the physician explored family problems or issues, requested interviews with family members, suggested or referred the patient, or inquired about employment or living environment). The second form was a self-administered genogram that the investigator completed as family information was obtained by the physician.

The genograms were reviewed to determine the extent of the family information recorded. Four categories of information were included: family structure, life events, repetitive patterns, and current household. Three study groups (baseline, experimental, and control) were compared on the genogram information categories and on the dependent variables: exploration of family or job issues, requests for interviews with other family members, and prescription counseling. Review of the genograms showed that the self-administered genograms (experimental and control groups) captured more family information than normally obtained by the physicians. This was an excellent seminal study especially because of the clear, easy-to-follow protocol Rogers and Cohn developed for the self-administered genogram. A computer program would make this type of research even better.

Given the extensive clinical and training uses of genograms and their strong theoretical foundation in Bowen theory, it is surprising that they have attracted the attention of so few researchers in family therapy. Foster et al. (2002) suggested that this may be because of the complexity of collecting and interpreting the rich array of data generated on genograms. They themselves are among the few who have undertaken genogram research, but they have preferred to focus their research on the process of doing genogram interviewing rather than on genogram information itself.

There are at least two different ways to think of genograms: first, as a clinical instrument to collect and organize data about a family's history, and second as a clinical tool to promote change in families by helping them understand themselves systemically. Foster and colleagues (2002) viewed this latter avenue as the most interesting for research. They considered the conjoint processing of the genogram with a systemically knowledgable therapist as more important than just obtaining a detailed and accurate record of the client's family history. Foster and her colleagues developed a manualized five-session genogram interview for premarital couples using a Bowen systems approach.

The objective of the first session was to gather basic genogram information. The interviewing process focused initially on each partner's family of origin issues rather than on couple issues, encouraging partners to examine what each was bringing to the relationship from his or her family of origin. This process helped create emotional space between the partners to gain perspective on themselves, each other, and their relationship.

The focus of the second session was to increase couples' curiosity about the ways family of origin patterns influence each partner and the dynamics of their relationship, and to encourage them to view their relationship as part of the evolving multigenerational process of their families.

The third session focused on what the partners learned in doing their homework. When partners veered off their own family, finding it easier to think systemically about the other's relationships, they were encouraged to come back to focus on their own families.

The fourth session focused on helping couples make connections between their families of origin and their couple relationship. Couples who did not identify conflict as a concern were encouraged to consider one or more issues that have some emotional power for them such as money, holiday rituals, attitudes about health, or relationships with extended family.

In the final session couples explored ways to integrate their experience working with their genogram and appreciating the larger familial context of their relationships.

These genogram interviews appeared to improve couples' relationships with each other and with their families of origin. The authors suggested such interviewing might be useful in helping partners develop specific skills, such as money management. They believe that genogram interviewing has great potential for teaching clients to think systemically, not just because of the visual graphic of the genogram, but also, and more importantly, because of the multiple ways it links the interviews to their relationships and family history. The same method would seem most valuable in facilitating couples' situating themselves and their families in religious, ethnic, racial, class, and gender contexts.

Using Genograms and Ecomaps in Clinical Practice

The literature affirms the therapeutic value of working collaboratively with clients in constructing genograms, thereby encouraging the clients' voices to be heard and empowering them to make their own discoveries about their family processes. Dunn and Levitt (2000) have discussed the need for integration of mutual client-therapist collaboration in the process of genogram construction. They have demonstrated through their own practice how such integration enhances the therapeutic power of the genogram, recommending changes in the training of marriage and family therapists to include genograms.

The use of the genogram has expanded in many other areas as well. It has become an accepted tool for spiritual assessment (Dunn & Dawes, 1999; Frame, 2000a, 2000b, 2001; Hodge, 2001, 2005a; Massey & Dunn, 1999), for therapy with children in foster care (Altshuler, 1999; Petry & McGoldrick, 2005), for providing comfort for those in palliative and hospice care (Hockley, 2000), for identification of cardiovascular risk (Wimbush & Peters, 2000), and for academic and career counseling (Daughhetee, 2001; Gibson, 2005; Granello, Hothersall, & Osborne, 2000; Malott & Magnuson, 2004). Publications have demonstrated how it allows for multiple definitions of the family through socially constructed genograms (Milewski-Hertlein, 2001) and, of course, as we have been discussing here, in couples and family therapy (Foster et al., 2002). Further, the genogram has been enhanced by the addition of ecomaps and ecograms, which depict the larger systems affecting the individual and family system (Hodge, 2000, 2005b; Jordan, 2004).

Olsen and colleagues (2004) have made a strong case for combining genograms, ecomaps, and genetic family trees (called pedigrees) to optimize healthcare assessments for nursing. We believe pedigree information should be incorporated on genograms rather than separately, and that such a comprehensive assessment makes absolute sense for multiple reasons. Olsen and her colleagues laid out the specific uses of such an assessment to:

- Guide identification of risk factors
- Inform patient and family clinical decisions vis-a-vis care management strategies, psychosocial support, education for reproductive decisions, risk reduction, prevention, screening, diagnosis, referral, and long-term management of disease
- Decide on testing strategies
- Establish patterns of inheritance
- Identify at-risk family members
- Determine reproductive options
- Distinguish genetics from other risk factors
- Enhance patient rapport
- Educate patients and families
- Examine communication patterns and barriers
- Explore emotional and behavioral patterns in an intergenerational context
- Help the family see itself as an interdependent group, connected in important ways
- Help family members see commonalities and uniqueness in other members
- Clarify options for changes in a family (e.g., rearranging household membership)
- Prevent isolation of one family member as "scapegoat" independent of whole family structure
- Portray overview of family connections to each other and to outside institutions
- Demonstrate access to and pattern of resources, clarifying what extra resources may be needed

Olsen and her colleagues (2004) also laid out the important issues around accuracy of information. Obviously accuracy increases with confirmation of one patient's memory by that of other family members, and by data incorporated from medical records. It is clear that the more a single record is updated and checked over time in different clinical settings, the more accurate it will be. This makes clear the value of using a genogram/ecomap/chronology that has been gathered over time and with input from various family members as well as from healthcare, social service, and other sources.

There are ethical and legal implications of such an assessment. Producing such an expanded account of a patient's interpersonal and ecological world raises issues of confidentiality and privacy and requires careful scrutiny. Information revealed about relatives and family members is confidential and can only be released with the consent of that individual. Yet, patients should be encouraged to discuss genetic information with their relatives, particularly if the future health of those relatives or their children may be affected. Deciding whom to tell and what may be necessary to tell are important considerations for patients and healthcare providers. Protecting privacy and confidentiality in research is also important. Of particular concern is the possibility that health insurance may be denied based on genetic information. Legislators have made an effort to protect patients' rights with the Health Insurance Portability & Accountability Act (HIPAA) of 1996 (Department of Health and Human Services), and more recently with the Genetic Information Nondiscrimination Act of 2005 (S. 306, H.R. 1227), which prohibits using genetic information to refuse or cancel insurance coverage.

Genograms in Qualitative Research

Genograms have proven to be a good fit for qualitative research, in which data is collected by observation, in-depth interviewing, and in various ways that allow the voices of the research participants to be heard (Beitin & Allen, 2005; Jordan, 2006; Petry, 2006). Its use in family therapy classrooms made it a natural choice for family therapy researchers, and it is a popular instrument because it encourages participants to tell their stories. Further, researchers in family therapy are interested in representing their data in aesthetic forms that bring their findings to life (Piercy & Benson, 2005) and using genograms is one way of doing that. The genogram is a widely accepted qualitative assessment tool (Marshall & Rossman, 1999;

Miles & Huberman, 1994; Strauss & Corbin, 1998). Genogram software programs that include a database will make genograms an outstanding tool for quantitative research as well because the database will increase the capability of storing, managing, and analyzing complex data.

Software Programs

Randy Gerson developed the first computerized genogram program, designed for the original Macintosh, in 1982. Since that time a number of other programs have been developed, mostly for genealogists but also some for clinicians, for example Genogram-Maker Millennium (2007, www.genogram.org), GenoPro (2007, www.GenoPro.com), and Wonderware (www.interpersonaluniverse.net). Some of these programs allow you to indicate critical family relationships such as fused, distant, abusive, and so on. Likewise, some of these programs assist with the depiction of separation, divorce, illnesses, substance abuse, pets and household composition, and, of course, color coding of different features, and come with tutorials and extensive help files. One of them, GenoPro, also has a hyperlink, which allows you to draw multiple genograms that include the same family members, while preserving and adding to the database information on each individual as you go along. The ability of a program to go beyond just a physical drawing and maintain a database will open up a world of research opportunities. Researchers will be able to analyze all genograms that have been included in it and study patterns we have been hypothesizing about for many years. Dan Morin, GenoPro's developer, is in the process of creating an option that will conform exactly to the genogram format used in this book. The program should be available in early 2008. For further information please visit their Web site, listed above, or contact Dan Morin at daniel.morin@danmorin.com. With this program's potential to create a large database for multiple levels of individual and family information as well to conform to a common genogram language, this software offers great promise.

Software that automatically creates a database as the genogram is constructed will open up amazing new possibilities for using genograms in quantitative research. The family therapy field has been criticized for lagging behind in research. This is probably because family therapy research is incredibly complex and geometrically harder than research on individual psychological processes. In addition the culture of family therapy has generally not valued research and many family therapy teachers have not been trained in evidenced-based models and methodologies (Sprenkle, 2003). The development of genogram software that is attached to a database will dramatically change this situation. It will open up new possibilities for the collaboration of clinicians and researchers, because, for the first time, it will make a primary clinical tool into a powerful research tool as well. This bridges the traditional distance between researchers and clinicians, who have had different agendas for data collection with clients. Clinicians wanted to do what was clinically appropriate in the moment and researchers wanted to collect data in measurable ways so that they could study large amounts of data efficiently. Researchers have been more interested in numbers and manualized interventions, whereas clinicians have been more interested in the art of intervention. Now the clinicians' most immediate tool for keeping track of the enormously complicated data on families will be available for research. It means that clinicians and patients will no longer have to fill out special forms or participate in research-designed interviews in order to contribute to research data on families. Instead, researchers will be able to study the data clinicians use and update from session to session as families are willing to tell more about their histories and experiences. The genogram as a tool for collecting data was always far superior to any questionnaire because it was modified over time as different family members' memories confirmed or elaborated the data collected in the initial assessment. But now this rich data can be studied in aggregate form, giving us the possibility of studying more accurate clinical information on family patterns that is gathered over time in a clinical context.

Let us consider some possible scenarios for research using a genogram database. The database will record all of the information that is entered, such as ages of family members (living and deceased), their interpersonal relationships, attributes such as birth place, ethnicity, physical and mental functioning, education, occupation, religion, sexual orientation, and income, and any other information that the clinician decides is relevant.

Imagine a database of genograms from which a researcher could track any specific theme—for example, "breast cancer and supportive networks." It would be possible, with a few clicks, to identify all genograms in which someone had breast cancer and compare them with regard to the level of support of the family and kinship network, assuming this information has been tracked in the genogram. The researcher could go forward in time to friendship networks or backward to the previous generations and historical experiences. Medical problems could be assessed in relation to the level of support of family and network relationships, the probability of other risk factors, and the financial resources available for the patient and her family. They could be considered in light of risks from previous family history or the strengths and resources of the previous generations (i.e., how did her grandmother and the family deal with it?).

The researcher would be able to choose almost any theme. Looking at a sample of genograms one may decide to track patterns of substance abuse correlated with ethnicity, occupation, marital status, or sexual orientation. Or examine the correlation of substance abuse with medical problems, physical disabilities, and relationship problems. One might decide to look at themes of family cutoffs and substance abuse, or substance abuse and physical or sexual abuse. The beauty of the database is that the clinician can enter as much information as is available, adding more details during each session. Yet attributes may be turned on or off to highlight different issues for the client or for the clinician's exploration, while all of the information remains stored in the database.

Ethical and Legal Implications

The ethical obligation to protect the privacy and obtain informed consent of participants in medical and psychosocial research is standard practice. However, special consideration is warranted for the responsibilities that arise when information involves family members. Indeed, this has become a topic of concern with respect to private information revealed in the publishing of family pedigrees and has resulted in ethical issues and lawsuits (Botkin, 2001; Botkin, McMahon, Smith, & Nash, 1998; Frankel

& Teich, 1993). Informed consent is routinely obtained from the patient, but it would be impossible to conduct any meaningful research if all family members mentioned on a genogram were required to give consent. Nevertheless, a database that holds private information of nonconsenting family members raises serious ethical implications. The software must allow for the clinician to have complete and accurate information for treatment, yet the research database must have a systematic method to disguise identities. Even with the names of family members deleted, however, researchers will need to take precautions to protect the privacy of everyone involved.

In sum, although genograms have been used in research for more than two decades, their potential has not even begun to be fully realized. A computerized genogram with a manualized inquiry and a database will create enormous opportunities for systemic research. In our view, the genogram is nothing less than the best available tool for clinical assessment and research on family systems.

Appendix

FOR THE CONVENIENCE OF TEACHERS AND CLINICIANS, this appendix provides summaries of some important materials and skeletal formats for doing genograms. It includes:

- A summary of the symbol standardization for doing genograms
- An outline for conducting a genogram interview
- An outline for genogram interpretation

Part 1: Genogram Format

Symbols

Symbols are used to describe basic family membership and structure. The genogram should also include significant others who lived with or cared for family members.

Family Interaction Patterns

Relationship indicators are optional. The clinician may prefer to note them on a separate sheet. They are among the least precise information on the genogram, but they may be key indicators of relationship patterns the clinician wants to remember.

Medical History

Because the genogram is meant to be an orienting map of the family, prioritizing the most important factors is essential. List the only major or chronic illnesses and problems, with dates when feasible or applicable.

Use *DSM-IV* categories or recognized abbreviations when appropriate (e.g., cancer: CA; stroke: CVA).

Other Family Information
Other family information of special importance should also be noted on the genogram:

- Ethnic background and migration date
- Religion or religious change
- Education
- Occupation or unemployment
- Military service
- Retirement
- Trouble with law
- Physical or sexual abuse or incest
- Obesity (indicate with an O to the lower right of the symbol)
- Alcohol or drug abuse
- Smoking (indicate with an S on the lower right of the symbol)
- Dates when family member left home (**LH 93**)
- Current location of family members
- Difficulty speaking the dominant language of the culture (indicate with an L on the lower right of the symbol)

It is useful to have a space at the bottom of the genogram for notes on other key information. This would include critical events, changes in the family structure since the genogram was made, hypotheses and other notations of major family issues or changes. These notations should always be dated and should be kept to a minimum, as every extra piece of information on a genogram complicates it and therefore diminishes its readability.

Part 2: Outline for a Brief Genogram Interview
Start With the Presenting Problem

- What help are they coming for at this moment?
- When did the problem begin?
- Who noticed it?
- How does each person view it?
- How has each responded?
- What were relationships in the family like prior to the problem?
- Has the problem changed relationships? How?
- What will happen if the problem continues?

Move to Questions About the Household Context

- Who lives in the household (name, age, gender)?
- How is each related?
- Where do other family members live?
- Were there ever similar problems in the family before?
- What solutions were tried in the past? Therapy? Hospitalization? Visits to doctor, religious helper, family member?
- What has been happening recently in the family?
- Have there been any recent changes or stresses?

Gather Information on Families of Origin

- Parents and stepparents (name, age, occupation, couple status, health status or date and cause of death)
- Siblings (name, age, birth order, occupation, couple status, children, health status or date and cause of death)

Inquire About Other Generations

- Grandparents (name, age, occupation, couple status, health status or date and cause of death)

Cultural Variables
- Cultural heritage of family members
- Religious or spiritual orientation of family members
- Family's migration history
- Gender roles and rules in the family

Life Events and Individual Functioning
- Traumatic or untimely deaths
- Stressors such as illness or job problems
- Medical or psychological problems
- Addictions
- Legal problems (arrests, loss of professional license, current status of litigation)
- Work or school achievement or difficulty

Family Relationships
- Special closeness of any family members, ability to read the other's mind
- Serious conflict or cutoff of any relationships
- Quality of couple relationship, parent-child relationships, sibling relationships
- Physical, emotional, or sexual abuse

Family Strengths and Balance
- Family roles: Who are the caretakers and the sick ones? The good ones and the bad ones? The successful ones and the failures? The warm ones and the cold, distant, or mean ones?
- Family resilience: What are the sources of hope? Humor, loyalty, courage, intelligence, warmth?
- Ability to connect with resources: love, friends, community, money, religious community, work, and so on

Part 3: Genogram Interpretation
Family Structure and Composition

Couple configurations

- Single-parent households can be stressful because of the obvious loss issues as well as loneliness, economic stress, child-rearing strains, and so on.
- Remarried households, where one or both parents have remarried after death or divorce, may involve problems over custody, visitation, imbalance of resources, jealousy, favoritism, loyalty conflicts, stepparent conflicts, stepsibling conflicts, and so on.

Siblings

- Birth order can have relevance for one's emotional and relational role in the family. For example, the oldest is more likely to be over-responsible, conscientious, and parental; youngest children may be more spoiled or childlike. Only children may be socially independent, less oriented toward peer relations, more adultlike at an earlier age, more anxious at times, and, like an oldest child, often the focus of parents' attention. All children after the oldest have to find some way to carve a niche for themselves.
- Timing of sibling births vis-a-vis what else was happening in the family at the time. For example, was there a birth right before or after a loss? (Such a situation often indicates an attempt to replace or make up for the loss.)
- Family's expectations or "program" for the child.
- Parental attitudes and biases regarding gender. Are males given preferred status? Or females? Are there alliances in the family by gender?

Family Place in the Life Cycle

In interpreting a genogram, you will also want to look at where individuals and the family as a whole are in the life cycle. Families progress through a series of stages or transitions, including leaving the home of origin, marriage, births, child rearing, and retirement. Upon reaching each milestone, the family must reorganize itself and move on successfully to the next phase. If patterns rigidify at transition points, families can have trouble adapting to a later phase (Carter & McGoldrick, 2004).

The clinician should note what life cycle transitions, if any, the family is adapting to, and how they have adapted to life cycle events in the past. When ages and dates do not add up in terms of how that family progressed through various stages, possible difficulties in managing that phase of the life cycle can be explored. For example, if adult children have not left home, one would want to explore any difficulties around beginning a new phase of the life cycle. Or, if a marriage occurred quickly after a loss, this may be a clue about issues of unresolved grief.

Pattern Repetition Across Generations

Because family patterns can be transmitted from one generation to the next, be alert to any cross-generational patterns that reveal themselves in the following areas:

Patterns of Functioning

Are there things about how this family functions that you see in previous generations also? These patterns could be adaptive (creativity, resilience, strengths) or maladaptive (battering, child abuse, alcoholism, suicide).

Patterns of Relationships

Look for patterns of closeness, distance, cutoffs, or conflicts repeating over generations. For example, a family might have a pattern of forming relational "triangles" with mother and father allied against a child.

Patterns Related to Position in Family

People in similar positions as a previous generation member tend to repeat the same patterns. For example, the only son of a man who spent time in prison during his twenties may pattern himself after his father and end up going to prison during his twenties. Or a person may remarry and form a similar family constellation to the one he or she grew up in. This factor may influence relationships with others in the same repetitive patterns.

Balance in Family Roles and Functioning

In well-functioning families, members' characteristics tend to balance out one another. For example, a gregarious social partner is balanced out by a more home-oriented spouse; a responsible older sibling is balanced out by an easygoing younger one. The roles and personalities of one provide a complementary fit with the other.

But some genograms show an imbalance in roles, with too many people vying for the same role of "caretaker," for example, or one person being responsible for too much. An alcoholic married to a caretaker, for instance, may seem a complementary fit, but ultimately this situation puts too much of a strain on the caretaker. Families may also show an imbalance in power between husbands and wives, brothers and sisters, darker- and lighter-skinned family members, or for some other reason, depending on class, abilities, parental preferences, family values, and so on. When imbalances appear, explore how the family handles them and what the implications would be of changing them to create a more equitable balance.

References

T HE BIBLIOGRAPHY HAS BEEN DIVIDED into three sections. The first includes references to the literature cited in the text. The second is a bibliography arranged by topic. The third includes biographical sources and is arranged alphabetically by family name.

Ahrons, C. (1998). *The good divorce*. New York: Harper Paperbacks.

Alexander, D., & Clark, S. (1998). Keeping "the family" in focus during patient care. In P. D. Sloane, L. M., Slat, P. Curtis, & M. H. Ebell (Eds.), *Essentials of family medicine* (3rd ed., pp. 25–39). Baltimore: Williams & Wilkins.

Ali, T. (1985). *An Indian dynasty*. New York: Putnam.

Almeida, R., Messineo, T., Woods, R., & Font, R. (1998). The cultural context model. In M. McGoldrick (Ed.), *Revisioning family therapy: Race, culture and gender in clinical practice*. New York: Guilford.

Altshuler, S. J. (1999, November/December). Constructing genograms with children in care: Implications for casework practice. *Child Welfare*, (6), 777–790.

Anderson, J. L. (1997). *Che Guevara: A revolutionary life*. New York: Grove Press.

Andrews, J. D. (1998). *Young Kennedys: The new generation*. New York: Avon.

Anzieu, D. (1986). *Freud's self analysis*. Madison, CT: International Universities Press.

Appignanesi, L., & Forrester, J. (1992). Freud's women. New York: Basic.

Baird, M. A., & Grant, W. D. (1994). Families and health. In R. B. Taylor, A. K. David, T. A. Johnson, Jr., D. M. Phillips, & J. E. Scherger (Eds.), *Family medicine principles and practice* (4th ed., pp. 10–15). New York: Springer-Verlag.

Baird, M. A., & Grant, W. D. (1998). Families and health. In R. B. Taylor, A. K. David, T. A. Johnson, Jr., D. M. Phillips, & J. E. Scherger (Eds.), *Family medicine principles and practice* (5th ed., pp. 26–31). Baltimore: Williams & Wilkins.

Bannerman, C. (1986). The genograms and elderly patients. *Journal of Family Practice, 23,* 426–427.

Barth, J. C. (1993). *It runs in my family: Overcoming the legacy of family illness.* New York: Brunner/Mazel.

Bateson, M. C. (1984). *With a daughter's eye.* New York: William Morrow.

Beitin, B. K., & Allen, K. R. (2005). Resilience in Arab American couples after September 11, 2001: A systems perspective. *Journal of Marital & Family Therapy, 31*(3), 25–267.

Bepko, C. S., & Krestan, J. (1985). *The responsibility trap: Women and men in alcoholic families.* New York: Free Press.

Bernikow, L. (1980). *Among women.* New York: Harper & Row.

Blumenthal, R. (2006). Hotel log hints as illicit desire that Dr. Freud didn't repress. *NY Times,* Dec. 24, pp. 1, 4.

Botkin, J. R. (2001). Protecting the privacy of family members in survey and pedigree research. *Journal of the American Medical Association, 285*(2), 207–211.

Botkin, J. R., McMahon, W. M., Smith, K. R., & Nash, J. E. (1998). Privacy and confidentiality in the publication of pedigrees. *Journal of the American Medical Association, 279*(22), 1808–1812.

Bowen, M. (1978). *Family therapy in clinical practice.* New York: Jason Aronson.

Boyd-Franklin, N. (1989). *Black families in therapy: A multisystems approach.* New York: Guilford.

Boyd-Franklin, N. (2006). *Black families in therapy: Understanding African-American experience* (2nd ed.). New York: Guilford.

Bradt, J. (1980). *The family diagram.* Washington DC: Groome Center.

Bragg, M. (1990). *Richard Burton: A life*. New York: Warner.

Brodie, F. M. (1974). *Thomas Jefferson: An intimate history*. New York: Norton.

Burke, J. L., & Faber, P. (1997). A genogrid for couples. *Journal of Gay and Lesbian Social Services, 7*(1), 13–22.

Callas, J. (1989). *Sisters*. New York: St. Martin's.

Campbell, C. (1998). *The real Diana*. New York: St. Martin's Press.

Campbell, T. L., McDaniel, S. H., Cole-Kelly, K., Hepworth, J., & Lorenz, A. (2002). Family interviewing: A review of the literature in primary care. *Family Medicine, 34*(5), 312–318).

Caplow, T. (1968). *Two against one. Coalitions in triads*. Englewood Cliffs, NJ: Prentice Hall.

Carson, C. (Ed.). (2001). *The autobiography of Martin Luther King*. New York: Warner.

Carter, B., & McGoldrick, M. (2005a). Coaching at various stages of the life cycle. In B. Carter & M. McGoldrick (Eds.), *The expanded family life cycle: Individual, family and social perspectives*, (3rd ed., pp. 436–454). Boston: Allyn & Bacon.

Carter, B., & McGoldrick, M. (Eds.). (2005b). *The expanded family life cycle: Individual, family and social perspectives: Classic edition*. Boston: Allyn & Bacon.

Carter, E. A. (1978). Transgenerational scripts and nuclear family stress: Theory and clinical implications. In R. R. Sager (Ed.), *Georgetown family symposium* (Vol. III, 1975–77). Washington, DC: Georgetown University.

Christie-Seely, J. (1986). *A diagnostic problem and family assessment. Journal of Family Practice, 22*, 329–339.

Clinton, B. (2005). *My life*. New York: Vintage.

Clinton Kelley, V., with J. Morgan (1994). *Leading with my heart: My life*. New York: Pocket Books.

Cohler, B. A., Hosteler, J., & Boxer, A. (1998). In D. McAdams & E. de St. Aubin (Eds.), *Generativity and adult development: Psychosocial perspective on caring and contributing to the next generation*. Washington, DC: American Psychological Association Press.

Colon, F. (1973). *In search of one's past: An identity trip*. Family Process, 12(4), 429–438.

Colon, F. (1978). Family ties and child placement. *Family Process, 17,* 189–312.

Colon, F. (1998). The discovery of my multicultural identity. In M. McGoldrick. (Ed.), *Revisioning family therapy: Race, culture and gender in clinical practice* (pp. 200–214). New York: Guilford.

Colon-Lopez, F. (2005). *Finding my face: Memory of a Puerto Rican American.* Victoria, BC, Canada: Trafford Publishing.

Congress, E. P. (1994). The use of culturagrams to assess and empower culturally diverse families. *Families in Society, 75*(9), 531–540.

Coupland, S. K., & Serovich, J. M. (1999, December). Effects of couples' perceptions of genogram construction on therapeutic alliance and session impact: A growth curve analysis. *Contemporary Family Therapy, 21*(4), 551–572.

Coupland, S. K., Serovich, J., & Glenn, J. E. (1995). Reliability in constructing genograms: A study among marriage and family therapy doctoral students. *Journal of Marital and Family Therapy, 21,* 251–264.

Crouch, M. A. (1986). Working with one's own family: Another path for professional development. *Family Medicine, 18,* 93–98.

Crouch, M., & Davis, T. (1987). Using the genogram (family tree) clinically. In M. A. Crouch & L. Roberts (Eds.), *The family in medical practice: A family systems primer* (pp. 174–192). New York: Springer-Verlag.

Crouch, M. A. (1989). A putative ancestry of family practice and family medicine: Genogram of a discipline. *Family Systems Medicine, 7*(2), 208–212.

Darkenwald, G. G., & Silvestri, K. (1992). Analysis and assessment of the Newark literacy campaign: A report to the Ford Foundation. (Grant #915-0298).

Daughhetee, C. (2001). Using genograms as a tool for insight in college counseling. *Journal of College Counseling, 4*(1), 73–76.

Davis, O., & Dee, R. (2000). *With Ossie and Ruby: In this life together.* New York: Harper Collins.

Dean, P. H. (1989). Paul Robeson. In E. Hill (Ed.), *Black heroes: Seven plays* (pp. 277–354). New York: Applause Theatre.

Donn, L. (2001). *The Roosevelt cousins.* New York: Knopf.

Dumas, C. A., Katerndahl, D. A., & Burge, S. K. (1995). Familial patterns in patients with infrequent panic attacks. *Archives of Family Medicine, 4*, 862–867.

Dunn, A. B., & Dawes, S. J. (1999). Spiritually-focused genograms: Keys to uncovering spiritual resources in African-American families. *Journal of Multicultural Counseling & Development, 27*(4), 240–255.

Dunn, A. B., & Levitt, M. M. (2000, July). The genogram: From diagnostics to mutual collaboration. *Family Journal: Counseling & Therapy for Couples & Families, 8*(3). 236–244.

Eissler, K. R. (1978). *Sigmund Freud: His life in pictures and words.* New York: Helen & Kurt Wolff, Harcourt Brace, Jovanovich.

Elder, G. (1986). Military times and turning points in mens' lives. *Developmental Psychology, 22*, 233–245.

Elder, G. (1992). Life course. In E. Borgatta & M. Borgatta (Eds.), *Encyclopedia of sociology* (Vol. 3, pp. 1120–1130), New York: Macmillan.

Elder, G. H., Jr. (1977). Family history and the life course. *Journal of Family History, 22*, 279–304.

Ellenberger, H. F. (1970). *The discovery of the unconscious: The history and evolution of dynamic psychiatry.* New York: Basic.

Engel, G. (1975). The death of a twin: Mourning and anniversary reactions: Fragments of 10 years of self-analysis. *International Journal of Psychoanalysis, 56*(l), 23–40.

Erikson Bloland, S. (1999, November). Frame: The power and cost of a fantasy. *Atlantic Monthly,* 51–62.

Fields, J. (2003). America's families and living arrangements: 2003. *Current Population Reports. P20-553.* Washington, DC: U.S. Census Bureau.

Fink, A. H., Kramer, L., Weaver, L. L., & Anderson, J. (1993). More on genograms: Modifications to a model. *Journal of Child and Adolescent Group Therapy, 3*, 203–266.

Fogarty, T. (1975). Triangles. *The Family Journal, 2*, 11–19. New Rochelle, NY: Center for Family Learning.

Folwarski, J. (1998). No longer an orphan in history. In M. McGoldrick (Ed.), *Revisioning family therapy* (pp. 239–252). New York: Guilford.

Fonda, J. (2006). *My life so far*. New York: Random House.

Fonda, P. (1998). *Don't tell dad*. New York: Hyperion.

Foster, M. A., Jurkovic, G. J., Ferdinand, L. G., & Meadows, L. A. (2002, January). Impact of the genogram on couples: A manualized approach. *Family Journal: Counseling & Therapy for Couples & Families, 10*(1), 34–40.

Frame, M. W. (2000a). Constructing religious/spiritual genograms. In R. E. Watts (Ed.). *Techniques in marriage and family counseling, Vol. 1. The family psychology and counseling series* (pp. 69–74). Alexandria, VA: American Counseling Assoc.

Frame, M. W. (2000b). The spiritual genogram in family therapy. *Journal of Marital and Family Therapy, 26*(92), 211–216.

Frame, M. W. (2001, April). The spiritual genogram in training and supervision. *Family Journal: Counseling & Therapy for Couple & Families, 9*(2), 109–115.

Frankel, M. S., & Teich, A. H. (Eds.) (1993). *Ethical and legal issues in pedigree research*. Washington, DC: Directorate for Science and Policy Programs, American Association for the Advancement of Sciences.

Freeman, E. L., & Strean, H. S. (1981). *Freud and women*. New York: Fredrick Ungar.

Freire, P. (1994). *The pedagogy of hope*. New York: Continuum.

Freud, E. L. 1960. *The letters of Sigmund Freud*. New York: Basic.

Freud, S. (1988). *My three mothers and other passions*. New York: New York University Press.

Friedman, H., Rohrbaugh, M., & Krakauer, S. (1988). The timeline genogram: Highlighting temporal aspects of family relationships. *Family Process, 27*, 293–304.

Friedman, L. J. (1999). *Identity's architect*. New York: Scribner.

Friesen, P., & Manitt, J. (1991). Nursing the remarried family in a palliative care setting. *Journal of Palliative Care, 6*(4), 32–39

Garrett, R. E., Klinkman, M., & Post, L. (1987). If you meet Buddha on the road, take a genogram: Zen and the art of family medicine. *Family Medicine, 19*, 225–226.

Gelb, A., & Gelb, B. (1987). *O'Neill*. New York: Harper & Row.

Genogram-Maker Millennium (2007). Online at *www.genogram.org*.

GenoPro (2007). Online at *www.genopro.com*.

Gewirtzman, R. C. (1988). The genogram as a visual assessment of a family's fugue. *Australian Journal of Sex, Marriage and Family, 9,* 37–46.

Gibson, D. (2005). The use of genograms in career counseling with elementary, middle, and high school students. *Career Development Quarterly, 53,* 353–362.

Gordon, J. S., Staples, J. K., Blyta, A., & Bytyqi, M. (2004). Treatment of posttraumatic stress disorder in postwar Kosovo high school students using mind-body skills groups: A pilot study. *Journal of Traumatic Stress, 17*(2), 143–147.

Granello D. H., Hothersall, D., & Osborne, A. L. (2000, March). The academic genogram: Teaching for the future by learning from the past. *Counselor Education and Supervision, 39*(3), 177–188

Grimberg, S. (1997). *Frida Kahlo.* North Dighton, MA: World Publications Group, Inc.

Guerin, P., Fogarty, T. F., Fay, L. F., & Kautto, J. G. (1996). *Working with relationship triangles.* New York: Guilford.

Hardy, K. V., & Laszloffy, T. A. (1995). The cultural genogram: Key to training culturally competent family therapists. *Journal of Marital and Family Therapy, 21*(3), 227–237.

Harmon, A. (2006, June 11). Who's your great-great-great-great-granddaddy? *New York Times,* section 4, p. 1.

Haskins, J. (1978). *Scott Joplin: The man who made ragtime.* Briarcliff Manor, NY: Scarborough.

Hays, E. R. (1967). *The extraordinary Blackwells.* New York: Harcourt Brace.

Hayden, T. (Ed.) (1998). *Irish hunger.* Boulder, CO: Roberts Reinhart.

Hayden, T. (2001). *Irish on the inside: In search of the soul of Irish America.* New York: Verso.

Hernandez, M., & McGoldrick, M. (2005). Migration and the family life cycle. In B. Carter & M. McGoldrick (Eds.), *The expanded family life cycle, Classic Edition* (pp. 169–174). Boston: Allyn & Bacon.

Hines, P .M. (2005). The family life cycle of African-American families living in poverty. In B. Carter & M. McGoldrick (Eds.), *The expanded family life cycle: Individual, family and social perspectives* (pp. 327–345). Boston: Allyn & Bacon.

Hockley, J. (2000). Psychosocial aspects in palliative care: Communicating with the patient and family. *Acta oncologica, 39*(8), 905–910.

Hodge, D. R. (2000, April). Spiritual ecomaps: A new diagrammmatic tool for assessing marital and family spirituality. *Journal of Marital and Family Therapy, 26*(2), 217–228.

Hodge, D. R. (2001 January/February). Spiritual genograms: A generational approach to assessing spirituality. *Families in Society, 82*(1), p. 35–48.

Hodge, D. R. (2005a). Spiritual life maps: A client-centered pictorial instrument for spiritual assessment, planning, and intervention. *Social Work, 50,* 77–87.

Hodge, D. R. (2005b). Spiritual ecograms: A new assessment instrument for indentifying clients' spiritual strengths in space and across time. *Familys in Society, 86,* 287–296.

Hof, L., & Berman, E. (1986). The sexual genogram. *Journal of Marital and Family Therapy, 12*(1), 39–47.

Holmes, T. H., & Masuda, M. (1974). Life change and illness susceptibility. ln B. S. Dohrenwend & B. Dohrenwend (Eds.), *Stressful life events: Their nature and effects* (pp. 45–72). New York: Wiley.

Holmes, T. H., & Rahe, T. H. (1967). The social adjustment rating scale. *Journal of Psychosomatic Research, 11,* 213–218.

Horn, M. (1980). Family ties: The Blackwells, a study in the dynamics of family life in nineteenth century America, (Ph.D. Dissertation, Tufts University).

Horn, M. (1983). Sisters worthy of respect: Family dynamics and women's roles in the Blackwell family. *Journal of Family History, 8*(4), 367–382.

Huygen, F. J. A. (1982). *Family medicine: The medical life history of families.* New York: Brunner/Mazel.

Imber Black, E. (Ed.). (1993). *Secrets in families and family therapy.* New York: Norton.

Imber Black, E. (1998). *The secret life of families.* New York: Bantam.

Ingersoll-Dayton, B., & Arndt, B. (1990). Uses of the genogram with the elderly and their families. *Journal of Gerontological Social Work, 15*(1-2), 105–120.

Johnson, P. (2005). *George Washington: Founding father*. New York: Harper Collins.

Jolly, W. M., Froom, J., & Rosen, M. G. (1980). The genogram. *Journal of Family Practice, 10*(2), 251–255.

Jones, E. (1953, 1954, 1955). *The life and work of Sigmund Freud* (3 volumes.). New York: Basic.

Jordan, K. (2004). The color-coded timeline trauma genogram. *Brief Treatment and Crisis Intervention, 4*(1), 57–70.

Jordan, K. (2006). The scripto-trauma genogram: An innovative technique for working with trauma survivors' intrusive memories. *Brief Treatment and Crisis Intervention, 6*(1), 36–51.

Kerr, M. E., & Bowen, M. (1988). *Family evaluation*. New York: Norton.

Krüll, M. (1986). *Freud and his father*. New York: Norton.

Kuehl, B. P. (1995). The solution-oriented genogram: A collaborative approach. *Journal of Marital and Family Therapy, 21*(3) 239–250.

Laird, J. (1996). Family-centered practice with lesbian and gay families. *Families in Society: Journal of Contemporary Human Services, 77*(9), 559–572.

Lerner, H. (1990). *The dance of intimacy*. New York: Harper Collins.

Lerner, H. (1994). *The dance of deception*. New York: Harper Collins.

Lerner, H. (1997). *The dance of anger*. New York: Harper Collins.

Lerner, H. (2002). *The dance of connection*. New York: Harper Collins.

Lerner, H. (2005). *The dance of fear*. New York: Harper Collins.

Like, R. C., Rogers, J., & McGoldrick, M. (1988). Reading and interpreting genograms: A systematic approach. *Journal of Family Practice, 26*(4), 407–412.

Lipset, D. (1980). *Gregory Bateson: The legacy of a scientist*. Englewood Cliffs, NJ: Prentice.

Maccoby, E. E. (1990). Gender and relationships: A developmental account. *American Psychologist, 45*(4), 513–520.

Malott, K. M., & Magnuson, S. (2004). Using genograms to facilitate undergraduate students' career development: A group model. *The Career Development Quarterly, 53*(4), pp. 178–186.

Mann, W. J. (2006). *Kate: The woman who was Hepburn*. New York: Henry Holt.

Maraniss, D. (1995). *First in his class: The biography of Bill Clinton*. New York: Touchtone.

Masson, J. (Ed.). (1985). *The complete letters of Sigmund Freud to Wilhelm Fleiss: 1887-1904*. Cambridge, MA: Belnap.

Masson, J. (1992). *The assault on truth*. New York: Harper Collins.

Massey, R. F., & Dunn, A. B. (1999). Viewing the transactional dimensions of spirituality through family prisms. *Transactional Analysis Journal, 29*(2), 113–129.

McGill, D. M. (1992). The cultural story in multicultural family therapy. *Families in Society: Journal of Contemporary Human Services, 73*, 339–349.

McGoldrick, M. (1989). Sisters. In M. McGoldrick, C. Anderson, & F. Walsh (Eds.), *Women in families* (pp. 244–266). New York: Norton.

McGoldrick, M. (1995). *You can go home again: Reconnecting with your family*. New York: Norton.

McGoldrick, M. (1996). *The legacy of unresolved loss: A family systems approach*. New York: Norton.

McGoldrick, M. (Ed.). (1998). *Revisioning family therapy: Race, culture and gender in clinical practice*. New York: Guilford.

McGoldrick, M., Broken Nose, M., & Potenza, M. (2005). Violence and the family life cycle. In B. Carter & M. McGoldrick (Eds.), *The expanded family life cycle: Individual, family and social perspectives, Classic edition* (pp. 470–491). Boston: Allyn & Bacon.

McGoldrick, M., & Carter, B. (2005a). Self in context: The individual life cycle in systemic perspective. In B. Carter & M. McGoldrick (Eds.), *The expanded family life cycle: Individual, family and social perspective, Classic edition* (pp. 27–46). Boston: Allyn & Bacon.

McGoldrick, M., & Carter, B. (2005b). Remarried families. In B. Carter & M. McGoldrick (Eds.), *The expanded family life cycle: Individual, family and social perspectives, Classic edition* (pp. 417–435). Boston: Allyn & Bacon.

McGoldrick, M., & Garcia-Preto, N. (2005). Cultural assessment. In M. McGoldrick, J. Giordano, & N. Garcia-Preto (Eds.), *Ethnicity and family therapy* (3rd ed., pp. 757–763). New York: Guilford.

McGoldrick, M., Giordano, J., & Garcia-Preto, N. (Eds.). (2005). *Ethnicity and family therapy* (3rd ed.). New York: Guilford.

McGoldrick, M., Loonan, R., & Wolsifer, D. (2006). Sexuality and culture. In S. R. Leiblum (Ed.), *Principles and practice of sex therapy* (4th ed., pp. 416–441). New York: Guilford.

McGoldrick, M., & Walsh, F. (2004). A time to mourn: Death and the family life cycle. In F. Walsh & M. McGoldrick (Eds.), *Living beyond loss* (2nd ed., pp. 27–46). New York: Norton.

McGoldrick, M., & Watson, M. (2005). Siblings through the life cycle. In B. Carter & M. McGoldrick (Eds.), *The expanded family life cycle: Individual, family and social perspectives, Classic edition* (pp. 153–168). Boston: Allyn & Bacon.

McIlvain, H., Crabtree, B., Medder, J., Strange, K. C., & Miller, W. L. (1998). Using practice genograms to understand and describe practice configurations. *Family medicine, 30*(7), 490–496.

McMillen, J. C., & Groze, V. (1994). Using placement genograms in child welfare practice. *Child Welfare, 73*(4), 307–318.

Medalie, J. H. (1978). *Family medicine: Principles and applications.* Baltimore: Williams & Wilkins.

Milewski-Hertlein, K. A. (2001, January/February). The use of a socially constructed genogram in clinical practice. *American Journal of Family Therapy, 29*(1), 23–28.

Moon, S. M., Coleman, V. D., McCollum, E. E., Nelson, T. S., & Jensen-Scott, R. L. (1993). Using the genogram to facilitate career decisions: A case study. *Journal of Family Psychology, 4*, 45–56.

Mullins, M. C., & Christie-Seely, J. (1984). Collecting and recording family data: The genogram. In J. Christie-Seely (Ed.), *Working with the family in primary care* (pp. 79–81). New York: Praeger.

Nabokov, V. (1959). *The real life of Sebastian Knight.* Norfolk, CT: New Directions.

Niederhauser, V. P. & Arnold, M. (2004). Assess health risk status for intervention and risk reduction. *Nurse Practiioner, 29*(2), 35–42.

Oestreich, J. R. (2006, February). The asterisks tell the story: What tangled webs operas can weave. That's where a five page diagram comes in. *New York Times*, p. C2.

Olsen, S. Dudley-Brown, S., & McMullen, P. (2004). Case for blending pedigrees, genograms, and ecomaps: Nursings' contribution to the "big picture." *Nursing & Health Sciences, 6*(4), 295–308.

Papp, P., Silverstein, O., & Carter, E. A. (1973). Family sculpting in preventive work with well families. *Family Process, 12*(25), 197–212.

Paul, N., & Paul B. B. (1986). A marital puzzle. New York: Norton.

Peluso, P. (2003). The ethical genogram: A tool for helping therapists understand their ethical decision-making roles. *The Family Journal, 11*(3), 286–291.

Petry, S. S. (2006). The impact on male therapists treating sex offenders: A phenomenological study with a focus on gender, race, and ethnicity. *Dissertation Abstracts International: SectionB: The Sciences and Engineering, 66*(9-B), 5143–5367.

Petry, S. S., & McGoldrick, M. (2005). Genograms in assessment and therapy. In G. P. Koocher, J. C. Norcross, & S. S. Hill (Eds.), *The psychologists' desk reference* (2nd ed., pp. 366–373).

Piercy, F. P., & Benson, K. (2005). Aesthetic forms of data representation in qualitative family therapy research. *Journal of Marital & Family Therapy, 31*(1), 107–119.

Pinderhughes, E. (1998). Black genealogy revisited: Restorying African-American family. In M. McGoldrick (Ed.), *Revisioning family therapy: Race, culture, and gender in clinical practice* (pp. 179–199). New York: Guilford.

Rainsford, G. L., & Schuman, S. H. (1981). The family in crisis: A case study of overwhelming illness and stress. *Journal of the American Medical Association, 246*(1), 60–63.

Rakel, R. E. (1977). *Principles of family medicine.* Philadelphia: W.B. Saunders.

Rigazio-DiGilio, S. A, Ivey, A. E., Kunkler-Peck, K. P., & Grady, L. T. (2005). *Community genograms: Using individual, family, and cultural narratives with clients.* New York: Teachers College Press.

Roazen, P. (1993). *Meeting Freud's family.* Amherst, MA: University of Massachusetts Press.

Robeson, P. (1988). *Here I stand.* Boston: Beacon.

Robinson, J. (1972). *I never had it made.* New York: Putnam.

Robinson, S. (1996). *Stealing home.* New York: Harper-Collins.

Rogers, J. C. (1990). Completion and reliability of the self-administered genogram (SAGE). *Family Practice, 7,* 149–151.

Rogers, J. C. (1994a). Can physicians use family genogram information to identify patients at risk of anxiety or depression? *Archives of Family Medicine, 3,* 1093–1098.

Rogers, J. C. (1994b). Impact of a screening family genogram on first encounters in primary care. *Journal of Family Practice, 4,* 291–301.

Rogers, J. C., & Cohn, P. (1987). Impact of a screening family genogram on first encounters in primary care. *Journal of Family Practice, 4,* 291–301.

Rogers, J. C., & Durkin, M. (1984). The semi-structured genogram interview: l. Protocol, ll. Evaluation. *Family Systems Medicine, 2*(25), 176–187.

Rogers, J. C., Durkin, M., & Kelly, K. (1985). The family genogram: An underutilized clinical tool. *New Jersey Medicine, 82*(11), 887–892.

Rogers, J. C., & Holloway, R. (1990). Completion rate and reliability of the self-administered genogram (SAGE). *Family Practice, 7,* 149–51.

Rogers, J. C., Rohrbaugh, M., & McGoldrick, M. (1992). Can experts predict health risk from family genograms? *Family Medicine, 24,* 209–215.

Rohrbaugh, M., Rogers, J. C., & McGoldrick, M. (1992). How do experts read family genograms? *Family Systems Medicine, 10*(1), 79–89.

Satir, V. (1988). *New peoplemaking.* Palo Alto, CA: Science and Behavior Books.

Scharwiess, S. O. (1994). Step-sisters and half-brothers: A family therapist's view of German unification and other transitional processes. *Contemporary Family Therapy, 16*(3), 183–197.

Scherger, J. E. (2005). The end of the beginning: The redesign imperative in family medicine. *Family Medicine, 37*(7), 513–516.

Schoeninger, D. (2007). *Cultural legacies.* Manuscript in preparation.

Scrivner, R., & Eldridge, N. S. (1995) Lesbian and gay family psychology. In R. H. Mikesell, D. Lusterman, & S. McDaniel (Eds.), *Integrating family therapy: Handbook of family psychology and systems therapy* (pp. 327–345). Washington, DC: American Psychological Association.

Shellenberger, S., Shurden, K. W., & Treadwell, T. W. (1988). Faculty training seminars in family systems, *Family Medicine, 20,* 226–227.

Shellenberger, S., Watkins Couch, K., & Drake, M. (1989). Elderly family members and their caregivers: Characteristics and development of the relationship. *Family Systems and Health, 7,* 317–322.

Sherman, M. H. (1990). Family narratives: Internal representations of family relationships and affective themes. *Infant Mental Health Journal, 11,* 253–258.

Shernoff, M. J. (1984). Family therapy for lesbian and gay clients. *Social Work, 39,* 393–396.

Shields, C. G., King, D. A., & Wynne, L. C. (1995). Interventions with later life families. In R. H. Mikesell, D. Lusterman, & S. McDaniel (Eds.), *Integrating family therapy: Handbook of family psychology and systems therapy* (pp. 141–158). Washington, DC: American Psychological Association.

Sloan, P. D., Slatt, L. M., Curtis, P., & Ebell, M. (Eds.). (1998). *Essentials of family medicine* (2nd ed.). Baltimore: Williams & Wilkins.

Sprenkle, D. H. (2003). Effectiveness research in marriage and family therapy: Introduction. *Journal of Marital & Family Therapy, 29*(1), 85–96.

Sproul, M. S., & Gallagher, R. M. (1982). The genogram as an aid to crisis intervention. *Journal of Family Practice, 14*(55), 959–960.

Steinglass, P., Bennett, L., Wolin, S., & Reiss, D. (1987). *The alcoholic family.* New York: Basic.

Sulloway, F. J. (1996). *Born to rebel: Sibling relationships, family dynamics and creative lives.* New York: Pantheon.

Swales, P. (1982). Freud, Minna Bernays, and the conquest of Rome: New light on the origins of psychoanalysis. *The New American Review, 1*(2/3), 1–23.

Swales, P. (1986). *Freud, his origins and family history.* UMDNJ-Robert Wood Johnson Medical School. November 15.

Taylor, R. B., David, A. K., Johnson, T. A., Jr., Phillips, D. M., & Scherger, J. E. (Eds.). (1998). *Family medicine principles and practice* (5th ed.). Baltimore: Williams & Wilkins.

Thomas, A. J. (1998). Understanding culture and worldview in family systems: Use of the multicultural genogram. *The Family Journal: Counseling and Therapy for Couples and Families, 6*(1), 24–31.

Tjaden, P., & Thoennes, N. (2000). *Full report of the prevalence, incidence, and consequences of violence against women* (Research Report). Washington, DC: National Institute of Justice and the Centers for Disease Control Prevention.

Toman, W. (1976). *Family constellation* (3rd ed.). New York: Springer.

Tomson, P. (1985). Genograms in general practice. *Journal of the Royal Society of Medicine Supplement, 78*(8), 34–39.

Troncale, J. A. (1983). The genogram as an aid to diagnosis of distal renal tubular acidosis. *Journal of Family Practice, 17,* 707–708.

Wachtel, E. F. (1982). The family psyche over three generations: The genogram revisited. *Journal of Marital and Family Therapy, 8*(35), 335–343.

Wallechinsky, D., & Wallace, I. (1975). *The people's almanac.* New York: Harper & Row.

Walsh, F. (Ed.). (2003). *Normal family processes* (3rd ed.). New York: Guilford.

Walsh, F. (1995). From family damage to family challenge. In R. H. Mikesell, D. D. Lusterman, & S. McDaniel (Eds.), *Integrating family therapy: Handbook of family psychology and systems therapy* (pp. 587–606). Washington, DC: American Psychological Association.

Walsh, F. (2006). *Strengthening family resilience* (2nd ed.). New York: Guilford.

Walsh, F. (Ed.). (1999). *Spiritual resources in family therapy.* New York: Guilford.

Watson, M. (1998). African-American sibling relationships. In M. McGoldrick (Ed.), *Revisioning family therapy: Race, culture and gender in clinical practice* (pp. 282–294). New York: Guilford.

Wattendorf, D. J., & Hadley, M. S. (2005). Family history: The three generation pedigree. *American Family Physician, 72*(3), 441–448.

Watts Jones, D. (1998). Towards an African-American genogram. *Family Process, 36*(4), 373–383.

Weber, T., & Levine, F. (1995). Engaging the family: An integrative approach. In R. H. Mikesell, D. D. Lusterman, & S. McDaniel (Eds.), *Integrating family therapy: Handbook of family psychology and systems therapy* (pp. 45–71). Washington, DC: American Psychological Association.

White, M. (2006). Personal communication.

White, M. B., & Tyson-Rawson, K. J. (1995). Assessing the dynamics of gender in couples and families: The gendergram. *Family Relations, 44*, 253–260.

Widmer, R. B., Cadoret, R. J., & North, C. S. (1980). Depression in family practice: Some effects on spouses and children. *Journal of Family Practice, 10*(1), 45–51.

Wimbush, F. B., & Peters, R. M. (2000). Identification of cardiovascular risk: use of a cardiovascular-specific genogram. *Public Health nursing, 17*(3), 148–154.

Wolpert, S. (1996). *Nehru.* new York: Oxford University Press.

Wonderware (2007). Online at *www.interpersonaluniverse.net.*

Wright, L. (1995, August). Double mystery. *New Yorker Magazine*, pp. 44–62.

Wright, L. M., & Leahey, M. (2000). *Nurses and families: A guide to family assessment and intervention* (3rd ed.). Philadelphia: F. A. Davis.

Wright, L. M., & Leahey, M. (1999). Maximizing time, minimizing suffering: The 15-minute (or less) family interview. *Journal of Family Nursing, 5*(3), 259–274.

Young-Bruel, E. (1988). *Anna Freud: A biography.* New York: Summit.

Zide, M. R., & Gray, S. W. (2000). The solutioning process: Merging the genogram and the solution-focused model of practice. *Journal of Family Social Work, 4*(1), pp. 3–19.

Zimroth, E. (2002). Marilyn at the Mikvah. In Y. Z. McDonough (Ed.), *All the available light: A Marilyn Monroe reader* (pp. 176–183). New York: Simon & Schuster.

Bibliography by Topic

Assessment Genograms and Systems Theory

Banmen, J. (2002, March). The Satir model: Yesterday and today. *Contemporary Family Therapy, 24*(1), 7–22.

Bowen, M. (1978). *Family therapy in clinical practice.* New York: Jason Aronson.

Bradt, J. (1980). *The family diagram.* Washington, DC: Groome Center.

Byng-Hall, J. (1995). *Rewriting family scripts.* New York: Guilford.

Caplow, T. (1968). *Two against one: Coalitions in triads.* Englewood Cliffs, NJ: Prentice Hall.

Carter, B., & McGoldrick, M. (Eds.). (2005). *The expanded family life cycle: Individual, family and social perspectives, Classic Edition.* Boston: Allyn & Bacon.

Carter, E. A. (1978). Transgenerational scripts and nuclear family stress: Theory and clinical implications. In R. R. Sager (Ed.), *Georgetown family symposium.* (Vol. III, pp. 1975–1977).Washington, DC: Georgetown University.

Christie-Seely, J. (1986). A diagnostic problem and family assesment. *Journal of Family Practice, 22,* 329–339.

Erdman, H. P., & Foster, S. W. (1986). Computer-assisted assessment with couples and families. *Family Therapy, 13*(1), 23–40.

Fleck, S. (1994). The family in health and disease. *New Trends in Experimental and Clinical Psychiatry, 10*(1), 41–51.

Fogarty, T. (1973). *Triangles. The Family.* New Rochelle. NY: Center for Family Learning.

Forster, J., Gilman, M., Gipson, D., Jackson, P., Reed, A., Wheeler, J., & Wray, M. (2000). On using genograms in therapy and training contexts. *Context, 49,* pp. 9–10.

Galindo, I., Boomer, E., & Reagan, D. (2006). *A family genogram workbook.* Kearney, NE: Morris Publishing.

Guerin, P. J. (Ed.). (1976). *Family therapy.* New York: Gardner.

Guerin, P., Fogarty, T. F., Fay, L. F., & Kautto, J. G. (1996). *Working with relationship triangles.* New York: Guilford.

Guerin, P. J., & Pendagast, E. G. (1976). Evaluation of family system and genogram. In P. Guerin (Ed.), *Family therapy* (pp. 450–464). New York: Gardner.

Haley, A. (1974). *Roots: The saga of an American family.* New York: Doubleday.

Hartman, A. (1995). Diagrammatic assessment of family relationships. *Families in Society, 76*(2), 111–122.

Karpel, M. A. (1994). *Evaluating couples: A handbook for practitioners.* New York: Norton.

Kent-Wilkinson, A. (1999). Forensic family genogram: An assessment and intervention tool. *Journal of Psychosocial Nursing and Mental Health Services, 37,* 52–56.

Kerr, M. E., & Bowen, M. (1988). *Family evaluation.* New York: Norton.

Krasner-Khait, B. (2000, Jan/Feb). Focusing beneath the surface: Genograms add insight to family research. *Ancestry, 18*(1), pp. 28–31.

Lewis, K. G. (1989). The use of color-coded genograms in family therapy. *Journal of Marital and Family Therapy, 15*(2), 169–176.

Lieberman, S. (1979). *Transgenerational family therapy.* London: Croom Helm.

Like, R. C., Rogers, J., & McGoldrick, M. (1988). Reading and interpreting genograms: A systematic approach. *Journal of Family Practice*, *26*(4), 407–412.

Magnuson, S., & Shaw, H. E. (2003, January). Adaptations of the multifaceted genogram in counseling, training and supervision. *Family Journal: Counseling & Therapy for Couples & Families*, *2*(1), 45–54.

Marlin, E. (1989). Genograms. Chicago: Contemporary Books.

McGoldrick, M. (1980). Problems with family genograms. *American Journal of Family Therapy*, *7*, 74–76.

McGoldrick, M. (1995). *You can go home again: Reconnecting with your family*. New York: Norton.

McGoldrick, M. (Ed.). (1998). *Revisioning family therapy: Race, culture and gender in clinical practice*. New York: Guilford.

Milewski-Hertlein, K. A. (2001, January/February). The use of a socially constructed genogram in clinical practice. *American Journal of Family Therapy*, *29*(1), 23–38.

Papadopoulos, L., Bor, R., & Stanion, P. (1997). Genograms in counselling practice. *Counselling Psychology Quarterly*, *10*(1) 17–28.

Pendagast, E. G., & Sherman, C. O. (1977). A guide to the genogram. *The Family*, *5*, 3–14.

Petry, S. S., & McGoldrick, M. (2003). Genograms in assessment and therapy. In G. P. Koocher, J. C. Norcross, & S. S. Hill (Eds.), *The psychologists' desk reference* (2nd ed., pp. 366–373). New York: Oxford University Press.

Richardson, R. W. (1987). *Family ties that bind: A self-help guide to change through family of origin therapy* (2nd ed.). Bellingham, WA: Self-Counsel Press.

Satir, V. (2000). *Conjoint family therapy*. Palo Alto, CA: Science and Behavior Books.

Satir, V. (1988). *New peoplemaking*. Palo Alto, CA: Science and Behavior Books.

Stanion, P., Papadopoulos, L., & Bor, R. (1997). Genograms in counselling practice. *Counselling Psychology Quarterly*, *10*(2), 139–148.

Starkey, P. J. (1981). Genograms: A guide to understanding one's own family system. *Perspectives in Psychiatric Care*, *19*, 164–173.

Stone, E. (1988). *Black sheep & kissing cousins: How our family stories shape us*. New York: Times Books.

Tomson, P. (1985). Genograms in general practice. *Journal of the Royal Society of Medicine Supplement, 78*(8), 34–39.

Van Treuren, R. R. (1986). Self perception in family systems: A diagrammatic technique. *Social Casework, 67*(5), 299–305.

Visscher, E. M., & Clore, E. R. (1992). The genogram: A strategy for assessment. *Journal of Pediatric healthcare, 6*, 361–367.

Wachtel, E. F. (1982). The family psyche over three generations: The genogram revisited. *Journal of Marital and Family Therapy, 8*(35), 335–343.

Walsh, F. (2003). *Normal family processes: Growing diversity and complexity* (3rd ed.). New York: Guilford.

Weber, T., & Levine, F. (1995). Engaging the family: An integrative approach. In R. H. Mikesell, D. D. Lusterman, & S. McDaniel (Eds.), *Integrating family therapy: Handbook of family psychology and systems therapy* (pp. 45–71). Washington, DC: American Psychological Association.

Career Counseling

Gibson, D. (2005). The use of genograms in career counseling with elementary, middle, and high school students. *Career Development Quarterly, 53*, 353–362.

Heppner, M. J., O'Brien, K. M., Hinkelman, J. M., & Humphrey, C. F. (1994). Shifting the paradigm: The use of creativity in career counseling. *Journal of Career Development, 21*(2), 77–86.

Magnuson, S. (2000, October). The professional genogram: Enhancing professional identity and clarity. *Family Journal: Counseling & Therapy for Couples & Families, 8*(4), 299–401.

Malott, K. M., & Magnuson, S. (2004). Using genograms to facilitate undergraduate students' career development: A group model. *Career Development Quarterly, 53*(4), pp. 178–186.

Moon, S. M., Coleman, V. D., McCollum, E. E., & Nelson, T. S. (1993). Using the genogram to facilitate career decisions: A case study. *Journal of Family Psychotherapy, 4*(1), 45–56.

Okiishi, R. W. (1987). The genogram as a tool in career counseling. *Journal of Counseling and Development, 66*(3), 139–143.

Splete, H., & Freeman-George, A. (1985). Family influences on the career development of young adults. *Journal of Career Development, 12*(1), 55–64.

Chronologies, Time, and Timelines

Elder, G. H., Jr. (1977). Family history and the life course. *Journal of Family History, 22,* 279–304.

Elder, G. (1986). Military times and turning points in mens' lives. *Developmental Psychology, 22,* 233–245.

Elder, G. (1992). Life course. In E. Borgatta & M. Borgatta (Eds.), *Encyclopedia of sociology* (Vol. 3, pp. 1120–1130). New York: Macmillan.

Hodge, D. R. (2005). Spiritual ecograms: A new assessment instrument for identifying clients' spiritual strengths in space and across time. *Families in Society, 86,* 287–296.

Jewett, C. (1982). *Helping children cope with separation and loss.* Harvard, MA: Harvard Common Press.

Stanton, M. D. (1992). The time line and the "why now?" question: A technique and rationale for therapy, training, organizational consultation and research. *Journal of Marital and Family Therapy, 18*(4), 331–343.

Coaching: Family of Origin Work

Bowen, M. (1978). *Family Therapy in Clinical Practice.* New York: Jason Aronson.

Carter, B. (1991). Death in the therapist's own family. In M. McGoldrick, C. Anderson, & F. Walsh (Eds.), *Living beyond loss: Death in the family* (pp. 273–283). New York: Norton.

Carter, B., & McGoldrick, M. (2005). Coaching at various stages of the life cycle. In B. Carter & M. McGoldrick (Eds.), *The expanded family life cycle: Individual, family, and social perspectives* (3rd ed. pp. 436–454). Boston: Allyn & Bacon.

Colon, F. (1973). In search of one's past: An identity trip. *Family Process, 12*(4), 429–438.

Colon, F. (1998). The discovery of my multicultural identity. In M. McGoldrick (Ed.), *Revisioning family therapy: Race, culture and gender in clinical practice* (pp. 200–214). New York: Guilford.

Colon, F. (2005). *Finding my face: Memoir of a Puerto Rican-American.* New York: Trafford.

Crouch, M. A. (1986). Working with one's own family: Another path for professional development. *Family Medicine, 18,* 93–98.

Ferber, A. (Ed.), (1972). *The book of family therapy.* New York: Science House.

Folwarski, J. (1998). No longer an orphan in history. In M. McGoldrick (Ed.), *Revisioning family therapy* (pp. 239–252). New York: Guilford.

Friedman, E. H. (1987). The birthday party revisited: Family therapy and the problem of change. In P. Titelman (Ed.), *The therapist's own family* (pp. 163–188). New York: Jason Aronson.

Herz, F. (Ed.). (1994). *Reweaving the family tapestry.* New York: Norton.

Lerner, H. (1990). *The dance of intimacy.* New York: Harper Collins.

Lerner, H. (1994). *The dance of deception.* New York: Harper Collins.

Lerner, H. (1997). *The dance of anger.* New York: Harper Collins.

Lerner, H. (2002). *The dance of connection.* New York: Harper Collins.

Lerner, H. (2005). *The dance of fear.* New York: Harper Collins.

Lowenstein, S. F. (1982). A feminist perspective. *Education and methods for clinical practice.*

Mahboubi, J., & Searcy, A. (1998). Racial unity from the perspective of personal family history: Where black or white entered our families. In M. McGoldrick (Ed.), *Revisioning family therapy: Race, culture, and gender in clinical practice* (pp. 229–238). New York: Guilford.

McGoldrick, M. (1998). Belonging and liberation: Finding a place called "home." In M. McGoldrick (Ed.), *Revisioning family therapy: Race, culture, and gender in clinical practice* (pp. 215–228). New York: Guilford.

McGoldrick, M., & Carter, B. (2001). Advances in coaching: Family therapy with one person. *Journal of Marital and Family Therapy, 27*(3), 281–300.

Pinderhughes, E. (1998). Black genealogy revisited: Restorying African-American family. In M. McGoldrick (Ed.), *Revisioning family therapy: Race, culture, and gender in clinical practice* (pp. 179–199). New York: Guilford.

Computerized Genograms

Chan, D. H., Donnan, S. P. B., Chan, N., & Chow, G. (1987). A microcomputer-based computerized medical record system for a general practice teaching clinic. *Journal of Family Practice, 24,* 537–541.

Ebell, M., & Heaton, C. (1988). Development and evaluation of a computer genogram. *Journal of Family Practice, 27,* 536–538.

Gerson, R., & McGoldrick, M. (1985). The computerized genogram. *Primary Care, 12,* 535–545.

Couples

Carter, B. (1996). *Love, honor and negotiate: Making your marriage work.* New York: Pocket Books.

Coupland, S. K., & Serovich, J. M. (1999, December). Effects of couples' perceptions of genogram construction on therapeutic alliance and session impact: A growth curve analysis. *Contemporary Family Therapy, 21*(4), 551–572.

Evans, C., & Stewart-Smith, S. (2000). Looking backwards, looking forward. *Context: The History and Future of Transgenerational Family Therapy, 49,* 23–24.

Foster, M. A., Jurkovic, G. J., Ferdinand, L. G., & Meadows, L. A. (2002, January). The impact of the genogram on couples: A manualized approach. *Family Journal: Counseling & Therapy for Couples & Families, 10*(1), 34–40.

Gerson, R., Hoffman, S., Sauls, S., & Ulrici, M. (1993). Family-of-origin frames in couples therapy. *Journal of Marital and Family Therapy, 19,* 341–354.

Golden, E., & Mohr, R. (2000, July). Issues and techniques for counseling long-term, later-life couples. *Family Journal: Counseling & Therapy for Couples & Families, 8*(3), 229–235.

Hof, L., & Berman, E. (1986). The sexual genogram. *Journal of Marital and Family Therapy, 12*(1), 39–47.

McGoldrick, M., & Garcia Preto, N. (1984). Ethnic intermarriage: Implications for therapy. *Family Process, 23*(3), 347–364.

McGoldrick, M., Loonan, R., & Wolsifer, D. (2006). Sexuality and culture. In S. R. Leiblum (Ed.), Principles and practice of sex therapy (4th ed., pp. 416–441). New York: Guilford.

Paul, N., & Paul, B. B. (1986). *A marital puzzle*. New York: Norton.

Peluso, P. R. (2003). The technical genogram: A tool for helping therapists understand their ethical decision-making styles. *The Family Journal: Counseling and Therapy for Couples and Families, 11*(3), 286–291.

Scarf, M. (1987). *Intimate partners: Patterns in love and marriage*. New York: Random House.

Sherman, R. (2000). The intimacy genogram. In R. E. Watts (Ed.), *Techniques in marriage and family counseling, Vol. 1. The family psychology and counseling series* (pp. 81–84). Alexandria, VA: American Counseling Association.

Wood, N. S., & Stroup, H. W. (1990). Family systems in premarital counseling. *Pastoral Psychology, 39*(2), 111–119.

Culture and Race

Boyd-Franklin, N. (1995). Therapy with African-American inner city families. In R. H. Mikesell, D. Lusterman, & S. McDaniel (Eds.), *Integrating family therapy: Handbook of family psychology and systems therapy* (pp. 357–371). Washington, DC: American Psychological Association.

Boyd-Franklin, N. (2006). *Black families in therapy: Understanding African-American experience* (2nd ed.). New York: Guilford.

Congress, E. P. (1994, November). The use of culturagrams to assess and empower culturally diverse families. *Families in Society*, 531–540.

Draper, C. V. (1999). Intrafamilial skin color socialization, racial identity attitude, and psychological well-being in African-American women. Dissertation Abstracts International: Section B: The Sciences & Engineering. 60 (1-B), July, 0363. US, Univ, Microfilms International

Dunn, A. B, & Dawes, S. J. (1999). Spiritually-focused genograms: Keys to uncovering spiritual resources in African-American families. *Journal of Multicultural Counseling & Development, 27*(4), 240–255.

Eddington, A. (1998). Moving beyond white guilt. *Transformation, 13*(3), 2–7.

Estrada, A. U., & Haney, P. (1998). Genograms in a multicultural perspective. *Journal of Family Psychotherapy, 9*(2), 55–62.

Frame, M. W. (1996, October). Counseling African-Americans: Integrating spirituality in therapy. *Counseling & Values, 41*(1), pp. 16-29.

Hardy, K. V., & Laszloffy, T. A. (1992). Training racially sensitive family therapists: Context, content and contact. *Families in Society, 73*(6), 363–370.

Hardy, K. V., & Laszloffy, T. A. (1995). The cultural genogram: Key to training culturally competent family therapists. *Journal of Marital and Family Therapy, 21*(3), 227–237.

Hodge, D. R. (2004a). Social work practice with Muslims in the United States. In A. T. Morales & B. W. Sheafor (Eds.), *Social work: A profession of many faces* (10th ed., pp. 443–469). Boston: Allyn & Bacon.

Hodge, D. R. (2004b). Working with Hindu clients in a spiritually sensitive manner. *Social Work, 49*, 27–38.

Hodge, D. R., & Williams, T. R. (2002). Assessing African-American spirituality with spiritual eco-maps. *Families in Society, 83*, 585–595.

Kaslow, F. (1995, September). Descendants of holocaust victims and perpetrators: Legacies and dialogue. *Contemporary Family Therapy*, 275–290.

Keiley, M. K., Dolbin, M., Hill, J., Karuppaswamy, N., Liu, Ting Natrajan, R., Poulsen, S., Robins, N., & Robinson, P. (2002, April). The cultural genogram: Experiences from within a marriage and family therapy training program. *Journal of Marital and Family Therapy, 28*(2), 165–178.

Kelly, G. D. (1990). The cultural family of origin: A description of a training strategy. *Counselor Education and Supervision, 30*(1), 77–84.

Lappin, J. (1983). On becoming a culturally conscious family therapist. *Family Therapy Collections, 6*, 122–136.

McGill, D. M. (1992). The cultural story in multicultural family therapy. Families in Society: *Journal of Contemporary Human Services, 73*, 339–349.

McGoldrick, M., Giordano, J., & Garcia-Preto, N. (Eds.). (2005). *Ethnicity and family therapy* (3rd ed.). New York: Guilford.

McIntosh, P. (1998). White privilege: Unpacking the invisible knapsack. In M. McGoldrick (Ed.), *Revisioning family therapy: Race, culture and gender in clinical practice* (pp. 147–152). New York: Guilford.

Odell, M., Shelling, G., Young, K. S., Hewett, D. H., et al. (1995). The skills of the marriage and family therapist in straddling multicultural issues. *American Journal of Family Therapy, 22*(2), 145–155.

Parnell, M., & Vanderkloot, J. (1992). Mental health services 2001: Serving a new America. *Journal of Independent Social Work, 5*(3-4), 183–203.

Poole, D. L. (1998). Politically correct or culturally competent? *Health & Social Work, 23*(3), 163–167.

Preli, R., & Bernard, J. M. (1993). Making multiculturalism relevant for majority culture graduate students. *Journal of Marital and Family Therapy, 19*(1), 5–16.

Rigazio-DiGilio, S. A., Ivey, A. E., Kunkler-Peck, K. P., & Grady, L. T. (2005). *Community genograms: Using individual, family, and cultural narratives with clients.* New York: Teachers College Press.

Salgado de Bernal, C., & Alvarez-Schwarz, M. (1990). The genogram as a training instrument for family therapists. *Revista Latinoamericana de Psicologia, 22*(3), 385–420.

Scharwiess, S. O. (1994). Step-sisters and half-brothers: A family therapist's view of German unification and other transitional processes. *Contemporary Family Therapy, 16*(3), 183–197.

Thomas, A. J. (1998). Understanding culture and worldview in family systems: Use of the multicultural genogram. *The Family Journal: Counseling and Therapy for Couples and Families, 6*(1), 24–31.

Watts Jones, D. (1998). Towards an African-American genogram. *Family Process, 36*(4), 373–383.

Woodcock, J. (1995). Healing rituals with families in exile. *Journal of Family Therapy, 17*(4), 397–409.

Divorce and Remarriage

Friesen, P., & Manitt, J. (1991). Nursing the remarried family in a palliative care setting. *Journal of Palliative Care, 6*(4), 32–39.

McGoldrick, M., & Carter, B. (2005). Remarried families. In B. Carter & M. McGoldrick (Eds.), *The expanded family life cycle: Individual, family and social perspectives.* (3rd ed., pp. 417–435). Boston: Allyn & Bacon.

Peck, J. S. (1988). The impact of divorce on children at various stages of the family life cycle. *Journal of Divorce, 12*(2-3), 81–106.

Sager, C. J., Brown, H. S., Crohn, H., Engel, T., Rodstein, E., & Walker, L. (1983). *Treating the remarried family.* New York: Brunner/Mazel.

Drug and Alcohol Abuse

Barthwell, A. G. (1995). Alcoholism in the family: A multicultural exploration. In M. Galanter (Ed.), *Recent developments in alcoholism: Vol. 12: Alcoholism and women* (pp. 387–407). New York: Plenum.

Bepko, C. S., & Krestan, J. (1985). *The responsibility trap: Women and men in alcoholic families*. New York: Free Press.

Dardia, T. (1989). *The thirsty muse: Alcohol and the American writer*. New York: Tichnor & Fields.

Darmsted, N., & Cassell, J. L. (1983). Counseling the deaf substance abuser. *Readings in Deafness, 7,* 40–51.

Hurst, N. C., Sawatzky, D. D., & Pare, D. P. (1996). Families with multiple problems through a Bowenian lens. *Child Welfare, 75*(6), 693–708.

Nowinski, J., & Baker, S. (1998). *The twelve-step facilitation handbook: A systematic approach to early recovery from alcoholism and addiction*. San Francisco: Jossey-Bass.

Stanton, M. D., & Heath, A. W. (1995). Family treatment of alcohol and drug abuse. In R. H. Mikesell, D. D. Lusterman, & S. McDaniel (Eds.), *Integrating family therapy: Handbook of family psychology and systems therapy* (pp. 529–541). Washington, DC: American Psychological Association.

Steinglass, P., Bennett, L., Wolin, S., & Reiss, D. (1987). *The alcoholic family*. New York: Basic.

Vukov, M. G., & Eljdupovic, G. (1991). The Yugoslavian drug addict's family structure. *International Journal of the Addictions, 26*(4), 415–422.

Wolin, S. J., Bennett, L. A., & Jacobs, J. S. (1988). Assessing family rituals in alcoholic families. In E. Imber-Black, J. Roberts, & R. Whiting (Eds.), *Rituals in families and family therapy* (pp. 230–256). New York: Norton.

Family Life Cycle

Campbell, T. L., McDaniel, S. H., Cole-Kelly, K., Hepworth, J., & Lorenz, A. (2002). Family interviewing: A review of the literature in primary care. *Family Medicine, 34*(5), 312–318.

Erlanger, M. A. (1997). Changing roles and life cycle transitions. In T. D. Hargrave & C. Midori Hanna (Eds.), *The aging family: New visions in theory, practice, and reality* (pp. 163–177), New York: Brunner/Mazel.

Gerson, R. (1995). The family life cycle: Phases, stages and crises. In R. H. Mikesell, D. D. Lusterman, & S. McDaniel (Eds.), *Integrating family therapy: Handbook of family psychology and systems therapy* (pp. 91–111). Washington, DC: American Psychological Association.

McAdams, D., & de St. Aubin, E. (Eds.), *Generativity and aduult development: How and why we care for the next generation.* Washington, DC: American Psychological Association.

Hadley, T., Jacob, T., Miliones, J., Caplan, J., & Spitz, D. (1974). The relationship between family developmental crises and the appearance of symptoms in a family member. *Family Process, 13,* 207–14.

McGoldrick, M. (2005). History, genograms and the family life cycle: Freud in context. In B. Carter & M. McGoldrick (Eds.), *The expanded family life cycle: Individual, family and social perspectives* (3rd ed., pp. 47–68). Boston: Allyn & Bacon.

Norris, J. E., & Tindale, J. A. (1994). *Among generations: The cycle of adult relationships.* New York: W. H. Freeman.

With Children

Altshuler, S. J. (1999, November/December). Constructing genograms with children in care: Implications for casework practice. *Child Welfare, 78*(6), 777–790.

Carr, A. (1997). Involving children in family therapy and systemic consultation. *Journal of Family Psychotherapy, 5*(1), 41–59.

Fink, A. H., Kramer, L., Weaver, L. L., & Anderson, J. (1993). More on genograms: Modifications to a model. *Journal of Child & Adolescent Group Therapy, 3*(4), 203–206.

Goodyear-Brown, P. (2001). The preschool play geno-game. In H. G. Kaduson & C. E. Schaefer (Eds.), *101 more favorite therapy techniques* (pp. 225–228). Northvale, NJ: Jason Aronson.

With Adolescents

Cole-Kelly, K., & Kaye, D. (1993). Assessing the family. In M. I. Singer, L. T. Singer, & T. M. Anglin (Eds.), *Handbook for screening adolescents at psychosocial risk* (pp. 1–40). New York: Macmillan.

With Young Adults

Daughhetee, C. (2001). Using genograms as a tool for insight in college counseling. *Journal of College Counseling.* 4(1), 73–76.

Magnuson, S. (2000, October). The professional genogram: Enhancing professional identity and clarity. *Family Journal: Counseling & Therapy for Couples & Families, 8*(4), 299–401.

Malott, K. M., & Magnuson, S. (2004). Using genograms to facilitate undergraduate students' career development: A group model. *The Career Development Quarterly, 53*(4), 178–186.

Santa Rita, E., & Adejanju, M. G. (1993). The genogram: Plotting the roots of academic success. *Family Therapy, 20*(1), 17–28.

Splete, H., & Freeman-George, A. (1985). Family influences on the career development of young adults. *Journal of Career Development, 12*(1), 55–64.

Vinson, M. L. (1995). Employing family therapy in group counseling with college students: Similarities and a technique employed in both. *Journal for Specialists in Group Work, 20*(4), 240–252.

With Expectant Families

Condon, J. J. (1985). Therapy of the expectant family: The fetus as a force to be reckoned with. *Australian & New Zealand Journal of Family Therapy, 6*(2), 77–81.

Evans, C., & Stewart-Smith, S. (2000). Looking backwards, looking forward. *Context, 49,* 23–24.

Holtslander, L. (2005). Clinical application of the 15-minute family interview: Addressing the needs of postpartum families. *Journal of Family Nursing, 11*(1), 5–18.

With Aging

Bannerman, C. (1986). The genogram and elderly patients. *Journal of Family Practice, 23*(5), 426–428.

Erlanger, M. A. (1990). Using the genogram with the older client. *Journal of Mental Health Counselling, 12*(3), 321–331.

Golden, E., & Mohr, R. (2000, July). Issues and techniques for counseling long-term, later-life couples. *Family Journal: Counseling & Therapy for Couples & Families, 8*(3), 229–235.

Gwyther, L. (1986). Family therapy with older adults. *Generations, 10*(3), 42–45.

Ingersoll-Dayton, B., & Arndt, B. (1990). Uses of the genogram with the elderly and their families. *Journal of Gerontological Social Work, 15*(1-2), 105–120.

Shellenberger, S., Watkins-Couch, K., & Drake, M. A. (1989). Elderly family members and their caregivers: Characteristics and development of the relationship. *Family Systems Medicine, 7*(3), 317–322.

Shields, C. G., King, D. A., & Wynne, L. C. (1995). Interventions with later life families. In R. H. Mikesell, D. Lusterman, & S. McDaniel (Eds.), *Integrating family therapy: Handbook of family psychology and systems therapy* (pp. 141–158). Washington, DC: American Psychological Association.

Family Play Genograms

Gil, E. (2003). Play genograms. In C. E. Sorit & L. L. Hecker (Eds.), *The therapist's notebook for children and adolescents: Homework, handouts, and activities for use in psychotherapy* (pp. 97–118). New York: Haworth Press.

Goodyear-Brown, P. (2001). The preschool play geno-game. In H. G. Kaduson & C. E. Schaefer (Eds.), *101 more favorite therapy techniques* (pp. 225–228). Northvale, NJ: Jason Aronson.

Petry, S. S., & McGoldrick, M. (2005). Genograms in assessment and therapy. In G. P. Koocher, J. C. Norcross, & S. S. Hill (Eds.), *The psychologists' desk reference* (2nd ed., pp. 366–373). New York: Oxford University Press.

Foster Care, Adoption, and Child Welfare

Allen, M. (1990). *Training materials for post adoption family therapy.* Iowa City, IA: National Center on Family Based Resources.

Altshuler, S. J. (1999, November/December). Constructing genograms with children in care: Implications for casework practice. *Child Welfare, 78*(6), 777–790.

Colon, F. (1978). Family ties and child placement. *Family Process, 17,* 289–312.

Finch, R., & Jaques, P. (1985). Use of the geneogram with adoptive families. *Adoption and Fostering, 9*(3), 35–41.

Flashman, M. (1991). Training social workers in public welfare: Some useful family concepts. *Journal of Independent Social Work, 5*(3-4), 53–68.

Groze, V., Young, J., & Corcran-Rumppe, K. (1991). *Post adoption resources for training, networking and evaluation services (PARTNERS): Working with special needs adoptive families in stress.* Washington DC: Department of Health and Human Services.

Hoyle, S. G. (1995). Long-term treatment of emotionally disturbed adoptees and their families. *Clinical Social Work Journal, 23*(4), 429–440.

McMillen, J. C., & Groze, V. (1994). Using placement genograms in child welfare practice. *Child Welfare, 73*(4), 307–318.

Pinderhughes, E. E., & Rosenberg, K. (1990). Family-bonding with high-risk placements: A therapy model that promotes the process of becoming a family. In L. M. Glidden (Ed.), *Formed families: Adoption of children with handicaps* (pp. 209–230). New York: Haworth.

Sandmeier, M. (1988). *When love is not enough: How mental health professionals can help special needs adoptive families.* Washington, DC: Child Welfare League of America.

Young, J., Corcoran-Rumppe, K., & Groze, V. K. (1992). Integrating special needs adoption with residential treatment. *Child Welfare, 71*(6), 527–535.

Gender and Gendergrams

Holmes, S. E., & Anderson, S. A. (1994). Gender differences in the relationship between differentiation experienced in one's family of origin and adult adjustment. *Journal of Feminist Family Therapy, 6*(1), 27–48.

Howe, K. (1990). Daughters discover their mothers through biographies and genograms: Educational and clinical parallels. *Women and Therapy, 10*(1-2), 31–40.

McGoldrick, M. (2005). Women through the family life cycle. In B. Carter & M. McGoldrick (Eds.), *The expanded family life cycle: Individual, family, & social perspectives* (2nd ed., pp. 106–123). Boston: Allyn & Bacon.

McGoldrick, M., Anderson, C., & Walsh, F. (1989). *Women in families: A framework for family therapy*. New York: Norton.

Rekers, G. A. (1985, summer). The genogram: Her story of a woman. *Women & Therapy, 4*(2), 9–15.

Softas-Nall, B. C., Baldo, T. D., & Diedemann, T. R. (1999). A gender-based, solution-focused genogram case: He and she across the generations. *The Family Journal, 7*, 177–190.

White, M. B., & Tyson-Rawson, K. J. (1995). Assessing the dynamics of gender in couples and families: The gendergram. *Family Relations, 44*, 253–260.

Genogram Variations, Ecomaps, Pedigrees, and Sociograms

Burke, J. L., & Faber, P. (1997). A genogrid for couples. *Journal of Gay and Lesbian Social Services, 7*(1), 13–22.

Friedman, H., Rohrbaugh, M., & Krakauer, S. (1988). The timeline genogram: Highlighting temporal aspects of family relationships. *Family Process, 27*, 293–304.

Friesen, P., & Manitt, J. (1991). Nursing the remarried family in a palliative care setting. *Journal of Palliative Care, 6*(4), 32–39.

Hardy, K. V., & Laszloffy, T. A. (1995). The cultural genogram: Key to training culturally competent family therapists. *Journal of Marital and Family Therapy, 21*(3), 227–237.

Hartman, A. (1995). Diagrammatic assessment of family relationships. *Families in Society, 76*(2), 111–122.

Hodge, D. R. (2000, April). Spiritual ecomaps: A new diagrammatic tool for assessing marital and family spirituality. *Journal of Marital and Family Therapy, 26*(2), 217–228.

Hof, L., & Berman, E. (1986). The sexual genogram. *Journal of Marital & Family Therapy, 12*, 39–47.

Holtslander, L. (2005). Clinical application of the 15-minute family interview: Addressing the needs of postpartum families. *Journal of Family Nursing, 11*(1), 5–18.

Lewis, K. G. (1989). The use of color-coded genograms in family therapy. *Journal of Marital & Family Therapy, 15*(2), 169–176.

Magnuson, S., & Shaw, H.E. (2003, January). Adaptations of the multifaceted genogram in counseling, training and supervision. *Family Journal: Counseling & Therapy for Couples & Families, 2*(1), 45–54.

McIlvain, H., Crabtree, B., Medder, J., Strange, K. C., & Miller, W. L. (1998). Using ractice genograms to understand and describe practice configurations. *Family Medicine, 30*(7), 490–496.

Olsen, S., Dudley-Brown, S., & McMullen, P. (2004). Case for blending pedigrees, genograms and ecomaps: Nursing's contribution to the 'big picture.' *Nursing and Health Sciences, 6*, 295–308.

Peluso, P. (2003). The ethical genogram: A tool for helping therapists understand their ethical decision-making roles. *The Family Journal, 11*(3), 286–291.

Praeger, S. C., & Martin, L. S. (1994). Using genograms and ecomaps in schools. *Journal of School Nursing, 10*, 34–40.

Rigazio-DiGilio, S. A, Ivey, A. E., Kunkler-Peck, K. P., & Grady, L. T. (2005). *Community genograms: Using individual, family, and cultural narratives with clients.* New York: Teachers College Press.

Sherman, R., & Fredman, N. (1986). *Handbook of structural techniques in marriage and family therapy.* New York: Brunner/Mazel.

Watts Jones, D. (1998). Towards an African-American genogram. *Family Process, 36*(4), 373–383.

White, M. B., & Tyson-Rawson, K. J. (1995). Assessing the dynamics of gender in couples and families: The gendergram. *Family Relations, 44*(3), 253–260.

Wright, L. M., & Leahey, M. (1999). Maximizing time, minimizing suffering: The 15-minute (or less) family interview. *Journal of Family Nursing, 5*, 259–274.

Wright, L. M., & Leahey, M. (2000). *Nurses and families: A guide to family assessment and intervention* (3rd ed.). Philadelphia: F. A. Davis.

Healthcare, Medicine, Nursing, Stress, Illness

Alexander, D., & Clark, S. (1998). Keeping "the family" in focus during patient care. In P. D. Sloane, L. M. Slatt, P. Curtis & M. H. Ebell (Eds.), *Essentials of family medicine* (3rd ed., pp. 25–39). Baltimore: Williams & Wilkins.

Baird, M. A., & Grant, W. D. (1998). Families and health. In R. B. Taylor, A. K. David, T. A. Johnson, Jr., D. M. Phillips, & J. E. Scherger (Eds.), *Family medicine principles and practice* (5th ed., pp. 26–31). Baltimore: Williams & Wilkins.

Barth, J. C. (1993). *It runs in my family: Overcoming the legacy of family illness.* New York: Brunner/Mazel.

Berolzheimer, N., Thrower, S. M., Koch-Hattem, A. (1993). Working with families. In P. D. Sloan, L. M. Slatt, & P. Curtis (Eds.), *Essentails of family medicine* (2nd ed., pp. 19–29). Baltimore: Williams & Wilkins.

Blossom, H. J. (1991). The personal genogram: An interview technique for selecting family practice residents. *Family Systems Medicine, 9*(2), 151–158.

Campbell, T. L., McDaniel, S. H., Cole-Kelly, K., Hepworth, J., & Lorenz, A. (2002). Family interviewing: A review of the literature in primary care. *Family Medicine, 34*(5), 312–318.

Christie-Seely, J. (1981). Teaching the family system concept in family medicine. *Journal of Family Practice, 13,* 391.

Craddock, N., McGuffin, P., & Owen, M. (1994). Darier's disease cosegregating with affective disorder. *British Journal of Psychiatry, 165*(2), 272.

Crouch, M., & Davis, T. (1987). Using the genogram (family tree) clinically. In M. A. Crouch & L. Roberts (Eds.), *The family in medical practice: A family systems primer* (pp. 174–192). New York: Springer-Verlag.

Crouch, M. A. (1989). A putative ancestry of family practice and family medicine: Genogram of a discipline. *Family Systems Medicine, 7*(2), 208–212.

Doherty, W. J., & Baird. M. A. (1983). *Family therapy and family medicine.* New York: Guilford.

Dudley-Brown, S. (2004). The genetic family history assessment in gastroenterology nursing practice. *Gastroenterology Nursing, 27,* 107–110.

Duhamel, F., & Dupuis, F. (2004). Guaranteed returns: Investing in conversations with families of patients with cancer. *Cancer Journal of Nursing, 8*, 68–71.

Engelman, S. R. (1988). Use of the family genogram technique with spinal cord injured patients. *Clinical Rehabilitation, 2*(1), 7–15.

Faucett, C. S. (Ed.). (1993). *Family psychiatric nursing.* St. Louis, MO: Mosby.

Fohs, M. W. (1991). Family systems assessment: Interventions with individuals having a chronic disability. *Career Development Quarterly, 39*(4), 304–311.

Fossum, A. R., Elam, C. L., & Broaddus, D. A. (1982). Family therapy in family practice: A solution to psychosocial problems? *Journal of Family Practice, 15*, 461.

Garrett, R. E., Klinkman, M., & Post, L., (1987). If you meet the Buddha on the road, take a genogram: Zen and the art of family medicine. *Family Medicine, 19*, 225–226.

Glimelius, B., Bilgegard, G., Hoffman, K., Hagnebo, C., Krale, G., Nordin, K., Nou, E., Persson, C., & Sjoden, P. (1993). A comprehensive cancer care project to improve the overall situation of patients receiving intensive chemotherapy. *Journal of Psychosocial Oncology, 11*(1), 17–40.

Greco, K. E. (2004). Nursing in the genomic era: Nurturing our genetic nature. *Medsurgical Nursing, 12*, 307–312.

Haas-Cunningham, S. M. (1994). The genogram as a predictor of families at risk for physical illness. *Dissertation Abstracts International, 54*(9-b) 4590.

Hockley, J. (2000). Psychosocial aspects in palliative care: Communicating with the patient and family. *Acta oncologica, 39*(8), 905–910.

Holmes, T. H., & Masuda, M. (1974). Life change and illness susceptibility. In B. S. Dohrenwend & B. Dohrenwend (Eds.), *Stressful life events: Their nature and effects* (pp. 45–72). New York: Wiley.

Holmes, T. H., & Rahe, T. H. (1967). The social adjustment rating scale. *Journal of Psychosomatic Research, 11*, 1967, 213–218.

Howkins, E., & Allison, A. (1996). Shared learning for primary health-care teams: A success story. *Nurse Education Today, 17*(3), 225–231.

Huygen, F. J. A. (1982). *Family medicine.* New York: Brunner/Mazel.

Huygen, F. J. A., van den Hoogen, H. J. M., van Eijk, J. T. M., & Smits, A. J. A. (1989). Death and dying: A longitudinal study of their medical impact on the family. *Family Systems Medicine, 7*, 374–384.

Jolly, W. M., Froom, J., & Rosen, M. G. (1980). The genogram. *Journal of Family Practice, 10*(2), 251–255.

Josse, J. (1993, May 1). The use of family trees in general practice. *Postgraduate Update,* 775–780.

Levine, F. B. (1997). The girl who went on strike: A case of childhood diabetes. In S. H. McDaniel, J. Hepworth, & W. J. Doherty (Eds.), *The shared experience of illness: Stories of patients, families, and their therapists* (pp. 58–72). New York: Basic.

Liossi, C., Hattira, P., & Mystakidou, K. (1997). The use of the genogram in palliative care. *Palliative Medicine, 11*(6), 455–461.

Massad, R. J. (1980). *In sickness and in health: A family physician explores the impact of illness on the family.* Philadelphia: Smith, Kline & French.

McDaniel, S. (1997). Trapped inside a body without a voice: Two cases of somatic fixation. In S. H. McDaniel, J. Hepworth, & W. J. Doherty (Eds.), *The shared experience of illness: Stories of patients, families, and their therapists* (pp. 274–290). New York: Basic.

McDaniel, S. H., Hepworth, J., & Doherty, W. J. (1992). *Medical family therapy.* New York: Basic.

McWhinney, I. R. (1981). *An introduction to family medicine.* New York: Oxford University Press.

Medalie, J. H. (1978). *Family medicine: Principles and applications.* Baltimore: Williams & Wilkins.

Milhorn, H. T. (1981). The genogram: A structured approach to the family history. *Journal of the Mississippi State Medical Association, 22*(10), 250–52.

Mullins, M. C., & Christie-Seely, J. (1984). Collecting and recording family data: The genogram. In J. Christie-Seely (Ed.), *Working with the family in primary care* (pp. 179–181). New York: Praeger.

Nieferhauser, V. P. (2004). Assess health risk status for intervention and risk reduction. *The Nurse Practitioner, 29*(2), 35–42.

Norwood, W. (1993). An initial exploration through the use of the genogram of the premorbid functioning of families with a person with a head injury. *Dissertation Abstracts International, 54*(3-A), 870.

Penn, P. (1983). Coalitions and binding interactions in families with chronic illness. *Family Systems Medicine, 1*(2), 16–25.

Puskar, K. (1996). Genogram: A useful tool for nurse practitioners. *Journal of Psychiatric and Mental Health Nursing, 3*, 55–60.

Rakel, R. E. (1977). *Principles of family medicine.* Philadelphia: W. B. Saunders.

Richards, W. R., Burgess, D. E., Peterson, F. R., & McCarthy, D. L. (1993). Genograms: A psychosocial assessment tool for hospice. *Hospital Journal, 9*, 1–12.

Richardson, H. B. (1945). *Patients have families.* New York: Commonwealth Fund.

Rolland, J. (1994). *Families, illness, and disability.* New York: Basic.

Rolland, J. (2005). Chronic illness and the family life cycle. In B. Carter & M. McGoldrick (Eds.), *The expanded family life cycle: Individual, family and social perspectives* (3rd ed., pp. 492–511). Boston: Allyn & Bacon.

Rosen, G., Kleinman, A., & Katon, W. (1982). Somatization in family practice: A biopsycho-social approach. *Journal of Family Practice, 14,* 493.

Schilson, E., Barun, K., & Hudson, A. (1993). Use of genograms in family medicine: A family physician/family therapist collaboration. *Family Systems Medicine, 11*(2), 201–208.

Schmidt, D. D. (1978). The family as the unit of medical care. *Journal of Family Practice, 7,* 303.

Shellenberger, S., & Phelps, G. (1997). When it never stops hurting: A case of chronic pain. In S. H. McDaniel, J. Hepworth, & W. J. Doherty (Eds.), *The shared experience of illness: Stories of patinets, families, and their therapists* (pp. 231–241). New York: Basic.

Sloan, P. D., Slatt, L. M., Curtis, P., & Ebell, M. (Eds.). (1998). *Essentials of family medicine* (2nd ed.). Baltimore: Williams & Wilkins.

Smilkstein, G. (1984). The physician and family function assessment. *Family Systems Medicine, 2*(3), 263–278.

Stavros, M. K. (1991). Family systems approach to sexual dysfunction in neurologic disability. *Sexuality and Disability, 9*(1), 69–85.

Taylor, R. B., David, A. K., Johnson, T. A., Jr., Phillips, D. M., & Scherger, J. E. (Eds.). (1998). *Family medicine principles and practice* (5th ed., pp. 26–31). Baltimore: Williams & Wilkins.

Wattendorf, D. J., & Hadley, M. S. (2005). Family history: The three-generation pedigree. *American Family Physician, 72*(3), 441–448.

Wimbush, F. B., & Peters, R .M. (2000). Identification of cardiovascular risk: Use of a cardiovascular-specific genogram. *Public Health Nursing, 17*(3) 148–154.

Wright, L. M., & Leahey, M. (1999). Maximizing time, minimizing suffering: The 15-minute (or less) family interview. *Journal of Family Nursing, 5,* 259–274.

Wright, L. M., & Leahey, M. (2000). *Nurses and families: A guide to family assessment and intervention* (3rd ed.). Philadelphia: F. A. Davis.

Lesbian and Gay Families and Networks

Burke, J. L., & Faber, P. (1997). A genogrid for couples. *Journal of Gay and Lesbian Social Services, 7*(1), 13–22.

Feinberg, J., & Bakerman, R. (1994). Sexual orientation and three generational family patterns in a clinical sample of heterosexual and homosexual men. *Journal of Gay and Lesbian Psychotherapy, 2*(2), 65–76.

Laird, J. (1996a). Family-centered practice with lesbian and gay families. *Families in Society: Journal of Contemporary Human Services, 77*(9), 559–572.

Laird, J., & Green, R. J. (Eds.). (1996). *Lesbians and gays in couples and families.* San Francisco: Jossey-Bass.

Magnuson, S., Norem, K., & Skinner, C. H. (1995). Constructing genograms with lesbian clients. *The Family Journal: Counseling and Therapy for Couples and Families, 3,* 110–115.

Scrivner, R., & Eldridge, N. S. (1995). Lesbian and gay family psychology. In R. H. Mikesell, D. D. Lusterman, & S. McDaniel (Eds.), *Integrating family therapy: Handbook of family pychology and systems therapy* (pp. 327–345). Washington, DC: American Psychological Association.

Shernoff, M. J. (1984). Family therapy for lesbian and gay clients. *Social Work, 39,* 393–396.

Slater, S. (1995). *The lesbian family life cycle.* New York: Free Press.

Weinstein, D. L. (1993). Application of family therapy concepts in the treatment of lesbians and gay men. *Journal of Chemical Dependency Treatment, 5*(1), 141–155.

Loss, Hospice, Death, and Trauma

Boss, P. (2004). Ambiguous loss. In F. Walsh & M. McGoldrick (Eds.), *Living beyond loss: Death in the family* (pp. 237–246). New York: Norton.

Bowen, M. (2004). Family reaction to death. In F. Walsh & M. McGoldrick (Eds.), *Living beyond loss: Death in the family* (pp. 47–60). New York: Norton.

Crosby, J. F. (1989). Museum tours in genogram construction: A technique for facilitating recall of negative affect. *Contemporary Family Therapy, 11*(4), 247–258.

Duhamel, F., & Dupuis, F. (2004). Guaranteed returns: Investing in conversations with families of patients with cancer. *Cancer Journal of Nursing, 8*, 68–71.

Early, B. P., Smith, E. D., Todd, L., & Beem, T. (2000). The needs and supportive networks of the dying: An assessment instrument and mapping procedure for hospice patients. *American Journal of Hospice and Palliative Care, 17*, 87–96.

Engel, G. (1975). The death of a twin: Mourning and anniversary reactions. Fragments of 10 years of self-analysis. *International Journal of Psychoanalysis. 56*(1), 23–40.

Ferra Bucher, J. S. (1991). Family interaction and suicide: Case studies from a transgenerational perspective. *PSICO, 21*(1), 41–64.

Gajdos, K. C. (2002). The intergenerational effects of grief and trauma. *Illness, Crisis & Loss, 10*(6), 304–317.

Jordan, K. (2004). The color-coded timeline trauma genogram. *Brief Treatment and Crisis Intervention, 4*(1), 57–70.

Jordan, K. (2006). *The scripto-trauma genogram: An innovative technique for working with trauma survivors' intrusive memories*. Oxford University Press.

Kuhn, J. (1981). Realignment of emotional forces following loss. *The Family, 5*(1), 19–24.

McDaniel, S. H., Hepworth, J., & Doherty, W. J. (1992). *Medical family therapy*. New York: Basic.

McGoldrick, M. (2004a). The legacy of loss. In F. Walsh & M. McGoldrick (Eds.), *Living beyond loss: Death in the family* (pp. 104–129). New York: Norton.

McGoldrick, M. (2004b). Echoes from the past: Helping families mourn their losses. In F. Walsh & M. McGoldrick (Eds.), *Living beyond loss: Death in the family* (pp. 50–78). New York: Norton.

McGoldrick, M., Schlesinger, J. M., Lee, E., Hines, P. M., Chan, J., Almeida, R., Petkov, B., Garcia-Preto, N., & Petry, S. (2004). Mourning in different cultures. In F. Walsh & M McGoldrick (Eds.), *Living beyond loss: Death in the family* (2nd ed., pp. 119–160). New York: Norton.

McGoldrick, M., & Walsh, F. (2004). A time to mourn: Death and the family life cycle. In F. Walsh & M. McGoldrick (Eds.), *Living beyond loss: Death in the family* (pp. 27–46). New York: Norton.

Mikesell, S. G., & Stohner, M. (1995). Infertility and pregnancy loss: The role of the family consultant. In R. H. Mikesell, D. D. Lusterman, & S. McDaniel (Eds.), *Integrating family therapy: Handbook of family psychology and systems therapy* (pp. 421–436). Washington, DC: American Psychological Association.

Richards, W. R., Burgess, D. E., Peterson, F. R., & McCarthy, D. L. (1993). Genograms: A psychosocial assessment tool for hospice. *Hospital Journal, 9,* 1–12.

Seaburn, D. B. (1990). The time that binds: Loyalty and widowhood. *Psychotherapy Patient, 6*(3-4), 139–146.

Walsh, F. (1978). Concurrent grandparent death and birth of schizophrenic offspring: An intriguing finding. *Family Process, 17,* 457–463.

Walsh, F., & McGoldrick, M. (2004a). *Living beyond loss: Death in the family*. New York: Norton.

Walsh, F., & McGoldrick, M. (2004b). Loss and the family: A systemic perspective. In F. Walsh & M. McGoldrick (Eds.), *Living beyond loss: Death in the family* (pp. 3–26). New York: Norton.

Whitman-Raymond, R. (1988). Pathological gambling as a defense against loss. *Journal of Gambling Behavior, 4*(2), 99–109.

Wortman, C., & Silver, R. (1989). The myths of coping with loss. *Journal of Counseling and Clinical Psychology, 57,* 349–357.

Migration

Hernandez, M., & McGoldrick, M. (2005). Migration and the family life cycle. In B. Carter & M. McGoldrick (Eds.), *The expanded family life cycle: Individual, family and social perspectives* (pp. 169–184). Boston: Allyn & Bacon.

Mirkin, M. (1998). The impact of multiple contexts on recent immigrant families. In M. McGoldrick (Ed.), *Revisioning family therapy: Race, culture and gender in clinical practice* (pp. 370–384). New York: Guilford.

Mock, M. (1998). Clinical reflections on refugee families: Transforming crises into opportunities. In M. McGoldrick (Ed.), *Revisioning family therapy: Race, culture and gender in clinical practice* (pp. 347–359). New York: Guilford.

Sluzki, C. (1998). Migration and the disruption of the social network. In M. McGoldrick (Ed.), *Revisioning family therapy: Race, culture and gender in clinical practice* (pp. 360–369). New York: Guilford.

Religion/Spirituality

Dunn, A. B., & Dawes, S. J. (1999). Spiritually-focused genograms: Keys to uncovering spiritual resources in African-American families. *Journal of Multicultural Counseling & Development, 27*(4), 240–55).

Frame, M. W. (1996). Counseling African-Americans: Integrating spirituality in therapy. *Counseling & Values, 41*(1), 16–29.

Frame, M. W. (2000a). Constructing religious/spiritual genograms. In R. E. Watts (Ed.), *Techniques in marriage and family counseling, Vol. 1. The family psychology and counseling series* (pp. 69–74). Alexandria, VA: American Counseling Assoc.

Frame, M. W. (2000b, April). The spiritual genogram in family therapy. *Journal of Marital and Family Therapy, 26*(92), 211–216.

Frame, M. W. (2001, April). The spiritual genogram in training and supervision. *Family Journal: Counseling & Therapy for Couple & Families, 9*(2), 109–115.

Hodge, D. R. (2000, April). Spiritual ecomaps: A new diagrammatic tool for assessing marital and family spirituality. *Journal of Marital and Family Therapy, 26*(2), 217–228.

Hodge, D. R. (2001, January/February). Spiritual genograms: A generational approach to assessing spirituality. *Families in Society, 82*(1), 35–48.

Hodge, D. R. (2001b). Spiritual assessment: A review of major qualitative methods and a new framework for assessing spirituality. *Social Work, 46*, 203–214.

Hodge, D. R. (2003). The intrinsic spirituality scale: A new six-item instrument for assessing the salience of spirituality as a motivational construct. *Journal of Social Service Research, 30*, 41–61.

Hodge, D. R. (2004a). Social work practice with Muslims in the United States. In A. T. Morales & B. W. Sheafor (Eds.), *Social work: A profession of many faces* (10th ed., pp. 443–469). Boston: Allyn & Bacon.

Hodge, D. R. (2004b). Spirituality and people with mental illness: Developing spiritual competency in assessment and intervention. *Families in Society, 85*, 36–44.

Hodge, D. R. (2004c). Working with Hindu clients in a spiritually sensitive manner. *Social Work, 49*, 27–38.

Hodge, D. R. (2005a). Spiritual life maps: A client-centered pictorial instrument for spiritual assessment, planning, and intervention. *Social Work, 50*, 77–87.

Hodge, D. R. (2005b). Spiritual ecograms: A new assessment instrument for identifying clients' spiritual strengths in space and across time. *Families in Society, 86*, 287–296.

Hodge, D. R. (2005c). Spiritual assessment in marital and family therapy: A methodological framework for selecting from among six qualitative assessment tools. *Journal of Marital and Family Therapy, 32*(4), 341–356.

Hodge, D. R., & Williams, T. R. (2002). Assessing African-American spirituality with spiritual eco-maps. *Families in Society, 83*, 585–595.

Poole, D. L. (1998). Politically correct or culturally competent? *Health & Social Work, 23*(3), 63–167.

Research on Genograms

Coupland, S. K., & Serovich, J. M. (1999, December). Effects of couples' perceptions of genogram construction on therapeutic alliance and session impact: A growth curve analysis. *Contemporary Family Therapy, 21*(4), 551–572.

Coupland, S. K., Serovich, J., & Glenn, J. E. (1995). Reliability in constructing genograms: A study among marriage and family therapy doctoral students. *Journal of Marital and Family Therapy, 21*(3), 251–263.

Daughhetee, C. (2001). Using genograms as a tool for insight in college counseling. *Journal of College Counseling, 4*(1), 73–76.

Dudley-Brown, S. (2004). The genetic family history assessment in gastroenterology nursing practice. *Gastroenterology Nursing, 27,* 107–110.

Dunn, A. B., & Levitt, M. M. (2000, July). The genogram: From diagnostics to mutual collaboration. *Family Journal: Counseling & Therapy for Couples & Families, 8*(3), 236–244.

Friedman, H. L., & Krakauer, S. (1992). Learning to draw and interpret standard and time-line genograms: An experimental comparison. *Journal of Family Psychology, 6*(1), 77–83.

Greenwald, J. L., Grant, W. D., Kamps, C. A., & Haas-Cunningham, S. (1998). The genogram scale as a predictor of high utilization in a family practice. *Family, Systems & Health, 16*(4), 375–391.

Hodge, D. R. (2005). Spiritual assessment in marital and family therapy: A methodological framework for selecting from among six qualitative assessment tools. *Journal of Marital and Family Therapy, 32*(4), 341–356.

Hurst, N. C., Sawatzky, D. D., & Pare, D. P. (1996). Families with multiple problems through a Bowenian lens. *Child Welfare, 75*(6), 693–708.

Milewski-Hertlein, K. A. (2001, January/February). The use of a socially constructed genogram in clinical practice. *American Journal of Family Therapy, 29*(1),23–38.

Perfetti, L. J. C. (1990). The base 32 method: An improved method for coding sibling constellations. *Journal of Marital and Family Therapy, 16*(2), 201–204.

Rigazio-DiGilio, S. A, Ivey, A. E., Kunkler-Peck, K. P., & Grady, L. T. (2005). *Community genograms: Using individual, family, and cultural narratives with clients.* New York: Teachers College Press.

Rogers, J. C. (1990). Completion and reliability of the self-administered genogram SAGE). *Family Practice, 7,* 149–151.

Rogers, J. C. (1994a). Can physicians use family genogram information to identify patients at risk of anxiety or depression? *Archives of Family Medicine, 3,* 1093–1098.

Rogers, J. C. (1994b). Impact of a screening family genogram on first encounters in primary care. *Journal of Family Practice, 4*, 291–301.

Rogers, J. C., & Cohn, P. (1987). Impact of a screening family genogram on first encounters in primary care. *Journal of Family Practice, 4*, 291–301.

Rogers, J. C., & Durkin, M. (1984). The semi-structured genogram interview: I. Protocol, II. Evaluation. *Family Systems Medicine, 2*(25), 176–187.

Rogers, J. C., Durkin, M., & Kelly, K. (1985). The family genogram: An underutilized clinical tool. *New Jersey Medicine, 82*(11), 887–892.

Rogers, J. C., & Holloway, R. (1990). Completion rate and reliability of the self-administered genogram (SAGE). *Family Practice, 7*, 149–51.

Rogers, J. C., & Rohrbaugh, M. (1991). The SAGE-PAGE trial: Do family genograms make a difference? *Journal of the American Board of Family Practice, 4*, 319–326.

Rogers, J. C., Rohrbaugh, M., & McGoldrick, M. (1992). Can experts predict health risk from family genograms? *Family Medicine, 24*, 209–215.

Rohrbaugh, M., Rogers, J. C., & McGoldrick, M. (1992). How do experts read family genograms? *Family Systems Medicine, 10*(1), 79–89.

Visscher, E. M., & Clore, E. R. (1992). The genogram: A strategy for assessment. *Journal of Pediatric healthcare, 6*, 361–367.

Schools and Other Larger Systems

Darkenwald, G. G., & Silvestri, K. (1992). *Analysis and assessment of the Newark literacy campaign: A report to the Ford Foundation.* (Grant #915-0298).

Daughhetee, C. (2001). Using genograms as a tool for insight in college counseling. *Journal of College Counseling, 4*(1), 73–76.

Friedman, E. H. (1985). *Generation to generation. Family process in church and synagogue.* New York: Guilford.

Granello, D. H., Hothersall, D., & Osborne, A. L. (2000, March). The academic genogram: Teaching for the future by learning from the past. *Counselor Education and Supervision, 39*(3), 177–188.

Okum, B. F. (1984) *Family therapy with school-related problems.* Rockville, MD: Aspen.

Praeger, S. C., & Martin, L. S. (1994). Using genograms and ecomaps in schools. *Journal of School Nursing, 10,* 34–40.

Rigazio-DiGilio, S. A, Ivey, A. E., Kunkler-Peck, K. P., & Grady, L. T. (2005). *Community genograms: Using individual, family, and cultural narratives with clients.* New York: Teachers College Press.

Shellenberger, S., & Hoffman, S. (1995). The changing family-work system. In R. H. Mikesell, D. D. Lusterman, & S. McDaniel (Eds.), *Integrating family therapy: Handbook of family psychology and systems therapy* (pp. 461–479). Washington, DC: American Psychological Association.

Siblings

Adler, A. (1959). *The practice and theory of individual psychology.* Paterson, NJ: Littlefield, Adams.

Bank, S. P., & Kahn, M. D. (1997). *The sibling bond.* New York: Basic.

Bass, D. M., & Bowman, K. (1990). Transition from caregiving to bereavement. The relationship of care-related strain and adjustment to death. *The Gerontologist, 30,* 135–142.

Bernikow, L. (1980). *Among women.* New York: Harper & Row.

Bowerman, C. E., & Dobash, R. M. (1974). Structural variations in inter-sibling affect. *Journal of Marriage and the Family, 36,* 48–54.

Brody, G. H., Stoneman, Z., & Burke, M. (1987). Child temperaments, maternal differential behavior, and sibling relationships. *Developmental Psychology, 23*(3), 354–362.

Carroll, R. (1988). Siblings and the family business. In M. D. Kahn & K. G. Lewis (Eds.), *Siblings in therapy: Life span and clinical issues* (pp. 379–398). New York: Norton.

Chappell, N. L. (1991). *Social supports and aging.* Toronto: Butterworths.

Cicirelli, V. G. (1989). Feelings of attachment to siblings and well-being in later life. *Psychology and Aging, 4,* 211–216.

Cicirelli, V. G. (1995). *Sibling relationships across the life span.* New York: Plenum.

Connidis, I. A. (1989a). Contact between siblings in later life. *Canadian Journal of Sociology, 14*, 429–442.

Connidis, I. A. (1989b). Family ties and aging. Toronto: Butterworths.

Connidis, I. A. (1989c). Siblings as friends in later life. *American Behavioral Scientist, 33*, 81–93.

Connidis, I., & Davies, L. (1990). Confidants and companions in later life. The place of family and friends. *Journal of Gerontology, 45*, 141–149.

Elder, G. H., Jr. (1962). Structural variations in child rearing relationship. *Sociometry, 25*, 241–262.

Falbo, T. (Ed.). (1984). *The single-child family*. New York: Guilford.

Fishel, E. (1979). *Sisters: Love and rivalry inside the family and beyond.* New York: William Morrow.

Gaddis, V., & Gaddis, M. (1973). *The curious world of twins*. New York: Warner.

Gold, D. T. (1987). Siblings in old age. Something special. *Canadian Journal on Aging, 6*, 199–215.

Gold, D. T. (1989). Sibling relationships in old age: A typology. *International Journal of Aging and Human Development, 28*, 37–51.

Holden, C. E. (1986). Being a sister: Constructions of the sibling experience. (Doctoral dissertation, University of Michigan). *Dissertation Abstracts International, 10*, SECB, PP4301.

Hoopes, M. H., & Harper, J. M. (1987). *Birth order roles and sibling patterns in individual and family therapy*. Rockville, MD: Aspen.

Jalongo, M. R., & Renck, M. A. (1985). Sibling relationships: A recurrent developmental and literary theme. *Childhood Education, 61*(5), 346–351.

Johnson, C. L. (1982). Sibling solidarity: Its origin and functioning in Italian-American families. *Journal of Marriage and the Family, 44*, 155–67.

Krell, R., & Rabkin, L. The effects of sibling death on the surviving child: A family perspective. *Family Process, 18*(4), 471–478.

Lamb, M. E., & Sutton-Smith, B. (1982). *Sibling relationships: Their nature and significance across the lifespan*. Hillsdale, NJ: Erbaum.

Leder, J. M. (1993). *Brothers and sisters: How they stage our lives*. New York: Ballantine.

Marcil-Gratton, N., & Legare, J. (1992). Will reduced fertility lead to greater isolation in old age for tomorrow's elderly? *Canadian Journal on Aging, 11*, 54–71.

Mathias, B. (1992). *Between sisters: Secret rivals, intimate friends*. New York: Delacorte.

McGhee, J. L. (1985). The effects of siblings on the life satisfaction of the rural elderly. *Journal of Marriage and the Family, 41*, 703–714.

McGoldrick, M. (1989). Sisters. In M. McGoldrick, C. Anderson, & F. Walsh (Eds.), *Women in families* (pp. 244–266). New York: Norton.

McGoldrick, M., & Watson, M. (2005). Siblings through the life cycle. In B. Carter & M. McGoldrick (Eds.), *The expanded family life cycle: Individual, family and social perspectives* (pp. 153–184). Boston: Allyn & Bacon.

McKeever, P. (1983). Siblings of chronically ill children: A literature review with implications for research and practice. *American Journal of Orthopsychiatry, 53*(2), 209–218.

McNaron, T. A. H. (Ed.). (1985). *The sister bond: A feminist view of a timeless connection*. New York: Pergamon.

Merrell, S. S. (1995). *The accidental bond: The power of sibling relationships*. New York: Times Books.

Miller, N. B., & Cantwell, D. P. (1978). Siblings as therapists: A behavioral approach. *American Journal of Psychiatry, 133*(4), 447–50.

Norris, J. E., & Tindale, J. A. (1994). *Among generations: The cycle of adult relationships*. New York: W. H. Freeman.

Notar, M., & McDaniel, S. A. (1986). Feminist attitudes and mother-daughter relationships in adolescence. *Adolescence, 21*(81), 11–21.

Nuckolls, C. W. (1993). *Siblings in South Asia: Brothers and sisters in cultural context*. New York: Guilford.

Rosenberg, B. G., & Sutton-Smith, B. (1964). Ordinal position and sex role identification. *Psychological Monographs, 70*, 297–328.

Rosenberg, B. G., & Sutton-Smith, B. (1969). Sibling age spacing effects on cognition. *Developmental Psychology, 1*, 661–669.

Sandmaier, M. (1994). *Original kin: Intimacy, choices and change in adult sibling relationships*. New York: Dutton.

Schmuck, R. (1963). Sex of sibling, birth order position, and female dispositions to conform in two-child families. *Child Development, 34*, 913–918.

Shanas, E., & Streib, G. F. (1965). *Social structure and the family*. Englewood Cliffs, NJ: Prentice-Hall.

Sulloway, F. J. (1996). *Born to rebel: Sibling relationships, family dynamics and creative lives*. New York: Pantheon.

Sutton-Smith, B., & Rosenberg, B. G. (1970). *The sibling*. New York: Holt, Rinehart & Winston.

Toman, W. (1976). *Family constellation*. (3rd ed.). New York: Springer.

L. E. Troll & B. F. Turner (Eds.). (1994). *Women growing older*. Thousand Oaks, CA: Sage.

Ulanov, A., & Ulanov, B. (1983). *Cinderella and her sisters: The envied and the envying*. Philadelphia: Westminster.

Vadasy, P. F., Fewell, R. R., Meyer, D. J., & Schell, G. (1984). Siblings of handicapped children: A developmental perspective on family interactions. *Family Relations, 33*(1), 155–167.

Valliant, G. (1977). *Adaptation to life*. Boston: Little, Brown.

Zukow, P. G. (Ed.). (1989). *Sibling interaction across cultures*. New York: Springer-Verlag.

Supervision and Training

Bahr, K. S. (1990). Student responses to genogram and family chronology. *Family Relations, 39*, 243–249.

Canzoneri, K. W. (1993). The development of systemic thinking in counselors-in-training: A descriptive analysis. *Dissertation Abstracts International, 53*(10-A) 3475–3476.

Deveaux, F., & Lubell, I. (1994, August). Training the supervisor: Integrating a family of origin approach. *Contemporary Family Therapy, 16*(4), 291–299.

Frame, M. W. (2001, April). The spiritual genogram in training and supervision. *Family Journal: Counseling & Therapy for Couple & Families, 9*(2), 109–115.

Getz, H. G., & Protinsky, H. O. (1994). Training marriage and family counselors: A family of origin approach. *Counselor Education and Supervision, 33*, 183–190.

Haber, R. (1997). *Dimensions of family therapy supervision: Maps and means.* New York: Norton.

Magnuson, S., & Shaw, H. E. (2003, January). Adaptations of the multifaceted genogram in counseling, training and supervision. *Family Journal: Counseling & Therapy for Couples & Families, 2*(1), 45–54.

Pistole, M. C. (1995). The genogram in group supervision of novice counselors: Draw them a picture. *Clinical Supervisor, 13*(1), 133–43.

Shore, W., Wilkmie, H., & Croughan-Minihane, M. (1994). Family of origin genograms: Evaluation of a teaching program for medical students. *Family Medicine, 26*, 238–243.

Thomas, V. K., & Striegel, P. (1994). Family of origin work for the family counselor. In C. H. Huber (Ed.), *Transitioning from individual to family counseling: The family psychology and counseling series, No. 2.* (pp. 21–30). Alexandria, VA: American Counselling Association.

Wells, V. K., Scott, R. G., Schmeller, L. J., & Hilmann, J. A. (1990). The family-of-origin framework: A model for clinical training. *Journal of Contemporary Psychotherapy, 20*(4), 223–235.

Therapy From Multiple Orientations

Anderson, W. T., Anderson, R. A., & Hovestadt, A. J. (1988). Intergenerational family therapy: A practical primer. In P. A. Keller & R. Heyman (Eds.), *Innovations in clinical practice: A source book,* 7 (pp. 175–188). Sarasota, FL: Professional Resource Press

Arrington, D. (1991). Thinking systems-seeing systems: An integrative model for systematically oriented art therapy. *Arts in Psychotherapy, 18*(3), 201–211.

Banmen, J. (2002. March). The Satir model: Yesterday and today. *Contemporary Family Therapy, 24*(1), 7–22.

Beck, R. L. (1987). The genogram as process. *American Journal of Family Therapy, 15*(4), 343–351.

Goodyear-Brown, P. (2001). The preschool play geno-game. In H. G. Kaduson, & C. E. Schaefer, (Eds.), *101 more favorite therapy techniques* (pp. 225–228). Northvale, NJ: Jason Aronson.

Hurst, N. C., Sawatzky, D. D., & Pare, D. P. (1996). Families with multiple problems through a Bowenian lens. *Child Welfare, 75*(6), 693–708.

Kent-Wilkinson, A. (1999). Forensic family genogram: An assessment and intervention tool. *Journal of Psychosocial Nursing and Mental Health Services, 37,* 52–56.

Kuehl, B. P. (1995). The solution-oriented genogram: A collaborative approach. *Journal of Marital and Family Therapy, 21*(3), 239–250.

Kuehl, B. P. (1996). The use of genograms with solution-based and narrative therapies. *The Family Journal: Counseling and Therapy for Couples and Families, 4,* 5–11.

Massey, R. F., Comey, S., & Just, R. L. (1988). Integrating genograms and script matrices. *Transactional Analysis Journal,18*(4), 325–335.

Mauzey, E., & Erdman, P. (1995). Let the genogram speak: Curiosity, circularity and creativity in family history. *Journal of Family Psychotherapy, 6*(2), 1–11.

Nicholl, W. G., & Hawes, E. C. (1985). Family lifestyle assessment: The role of family myths and values in the client's presenting issues. *Individual Psychology: Journal of Adlerian Theory, Research & Practice, 41*(2), 147–160.

Sherman, R. (1993). Marital issues of intimacy and techniques for change: An Adlerian systems perspective. *Journal of Adlerian Therapy, Research and Practice, 49*(3-4), 318–329.

Sproul, M. S., & Galagher, R. M. (1982). The genogram as an aid to crisis intervention. *Journal of Family Practice, 14*(55), 959–60.

Woolf, V. V. (1983). Family network systems in transgenerational psychotherapy: The theory, advantages and expanded applications of genograms. *Family Therapy, 10*(35), 119–137.

Zide, M. R., & Gray, S. W. (2000). The solutioning process: Merging the genogram and the solution-focused model of practice. *Journal of Family Social Work, 4*(1) 3–19.

Videotapes on Genograms

McGoldrick, M. (1996). *The legacy of unresolved loss: A family systems approach*. New York: Norton.

Violence: Physical and Sexual Abuse

Gewirtzman, R. C. (1988). The genogram as a visual asessment of a family's fugue. *Australian Journal of Sex, Marriage and Family, 9*(1), 37–46.

Hurst, N. C., Sawatzky, D. D., & Pare, D. P. (1996). Families with multiple problems through a Bowenian lens. *Child Welfare, 75*(6), 693–708.

Nichols, W. C. (1986). Understanding family violence: An orientation for family therapists. *Contemporary Family Therapy, 8*(3), 188–207.

Biographical References

Adams Family

Levin, P. L. (1987). *Abigail Adams*. New York: St. Martin's.

Musto, D. (1981). The Adams Family. *Proceedings of Massachusetts Historical Society, 93*, 40–58.

Nagel, P. C. (1983). *Descent from glory: Four generations of the John Adams family*. New YorK: Oxford University Press.

Nagel, P. C. (1987). *The Adams women*. New York: Oxford University Press.

Shepherd, J. (1975). *The Adams chronicles: Four generations of greatness*. Boston: Little, Brown.

Alfred Adler

Adler, A. (March 1984, August 1984). Personal interviews.

Adler, K. (August, 1984a). Personal interview.

Adler, K. (August, 1984b). Personal communication.

Ansbacher, H. (1984). Personal communication.

Ansbacher, H. L. (1970). Alfred Adler: A historical perspective. *American Journal of Psychiatry, 127*, 777–782.

Ellenberger, H. F. (1970). *The discovery of the unconscious: The history and evolution of dynamic psychiatry*. New York: Basic.

Furtmuller, C. (1979). Alfred Adler: A biographical essay. In H. L. Ansbacher & R. R. Ansbacher (Eds.), *Superiority and social interest: A collection of later writings* (pp. 311–394). New York: Norton.

Hoffman, E. (1994). *The drive for self: Alfred Adler and the founding of individual psychology*. New York: Addison-Wesley.

Rattner, J. (1983). *Alfred Adler*. New York: Frederick Ungar.

Sperber, M. (1974). *Masks of loneliness: Alfred Adler in perspective*. New York: Macmillan.

Stepansky, P. E. (1983). *In Freud's shadow: Adler in context*. Hillsdale, NJ: The Analytic Press.

Louis Armstrong

Armstrong, L. (1954). *Satchmo: My life in New Orleans*. New York: Perseus.

Bergreen, L. (1997). *Louis Armstrong: An extravagant life*. New York: Broadway.

Brothers, T. (Ed.). (1999). *Louis Armstrong in his own words*. New York: Oxford University Press.

Collier, J. L. (1983). *Louis Armstrong: An American genius*. New York: Oxford University Press.

Giddins, G. (1988). *Satchmo: The genius of Louis Armstrong*. New York: Perseus.

Terkel, S. (1975). *Giants of jazz*. New York: The New Press.

Bateson/Mead Family

Bateson, M. C. (1984). *With a daughter's eye*. New York: William Morrow.

Bateson, M. C. (1988). *Peripheral visions*. New York: Morrow.

Bateson, M. C. (1990). *Composing a life*. New York: Atlantic Monthly Press.

Cassidy, R. (1982). *Margaret Mead: A voice for the century*. New York: Universe.

Grosskurth, P. (1988). *Margaret Mead: A life of controversy*. London Penguin.

Howard, J. (1984). *Margaret Mead: A life*. New York: Ballantine.

Lipset, D. (1980). *Gregory Bateson: The legacy of a scientist*. Englewood Cliffs, NJ: Prentice.

Mead, M. (1972). *Blackberry winter, my earlier years*. New York: Simon & Schuster.

Rice, E. (1979). *Margaret Mead: A portrait*. New York: Harper & Row.

Alexander Graham Bell

Bruce, R. V. (1973). *Bell: Alexander Graham Bell and the conquest of solitude*. Boston: Little, Brown.

Eber, D. H. (1982). *Genius at work: Images of Alexander Graham Bell*. New York: Viking.

Gray, C. (2006). *Reluctant genius: Alexander Graham Bell and the passion for invention*. New York: Abcade.

Grosvenor, E. S., & Wesson, M. (1997). *Alexander Graham Bell*. New York: Abrams.

Mackay, J. (1997). *Alexander Graham Bell: A life*. New York: Wiley.

Blackwell/Stone/Brown Family

Cazden, E. (1983). *Antoinette Brown Blackwell: A biography*. Old Westbury, New York: The Feminist Press.

Hays, E. R. (1967). *Those extraordinary Blackwells*. New York: Harcourt Brace.

Horn, M. (1980). Family ties: The Blackwells, a study of the dynamics of family life in nineteenth century America. (Ph.D. Dissertation, Tufts University).

Horn, M. (1983). Sisters worthy of respect: Family dynamics and women's roles in the Blackwell family. *Journal of Family History, 8*(4), 367–382.

Wheeler, L. (Ed.). (1981). *Loving warriers: Selected letters of Lucy Stone and Henry B. Blackwell, 1853 to 1893*. New York: Dial.

British Royal Family

Bradford, S. (1996). *Elizabeth*. New York: Riverhead.

Campbell, C. (1998). *The real Diana*. New York: St. Martin's.

Davies, N. (1998). *Queen Elizabeth II: A woman who is not amused*. New York: Carol Publishing.

Delderfield, E. R. (1998). *Kings and queens of England and Great Britain* (3rd ed.). Devon, England: David & Charles.

Fearon, P. (1996). *Behind the palace walls. The rise and fall of Britain's royal family*. Secaucus, NJ: Carol Publishing.

Kelley, K. (1997). *The royals*. New York: Warner.

Morton, A. (1997). *Diana: Her true story*. New York: Simon & Schuster.

Brontë Family

Bentley, P. (1969). *The Brontës and their world*. New York: Viking.

Cannon, J. (1980). *The road to Haworth: The story of the Brontës' Irish ancestry*. London: Weidenfeld and Nicolson.

Chadwick, E. H. (1914). *In the footsteps of the Brontës*. London: Sir Isaac Pitman & Sons.

Chitham, E. (1986). *The Brontës' Irish background*. New York: St. Martin's.

Chitham, E. (1988). *A life of Emily Brontë*. New York: Basil Blackwell.

Chitham, E., & Winnifrith, T. (1983). *Brontë facts and Brontë problems*. London: Macmillan.

du Maurier, D. (1961). *The infernal world of Branwell Brontë*. Garden City, NY: Doubleday.

Frazer, R. (1988). *The Brontës: Charlotte Brontë and her family*. New York: Crown.

Gaskell, E. (1975). *The life of Charlotte Brontë*. London: Penguin.

Gerin, W. (1961). *Branwell Brontë*. London: Thomas Nelson & Sons.

Gerin, W. (1971). *Emily Brontë: A biography*. London: Oxford University Press.

Hannah, B. (1988). *Striving toward wholeness*. Boston: Signpress.

Hanson, L., & Hanson, E. (1967). *The four Brontës*. New York: Archon.

Hardwick, E. (1975). *Seduction and betrayal: Women and literature*. New York: Vintage.

Hinkley, L. L. (1945). *The Brontës: Charlotte and Emily*. New York: Hastings House.

Hopkins, A. B. (1958). *The father of the Brontës*. Baltimore: Johns Hopkins Press.

Lane, M. (1969). *The Brontë story*. London: Fontana.

Lock, J., & Dixon, W. T. (1965). *A man of sorrow: The life, letters, and times of Reverend Patrick Brontë*. Westport, CT: Meckler.

Mackay, A. M. (1897). *The Brontës: Fact and fiction*. New York: Dodd, Mead.

Maurat, C. (1970). *The Brontës' secret*. Translated by M. Meldrum. New York: Barnes & Noble.

Moglen, H. (1984). *Charlotte Brontë: The self conceived*. Madison: University of Wisconsin Press.

Morrison, N. B. (1969). *Haworth harvest: The story of the Brontës*. New York: Vanguard.

Peters, M. (1974). *An enigma of Brontës*. New York: St. Martins.

Peters, M. (1975). *Unquiet Soul: A biography of Charlotte Brontë*. New York: Atheneum.

Ratchford, F. W. (1964). *The Brontës' web of childhood*. New York: Russell & Russell.

Raymond, E. (1948). *In the steps of the Brontës*. London: Rich & Cowan.

Spark, M., & Stanford, D. (1960). *Emily Brontë: Her life and work*. London: Arrow.

White, W. B. (1939). *The miracle of Haworth: A Brontë story*. New York: E. P. Dutton.

Wilks, B. (1986a). *The Brontës: An illustrated biography*. New York: Peter Bedrick. (Originally published by Hamlyn Publishing Group in 1975.)

Wilks, B. (1986b). *The illustrated Brontës of Haworth*. New York: Facts on File Publications.

Winnifith, T. Z. (1977). *The Brontës and their background: Romance and reality*. New York: Collier.

Wright, W. (1893). *The Brontës in Ireland*. New York: D. Appleton.

Burton/Taylor Family

Bragg, M. (1990). *Richard Burton: A life*. New York: Warner.

Ferris, P. (1981). *Richard Burton*. New York: Coward, McCann & Geoghegan.

Kelley, K. (1981). *Elizabeth Taylor: The last star*. New York: Simon & Schuster.

Morley, S. (1988). *Elizabeth Taylor*. New York: Applause.

Bush Family

Kelley, K. (2004). *The family: The real story of the Bush dynasty*. New York: Doubleday.

Minutaglio, B. (2001). *First son: George W. Bush and the Bush family dynasty*. New York: Three Rivers.

Phillips, K. (2004). *American dynasty: Aristocracy, fortune, and the politics of deceit in the house of Bush*. New York: Viking.

Wright, E. (2006). *Celebrity family ties*. New York: Barnes & Noble.

Callas Family

Allegri, R., & Allegri, R. (1997). *Callas by Callas*. New York: Universe.

Callas, J. (1989). *Sisters*. New York: St. Martin's.

Moutsatos, K. F. (1998). *The Onassis women*. New York: Putnam.

Stassinopoulos, A. (1981). *Maria Callas: The woman behind the legend*. New York: Simon & Schuster.

Clinton Family

Brock, D. (1996). *The seduction of Hillary Rodham*. New York: The Free Press.

Clinton, B. (2005). *My life*. New York: Vintage.

Clinton, R. (1995). *Growing up Clinton*. Arlington, TX: Summit.

Kelley, V., with J. Morgan (1994). *Leading with my heart: My life*. New York: Pocket Books.

King, N. (1996). *The woman in the White House*. New York: Carol.

Maraniss, D. (1988). *The Clinton enigma*. New York: Simon & Schuster.

Maraniss, D. (1995). *First in his class: The biography of Bill Clinton*. New York: Touchstone.

Morris, R. (1996). *Partners in power*. New York: Henry Holt.

Warner, J. (1993). *Hillary Clinton: The inside story*. New York: Signet.

Einstein Family

Clark, R. W. (1971). *Einstein: The life and times*. New York: Avon.

Highfield, R., & Carter, P. (1993). *The private life of Albert Einstein*. New York: St. Martin's.

Pais, A. (1994). *Einstein lived here*. New York: Oxford University Press.

Renn, J., & Schulmann, R. (1995). *Albert Einstein/Mileva Maric: The love letters*. Princeton: NJ Princeton University Press.

Specter, M. (1994, July 22). Einstein's son? It's a question of relativity. *New York Times*, p. 1.

Sullivan, W. (1987, May 3). Einstein letters tell of anguished love affair. *New York Times*, p. 1.

Erikson Family

Erikson Bloland, S. (1999, November). Fame: The power and cost of a fantasy. *Atlantic Monthly*, 51–62.

Erikson Bloland, S. (2005). *In the shadow of fame: A memoir by the daughter of Erik H. Erikson*. New York: Viking.

Friedman, L. J. (1999). *Identity's architect*. New York: Scribner.

Farrow Family

Farrow, M. (1997). *What falls away: A memoir*. New York: Bantam.

Fonda Family

Collier, P. (1992). *The Fondas*. New York: Putnam.

Fonda, A. (1986). *Never before dawn: An autobiography*. New York: Weindenfeld & Nicolson.

Fonda, J. (2006). *My life so far*. New York: Random House.

Fonda, P. (1998). *Don't tell dad*. New York: Hyperion.

Guiles, F. L. (1981). *Jane Fonda: The actress in her time*. New York: Pinnacle.

Hayward, B. (1977). *Haywire*. New York: Alfred Knopf.

Kiernan, T. (1973). *Jane: An intimate biography of Jane Fonda*. New York: Putnam.

Sheed, W. (1982). *Clare Booth Luce*. New York: E. P. Dutton.

Springer, J. (1970). *The Fondas*. Secaucus, NJ: Citadel.

Teichman, H. (1981). *Fonda: My life*. New York: New American Library.

Foster Family

Foster, B., & Wagener, L. (1998). *Foster child*. New York: Signet.

Chunovic, L. (1995). *Jodie: A biography*. New York: Contemporary Books.

Sigmund Freud

Anzieu, D. (1986). *Freud's self analysis*. Madison, CT: International Universities Press.

Appignanesi, L., & Forrester, J. (1992). *Freud's women*. New York: Basic.

Bernays, A. F. (Nov. 1940). *My brother Sigmund Freud*. The American Mercury, II 336–340.

Bernays, E. (Aug. 8, 1984). Personal interview.

Bernays, H. (Aug. 8, 1984).Personal interview.

Blumenthal, R. (2006, December 24). Hotel log hints at illicit desire that Dr. Freud didn't repress. *New York Times*, pp. 1, 4.

Carotenuto, A. (1982). *A secret symmetry: Sabina Spielrein between Jung and Freud*. New York: Pantheon.

Clark, R. W. (1980). *Freud: The man and the cause*. New York: Random House.

Eissler, K. R. (1978). *Sigmund Freud: His life in pictures and words*. New York: Helen & Kurt Wolff, Harcourt Brace, Jovanovich.

Freeman, L., & Strean, H. S. (1981). *Freud and women*. New York: Frederick Ungar Publishing Company.

Freud, E. L. 1960. *The letters of Sigmund Freud*. New York: Basic.

Freud, M. (1982). *Sigmund Freud: Man and father*. New York: Jason Aronson.

Freud, S. (1988). *My three mothers and other passions*. New York: New York University Press.

Gay, P. (1988). *Freud: A life for our time*. New York: Norton.

Gay, P. (1990). *Reading Freud*. New Haven, CT: Yale University Press.

Glicklhorn, R. (1979) The Freiberg period of the Freud family. *Journal of the History of Medicine, 24*, 37–43.

Jones, E. (1953, 1954, 1955). *The life and work of Sigmund Freud* (3 volumes). New York: Basic.

Krüll, M. (1986). *Freud and his father*. New York: Norton.

Mannoni, O. (1974). *Freud*. New York: Vintage.

Margolis, D. P. (1996). *Freud and his mother*. Northvale, NJ: Jason Aronson.

Masson, J. (Ed.). (1985). *The complete letters of Sigmund Freud to Wilhelm Fliess: 1887-1904*. Cambridge, MA: Belnap.

Masson, J. (1992). *The assault on truth*. New York: Harper Collins.

McGoldrick, M., & Gerson, R. (1985). *Genograms in family assessment*. New York: Norton.

McGoldrick, M., & Gerson, R. (1988). Genograms and the family life cycle (pp. 164–189). In B. Carter & M. McGoldrick (Eds.), *The changing family life cycle*. Boston: Allyn & Bacon.

McGoldrick, M., & Gerson, R. (1998). History, genograms, and the family life cycle: Freud in context. In B. Carter & M. McGoldrick (Eds.), *The expanded family life cycle: Individual, family, and social perspectives* (3rd ed., pp. 47–68). Boston: Allyn & Bacon.

Peters, U. H. (1985). *Anna Freud: A life dedicated to children*. New York: Shocken.

Roazen, P. (1993). *Meeting Freud's family*. Amherst, MA: University of Massachusetts Press.

Ruitenbeek, H. M. (1973). *Freud as we knew him*. Detroit, MI: Wayne State University.

Schur, M. (1972). *Freud: Living and dying*. New York: International Universities Press.

Swales, P. (1982). Freud, Minna Bernays, and the conquest of Rome: New light on the origins of psychoanalysis. *The New American Review, 1*(2/3), 1–23.

Swales, P. (1987). What Freud didn't say. UMDNJ-Robert Wood Johnson Medical School. May 15.

Young-Bruel, E. (1988). *Anna Freud: A biography*. New York: Summit.

Che Guevara

Anderson, J. L. (1997). *Che Guevara: A revolutionary life*. New York: Grove Press.

Deutschmann, D. (Ed.) (2006). *Che: A memoir by Fidel Castro*. Melbourne: Ocean Press.

James, D. (2001). *Che Guevara: A biography*. New York: Cooper Square Press.

Ortiz, V. (1968). *Che Guevara: Reminiscences of the Cuban revolutionary war*. New York: Monthly Review Press.

Sinclair, A. (1970). *Che Guevara*. New York: Viking.

Henry VIII

Fraser, A. (1994). *The wives of Henry VIII*. New York: Vintage.

Lindsey, K. (1995). *Divorced, beheaded, survived: A feminist reinterpretation of the wives of Henry VIII*. New York: Addison-Wesley

Hepburn/Tracy Family

Anderson, C. (1988). *Young Kate*. New York: Henry Holt.

Carey, G. (1983). *Katharine Hepburn: A Hollywood yankee*. New York: Dell.

Davidson, B. (1987). *Spencer Tracy: Tragic idol*. New York: Dutton.

Edwards, A. (1985). *A remarkable woman: A biography of Katherine Hepburn*. New York: Simon & Schuster.

Higham, C. (1981). *Kate: The life of Katharine Hepburn*. New York: Signet.

Kanin, G. (1988). *Tracy and Hepburn: An intimate memoir*. New York: Donald I. Fine.

Mann, W. J. (2006). *Kate: The woman who was Hepburn*. New York: Henry Holt.

Morley, S. (1984). *Katherine Hepburn*. London: Pavilion.

Parish, J. R. (2005). *Katherine Hepburn: The untold story*. New York: Advocate.

Jefferson Family

Binger, C. (1970). *Thomas Jefferson: A well-tempered mind*. New York: Norton.

Brodie, F. M. (1974). *Thomas Jefferson: An intimate history*. New York: Norton.

Fleming, T. J. (1969). *The man from Monticello*. New York: Morrow.

Gordon-Reed, A. (1997). *Thomas Jefferson and Sally Hemings*. Charlottesville, VA: University of Virginia Press.

Halliday, E. M. (2001). *Understanding Thomas Jefferson*. New York: Harper Collins.

Lanier, S., & Feldman, J. (2000). *Jefferson's children*. New York: Random House.

Smith, D. (1998, November 7). The enigma of Jefferson: Mind and body in conflict. *New York Times*, B 7–8.

Wills, G. (2003). *Negro president*. Boston: Houghton Mifflin.

Woodson, B. W. (2001) *A President in the family: Thomas Jefferson, Sally Hemings and Thomas Woodson*. Westport, CT: Praeger.

Joplin Family

Berlin, E. A. (1994). *King of Ragtime: Scott Joplin and his era*. New York: Oxford University Press.

Curtis, S. (2004). *Dancing to a black man's tune: The life of Scott Joplin*. Columbia, MO: University of Missouri Press.

Gammond, P. (1975). *Scott Joplin and the ragtime era*. New York: St. Martin's.

Haskins, J. (1978). *Scott Joplin: The man who made ragtime*. Briarcliff Manor, NY: Scarborough.

Preston, K. (1988). *Scott Joplin: Composer*. New York: Chelsea House.

Berlin, E. A biography of Scott Joplin, retrieved 2006. www.scottjoplin.org/biography.htm.

Jung Family

Bair, D. (2003) *Jung: A biography*. New York: Little, Brown.

Broome, V. (1981). *Jung: Man and myth*. New York: Atheneum.

Hannah, B. (1981). *Jung: His life and work; A biographical memoir*. New York: Perigee, Putnam.

Jung, C. G. (1961). *Memories, dreams, reflections*. (Recorded and edited by Aniela Jaffe, translated by R. Winston & C. Winstons). New York: Vintage.

Stern, P. J. (1976). C. G. *Jung: The haunted prophet*. New York: Delta, Deli.

Kahlo/Rivera Families

Alcantara, I., & Egnolff, S. (1999). *Frida Kahlo and Diego Rivera*. New York: Prestel Verlag.

Drucker, M. (1991). *Frida Kahlo*. Albuquerque, NM: University of New Mexico Press.

Grimberg, S. (2002). *Frida Kahlo*. North Digton, MA: World Publications.

Herrera, H. (1983). *Frida: A biography of Frida Kahlo*. New York: Harper & Row.

Herrera, H. (1984). *Frida*. New York: Harper Collins.

Herrera, H. (1991). *Frida Kahlo: The paintings*. New York: Harper Collins.

Kahlo, F. (2001). *The diary of Frida Kahlo: An intimate self-portrait*. Toledo, Spain: Abradale.

Kahlo, F. (1995). *The letters of Frida Kahlo: Cartas apasionadas*. San Francisco: Chronicle.

Kettenmann, A. (2002). *Frida Kahlo, 1907-1954: Pain and passion*. New York: Barnes & Noble Books. (Original publication 1992, Cologne, Germany: Benedikt Taschen Verlag GmbH.)

Marnham, P. (1998). *Dreaming with his eyes open: A life of Diego Rivera*. New York: Knopf.

Rivera, D. (1991). *My art, my life*. New York: Dover.

Tibol, R. (1983). *Frida Kahlo: An open life*. Albuquerque, NM: University of New Mexico Press.

Kennedy Family

Andrews, J. D. (1998). *Young Kennedys: The new generation*. New York: Avon.

Collier, P., & Horowitz, D. (1984). *The Kennedys*. New York: Summit.

Davis, J. (1969). *The Bouviers: Portrait of an American family*. New York: Farrar, Straus, Giroux.

Davis, J. (1984). *The Kennedys: Dynasty & Disaster*. New York: McGraw-Hill.

Davis, J. (1993). *The Bouviers: From Waterloo to the Kennedys and beyond*. Washington, DC: National Press.

DuBois, D. (1995). *In her sister's shadow: The bitter legacy of Lee Radziwell*. New York: St. Martin's.

Gibson, B., & Schwarz, T. (1993). *The Kennedys: The third generation*. New York: Thunder Mouth's Press.

Hamilton, N. (1992). *JFK reckless youth*. New York: Random House.

Heymann, C. D. (1989). *A woman named Jackie*. New York: New American Library.

James, A. (1991). *The Kennedy scandals and tragedies.* Lincolnwood, IL: Publications Internations.

Kearns Goodwin, D. (1987). *The Fitzgeralds and the Kennedys.* New York: Simon & Schuster.

Kelley, K. (1978). *Jackie Oh!* Secaucus, NJ: Lyle Stuart.

Kennedy, R. (1974). *Times to remember.* New York: Bantam.

Klein, E. (1998). *Just Jackie: Her private years.* New York: Ballantine.

Klein, E. (2003). *The Kennedy curse.* New York: St. Martin's.

Latham, C., & Sakol, J. (1989). *Kennedy encyclopedia.* New York: New American Library.

Leamer, L. (2001). *The Kennedy men: 1901-1963.* New York: Harper Collins.

Maier, T. (2003). *The Kennedys: America's emerald kings.* New York: Basic.

McTaggart, L. (1983). *Kathleen Kennedy: Her life and times.* New York: Dial.

Moutsatos, K. F. (1998). *The Onassis women.* New York: Putnam.

Rachlin, H. (1986). *The Kennedys: A chronological history 1823-present.* New York: World Almanac.

Rainie, H., & Quinn, J. (1983) *Growing up Kennedy: The third wave comes of age.* New York: G. P. Putnam's Sons.

Saunders, F. (1982). *Torn lace curtain: Life with the Kennedys.* New York: Pinnade.

Wills, G. (1981). *The Kennedy imprisonment: A mediation on power.* New York: Little, Brown.

Martin Luther King Family

Carson, C. (Ed.). (2001). *The autobiography of Martin Luther King.* New York: Warner.

Franklin, V. P. (1998). *Martin Luther King, Jr. Biography.* New York: Park Lane Press.

King, M. L., Sr., with C. Riely (1980). *Daddy King: An autobiography.* New York: Morrow.

Lewis, D. L. (1978). *King: A biography* (2nd ed.). Chicago: University of Illinois Press.

Oates, S. B. (1982). *Let the trumpet sound: The life of Martin Luther King, Jr.* New York: New American Library.

Marilyn Monroe

Zimroth, E. (2002). Marilyn at the Mikvah. In Y. Z. McDonough (Ed.), *All the available light: A Marilyn Monroe reader*, (pp. 176–183). New York: Simon & Schuster.

Nehru/Gandhi Family

Ali, T. (1985). *An Indian dynasty.* New York: Putnam.

Frank, K. (2002). *Indira: The life of Indira Nehru Gandhi.* New York: Houghton-Mifflin.

Tharoor, S. (2003). *Nehru: The invention of India.* New TYork: Arcade Publishing.

Wolpert, S. (1996). *Nehru.* New York: Oxford University Press.

O'Neill Family

Black, S. (1999). *Eugene O'Neill: Beyond mourning and tragedy.* New Haven, CT: Yale University Press.

Bowen, C. (1959). *The curse of the misbegotten.* New York: McGraw-Hill.

Gelb, A., & Gelb, B. (1987). *O'Neill.* New York: Harper & Row.

Scovell, J. O. *Living in the shadows.* New York: Time Warner.

Sheaffer, L. (1968). *O'Neill: Son and playwright.* Boston: Little, Brown.

Sheaffer, L. (1973). *O'Neill: Son and artist.* Boston: Little, Brown.

Reich Family

Mann, W. E., & Hoffman, E. (1980). *The man who dreamed of tomorrow: The life and thought of Wilhelm Reich.* Los Angeles: Tarcher.

Reich, L. O. (1969). *Wilhelm Reich: A personal biography*. New York: Avon.

Sharaf, J. (1983). *Fury on earth: A biography of Wilhelm Reich*. New York: St. Martin's.

Wilson, C. (1981). *The quest for Wilhelm Reich: A critical biography*. Garden City, NY: Anchor Press/Doubleday.

Robeson Family

Dean, P. H. (1989). Paul Robeson. In E. Hill (Ed.), *Black heroes: Seven plays* (pp. 277–354). New York: Applause Theatre.

Duberman, M. B. (1988). *Paul Robeson*. New York: Knopf.

Ehrlich, S. (1988). *Paul Robeson: Singer and actor*. New York: Chelsea House.

Larsen, R. (1989). *Paul Robeson: Hero before his time*. New York: Franklin Watts.

Ramdin, R. (1987). *Paul Robeson: The man and his mission*. London: Peter Owen.

Robeson, P. (1988). *Here I stand*. Boston: Beacon.

Robinson Family

Falkner, D. (1995). *Great time coming: The life of Jackie Robinson from baseball to Birmingham*. New York: Simon & Schuster.

Rampersad, A. (1997). *Jackie Robinson: A biography*. New York: Knopf.

Robinson, J. (1972). *I never had it made*. New York: Putnam.

Robinson, R. (1996). *Jackie Robinson: An intimate portrait*. New York: Abrams.

Robinson, S. (1996). *Stealing home*. New York: HarperCollins.

Tygiel, J. (1997). *Baseball's great experiement: Jackie Robinson and his legacy*. New York: Oxford University Press.

Roosevelt Family

Asbell, B. (Ed.). (1982). *Mother and daughter: The letters of Eleanor and Anna Roosevelt*. New York: Coward McCann & Geoghegan.

Bishop, J. B. (Ed.). (1919). *Theodore Roosevelt's letters to his children*. New York: Charles Scribner's Sons.

Brough, J. (1975). *Princess Alice: A biography of Alice Roosevelt Longworth*. Boston: Little, Brown.

Collier, P., with D. Horowitz (1994). *The Roosevelts*. New York: Simon & Schuster.

Cook, B. W. (1992). *Eleanor Roosevelt 1884-1933. A life: Mysteries of the heart* (Vol. 1). New York: Viking Penguin.

Donn, L. (2001). *The Roosevelt cousins*. New York: Knopf.

Felsenthal, C. (1988). *Alice Roosevelt Longworth*. New York: G. P. Putnam's Sons.

Fleming, C. (2005). *Our Eleanor*. New York: Simon & Schuster.

Fritz, J. (1991). *Bully for you: Teddy Roosevelt*. New York: G. P. Putnam's Sons.

Hagedorn, H. (1954). *The Roosevelt family of Sagamore Hill*. New York: Macmillan.

Kearns Goodwin, D. (1994). *No ordinary time. Franklin and Eleanor Roosevelt: The home front in World War II*. New York: Simon & Schuster.

Lash, J. P. (1971). *Eleanor and Franklin*. New York: Norton.

McCullough, D. (1981). *Mornings on horseback*. New York: Simon & Schuster.

Miller, N. (1979). *The Roosevelt chronicles*. Garden City, NY: Doubleday.

Miller, N. (1983). *FDR: An intimate biography*. Garden City, NY: Doubleday.

Miller, N. (1992). *Theodore Roosevelt: A life*. New York: Morrow.

Morgan, T. (1985). *FDR: A biography*. New York: Simon & Schuster.

Morris, E. (1979). *The rise of Theodore Roosevelt*. New York: Ballantine.

Pringle, H. F. (1931). *Theodore Roosevelt*. New York: Harcourt, Brace, Jovanovich.

Roosevelt, E. (1984). *The autobiography of Eleanor Roosevelt*. Boston: G. K. Hall.

Roosevelt, E., & Brough, J. (1973). *The Roosevelts of Hyde Park: An untold story*. New York: Putnam.

Roosevelt, E., & Brough, J. (1975). *A rendezvous with destiny: The Roosevelts of the White House*. New York: Dell.

Roosevelt, J. (1976). *My parents: A differing view*. Chicago: The Playboy Press.

Roosevelt, T. (1925). *An autobiography*. New York: Charles Scribner's Sons.

Teichman, H. (1979). *Alice: The life and times of Alice Roosevelt*. Englewood Cliffs: NJ: Prentice-Hall.

Youngs, W. T. (1985). *Eleanor Roosevelt: A personal and public life*. Boston: Little, Brown.

Turner Family

Bibb, P. (1997). *Ted Turner: It ain't as easy as it looks*. Boulder, CO: Johnson.

Goldberg, R., & Goldberg, G. J. (1995). *Citizen Turner*. New York: Harcourt, Brace.

Queen Victoria

Auchincloss. L. (1979). *Persons of consequence: Queen Victoria and her circle*. New York: Random House.

Benson, E. F. (1987). *Queen Victoria*. London: Chatto & Windus.

Hibbert, C. Queen Victoria in her letters and journals. London: Penguin.

James, R. R. (1984). *Prince Albert*. New York: Knopf.

Strachey, L. (1921). *Queen Victoria*. New York: Harcourt, Brace, Jovanovich.

Weintraub, S.(1987). *Victoria*. New York: E. P .Dutton.

Wilson, E. (1990). *Emminent victorians*. New York: Norton.

Woodham-Smith, C. (1972). *Queen Victoria*. New York: Donald Fine.

George Washington

Bourne, M. A. (1982). *First family: George Washington and his intimate relations*. New York: Norton.

Ellis, J. J. (2004). *His excellency: George Washington*. New York: Knopf.

Furstenberg, F. (2006). *In the name of the father: Washington's legacy, slavery and the making of a nation*. New York: Penguin.

Johnson, P. (2005). *George Washington: The founding father*. New York: Harper Collins.

McCullough, D. (2005). *1776*. New York. Simon & Schuster.

Mitchell, S. W. (1904). *The youth of Washington*. New York: The Century Company.

Moore, C. (1926). *The family life of George Washington*. Boston: Houghton Mifflin.

Randall, W. S. (1997). *George Washington: A life*. New York: Henry Holt.

Wiencek, H. (2003). *An imperfect god: George Washington, his slaves and the creation of America*. New York: Farrar, Strauss & Giroux.

Index

Note: Genograms are indicated by italicized page numbers. Pages of the color insert are preceded by "C." Figures are indicated by "f" following a page number.